Prehistory of the Indo-Malaysian Archipelago

Peter Bellwood

Reader in Prehistory
The Australian National University

ACADEMIC PRESS
(Harcourt Brace Jovanovich, Publishers)

Sydney Orlando San Diego New York
London Toronto Montreal Tokyo

ACADEMIC PRESS AUSTRALIA
Centrecourt, 25–27 Paul Street North
North Ryde, N.S.W. 2113

United States Edition published by
ACADEMIC PRESS INC.
Orlando, Florida 32887

United Kingdom Edition published by
ACADEMIC PRESS, INC. (LONDON) LTD.
24/28 Oval Road, London NW1 7DX

Printed in Australia

National Library of Australia Cataloguing-in-Publication Data

---

Bellwood, Peter S. (Peter Stafford), 1943- .
Prehistory of the Indo-Malaysian archipelago.

ISBN 0 12 085370 1.
ISBN 0 12 085371 X (pbk).

1. Man, Prehistoric - Indonesia. 2. Man, Prehistoric - Malaysia. 3. Indonesia - Antiquities. 4. Malaysia - Antiquities. I. Title.

959'.01

Library of Congress Catalog Card Number: 85-47791

Contents

Preface

This book presents a multidisciplinary reconstruction of the prehistory of the modern nations of Indonesia and Malaysia, as viewed from the perspective of the whole South-East Asian and Australasian region. Since modern nation boundaries have little meaning for the student of the remote past, I refer to the region in the following chapters as "the Indo-Malaysian Archipelago". Several interlinked aspects of prehistory are reviewed, mainly from data produced by the disciplines of biological anthropology, linguistics and archaeology, and the overall time-span runs from about 2 million years ago to approximately AD 1000. In general, the book ceases with the historical civilisations of the first millennium AD, although it should be realised that prehistory *sensu stricto* continued in some remote regions to almost the present day.

I would like to acknowledge here the assistance of many of my colleagues who have read parts of the work. These include Robert Blust of the University of Hawaii, Roger Green of the University of Auckland, and Australian National University colleagues John Chappell, James Fox, Geoffrey Hope, Robert Kirk, Margot Lyon, Douglas Miles, Cecilia Ng, Alan Thorne and Daryl Tyron. Helmut Loofs-Wissowa first suggested that I undertake the project. The Department of Prehistory and Anthropology at the Australian National University provided invaluable staff assistance, and in this regard I would like to thank Louise Johnson for typing, Joan Goodrum, Mandy Mottram and Val Lyons for drawing the maps and charts, and Robert Dowhy and Karen Edwards for photographic work.

Dating

In general, I do not give full radiocarbon determinations with laboratory numbers in the text, and interested archaeologists can locate these through the references (see Bronson, in press, for a full listing from South-East Asia). Archaeological sites from about 6000 BC onwards are given approximate BC or AD dates according to historical data or the calibrated radiocarbon chronology presented by Klein *et al.* (1982). Radiocarbon dated sites older than 8000 years are given bp or bc (that is uncalibrated) dates, or simply given a "... years ago" approximation.

Pronunciation and placenames

In Indonesian placenames the "c" is pronounced "ch" as in English "church", "ng" as in "singer", and "ngg" as in "finger". Most placenames are given in their modern Indonesian or Malaysian versions, but some which have commonly used versions in English, such as Java, Sumatra, Lesser Sundas and Moluccas, are kept as such (Indonesian versions are Jawa, Sumatera, Nusatenggara and Maluku). I have also used the term "Malaya" throughout in place of the more formal West or Peninsular Malaysia.

I am not an authority on the pronunciation of Chinese placenames, although many occur in this book. Peking, Yellow and Yangtze are given as in present English, but all other placenames in the People's Republic are given in Pinyin spelling — I give an appendix at the back with Wade-Giles equivalents. Taiwanese names are all in Wade-Giles romanisation.

For my Mother

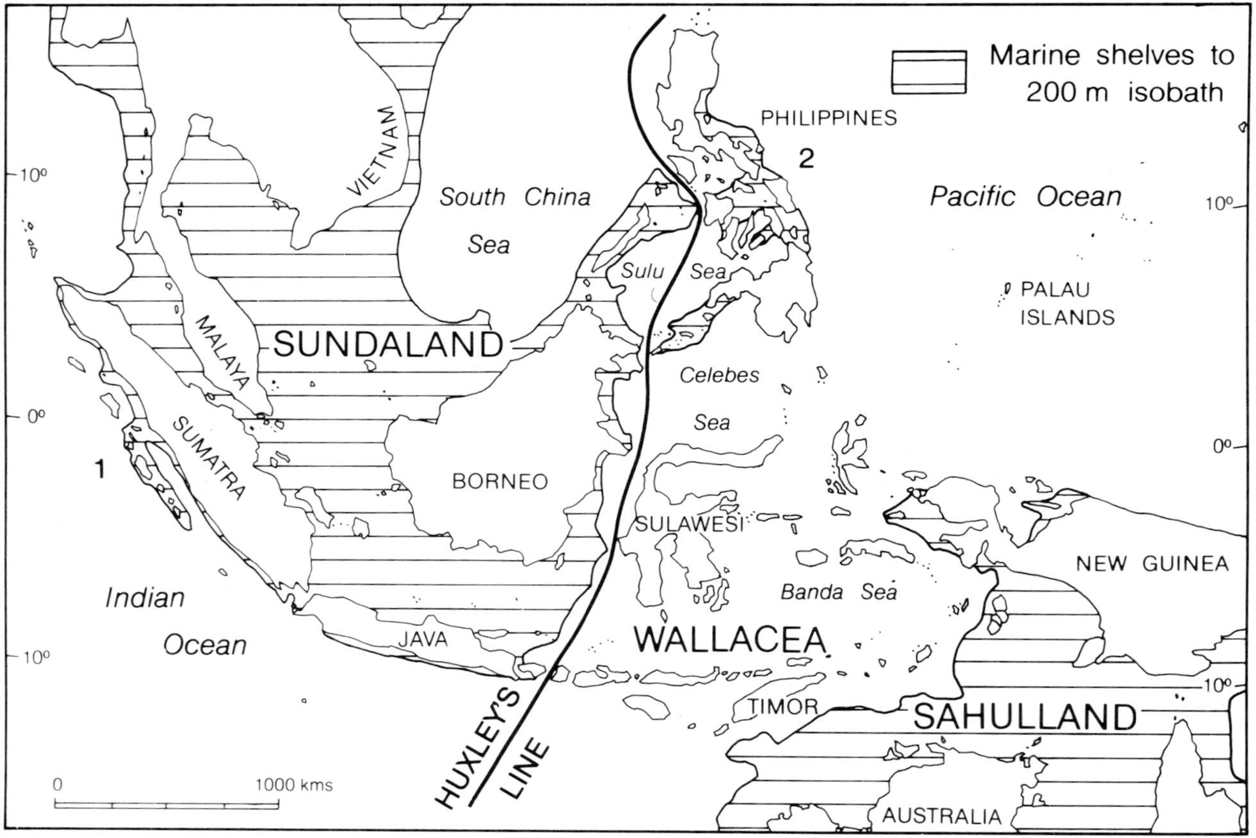
Marine shelves to 200 m isobath
PHILIPPINES
2
Pacific Ocean
PALAU ISLANDS
VIETNAM
South China Sea
Sulu Sea
Celebes Sea
SUNDALAND
MALAYA
SUMATRA
1
BORNEO
SULAWESI
Banda Sea
NEW GUINEA
Indian Ocean
JAVA
WALLACEA
TIMOR
SAHULLAND
AUSTRALIA
HUXLEY'S LINE
0
1000 kms
10°
0°
10°

1
The Environmental Background: Present and Past

The Indo-Malaysian Archipelago (Fig. 1.1) demonstrates a certain unity in human terms today, in the sense that all its indigenous populations (with restricted exceptions in Malaya and the far east of Indonesia) belong to the same Austronesian-speaking major ethnolinguistic group of mankind. Furthermore, they belong also (with minor exceptions) to the southern branch of the Mongoloid physical stock of mankind — the most numerous and expansive group in human prehistory.

However, the picture has not always been thus. Both the humans and the archipelago have changed in complex ways in the past. It is now necessary to introduce the archipelago itself from a basically geographical and environmental viewpoint in order to understand some of these changes. My object here is not to compete with the numerous standard geographical treatises on the region, but rather to emphasise aspects of the environment, past and present, which are likely to have direct interpretative value for the prehistoric record of the last 2 million years.

I. The Indo-Malaysian Archipelago

Our main area of interest includes all the islands of Indonesia and Malaysia (including the Malay Peninsula south of Thailand). The Philippines are also a part of the Indo-Malaysian Archipelago, and although they lie outside the main area of concern they will merit extended comment in later sections. Indeed, the prehistory of Indonesia in particular is very closely tied with that of the Philippines, especially in its later stages during the period of expansion of the Austronesian-speaking peoples. Adjacent regions which will also require extended comment in some following sections include Taiwan, the countries of Mainland South-East Asia (especially Thailand and Vietnam), China (especially the southern half), and the Australasian territories of

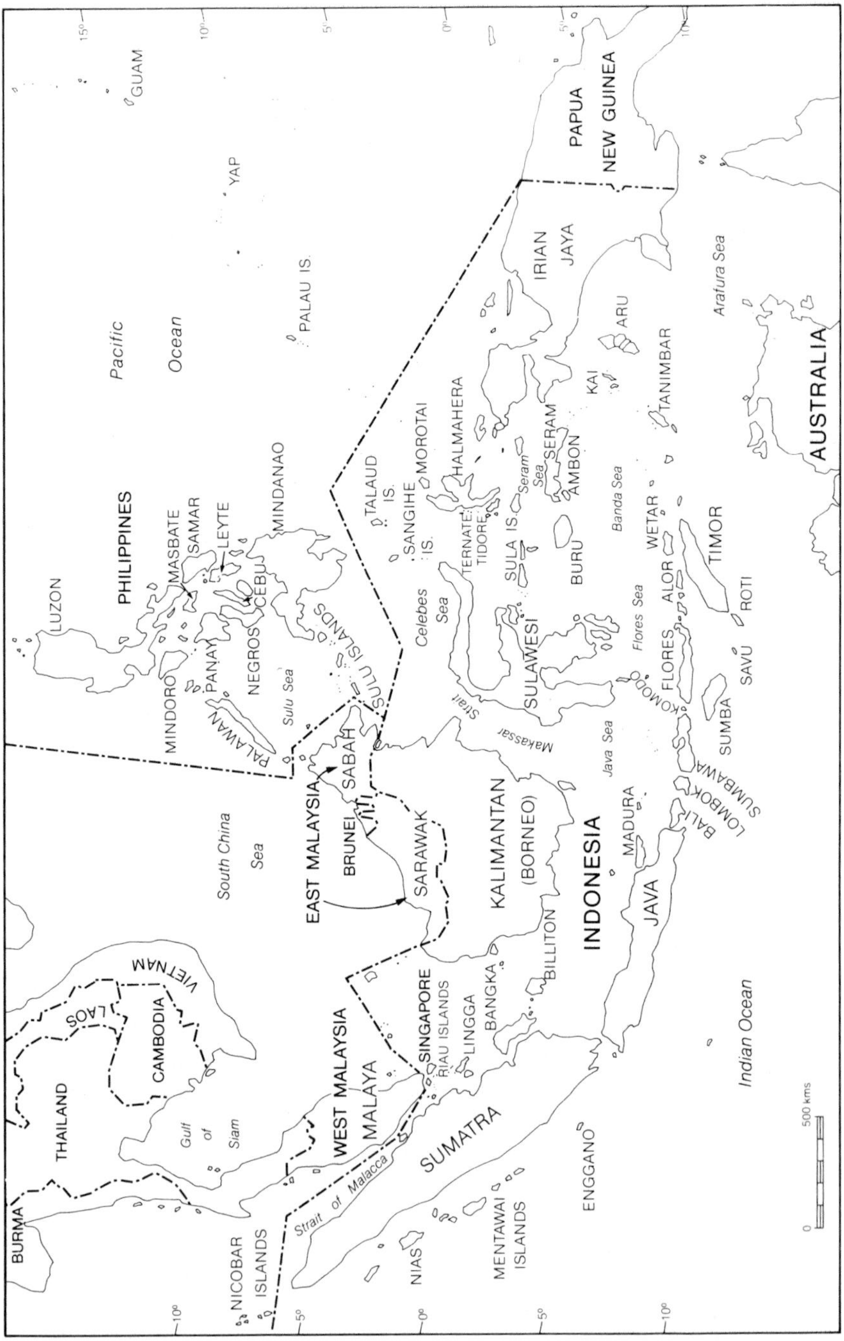
GUAM
YAP
PALAU IS.
Pacific
Ocean
PHILIPPINES
LUZON
MASBATE
SAMAR
LEYTE
MINDANAO
CEBU
NEGROS
PANAY
MINDORO
PALAWAN
Sulu Sea
SULU ISLANDS
South China
Sea
EAST MALAYSIA
SABAH
BRUNEI
SARAWAK
KALIMANTAN
(BORNEO)
Celebes
Sea
TALAUD
IS.
SANGIHE
IS.
MOROTAI
HALMAHERA
TERNATE
TIDORE
SULA IS.
Seram
Sea
SERAM
AMBON
BURU
SULAWESI
Makassar
Strait
IRIAN
JAYA
PAPUA
NEW GUINEA
ARU
KAI
TANIMBAR
Arafura Sea
AUSTRALIA
Banda Sea
WETAR
TIMOR
ALOR
ROTI
Flores Sea
FLORES
KOMODO
SAVU
SUMBA
SUMBAWA
LOMBOK
BALI
Java Sea
MADURA
JAVA
INDONESIA
BILLITON
BANGKA
LINGGA
RIAU ISLANDS
SINGAPORE
WEST MALAYSIA
MALAYA
VIETNAM
LAOS
CAMBODIA
THAILAND
Gulf
of
Siam
BURMA
NICOBAR
ISLANDS
Strait of Malacca
SUMATRA
NIAS
MENTAWAI
ISLANDS
ENGGANO
Indian Ocean
500 kms
0
15°
10°
5°
0°

Australia and New Guinea. New Guinea, the western half of which is politically now a part of Indonesia, is not included in the Indo-Malaysian Archipelago as here defined.

As defined for the purposes of this book, the "core region" of the Indo-Malaysian Archipelago extends from about 7° N (northern Malaya and Borneo) to 11° S (Sumba and Timor), and from the western tip of Sumatra to the Moluccas. The region is about 4200 km long by 2000 km from north to south, and supports about 1.8 million km^2 of dry land, of which about 80% lies in Indonesia; the remainder being in Malaysia (Malaya, plus the states of Sarawak and Sabah on Borneo) and Brunei.

The islands of this region clearly differ much in size; Borneo covers 736 000 km^2 (only slightly smaller than New Guinea), Sumatra comes next with 435 000 km^2, then Sulawesi (172 000), the Malay Peninsula (138 000 within Malaysia) and Java (127 000). It is obvious that the islands of western Indonesia are in general bigger than those of eastern Indonesia (except for Sulawesi), and the reasons for this lie in the structure of the archipelago.

A. The Shelves and Basins

To understand the human prehistory of Indonesia it is necessary to know something of the geological, climatic and biotic history of the archipelago. I will commence with some geology.

The Indo-Malaysian islands, "the remarkable festoon of islands that swing around the equator in the East Indies" (Umbgrove 1949), fall into three very fundamental structural divisions. The first, in the west, comprises the Sunda continental shelf. The second, attached to its Indian Ocean edge, and extending east towards New Guinea, comprises the volcanic Sunda-Banda arcuate mountain and trench system. The third, in the north-east, comprises the Sulawesi-Philippine and Halmahera volcanic arc systems, buckled towards Asia from the Pacific (Fig. 1.2).

The Sunda continental shelf (Tjia 1980), which has the largest area of submerged shelf in the world, has an old and tectonically fairly stable core which has had very little recent volcanic activity. Much of it today lies beneath the sediments of the South China and Java Seas as a virtual peneplain worn down by erosion, and present land areas which rise above the old submerged shelf core include Malaya, Borneo, and the northern coastal lowlands of Sumatra and Java. The volcanic mountains of Sumatra and Java are actually members of the Sunda-Banda arc system, to be described next, which have formed around the Indian Ocean rim of the Sunda shelf.

Fig. 1.1. The Indo-Malaysian Archipelago (Malaysia and Indonesia), together with adjacent regions.

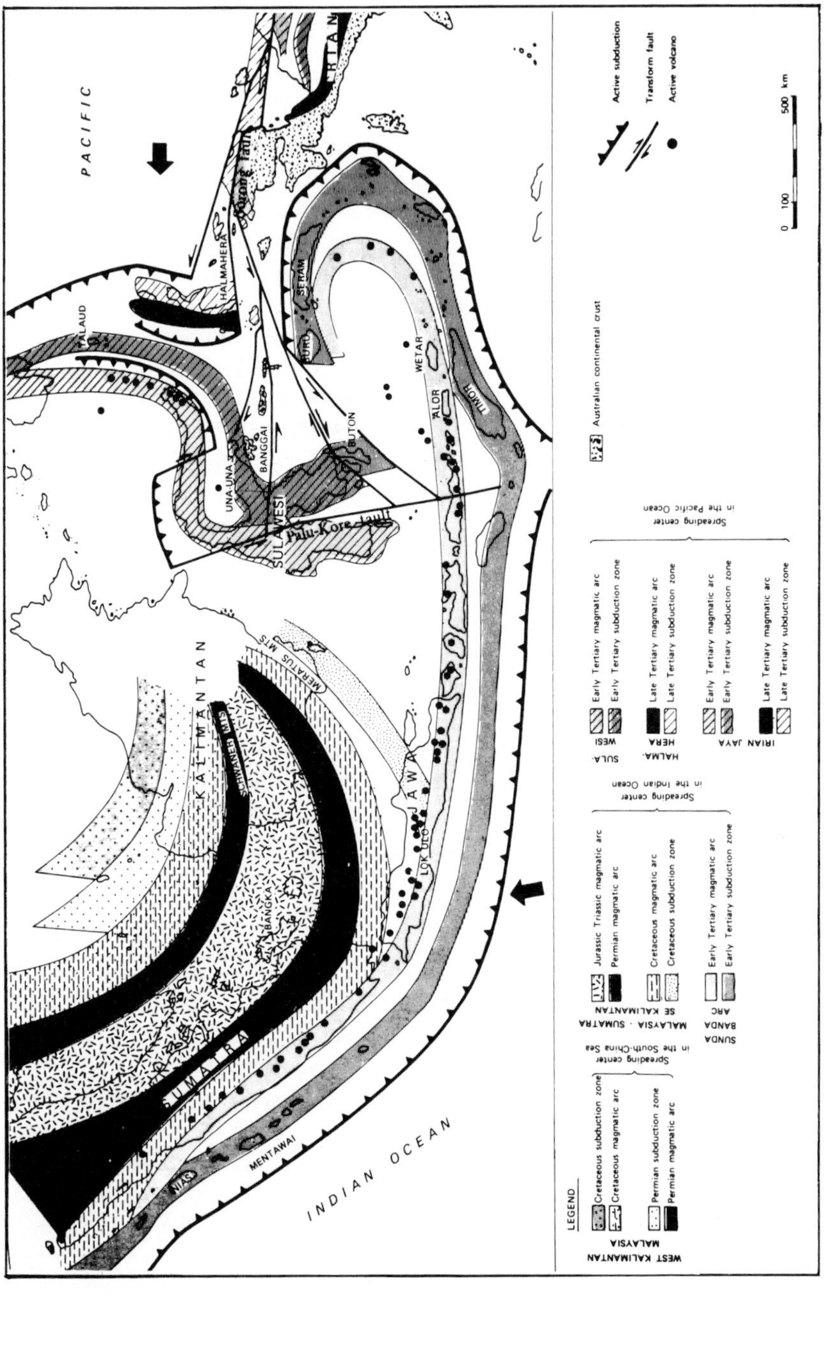
PACIFIC
INDIAN OCEAN
KALIMANTAN
SUMATRA
JAWA
SULAWESI
HALMAHERA
TALAUD
UNA-UNA
BANGGAI
BUTON
BURU
SERAM
WETAR
ALOR
TIMOR
BANGKA
NIAS
MENTAWAI
LOK ULO
SCHWANER MTS
MERATUS MTS
Palu-Kore fault
Sorong fault
LEGEND
WEST KALIMANTAN MALAYSIA
Cretaceous subduction zone
Cretaceous magmatic arc
Permian subduction zone
Permian magmatic arc
Spreading center in the South-China Sea
MALAYSIA - SUMATRA SE KALIMANTAN
Jurassic Triassic magmatic arc
Permian magmatic arc
Cretaceous magmatic arc
Cretaceous subduction zone
SUNDA BANDA ARC
Early Tertiary magmatic arc
Early Tertiary subduction zone
Spreading center in the Indian Ocean
SULA-WESI
Early Tertiary magmatic arc
Early Tertiary subduction zone
HALMA-HERA
Late Tertiary magmatic arc
Late Tertiary subduction zone
Early Tertiary magmatic arc
Early Tertiary subduction zone
IRIAN JAYA
Late Tertiary magmatic arc
Late Tertiary subduction zone
Spreading center in the Pacific Ocean
Australian continental crust
Active subduction
Transform fault
Active volcano
0 100 500 km

However, it is clear that any attempt to define the extent of an "original" Sunda shelf would be pointless, since it has been growing outwards from Asia since at least the Permian period. For present purposes it is more convenient to refer to the general western Indonesian shelf land mass as *Sundaland* (see Fig. 1.3); an area which of course contains a large portion of the present Sunda-Banda arc.

The Sunda-Banda arc includes the highland spines of Sumatra, Java and the Lesser Sundas, and forms one of the most remarkable arcuate volcanic mountain chains in the world. It is now assumed to have been formed by subduction of the bed of the Indian Ocean beneath Sumatra and Java, and the arc continues eastwards beyond these islands to become curled back on itself in eastern Indonesia through collision with the resistant Sahul continental shelf, which joins Australia and New Guinea. The process of subduction, described briefly for this region by Ollier (1980), has led to the upwarping of two parallel mountain chains, the inner one volcanic, the outer of uplifted marine sediments without active volcanoes. The inner volcanic chain includes 82 active volcanoes, which extend in a curve from Sumatra, through Java and the Lesser Sundas, eventually to curl right around the eastern edge of the Banda Sea and to end south of Seram. Outside this arc is a deep marine trench, and then the other non-volcanic outer arc rises beyond the trench to support the small islands off the western coast of Sumatra, plus Sumba, Timor, Seram and Buru.

So far, we have two major structural regions in Indonesia: the Sunda shelf, and the Sunda-Banda mountain arc system wrought against its edge and beyond it. The latter is still in active construction, as witnessed by numerous volcanic eruptions (such as the famous Krakatoa eruption of 1883) and earthquakes. The third region is not so clearly defined and includes the remaining parts of eastern Indonesia. The Philippines and Sulawesi lie on a similar double arc to the Sunda-Banda arc, and other such arcs continue northwards around the western Pacific rim through the Ryukyu Islands, Japan and the Aleutians. Part of a smaller double arc also appears in Halmahera, further towards the Pacific. Some textbooks show the Sulawesi-Philippine and Sunda-Banda arcs as one continuous formation (e.g. Spencer and Thomas 1971: Fig. 6.12), but recent studies in the rather complex field of plate tectonics in eastern Indonesia show that this may not be the case. Accounts of the formation of the whole Indo-Malaysian region have recently been given by Katili (1974; 1975), while a different explanation has been given by Audley-Charles *et al.* (1972; see also Audley-Charles 1981).

Katili's reconstructions (see Fig. 1.2) apply to Sundaland as well as to

Fig. 1.2. The structure of the Indo-Malaysian Archipelago (large black arrows denote directions of plate movements). From Katili and Hartono 1979. Courtesy: Geologie en Mijnbouw.

eastern Indonesia. He regards Sundaland as the result of a series of five successive volcanic arcs which have been forming since Permian times; the earliest being represented in the older eroded northerly parts of the shelf, the latest being the present Sunda-Banda arc, which attained its present configuration during the Pliocene, by which time the emergence of Java was underway (see also Umbgrove 1949).

In early Tertiary times (according to Katili) the Sunda-Banda arc was straighter than it is now, and lacked its eastern sharp return. By this time the Sulawesi-Philippine arc was also in formation to its north, on the western edge of the Pacific, while the Halmahera arc is regarded as being of later date — Middle to Late Miocene. The Sunda-Banda and Sulawesi-Philippine arcs have different mineral characteristics, and are regarded by Katili as of quite separate origin. However, Hamilton (1979: Fig. 77) shows them as a single system in the Early Miocene (about 20 million years ago), to be sundered by later tectonic movements.

While these arcs were forming, Australia was drifting northwards towards its present position, a process which is apparently continuing at the rate of about 40 km per million years. The result of this was that the Banda arc was bent back upon itself during the Pliocene into its present shape, while the rotation of New Guinea westwards across the northern edge of the Australian continent pushed the once-separate inner and outer arc systems of Sulawesi and Halmahera into each other, thus giving the peculiar four-armed formations seen in these islands today. The region between the ends of the Sulawesi and Banda arcs is regarded as a plate collision and major fault zone by Katili, where no arcs have been able to develop.

The rather different theory of Audley-Charles *et al.* (1972; see also Carter *et al.* 1976; Audley-Charles 1981) suggests that the two eastern arms of Sulawesi, the islands of the outer Banda arc (Timor, Seram, Buru), and Halmahera were once part of the Australian continental shelf, and that they reached their present positions during the Pliocene through complex processes involving continental drift and rotation since Australia began its northward migration from Gondwanaland early in the Tertiary (about 55 million years ago). This view is supported by some recent palaeomagnetic results from Sulawesi (Haile 1978), and Hamilton (1979: Fig. 81) considers Banggai and the Sula Islands off the eastern arm of Sulawesi to be displaced crustal fragments from New Guinea. The theory as a whole thus suggests that the present Sunda-Banda arc is a "weld" of two once-separate orogenic systems. However, as Ollier notes, "the impressive continuity of the present-day arc makes this seem rather unlikely" (Ollier 1980:8), and Eocene mammal fossils from Timor are of Indo-Malaysian rather than Australian affinity (Minchen Chow *et al.* 1983).

It is not my task to pass further judgement on these hypotheses of island formation. They are of great interest, and do suggest that the archipelago was

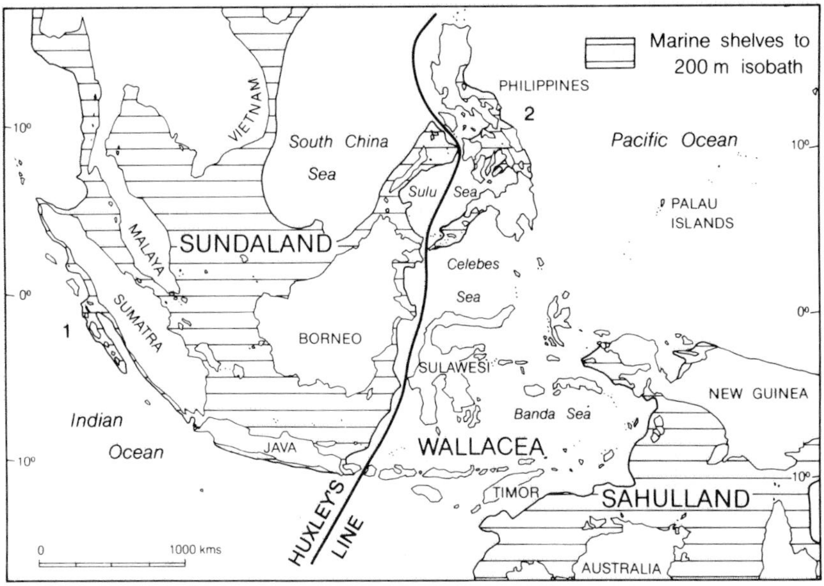

Fig. 1.3. Major biogeographical divisions in the Indo-Malaysian region. (1) The Mentawai Islands as a whole have probably not been joined to Sumatra since the Middle Pleistocene (Vernon Weitzell, personal communication). (2) Separate Philippine landmasses during glacial periods of low sea-level would probably have comprised (a) Greater Luzon; (b) Mindanao; Samar and Leyte; (c) Masbate, Panay, Negros and Cebu; (d) Bohol; (e) Mindoro; (f) Palawan (Heaney 1985).

already a close approximation to its present shape when hominids first entered the area, presumably in the Early Pleistocene. In terms of human and biotic developments the major structural divisions can be rearranged to make two basic divisions of more relevance for prehistory. These are *Sundaland* and *Wallacea*, with a third area, *Sahulland*, to the east (Fig. 1.3).

B. Sundaland

Sundaland comprises the regions on or attached to the present Sunda shelf, that is Malaya, Sumatra, Java, Borneo, Palawan, and other small groups such as the Riau and Lingga Islands. Its eastern edge is marked by Huxley's Line of biogeographers, not to be confused with its better known antecedent the Wallace Line, which runs south of the Philippines. Much of this area is now covered by shallow sea, but virtually all of it (2.2 Mkm^2) would have been exposed as dry land by low sea-levels for long periods during the Pleistocene, and especially at the peak of the last glaciation about 18 000 years ago. Drowned river channels and sediments in the beds of the South China and

Java Seas show this very clearly, and these will be described in more detail later. Huxley's Line runs between Bali and Lombok, Borneo and Sulawesi, Borneo and the Sulu Archipelago, then up to include the Calamianes and Palawan, and finally off into the Pacific between Luzon and Taiwan. The eastern edge of Sundaland, between Borneo and Sulawesi, is partially marked by the remarkable Great Sunda Reef — a partly-drowned coral reef which extends out from Borneo into the Strait of Makassar to within 44 km of Sulawesi (Bemmelen 1949: Fig. 4), and which must originally have grown from the old emergent coastline.

C. Wallacea

The term "Wallacea", after Alfred Russel Wallace, the 19th century naturalist, was first introduced into the zoogeographical literature by Dickerson in 1928. Dickerson defined the region as that between Huxley's Line and Weber's Line — a line in eastern Indonesia which is believed to mark a 50:50 balance between the Oriental and Australian faunas. In this book, however, I will adopt a definition which is more relevant for prehistory; Wallacea includes all those islands which lie between the continental shelves of Sundaland and Sahulland, that is the Lesser Sundas from Lombok eastwards, Sulawesi, the Moluccas, and the Philippines (with Sulu, but not Palawan).

Wallacea has evolved as a zone of enormous crustal instability, and now exists as a number of islands separated by deep ocean basins (particularly the Sulu, Sulawesi and Banda Seas), the whole formed by rapid processes of uplift and downfaulting. This area has never formed a continuous land bridge between Asia and Australia, and all faunal, floral and human dispersals through it must have involved water crossings. Some of the enclosed seas have particularly impressive features; for instance, the Sulu Sea is 4633 m deep, and yet is totally enclosed by high ridges which never sink more than 380 m below sea-level. This means that the temperature of this sea remains fairly even from top to bottom, without the rapid cooling with depth found in the great oceans (Molengraaff 1921). The islands of Wallacea rise from the continuous undersea ridges of the region, and the rate of uplift has been very rapid in places; corals of presumed Pleistocene date have been reported from an altitude of 1300 m in Timor, and many islands have series of raised coral coastal terraces. On the other hand, corals have been found to depths of 1633 m in the bed of the Seram Sea, so downfaulting of great magnitude has also occurred.

D. Sahulland

The Sahul shelf forms a shallow, drowned, and tectonically stable link between the Australian continent and the massive island of New Guinea —

it is the Australasian equivalent of the Sunda shelf. The term "Sahulland" may be used to denote the New Guinea–Australian land masses when both were joined together during periods of low sea-level. Environmental changes in northern Sahulland, particularly during the later Pleistocene and Holocene, are of particular significance for an understanding of similar events in Sundaland.

II. The Indo-Malaysian Environment

A. Climate

Since the whole region lies well within the tropics it need hardly be stressed that temperatures are uniformly hot and vary very little throughout the day or from season to season. The only major variation in temperature occurs with altitude (average temperature drops 1°C every 160 m), but even on the highest peak in the region (Mt Kinabalu in Sabah, 4104 m) the temperature never gets colder than an occasional night-time frost. The only permanent glaciers occur to the east in New Guinea, but only 8 km^2 of the total 805 000 km^2 of the island are so covered.

The crucial climatic feature in the region is the rainfall, and for general purposes it is useful to recognise two major zones (Fig. 1.4).

a. The zone, within approximately 5° of the equator, where rain occurs all year round. Most regions do have two slight rainfall peaks, but for practical purposes the rainfall is frequent, heavy, reliable, and the evergreen rainforest grows luxuriantly in constantly damp or wet soils. Malaya, Sumatra, western Java, Borneo, central Sulawesi, the southern and eastern Philippines and parts of the Moluccas fall generally in this zone, which I will henceforth term "equatorial".
b. The zone which extends beyond the equatorial zone both north and south of the equator, and which is characterised by clearly differentiated wet and dry seasons. Within the Indo-Malaysian Archipelago this zone in fact forms the warmer equatorward part of a world-wide intermediate tropical zone (Harris 1980) which is characterised by winter dry seasons of between 2.5 and 7.5 months in length. Within South-East Asia the intermediate tropical zone includes the mainland north of the Malay Peninsula, the western and northern Philippines, and southern Sulawesi and the Lesser Sunda islands from central Java eastwards. The zone ultimately fades into the temperate climates of China, and the deserts of central Asia and Australia. Because of the presence of the dry season, and occasional severe droughts, forests tend to be more open and have a deciduous tendency.

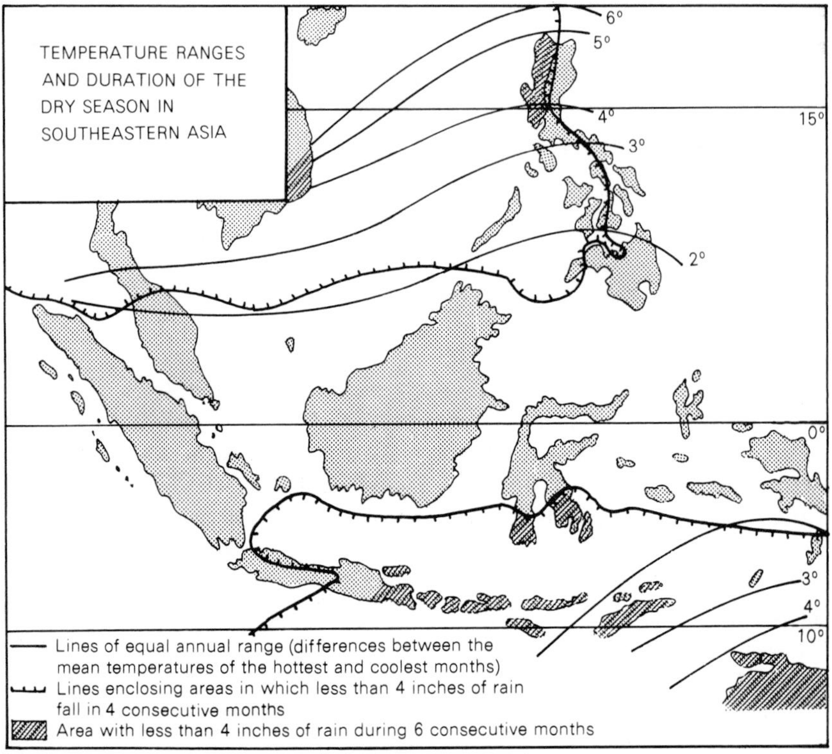

Fig. 1.4. Climatic regimes in the Indo-Malaysian Archipelago. After Robequain 1954. Courtesy: Editions Payot.

To explain these rainfall variations I can only try to summarise a topic which is really very complex (see Mizukoshi 1971; Dobby 1976). A major feature of global air circulation concerns the constant exchange of air (which flows as winds) between the equator and the poles. In the tropics, warm air is constantly rising, and this warm air flows polewards at intermediate altitudes. It cools, sinks in the latitudes of about 20–30°, and flows equatorwards again as the trade winds (these blow from the north-east in the northern hemisphere, and from the south-east in the southern hemisphere). The tropical zone where the trade winds meet and where air convection is strongest is termed the Intertropical Front, or Intertropical Convergence Zone. This front is not fixed in position, but moves seasonally according to temperatures in the continental interiors of Asia and Australia.

In January the Asian interior is cold, the Australian interior hot — the resulting pressure gradient outwards from Asia deflects the Intertropical Front southwards into the southern part of Indonesia and the northern tip of Australia (to about 10–12° south). These areas then receive their rainy season (southern summer) because the front is a constant formation zone of depressions and squalls. In the northern summer (July) the front is pushed far to the north (up to 32° north), and Mainland South-East Asia and the northern Philippines then get their wet seasons. The equatorial regions proper tend to have a double wet season because the front passes over them twice in each year.

However, the Intertropical Front is not the only factor which brings rain to the intermediate tropical regions, for when it lies in the northern hemisphere in the northern summer the southern hemisphere trade winds are sucked across the equator and bring further moisture from the seas which they cross. The same happens in reverse in January, when the northern trades tend to flow further south (although they do not get deflected so far since Australia, as a smaller continent, has a much weaker influence than Asia). These extended trade winds become the monsoons, which are usually named after their directions; however, it should be stressed that these directions vary from place to place and by deflection across the equator, and their effects can be varied locally by relief and position. For instance, the north-east coast of Malaya, in the northern hemisphere, has its wet season in November–January, actually the southern summer. This is because wet trade winds blow directly on to the coast at this time of the year from the South China Sea.

These climatic variations are of great importance for recent prehistory, and postulated changes in them are also of great importance in the Pleistocene — I will be describing some evidence for changes in due course. Typhoons and hurricanes also form in the intermediate tropical zone, but generally occur outside our area of interest. They are common in the northern Philippines, where they blow in from the Pacific Ocean, and likewise in northern Australia and the islands of Melanesia and Polynesia. They are almost unheard of in Indonesia and Malaysia.

B. Landforms and Soils

Humans, animals and plants depend not only on climate for their existence, but also on the nature of the ground upon which they live. In the Indo-Malaysian Archipelago there are some very important variations in landforms and soils, and these variations lie at the base of the enormous differences in population density which are seen today between such islands as Java and Borneo. It is my suspicion that they were equally important in prehistoric times.

The main soils of the equatorial ever-wet region are yellow to red leached lateritic formations, often called latosols. These soils are rich in iron and aluminium, are generally acidic, tend often to be heavy sticky clays, and are generally low in plant nutrients and organic matter. They do, indeed, support dense and luxuriant forests, but these are products of long evolution whereby 50–80% of the nutrients are accumulated in the biomass and constantly recycled in the upper layers of the soil as vegetation grows, dies, and decays. Once these forests are cleared the cycle is broken, since the nutrients simply leach away through the exposed soil, often with disastrous results.

These lateritic soils are generally characteristic of the equatorial and non-volcanic lowlands of Sumatra, the Malay Peninsula, Borneo, Sulawesi and western New Guinea. Today they support low populations, since they are fairly infertile, unsuited in traditional cultivation systems to anything but shifting agriculture, and hard for reasons of structure and excessive rainfall to bring under irrigated and terraced rice. Furthermore, the forest itself is ever-wet, hard to clear and burn with simple equipment, and subject to very rapid regrowth of weeds and secondary vegetation. In addition, many coastal regions of the Malay Peninsula, eastern Sumatra and southern and western Borneo (the drowned gentle slopes of Sundaland) have extensive areas of lowland peat soils (Polak 1975), which are very difficult for any simple economy apart from sago management.

However, the soil patterns change when we move into south-eastern Indonesia, from central Java through the Lesser Sundas. Here the soil is constantly enriched by the fertile outpourings of the many volcanoes, particularly where the products are of basic rather than acidic composition, as they are in central and eastern Java, Bali, Lombok, and also the Minahasa Peninsula of northern Sulawesi. Most (but not all) of the Sumatran volcanoes are more acidic in this respect, and consequently produce soils less favourable for agriculture.

This volcanic replenishment means that the normal tropical trends of leaching and nutrient loss in soils are constantly reversed, and the resulting volcanic ashes are often firm and ideally "carveable" for purposes of rice terrace construction, as any visitor to Bali or eastern Java will observe. This lucky combination does not cease here, for these regions have a climate with a definite dry season; this lessens the rate of soil leaching, and also promotes a partially deciduous and more open vegetation which is an easier target for agricultural societies than the ever-wet equatorial rainforest. However, this monsoonal vegetation is fragile when subjected to clearance, perhaps more so than the equatorial rainforest, and degraded lands in these regions tend to degenerate to extensive grasslands, particularly where droughts are common.

The present-day results of these differences were very clearly pointed out by Mohr as long ago as 1945. From a census taken in 1930 he was able to show that Java and Madura had average densities of over 300 persons per km^2, Bali and Lombok about 175, Sulawesi 22, Borneo 4, and Irian Jaya only 0.73. These figures, even if now outdated (Java had a density of 733 persons per km^2 in 1983), still tell a very important tale, although we must be fair and admit that the high Javanese densities are very much due to the introduction of intensive agricultural techniques, including permanent dry-field cultivation, by the Dutch after 1830. Nevertheless, Mohr was able to show very convincingly how high population densities in Indonesia depend on a combination of basic volcanic soils, a non-excessive rainfall (with a good dry season for cereal ripening and harvest), and a dependence on rice cultivation in permanent irrigated fields. He concluded "in the Netherlands Indies the population density is a function of the nature of the soil, and this is a function of the presence of active volcanoes" (Mohr 1945: 262). These differences in soil qualities, when combined with climate, are very important for reconstructing patterns of prehistoric agriculture in the archipelago.

One final point of importance concerns the rate of erosion and landform change in the tropics; archaeological sites are not only hard to find in dense vegetation, but land surfaces can change very rapidly in geomorphological terms. Caves and rock-shelters are common in South-East Asia, but few appear to contain deposits much older than 20 000 years; this circumstance may mean that in many cases the caves were buried and thus not available for habitation until geologically recent times, although the possibility that Pleistocene human occupation in equatorial regions was very sparse will also be discussed in Chapter 6. The prevailing high rates of erosion also obviously affect open sites, causing rapid destruction or burial. Some idea of the sheer power of erosional processes in these latitudes can be derived from geomorphic observations; the Solo River of Java carries 50 times more sediment by water volume than does the Rhine (Robequain 1954:26), and Haile (1968:278) has suggested that surfaces exposed to active erosion in the Baram region of Sarawak could have been eroded by as much as 750 m in the past 2 million years. In the same vein Hanbury-Tenison (1980) states that limestone surfaces in the Gunung Mulu region of northern Sarawak are eroding at a rate of 0.5 mm per year, or about 1000 m in 2 million years, about ten times the rate of limestone erosion in the United Kingdom.

C. The Flora and Fauna

The Indo-Malaysian Archipelago forms part of the "Malesia" of botanists; in its ever-wet equatorial regions the evergreen mixed Dipterocarp rainforest forms

> ...the most complex terrestrial ecosystem in the world. Below about 1000 metres above sea level the forest canopy lies between thirty and fifty metres above the ground and shelters a more or less dense undergrowth of smaller shade-tolerant trees, shrubs and saplings criss-crossed by lianes and studded with epiphytes... (Walker 1980:21).

Botanists are always eager to quote impressive statistics about this vegetation: within Malesia about 10% of all the plant species in the world, 25% of the genera, and over 50% of the families are represented. Over 25 000 species of flowering plants occur in the region, with 11 000 on Borneo alone. Associated with this variety is a rarity of extensive stands of single tree species. Extreme spatial variation is the rule, and no less than 780 species of trees have been recorded from a single 10 ha plot in northern Sarawak (Hanbury-Tenison 1980); the United Kingdom has a total of only 35 native tree species.

This equatorial rainforest is characteristic of the lowland regions without dry seasons which run along the equator, but in eastern Java, the Lesser Sunda Islands and the southern tips of Sulawesi, the longer dry season has favoured more open monsoon forests with a deciduous tendency, characterised by stands of casuarina, teak, sandalwood and eucalypts. In western Java, southern Sumatra and northern Malaya there is a shorter 3–5 week dry season which also encourages some elements of this type of forest (Ashton 1972). Local ecological variations also cross-cut the major climatic patterns, to give such specialised ecosystems as the coastal mangrove swamps, the limestone forests and the high mountain moss forests.

From a human prehistoric perspective, it is the broad distinction between the equatorial and the monsoonal forests which is likely to be of the greatest significance on a large scale. Modern plant geography also reflects factors concerning the geological history of the Indonesian region which are of importance for human prehistory. The floras of Sundaland are of Asian origin and are very rich in species, a reflection partly of the frequency of dry-land connections across the subcontinent in the past. The floras of Wallacea, on the other hand, have fewer species, higher proportions of endemic species, and a larger Australian element; some species of eucalypts extend as far as Sulawesi and the southern Philippines, and *Agathis* species have spread from New Guinea through equatorial Indonesia to as far as Malaya. Wallacea may be regarded as a transition zone between two ancient continental areas with very different floras.

The differences between Sundaland and Wallacea in terms of flora are also reflected in the distributions of animal species, particularly the large mammals which have a fairly prolific fossil record. Basically, Sundaland has an Asian placental mammal fauna which includes many species ranging in size from the elephant downwards; Wallacea, on the other hand, has fewer species and a greater proportion of endemic ones, with an increasing Australian marsupial element in the east (Fig. 1.5). (For general surveys see Jacobs 1974, Whitmore 1975, 1981).

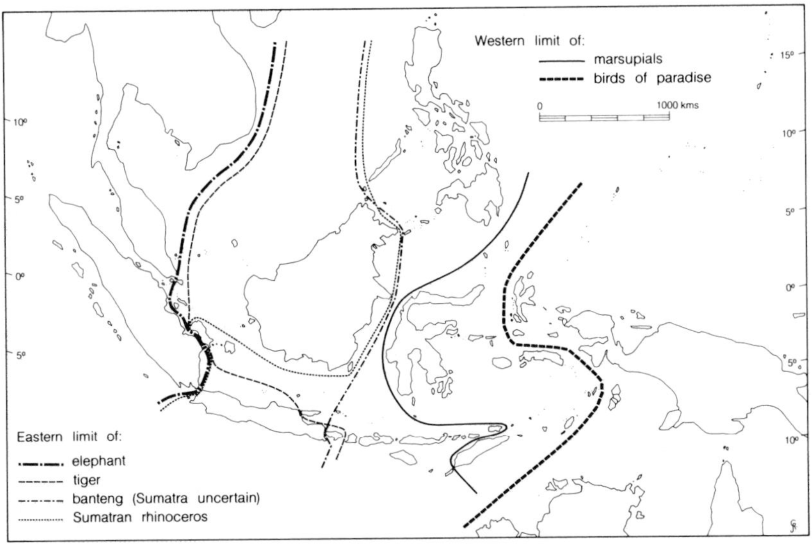

Fig. 1.5. The boundaries of some selected animal species in the Indo-Malaysian Archipelago. The Javan rhinoceros (*Rhinoceros sondaicus*) occurs on Sumatra and Java, but not Borneo, where the Sumatran rhinoceros (*Dicerorhinus sumatrensis*) occurs alone today (but see Chapter 6, Section IIB). After Atlas 1938, Blad 7b.

D. Biogeographical Boundaries

The sluggishness or absence of faunal dispersal across Huxley's Line into the eastern part of the archipelago is clearly of importance for human dispersal. There have been no major Wallacean land bridges of anything more than a very ephemeral nature within the past 2 million years, an observation underlined by biogeographical as well as geological considerations.

The most important of the biogeographical boundaries is Huxley's Line, the eastern edge of Sundaland (see Fig. 1.3). This is the line beyond which the Sundaland fauna drops off markedly into endemicity and species depletion. I should make one point very clear — Sundaland and Australia have never been joined by continuous dry land, and virtually all faunal dispersals into Wallacea have involved sea crossings, apart from the few land bridge cases reviewed below. Of placental mammals, only rats and bats are distributed from Sundaland right through to Sahulland, and of marsupials a number have spread into the eastern Lesser Sundas and Moluccas, but only *Phalanger* (the cuscus) ever reached Sulawesi. The zone defined as Wallacea (between the Sunda and Sahul shelves) is in fact a zone with a partly endemic fauna of mixed Asian and Australian elements, with the former generally being dominant.

Discussions of the significance of Huxley's Line have been numerous, and there is still much disagreement about how to subdivide the Wallacean region in zoogeographical terms (see Scrivenor *et al.* 1942–3; Mayr 1945; Darlington 1957:462–72; Simpson 1977). The line works quite well for freshwater fish, mammals and birds (in that order), but is less marked for insects and plants. It also works well between Borneo and Sulawesi, but the Philippine and Lesser Sunda boundaries are hazy. Although Oriental bird faunas drop off sharply down the Lesser Sunda chain from Java, it appears that the reasons are more to do with changing ecology than with the mere presence of sea gaps (Lincoln 1975). Furthermore, there is no sharp break in plant distributions down the Lesser Sundas (Jacobs 1974; Flenley 1979), while the break is sharper from Borneo (with 280 species of Dipterocarps) to Sulawesi (with only 45). In general, it is best to regard Wallacea as a zone of transition rather than as a zone of barriers.

III. The Pleistocene and World-wide Changes in Environment

Having discussed some elements of the natural environment in remote geological time and at the present day, I will now turn to the fundamental question of variations in climates, land–sea distributions, floras and faunas in the archipelago during the Pliocene and Pleistocene periods. However, in order to document environmental changes in the Pleistocene it is necessary to search the literatures of a number of complex and rapidly expanding disciplines in the general fields of the earth sciences and the natural sciences. There are many viewpoints to explain any given set of phenomena, and rapid obsolescence of any bright new idea seems to be an occupational hazard. I hope my more scientific colleagues will bear with me while I try to set their data in a perspective relevant for human prehistory.

It is sometimes hard to realise what tremendous changes have taken place in concepts of the Pleistocene over the past few years. When I was a student in the middle 1960s, it was still quite reasonable to equate the Pleistocene period in Europe and North America with a sequence of only four or five glaciations with intervening interglacials, and to assume that temperate glaciations correlated with tropical pluvials. It is now believed that there have been perhaps 20 glaciations within the past 2 million years, and glaciations tend to produce dry conditions in low latitudes, not pluvials. Changes in knowledge of chronology and sea-level variations have been equally dramatic.

A. The Pleistocene Period: Definition and Chronology

Concerning overall chronology, the boundary between the Pliocene and Pleistocene periods has been dated in the past according to three different criteria (Goudie 1983): the onset of mid-latitude glaciation, and certain changes in marine or terrestrial faunas. The present cycle of mid-latitude glaciation started about 2.5 to 3.2 million years ago (Shackleton and Opdyke 1977), and earlier cycles can be traced back into the Tertiary. However, most scholars today accept a Plio-Pleistocene boundary based on the appearance of certain new species of cool temperature foraminifera in the oceans between about 1.5 and 2 million years ago; this change is marked at 1.6 million years ago by the Calabrian fauna of the Mediterranean (Haq *et al.* 1977), and a similar change also occurs in the Pacific. The Villafranchian land mammal fauna, once considered to appear in the Early Pleistocene, is now known to go back well into the Pliocene and is no longer acceptable as a boundary marker.

It is, of course, apparent that both the Pliocene and the Pleistocene are rather artificial divisions of convenience — there are no indications of any really major world-wide environmental changes which took place in this particular boundary time span, and hence there is no world-wide clear boundary (Flint 1971). This is even more true of South-East Asia, where it is perhaps hardly justifiable to separate a Pleistocene from a Pliocene at all. However, the terminology is too deep-rooted to tamper with at this stage, and I will follow the international chronology adopted for Java by Orchiston and Siesser (1982) and place the Pliocene-Pleistocene boundary at 1.6 million years ago.

The question remains of subdivisions within the Pleistocene. It has been the tradition in the past to place hominid remains, animal faunas and stone tool assemblages into a framework of Early, Middle and Late Pleistocene, and there have been a number of strong debates between scholars, particularly with respect to Javanese faunas and stone tools, as to which division a particular fauna or industry belongs. The problem is well illustrated in Bemmelen's geological survey (1949): on page 93 Koenigswald placed the Kali Glagah and Ci Julang faunas of Java in the Pliocene, while on page 99 Bemmelen himself (following Movius) placed these faunas in the Lower (Early) Pleistocene. Likewise, Koenigswald (in the above survey) considered the Jetis fauna of Java to be Lower Pleistocene, while Hooijer (1956; 1968) placed it in the Middle Pleistocene. The situation is becoming even more confused today with the publication of conflicting radiometric dates, and it is clear that there are no pan-South-East Asian major changes in environments, hominids or faunas which can be recognised as unequivocal boundary markers. I will therefore follow Orchiston and Siesser (1982) and modern African Pleistocene specialists and refer to the period between 1.6 million and

700 000 years ago as Early Pleistocene, between 700 000 and 125 000 years ago as Middle Pleistocene, and from 125 000 to 10 000 years ago as Late Pleistocene. These divisions are for chronological convenience only, and it will be noted that they are not of equal duration. The Late Pleistocene is the only division with a firm environmental record in South-East Asia, and it equates with the last interglacial and last glacial of the temperate Pleistocene chronologies. Finally, I place the Pleistocene–Holocene boundary at 10 000 years ago following convention; this date probably falls somewhere near the centre of the world-wide postglacial warming trend.

B. The Consequences of Mid-latitude Glaciation

According to present theories (Beaty 1978; Chappell 1978; Covey 1984) the mid-latitude glaciations of the past 3 million years have been caused by the interactions of a number of phenomena. Cyclical causes may include variations in the intensity of solar radiation, and variations in the earth's trajectory and the slope of its axis. Other less cyclical causes may include the frequency of ash clouds from volcanic activity, and periods of continental uplift in high latitudes. At peaks of glaciation the icesheets covered three times their present area and extended deep into Europe and North America. During interglacials, conditions returned to something like those of the present, and within the glacials themselves there occurred short warm phases called interstadials, when conditions ameliorated to intermediate levels.

The major world-wide effects of glaciation were to lower sea-levels, vegetation zones and temperatures, and these changes were all felt quite strongly in tropical latitudes. For instance, in the fairly intensively studied highlands of New Guinea (Walker 1978; Flenley 1979; Hope 1980), icesheets covered about 2000 km^2 (only 8 km^2 now) at the last glacial peak of 18 000 years ago, the snow line was lowered to 1100 m below its present altitude, the tree line was lowered by about 1600 m, average highland temperatures dropped by 7–7.5° C, and 57 200 km^2 of land below the ice were under grassland (as opposed to only 5000 km^2 now). In South-East Asia the effects of pre-existing permanent glaciers are still traceable on the summit of Mt Kinabalu on Borneo (Flenley and Morley 1978), although any which might have occurred on the high volcanoes of Java and Sumatra will have left no traces owing to subsequent volcanic activity.

As a result of these changes caused by glaciation, tropical climates on large land masses became drier, rainforests shrank in extent, land bridges were exposed in the Indo-Malaysian Archipelago, and humans, animals and plants were subjected to alternating phases of island contact and island isolation.

C. The Cycles of Glacials and Interglacials

Until the 1960s, Pleistocene climatic cycles were traced mainly from studies of glacial geomorphology in temperate latitudes; the tropics remained rather remote and mysterious. However, in the past 20 years knowledge has been revolutionised by the results derived from deep-sea cores, and also from studies on deeply stratified terrestrial gastropod and pollen bearing soils. Sediments in the beds of the oceans contain shells of tiny marine micro-organisms, and these shells contain oxygen in two isotopic forms; ^{16}O and ^{18}O. during glaciations, the vast quantities of water trapped in the icesheets immobilised large amounts of ^{16}O, and the cold seas were thus relatively rich in ^{18}O. In interglacials the ratios were reversed. Fluctuations in these ratios have been plotted from deep-sea cores for the duration of the Pleistocene in several areas, and since they are thought to reflect partly the waxing and waning of continental glaciers they give very good evidence for Pleistocene climatic and sea-level cycles.

One very important core, drilled in the seas of the Solomon Islands, showed that there had been at least seven full glacial maxima with low sea-levels since the Matuyama to Brunhes reversal of the earth's magnetic field about 700 000 years ago (Shackleton and Opdyke 1973; Shackleton 1982). It is now known that there have been about 20 full glacials within the past 2 million years, and the same number of intervening true interglacials, plus periodic intermediate interstadials within the glacials themselves. This record has come from deep-sea cores, deep pollen bearing soil profiles in France and Greece, from gastropod faunas in loess deposits in central Europe, and also from the dating of coral reefs as indicators of past sea-levels (Butzer 1976; Donk 1976; Wright 1976; Chappell and Thom 1977; Fink and Kukla 1977; Kukla 1977, 1981; Chappell 1983). There is still some disagreement about the duration of the glacial–interglacial cycles, but present views seem to favour long glacials of about 100 000 years separated by much shorter interglacials of about 10 000 to 30 000 years (Wright 1976; Beaty 1978; Imbrie and Imbrie 1979; Kukla 1981; Covey 1984).

Two other general observations emerge; the glacials have become more severe within the past one million years, and the glacial waxing and waning cycles themselves are not totally regular. Glacial retreats appear to have been much more rapid than glacial advances (Fig. 1.6 Top), and this high rate of environmental change is important for any consideration of the emergence of the present world environmental regime at the end of the last glaciation.

D. World Sea-level Changes during the Pleistocene

Large scale glaciation implies a lowering of world absolute sea-level, owing to the immobilisation of vast quantities of water in the icesheets. If it is

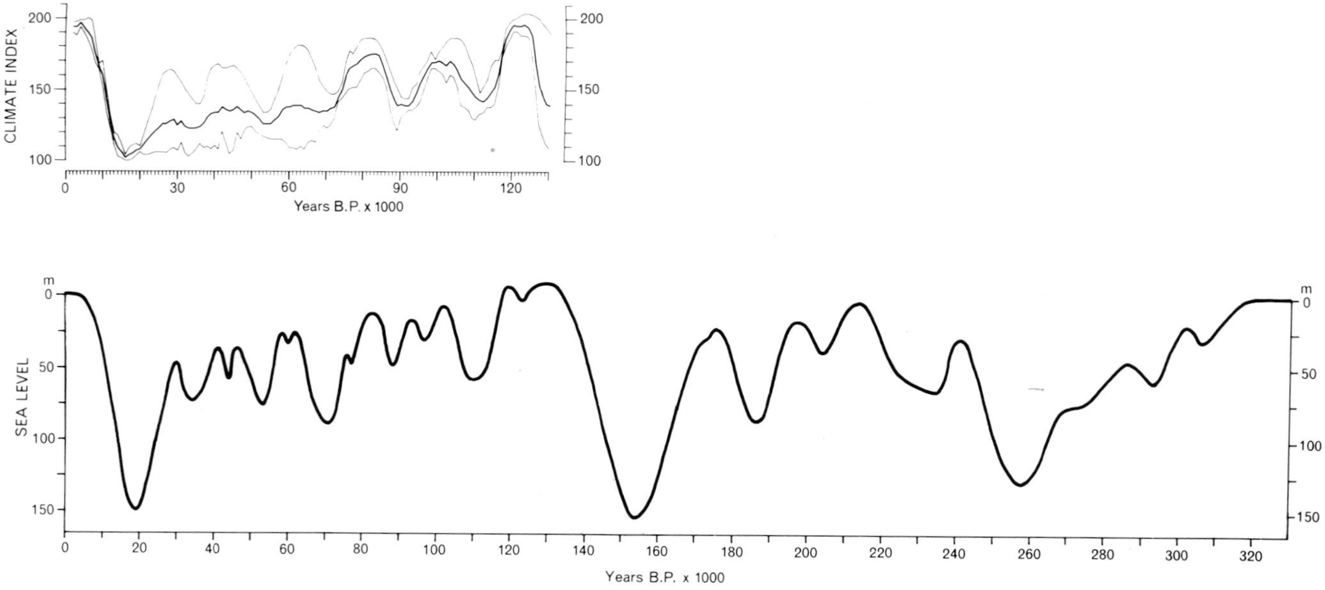

Fig. 1.6. Top: climatic severity index for the past 130 000 years derived from pollen, sea-level and oxygen isotope data. The vertical scale is relative: 100 units correspond to peak glacial conditions; 200 units to the climatic peak of the mid-Holocene. Uncertainty ranges are also indicated. After Kukla 1981. Courtesy: D. Reidel Publishing Company. Bottom: a sea-level curve for the past 330 000 years based on data from the Huon Peninsula, north-eastern New Guinea. Prepared by John Chappell (see Chappell 1982, 1983, for further details).

accepted, from the oxygen isotope record, that there have been 20 glacial–interglacial cycles within the past 2 million years, then world sea-levels must have gone through 20 major cycles of glacial falling and interglacial rising, not to mention interstadial fluctuations. Magnitudes of these absolute fluctuations have always been hard to estimate, and the most direct indicators come from observations of drowned shelf topography and the dating of old coastline markers such as coral reefs and mangrove timbers.

However, the calculations are not simple, since the earth's surface is not a rigid unmoving formation washed by fluctuating water levels. It can move in a very dynamic fashion itself, partly through the mechanism of isostasy, which compensates for the imposition of variable loads such as icesheets and oceans at changing times and places on its surface (Chappell 1974; Clark *et al.* 1978). In general, water, ice or sediment loads promote sinking, while relief from such loads will allow slow upward rebound. These processes are complicated and details need not be of further concern, except to note that isostatic adjustment processes will have operated mainly in the intermittently-drowned Sunda and Sahul shelf regions, while many of the Wallacean islands are subject to other kinds of tectonic instability, so that they themselves can rise and fall independently of sea-level changes at quite rapid rates. Northern Timor, for instance, seems to be rising at the fairly rapid rate of 0.5 m per thousand years (Chappell and Thom 1977), and north-east New Guinea at up to 4 m per thousand years. As Chappell (1982) has recently pointed out, each region of the earth must be studied independently with respect to local correlations between the surfaces of land and sea over time.

At present, the sea is at a high absolute level in terms of Pleistocene fluctuations, and the present level was previously attained during the last interglacial, about 120 000 years ago (Fig. 1.6 Bottom). At the last glacial maximum, 18 000 years ago, the sea-level is widely estimated to have been between 100 and 150 m below that of the present (Gohara 1976; Chappell and Thom 1977; Batchelor 1979), and a high-to-low overall swing of about this magnitude may have occurred approximately every 100 000 years going back to one million years ago. The swings before one million years ago seem to have been of slightly decreasing magnitude.

When we come to consider more detailed aspects of these fluctuations we find ourselves very much confined to the last 120 000 years, for which there are obviously more data than for previous cycles. The last interglacial had a fairly short duration, between about 130 000 and 120 000 years ago (Kukla 1981; Chappell 1983), and the seas were at around present absolute levels at this time. Following this, according to the charts of Chappell and Thom for the Huon Peninsula of New Guinea (1977: Fig. 1; Chappell 1982, 1983) the sea-levels fluctuated between relative low points at about 115 000, 90 000, 55 000, 35 000 and 18 000 years ago, and intervening high points at about 105 000, 80 000, 60 000, 40 000 and 28 000 years ago. However, none of these intervening highs appear to have attained the level of the present, and the "high" of 28 000 years ago may have reached only 60 m below present, according to recent evidence from the Sunda shelf off western Malaya (Geyh *et al.* 1979). A chart for Japan (Gohara 1976) also shows a "high" at about 65 m below present at 25 000 to 26 000 years ago, followed by the major last glacial drop to a suggested 130 m below present at about 20 000 years ago. The implications of these figures are that high stands like that of the present and low stands like that of 18 000 BP were relatively short-lived events during the Pleistocene, and average absolute levels would have been between 30 and 80 m below present for much longer periods.

These fluctuations in sea-level are of great potential importance for prehistory, since low levels make islands larger and also tend to produce land bridges. Shortened sea crossings are particularly important when considering the first settlement of Australia, and this could relate to one of the low points from 35 000 years ago or before (cf. Birdsell 1977), although this remains only surmise at present. One major problem is that there is still no real agreement on a precise absolute sea-level curve; I have referred to that of Chappell and Thom above since it is based on evidence from New Guinea, close to our area of interest. On the other hand, results from other parts of the world are often in conflict (Marcus and Newman 1983), probably owing to local tectonic and isostatic movements, and it would be unwise to demand too much precision at present; for instance, compare the conflicting results of Giresse and Davies (1980) from Africa, Cronin *et al.* (1981) from the United States Atlantic coastal plain, and Geyh *et al.* (1979) from the Strait of Malacca.

One final matter concerns the disputed question of a world sea-level slightly above that of the present during the Holocene. There are raised marine deposits in Japan (Gohara 1976), Malaya (Tjia 1970, 1980; Ashton 1972) and Java (Thommeret and Thommeret 1978) which suggest that sea-levels could have been up to 6 m above present during a warm phase of the Holocene between about 6000 and 3000 years ago (see also Haile 1971; Lamb 1982). These deposits may reflect tectonic or isostatic movement rather than an actual rise in absolute sea-level (Chappell 1982), but they do still indicate that parts of Sundaland may have been *relatively* more drowned then than they are now. The magnitude of the difference is very small, although the potential here for the destruction of early Holocene archaeological sites is clearly of great importance (see Chapter 6).

IV. The Environmental History of the Indo-Malaysian Archipelago during the Pliocene and Pleistocene

During the Miocene period (23 million to 5 million years ago) and the Pliocene (5 million to 1.6 million years ago) the archipelago gradually took

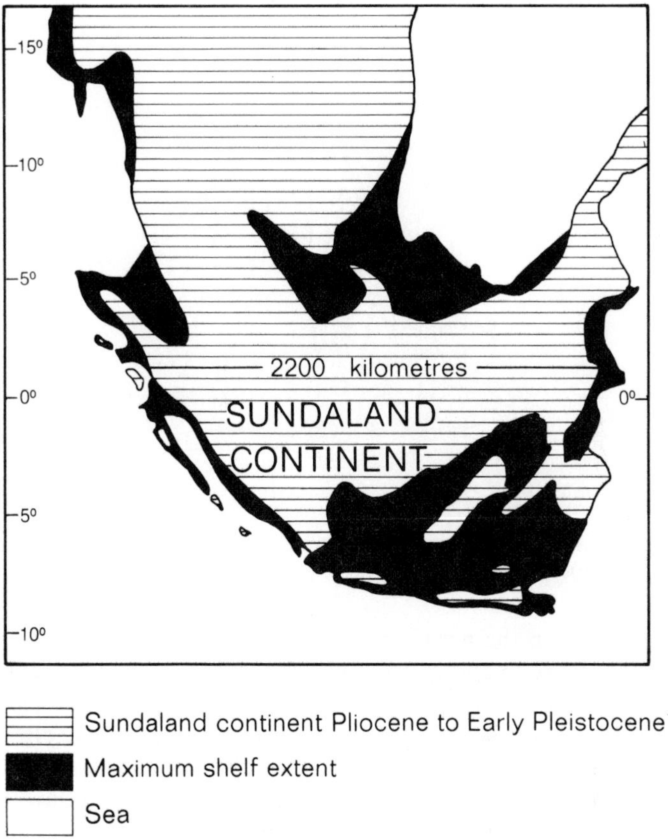

Fig. 1.7. The possible geographical extent of Sundaland in the Late Pliocene and Early Pleistocene. After Batchelor 1979. Courtesy: Geologie en Mijnbouw.

on its present shape, as a result of continuing island arc formation, and the constant pressure after 15 million years ago of the Australian continental plate in the east. By the end of the Pliocene, Sundaland already formed a large emerging continent some 2000 km from east to west (Fig. 1.7), incorporating much of the present land masses of Malaya, Sumatra and Borneo. Some parts of Java had also emerged, although there is current debate on the geography of the island at this time (Braches and Shutler 1983–4).

A. The Pliocene in Java, the Lesser Sundas and Sulawesi

In the earlier Pliocene a mammal fauna with strong Indian affinities (called "Siva-Malayan" by Koenigswald, and related to the Eurasian Villafranchian)

Fig. 1.8. A male *Stegodon*; in females the tusks were shorter and more widely spaced. From Kurten 1971. Courtesy: Weidenfeld Ltd.

gained a footing in the newly-emerging western and central Java. Its main Kali Glagah phase is known from coastal estuarine deposits, and animals present include extinct species of elephant, *Stegodon* (a proboscid distantly related to the elephants, see Fig. 1.8), hippopotamus, deer, pig and large felines (but apparently no hominids or forest primates), and the whole assemblage with its numerous browsing animals seems to have been well suited to both forested and more open parkland landscapes.

Although there can be no real certainty with respect to date, it appears that the Pliocene was also a time of two important faunal dispersals eastwards, neither on present evidence involving early hominids. One of these took place from Java along the Lesser Sundas to Flores and Timor, and the other was from Borneo to Sulawesi (possible contemporary movements from Borneo to the Philippines are not really of concern here). The link to Sulawesi is documented by the Cabenge fauna from several localities in the Walanae Valley in the south-western part of the island. This contains species of *Stegodon*, elephant (a small species derived from a larger Pliocene population on Sundaland, Maglio 1973), pig, and the pig-like babirusa and buffalo-like anoa (two of the odd mammals of Sulawesi which have survived the isolation of the Pleistocene to the present day). A significant chronological marker in this fauna is a giant land tortoise (*Geochelone*), which appears to have disappeared from Java before the end of the Pliocene Kali Glagah faunal phase (Sondaar 1981). It was once thought that the Cabenge fauna arrived in Sulawesi via a land bridge through the Sangihe Islands from the

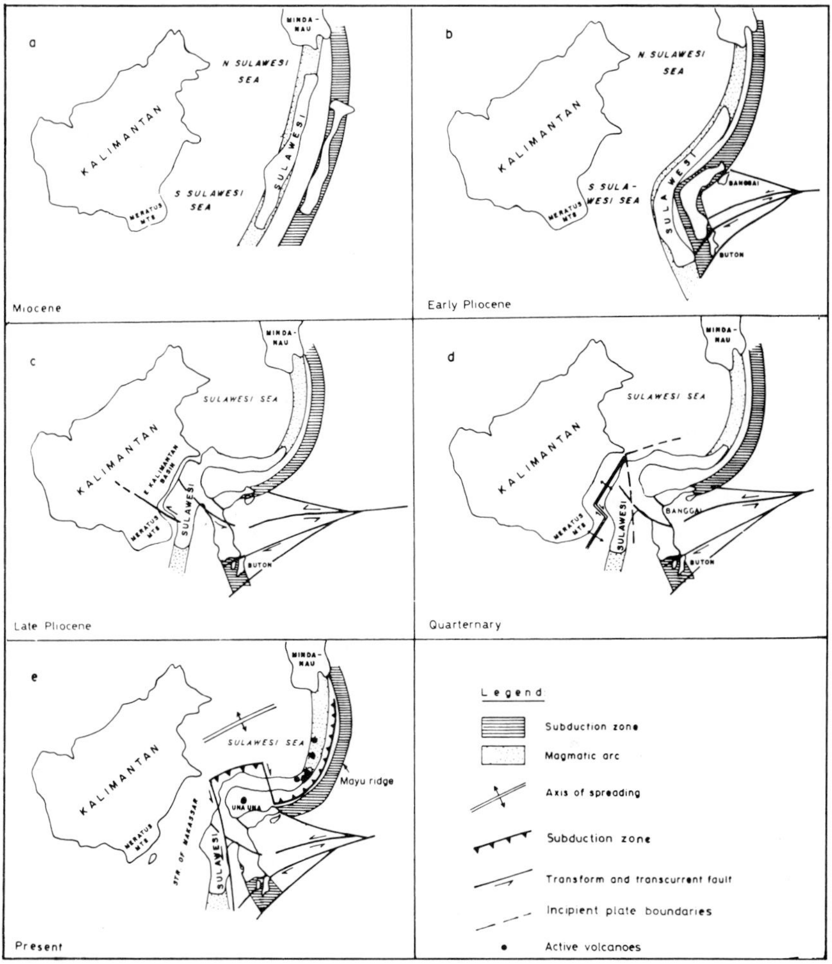

Fig. 1.9. The geological evolution of Sulawesi from Miocene times to the present, according to Katili (1978). Courtesy: Elsevier Science Publishers B.V.

Philippines and China, but it is now agreed that it is of Sundaland origin (Groves 1976; Bartstra 1977; Sartono 1979a).

How did the fauna get to Sulawesi? It is hard to imagine that all these species swam across the present distance from Borneo, and Groves (1976) has proposed a Pliocene land bridge from Java, while Katili (1978) has suggested that western Sulawesi was actually joined to eastern Borneo in the Pliocene, as a result of pressure from the Australian continental plate (Fig. 1.9).

However, there seems little doubt that any such land bridge would have been short-lived (Audley-Charles 1981; Cranbrook 1981), and the absence of a land bridge throughout the following Pleistocene period is also well-documented by Sulawesi's more recent fauna; the only other major species to reach the island by natural means since the period of the Cabenge fauna are cuscuses (*Phalanger*, a marsupial genus) from New Guinea via the Moluccas, and macaque monkeys from Borneo (deer and civet cats are probably recent human introductions). Of the Cabenge fauna itself, only Celebes pig, babirusa and anoa have survived to the present.

The evidence for a land bridge along the Lesser Sunda chain from Java to Timor is rather more tenuous. As with Borneo and Sulawesi the glacial sea-level changes would have been insufficient to bridge all the gaps, and even if tectonic movements of the seabed are invoked it seems unlikely that a continuous bridge ever ran all the way to Timor. The fossil faunas of the Lesser Sundas are simply too impoverished, and consist only of *Geochelone* tortoises from Timor (Sondaar, 1981, disputes that these belong to the same species as those from Java), sporadic rodent species, and species of *Stegodon*. The latter, however, are of particular importance for the land bridge question because it has recently been discovered that separate large and dwarfed species, probably derived from *Stegodon trigonocephalus* of Java, once existed in Mindanao, Sulawesi, Flores and Timor (Hooijer 1975, 1967–8; Sartono 1969, 1973), and one species of uncertain size existed on Sumba as well (Sartono 1979b; Hooijer 1981). To explain these distributions Audley-Charles and Hooijer (1973, see also Hooijer 1975) have suggested that Flores and Timor were joined by a land bridge through Alor in the Late Pliocene or Early Pleistocene, prior to subsidence of the (now 3000 m deep) Timor Sea, and also that Flores was similarly joined to south-western Sulawesi.

Other scholars have been loath to accept these postulated land bridges owing to the degree of tectonic movement which they demand, and a contrary theory is favoured by Sondaar (1981). This theory suggests that the *Stegodon* and tortoise species were able to move from Sundaland into the Lesser Sundas independently, perhaps by swimming. *Stegodon* thereafter could have undergone independent dwarfing as a result of restriction to relatively small islands, and the tortoises could have undergone separate selection for reptilian gigantism (both these processes for large mammals and reptiles are known from other islands). If Sondaar is right (and see Hooijer 1982 for disagreement) then a land bridge from either Java or Sulawesi to Timor is not required, but it seems that neither possibility can be conclusively proven and lively debate will doubtless continue.

B. The Pleistocene in Java

Prior to the beginning of the Pleistocene a new fauna had appeared in Java (see Chapter 2, Fig. 2.5 for site locations). It was called "Sino-Malayan" by

Koenigswald, since it shares more species with southern China than did the preceding Siva-Malayan fauna. It is also much richer in species, including many which still exist today. This fauna develops through three overlapping stages; traditionally termed Jetis (the earliest), Trinil, and Ngandong (but see Vos *et al.* 1982 for a suggested rearrangement of this scheme). New appearances in the Jetis (Koenigswald 1949; Hooijer 1968; Medway 1972) include rhinoceros, forest primates such as the gibbon and orang utan, and of course hominids. In addition, the fauna contains a very wide range of large herbivores such as elephant, cattle, buffalo, deer, pig and hippopotamus, and carnivores such as tiger, bear, panther and dogs of the *Cuon* genus.

The best record of human and faunal evolution in Java comes from a rather dramatic locality known as Sangiran (Fig. 1.10), where a domed formation of Pliocene and Pleistocene deposits has been cut open and exposed by the Cemoro River, a tributary of the much larger Solo. The crater-like exposure here measures approximately 6 by 4 km, and in its rather dissected base are exposed Pliocene estuarine sediments upon which lie patches of terrestrial Pleistocene formations (Matsu'ura 1982). During Late Pliocene times the region around Sangiran was still partly under the sea, and it appears that a long marine strait occupied much of the area of the present Solo Valley. Sangiran seems to have been quite near the coastline, since recent pollen analyses of the Pliocene estuarine sediments have indicated the presence of mangroves, *nipah* palms and pandanus trees (Sémah 1982a).

Above the Pliocene estuarine deposits in Sangiran come two major terrestrial formations: the Pucangan and the succeeding Kabuh. The Pucangan formation is exposed through a total thickness of about 200 m, and comprises mainly lacustrine black clays with two periods of marine estuarine transgression (Sémah *et al.* 1981; Bartstra 1974). The base of the Pucangan has thick estuarine deposits which contain shark teeth and shells of oysters, mother of pearl, and other bivalves. The pollen analyses support the stratigraphy in suggesting a gradual emergence of the land around Sangiran during Pucangan times, and the mangroves were slowly replaced by dry land vegetation with both rainforest and open country characteristics (Sémah 1982a,b). The Pucangan beds contain the Jetis fauna described above, together with the earliest hominids.

Above the Pucangan beds at Sangiran lie the Kabuh alluvial beds which contain the Trinil fauna; these beds are between 30 and 45 m thick, and have also produced the bulk of the hominid finds. Pollen from the Kabuh layers at Sangiran is predominantly of non-arboreal type (Gramineae, Cyperaceae), but rainforest continued to exist in the general region. It may be that volcanic eruptions promoted some open vegetation at the expense of forest (Sémah 1982a), and the possibility that the climate periodically had a longer dry season than now might also be considered.

The ages of these deposits are difficult to determine, and there is still much disagreement. Ninkovitch and Burckle (1978) have dated the base of the

Fig. 1.10. Top: the dissected Sangiran dome, central Java. Bottom: the Solo River at Trinil, central Java.

Pucangan beds at Sangiran to between 1.9 and 2.1 million years ago according to diatom correlations, and an age for the boundary between the Pucangan and the overlying Kabuh beds of either 950 000 or 700 000 years has been suggested by Sémah *et al.* (1981; Sémah 1982), from evidence for a palaeomagnetic reversal in the sediments. Siesser and Orchiston (1978) have suggested that foraminifera found in sediment attached to one of the most ancient hominid mandibles from Java (the *Pithecanthropus* mandible C from the Pucangan formation at Sangiran) are at least 1.6 million years old, and the lower marine facies of the Pucangan at Perning in eastern Java may date back well into the Late Pliocene (Sartono *et al.* 1981).

A date as recent as 700 000 or even 950 000 years ago for the Pucangan-Kabuh boundary poses some problems, however, since the Kabuh formation at Sangiran has recently produced an apparently reliable potassium-argon date of 1.2 million years (Curtis 1981:16). The status of this sample has been questioned by Pope (1984), but if it is correct then it clearly contradicts the suggested palaeomagnetic dates for the end of the Pucangan, and it seems to me that it would be unwise to be too precise about the overall ages of the Pucangan and Kabuh formations at this stage of research; the boundary between the two may not in fact be synchronous over the whole of central and eastern Java.

A "best fit" chronological scheme for central Java which favours a long chronology has recently been presented by Orchiston and Siesser (1982), and I have incorporated their conclusions in Fig. 1.11. They place the base of the Pucangan beds between 2.5 and 3 million years ago, and the Pucangan-Kabuh boundary between 1.2 and 1.4 million years ago. Also shown in Fig. 1.11 are the younger chronological estimates favoured by Pope (1984), and supported by Bartstra (1983). Given current disagreements it seems best to regard the Jetis and Trinil faunas as a continuous and intergrading sequence spanning the period from perhaps 2 million to about 500 000 years ago, and the *Homo erectus* fossils, to be described in Chapter 2, apparently made their appearance after 1.7 million years ago (the date favoured by Orchiston and Siesser) or after 1.3 million years ago (the date favoured by Pope, and also by Matsu'ura 1982).

The Jetis and Trinil faunas comprise a mixture of forest and parkland forms which presumably continued across a non-fossiliferous hiatus in the Middle Pleistocene represented by the volcanic Notopuro deposits, into the late Middle and Late Pleistocene Ngandong fauna. After the Notopuro tuffs and lahars were deposited in central Java the area was subject to uplift, causing river rejuvenation and terrace formation. The Ngandong fauna has been found on one of these terraces in the Solo Valley, and all its genera apart from *Stegodon* are still living; it may be regarded as the direct ancestor of the present fauna of Java.

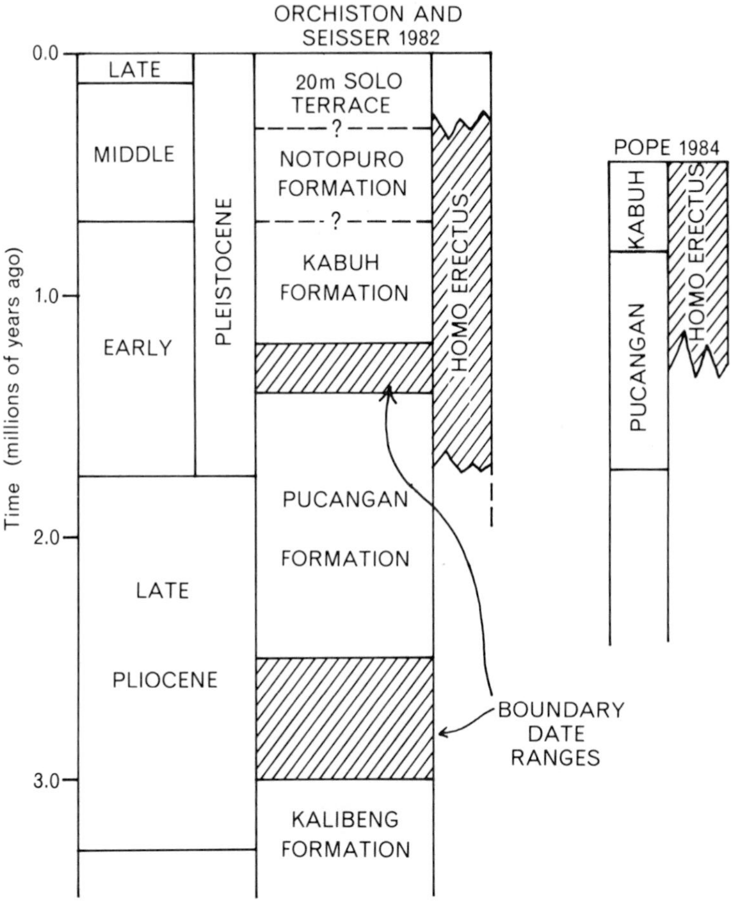

Fig. 1.11. Possible chronological and stratigraphic schemes for the Late Pliocene and Pleistocene in central and eastern Java. After Orchiston and Siesser (1982); Pope (1984).

C. Pleistocene Land–Sea Relationships in the Indo-Malaysian Archipelago

The question of sea-level relative to land surface level during the Pleistocene in Sundaland now arises, and possibly the surface of this vast area was indeed repeatedly flooded and then exposed in recurrent cycles of about 120 000 years, as the record from deep-sea cores might suggest. At present this possibility cannot be easily assessed, and the opinions published to date suggest several lines of disagreement. For instance, Batchelor (1979) has recently claimed that the Sunda shelf off western Malaya has submarine fan and braided stream deposits which show that it was emergent almost continuously until about 500 000 years ago, and even thereafter was not submerged to present levels until the last interglacial, only about 120 000 years ago. On the other hand, Tjia (1980) seems clearly unwilling to accept such a continuously low relative sea-level in the Early and Middle Pleistocene, and there are some zoological arguments to suggest that Sundaland must have been separated into islands for quite long periods going back into the Pliocene; Chivers (1977) believes that such periodic geographical isolation is required to explain gibbon speciation since this period, and Musser (1982) presents a similar viewpoint for rats.

This apparent difference of opinion about the possibility of a periodic drowning of Sundaland in the Early and Middle Pleistocene cannot easily be resolved at present, mainly because the sea-level history of Sundaland cannot simply be read from world absolute sea-level curves; even if isostatic compensation is allowed for there is always the unknown possibility that localised tectonic movement has occurred. However, if the latter is arbitrarily discounted, then the general shallowness of the present seas over the Sunda shelf would indicate that a drop of only 50 m with respect to the present land surface would be sufficient to join up Malaya, Sumatra, Java and Borneo into a sizeable continent. Sundaland could therefore have been exposed as a continental area of varying size for the greater part of the Pleistocene, and its present island configuration may be unusual in terms of geological time.

The surface of Sundaland as an emerged continent contains some interesting features. The shallow shelves of the South China and Java Seas are incised by a number of fossil river channels; between Sumatra and western Borneo there are three major ones, termed by Haile (1973) the Anambas, North Sunda (with the Proto-Kapuas as a tributary) and Proto-Lupar valleys. These can be clearly followed to the edge of the Sunda shelf at a depth of about 100 m (Fig. 1.12). Two large parallel rivers also ran along the bed of the Java Sea between Java and Borneo towards the Strait of Makassar (Umbgrove 1949; Verstappen 1975). Similarities in freshwater fish species between eastern Sumatra and western Borneo indicate that the rivers of these islands were once linked; the Musi of Sumatra and the Kapuas of Borneo in particular were once part of the North Sunda river system. On the other hand, some of these large rivers clearly served as faunal and floral divides of some magnitude; Ashton (1972) has pointed out that the Dipterocarp forest trees show some sharp breaks in distribution at the Lupar River in western Borneo, and the presence of the large rivers between Java and Borneo may have slowed down faunal dispersals between these two islands in the Pleistocene.

D. Environmental Conditions of the Last Glaciation in the Indo-Malaysian Archipelago

The environmental fluctuations of the past 120 000 years, since world climate and sea-level were last at around their present configurations, are rapidly

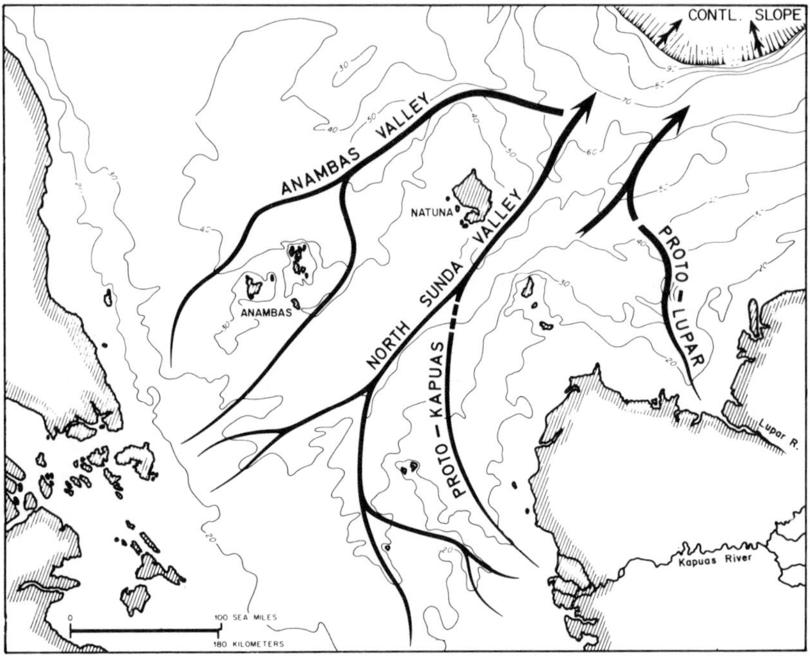

Fig. 1.12. The submarine topography of the northern Sunda shelf. From Haile 1973. Courtesy: Tsukiji Shokan.

becoming quite well-plotted. As noted above the major results come from oxygen isotope determinations, pollen analysis and sea-level studies. A graph of relative climatic severity over the past 130 000 years has recently been prepared by Kukla (1981), see Fig. 1.6 Top, and this shows quite clearly how relative severity increased gradually and slowly, despite fluctuations, until the last glacial maximum at about 18 000 years ago. The amelioration since then has been relatively very rapid indeed, and this is important for the rate of the last major sea-level rise; it has been estimated that parts of the Sahul shelf may have been drowned at rates of 25–45 m horizontal migration per year (Andel *et al.* 1967), although this movement was interrupted by occasional stillstands. Rates of vertical sea-level rise probably rose to maxima between 1.0 and 1.5 m per century (Chappell and Thom 1977:285). On the Sunda shelf, Haile (1973) has postulated a very rapid drowning of the course of the Proto-Lupar River, although this could involve local tectonic downwarping as well.

If we now focus on the last 40 000 years, for which there is increasingly good archaeological and environmental evidence, there is fairly widespread agreement on a temperate latitude cold phase around 35 000 years ago, with a following interstadial which peaked somewhere between 30 000 and 25 000 years ago. After 25 000 years ago the temperature began to downcurve again, to reach a nadir at about 18 000 years ago. Climates and sea-levels then returned to approximate present conditions by around 8000 years ago, and in some parts of the world the mid-Holocene climate was perhaps a little warmer and wetter than at present (Kutzbach 1981; Lamb 1982).

The conditions of the last glacial maximum in the tropics are of most interest here, and it is now becoming clear that some of these areas were considerably drier at this time, with evidence for relative aridity, decline of forest biomass, drying of lakes and extensions of deserts in Australia, Africa, the Middle East, India and South America (Williams 1975; Hamilton 1976; Simpson and Haffer 1978; Flohn 1981; CLIMANZ 1983). The Bay of Bengal waters were more saline than now, and this has been taken to reflect a decrease in summer monsoon rainfall and a consequent decrease in the quantity of fresh water entering the ocean from rivers (Duplessy 1981, 1982).

The evidence for Indo-Malaysian climatic conditions at 18 000 years ago is not as clear as it is for some of the larger tropical continental areas, partly because this area is relatively complex in terms of land–sea and altitudinal patterning. For instance, in terms of temperature it is apparent that New Guinea Highland averages fell to about 7–7.5° C below present averages (see Section IIIB), and tree and snow lines fell by between 1000 and 1600 m. For highland Taiwan a similar drop in average temperature of 5–9° C has been suggested by Tsukada (1966). Such dramatic plunges in average temperature probably did not occur in the tropical lowlands, however, and last glacial estimates for Sundaland locations near sea-level tend to fall between 2 and 5° C below present (Peterson 1969; Verstappen 1975; Batchelor 1979). New data derived from oxygen isotope analyses of coral reef shells from the Huon Peninsula of Papua New Guinea (Aharon 1983) suggest that tropical sea-surface temperature could have dropped by as much as 6° C below present during the last glacial maximum, but this figure is higher than that derived by a number of recent palaeoclimatic simulation studies (e.g. CLIMAP 1976; Manabe and Hahn 1977; Budd 1983). It is unfortunate that there are as yet no pollen sequences covering the last glacial in the lowland equatorial regions of South-East Asia, and while the evidence does seem to me to favour a lowland temperature drop of some extent it was probably of less magnitude than at high altitudes.

Turning now to rainfall, we may recall that through much of the Pleistocene both Sundaland and Sahulland would have been above sea-level as large continental areas, and periods of drowning like the present probably only occurred for short periods. The period of continentality at the maximum of the last glaciation would certainly have produced drier climates. Lower temperatures would reduce convectional rainfall, and winds would tend to be drier since they would cross larger land areas and cooler seas. High latitude glaciation would cause an increased pressure gradient between the Asian and Australian continents and the equator, and the Intertropical Front may have moved outside the limits of the Indo-Malaysian Archipelago for longer periods than it does now. Dry seasons would become longer, and even the equatorial regions could have experienced briefer and smaller rainfall maxima (Verstappen 1975; Batchelor 1979). Verstappen (1975:10) has suggested that average rainfall in Sundaland could have been reduced by as much as 30% during the last glaciation.

All this suggests that the Indo-Malaysian Archipelago would probably have had much larger areas of monsoon forest during the last glaciation, even if the inner core regions of equatorial forest in Sundaland and New Guinea were relatively little affected. The rainforest itself has certainly maintained a stable composition in Borneo since the Miocene (Muller 1975), but there possibly were landscapes with longer dry seasons and more open vegetation during the successive Pleistocene glaciations, perhaps around the fringes of the Sunda shelf, along which open forest mammals and hominids could have passed more freely southwards across the equator. This possibility was pointed out from a floral viewpoint some years ago by Steenis (1961, 1965; see also Scrivenor *et al.* 1942–3:148), who showed that several species of Leguminosae and grasses adapted to long dry seasons occur in the northern and southern monsoonal areas, but with sharp gaps in distribution in equatorial Indonesia at the present time (Fig. 1.13). To explain these disjunct distributions Steenis suggested that dry season zones or corridors had been more extensive in the past, particularly through Sulawesi and the Philippines. This need not of course imply the presence of continuous land bridges in this eastern region (Flenley 1979), and any dry season zones across Sundaland itself may have been fairly restricted in geographical and temporal extent; they were certainly never extensive enough to break up the overall distribution of the equatorial Dipterocarp rainforest (Ashton 1972; Walker 1982).

Other geomorphic observations fill out this picture of late glacial dryness, especially in and around Sundaland. Verstappen (1975) has suggested that the coarse alluvial and colluvial deposits of the last glacial in Malaya indicate tree savanna conditions with considerable erosion and valley filling, and terrestrial deposits beneath the sea on the Sunda shelf include bauxite and laterite pans, kankar nodules, and possibly braided stream deposits, all suggesting past seasonal climates. Confirmatory evidence for a shrinking of rainforests during glacial periods in the tropics has also been claimed by Shackleton (1977) from curves of variation in carbon-13 content in equatorial Pacific foraminifera; he suggests that plant biomass and associated humus, especially in the tropics, increased by a factor of three during the warming phase of 14 000 to 8000 years ago.

The Sahul shelf has produced similar evidence for glacial dryness. Andel *et al.* (1967) have suggested that it received only between one-third and one-

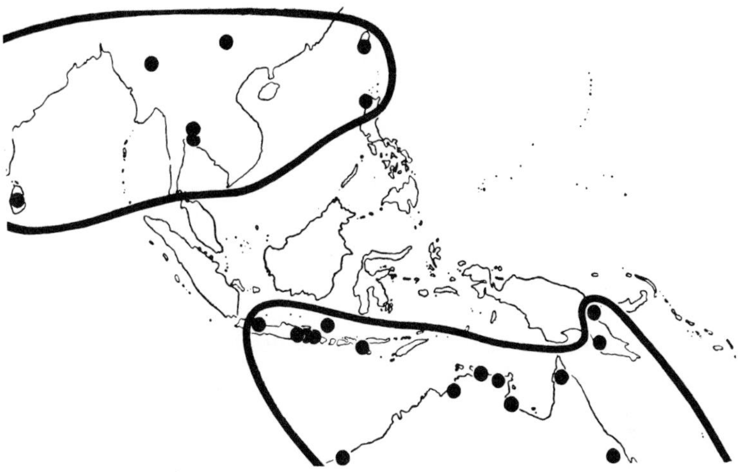

Fig. 1.13. The disjunct distribution of the plant species *Rhynchosia minima*, which grows under strong dry season conditions. From Steenis 1961. Courtesy: Herbarium Bogoriense.

half of its present rainfall in the last glaciation, and Nix and Kalma (1972) have reconstructed an open woodland vegetation for the shelf at this time, with a considerable restriction of the southwards extent of the New Guinea rainforest. For Timor, pollen sequences from deep-sea cores from the Timor Trough (Zaklinskaya 1978) suggest periodically cooler conditions in the Middle–Late Pleistocene than at present.

Some other non-climatic differences between continental (glacial) and island (interglacial) phases of Sundaland have recently been outlined by Dunn and Dunn (1977). For instance, at a sea-level 100 m below the present, Sundaland had about twice as much exposed land as it does now, but only about 47% of the coastline. Furthermore, a much greater proportion of this coastline would have had ideal shallow gradients for the support of extensive mangrove swamps (Biswas 1973); rather hostile environments for coastal economies with simple technologies. These are important observations, for many ancient economies in this part of the world depended on the sea, and periods of high sea-level are clearly favourable in this respect. On the other hand, interglacial conditions would not favour inland economies based on the hunting of herd animals in open parkland environments.

Dunn and Dunn also note another important fact; the Sunda shelf is not flat, and the exact extent of the continent would vary with sea-level. For instance, Palawan Island, technically speaking a part of Sundaland, is separated from Borneo by a channel 140 m deep, and since it also has an impoverished mammal fauna it clearly was not linked to Borneo for long periods (although it certainly was linked at some point during the Pleistocene). Java also may have been an island at times when Sumatra and Borneo were joined to Malaya, since it also has some faunal peculiarities.

We are not really in a position yet to state clearly what impact these Pleistocene climatic and environmental fluctuations had on the floras and faunas (including humans) of the Indo-Malaysian region. The most recent bout of animal extinction in the early Holocene does give some interesting hints, but it is clear that these fluctuations in the Indo-Malaysian latitudes did not have such a massive ecological impact as those recorded for periodically-glaciated temperate regions such as Europe and North America.

E. Animal Extinctions and Habitat Shifts in Sundaland in the Late Pleistocene and Holocene

Medway (1972) has noted that out of 200 extinctions world-wide during the Late Pleistocene, only 11 have occurred in South-East Asia. The 32 000 year old fauna of Niah in Sarawak has a giant pangolin as its only truly extinct species (Harrisson *et al.* 1961); a very different story from the record of animal extinction in the Late Pleistocene in Eurasia, North America and Australia.

Table 1.1 lists some approximately dated examples of Late Pleistocene and Holocene extinction or habitat shift in Sundaland. In a recent review, Medway (1977a) has argued against any major human role in this pattern, and has suggested that the rapid environmental fluctuations of the Late Pleistocene, especially the final glacial maximum and the subsequent rapid amelioration to warmer, wetter and more forested conditions, may have been the main causes. However, extinction of the Palawan deer seems to have been recent enough for human predation to be considered as a cause, while the giant pangolin appears to have vanished long before the end of the last glacial.

Of these animals the giant pangolin is the only totally extinct species, the rest are merely locally extinct. *Cervus eldi* and wild water buffalo no longer exist in Indonesia today. The gymnure and badger from Niah both survive today on the higher slopes of Mount Kinabalu in Sabah, and their presence in the Late Pleistocene at Niah supports the evidence for a cooler climate during that period. Medway (1977a) has also suggested that the giant pangolin would have required larger termitaria for its food supplies than exist in equatorial rainforests today, and this again suggests a more open environment in this part of Borneo in the Late Pleistocene.

When looking at modern animal distributions (excluding human transportation of such species as deer, monkey, civet cat and pig) we find some puzzling patterns (see Fig. 1.5). Elephants occur in Sumatra and Malaya, are extinct in Java, and never seem to have occurred in Borneo prior to recent introductions (Harrisson 1978); the Sumatran rhinoceros occurs in Sumatra, Malaya and Borneo, but the Javan rhinoceros lives only in Java, Malaya, and

Table 1.1. Late Pleistocene and Holocene extinctions in Sundaland

Species	Site	Last recorded date of local or regional existence	Reference
Manis palaeojavanica (giant pangolin)	Niah Caves, Sarawak	c. 30 000 bc	Medway, 1977a
Tapirus indicus [2] (Malayan tapir)	"	c. 6 000 bc	"
Hylomys suillus [1] (lesser gymnure, an insectivore)	"	Late Pleistocene?	"
Melogale orientalis [1] (ferret badger)	"	early Holocene?	"
Rhinoceros sondaicus [2] (Javanese rhinoceros)	Madai Caves, Sabah	6 000 bc	Cranbrook, in press a
Cuon sp.[2] (the dhole, a wild canid)	"	6 000 bc	Cranbrook, in press b (provisional identification only)
small deer[1] (species unknown)	Guri Cave, Palawan	3 000 BC	Fox, 1970
Elephas maximus [3] (Indian elephant)	Gua Lawa Cave, central Java	early Holocene?	Medway, 1972
Bubalus sp.[4] (water buffalo)	"	"	"
Neofelis nebulosa [3] (clouded leopard)	"	"	"
Cervus eldi [4] (a deer)	"	"	"

(1, locally extinct; 2, extinct on Borneo; 3, extinct on Java; 4, extinct in Indonesia)

southern Sumatra; wild banteng cattle live in Java, Borneo and Malaya, but are not certainly known in Sumatra; the tiger occurs in Malaya, Sumatra and Java, but not in Borneo. This list could continue, but I merely wish to point out the existence of these disjunct distributions. The reasons appear to be mainly ecological: ever-wet climates versus seasonal climates and vegetation; the presence of large rivers acting as faunal barriers; the compression of environmental zones against ocean or mountain barriers; and the possibility that some islands were cut off before others by rising sea-levels.

Having looked at the histories of the environments, climates and faunas of the Indo-Malaysian Archipelago from the Pliocene through to the Holocene, it is time to turn to the history of a major mammal species I have so far rather ignored: the human species.

2
Homo erectus in Sundaland

In 1891, a young Dutchman named Eugene Dubois commenced what has now been almost a century of human fossil discovery outside Europe: a century which has witnessed some profound changes in scientific views of human origins. Dubois entered, and changed, the history of anthropology in October 1891 near the village of Trinil, in the middle Solo Valley in central Java. His discovery, a skull-cap (or calotte) of apparent human form, belonged to an archaic human species which he called *Pithecanthropus erectus*.

Since 1891, many more finds have come to light in Java and the rest of the world, and in this section I intend to review the significance of the Javanese *erectus* populations in their general Old World setting. There are now so many articles and sections of textbooks which discuss the finer physical characteristics of these fossils that I will limit myself in this regard to a few central observations. The overall perspective is what is really of concern here.

During the past 25 years, fossil discoveries in the East African nations of Tanzania, Kenya and Ethiopia have completely overturned previous theories, which quite frequently postulated an Asian centre for the earliest phases of human evolution. This latter view was not, of course, surprising, since most of the major finds during the period from the 1920s to the Second World War had been made in Java and at Zhoukoudian in China, with the exception of the Australopithecines of South Africa, who at that time had yet to achieve full recognition as potential human ancestors.

Scientific understanding of the course of human evolution today is naturally founded on a much fuller fossil record than it was even 20 years ago, and the confident assertions of palaeoanthropologists might lead to a belief that many important problems have been solved, despite their own often fundamental disagreements with each other's interpretations. Common sense, however, would suggest that many surprises may still lie buried in different parts of the Old World, although the advances have certainly been impressive, as one can see by merely comparing recent textbooks with those published about 10 years ago. Palaeoanthropology has come a very long way indeed since theories of a giant ape ancestry for man were published by

Weidenreich as recently as 1945 and 1946. Weidenreich himself was of course a respected and very competent scholar who made fundamental contributions to the study of fossil man in China and Java, but unfortunately for him he produced his more general theory too soon (an occupational hazard which doubtless is always with us!)

I. The Antecedents

The oldest primate genus which is thought by many palaeoanthropologists to contain the first recognisable stage of emergent hominid form is *Ramapithecus* (Pilbeam 1980; Kay 1981; Simons 1981). Mandibles and teeth of this genus have been found in Kenya, Hungary, Turkey, Pakistan and southern China (Yunnan Province), and dates fall in the Miocene period between 14 million years ago in Kenya to perhaps as recently as 6 million years ago in Pakistan (Curtis 1981). At least three or four different sized species are apparently represented, and some specimens appear to indicate certain potentially hominid trends in dentition, such as reduced canines and relatively large molar teeth.

The South Chinese *Ramapithecus* remains come from lignite deposits at Shihuiba in Lufeng County, Yunnan, and are estimated to be about 8 million years old (Woo 1980; Simons 1981). Wu (1982) has recently announced the exciting information that two almost intact skulls of *Ramapithecus* are now known, and these show a position of the foramen magnum more forward than that in modern apes. This could suggest a trend towards bipedal stature, but speculation on this is rather premature at the moment.

Does the human line descend from a *Ramapithecus* species? Most palaeoanthropologists now seem to think so, although Wolpoff (1982) has cautioned against regarding the whole genus as hominid contra pongid, and sees it instead as a widespread complex of species which may have been ancestral to humans, chimpanzees and gorillas in Africa, and in Asia to the orang utan and to an extinct Plio-Pleistocene giant ape with hominid-like dental characteristics (*Gigantopithecus*). There is also genetic evidence from similarities in amino acid chains which supports the view that the divergence of humans, chimpanzees and gorillas from a common ancestor postdates most of the time-span of *Ramapithecus* (Pilbeam 1984), and the most likely hypothesis now for hominid origins would propose speciation from a localised and late Ramapithecine population in tropical Africa.

The Ramapithecines are unfortunately followed by a world-wide gap in the hominid record until the Australopithecines appear in Africa from about 4 million years ago, and in increasing numbers of sites from about 3 million years ago. These African hominids of the Pliocene undoubtedly contain some

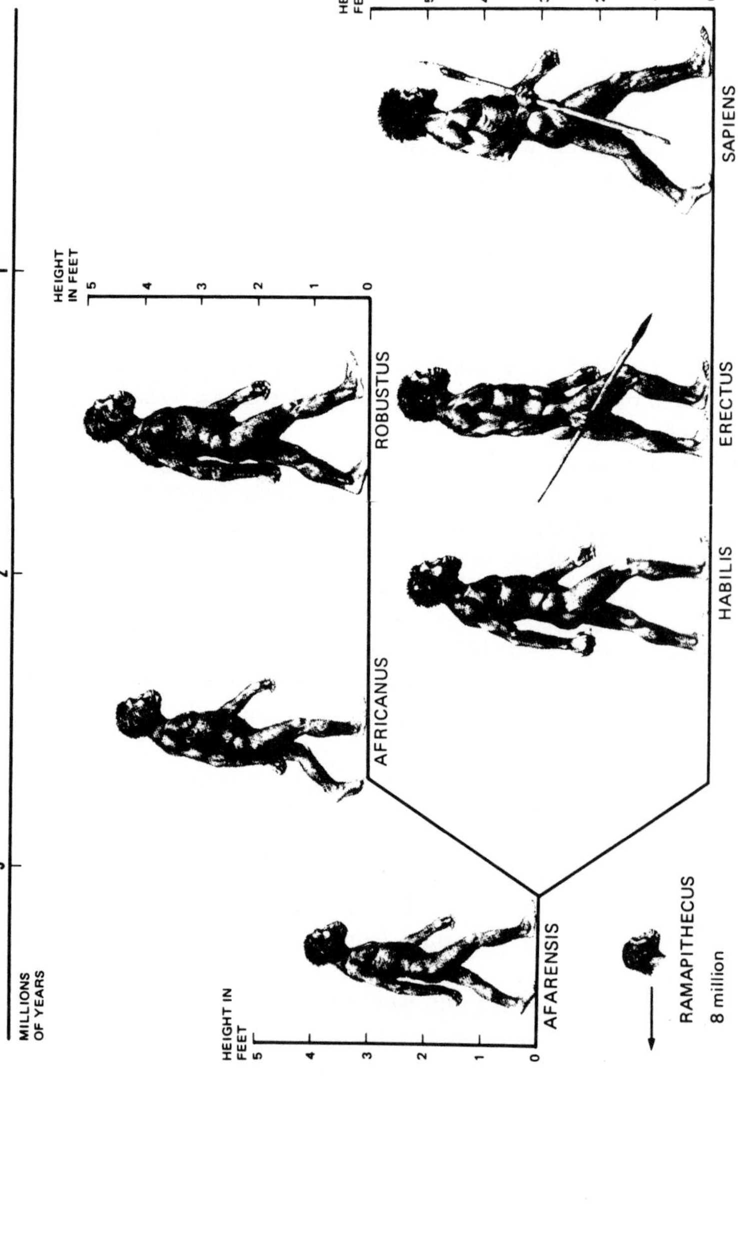

Fig. 2.1. A possible (but still controversial) family tree for human and Australopithecine evolution in Africa. From Johanson and Edey 1981. Courtesy: Sterling Lord Agency.

of the basic physical and cultural roots of our humanity. At present, there are continuing strong debates about how many species of *Australopithecus* are represented in the African record, which one evolved into *Homo*, and the apparent fates of the one or more species which do not have obvious descendants. However, there does now seem to be a growing agreement that the Pliocene members of the genus formed a single evolving chronospecies until it split about 2.5 million years ago into a *Homo* lineage and a separate robust Australopithecine lineage, the latter becoming extinct before one million years ago (Fig. 2.1). There is still clear disagreement about which regional group of Australopithecines evolved into the *Homo* lineage, with some authorities favouring an Ethiopian centre, others being less willing to be specific; Konigsson (1980) contains good debates on these matters. For my purposes it is not necessary to be specific about taxonomic variation within the Australopithecines, since the weight of evidence for an emergence of the genus *Homo* from an Australopithecine ancestor somewhere in Africa is now overwhelming, as is the evidence for the continued existence of one or more species of robust Australopithecine alongside *Homo* in East Africa.

Purely cultural developments in Africa prior to 2 million years ago are hard to identify, and they are likely to be heavily embedded in a biological developmental matrix which involved changes towards bipedal posture, increasing hand flexibility, greater cranial capacity, and the hominid grinding and chewing dentition. The Australopithecines had attained a habitual bipedal posture by at least 3.6 million years ago, according to a series of footprints preserved at Laetoli in Tanzania (Leakey 1981), but the expansion of the brain seems to have occurred mainly later with the genus *Homo*. Sexual body size dimorphism is marked among the early hominids, who probably existed on a fairly omnivorous meat and plant diet derived from territories located close to rivers and lakes (Boaz 1977). During the period of transition to the genus *Homo*, between 2.5 and 2 million years ago, there is already direct evidence for stone tool use, and inferred but disputed evidence (Binford 1983) for regular dwelling places or campsites, and for the evolution of such concepts as the nuclear family, kinship, the incest taboo, and basic human language (Isaac 1980; Wilson 1980; Lovejoy 1981).

The earliest *Homo* fossils are referred to the species *Homo habilis* by many recent writers, and Tobias (1981) has set out some of the differences which he believes can be used to separate *Homo* from *Australopithecus*; perhaps the most important difference is the relatively rapid change in cranial shape from a bell-shaped towards a more vertical-sided cross-section, and there is also a correlated increase in cranial capacity (Fig. 2.2). From a practical viewpoint, the *Homo* lineage can only be clearly recognised after a point in time when it can be seen to be coexistent with a separate robust Australopithecine lineage, and this point appears to be a little over 2 million years ago.

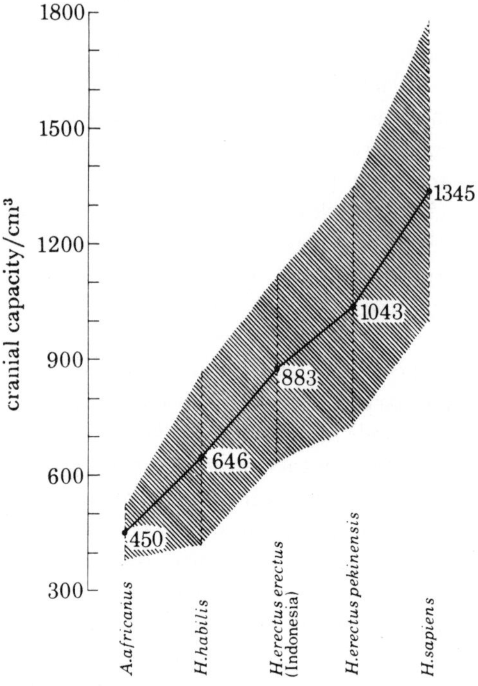

Fig. 2.2. The pattern of cranial capacity increase in human evolution over the past 3 million years (shading indicates 95% population limits). From Tobias 1981. Courtesy: The Royal Society, P. V. Tobias.

Prior to this time there is insufficient differentiation in the Australopithecines to allow widely agreed identification of the specific *Homo*-ancestral population. But from this time on, *Homo* evolved separately through the *habilis* (approximately 2 million years ago), *erectus* (1.7 million to c. 300 000 years ago?) and *sapiens* grades.

Definitions of these chronospecies are necessarily a little arbitrary, and those fossils normally placed in the *habilis* grade could equally be regarded as evolved Australopithecines, but in general the *habilis* remains from Olduvai Gorge and other localities in East Africa belonged to a small bipedal hominid with a body weight of around 20–30 kg and a cranial capacity averaging 650 cm^3. The earliest *erectus* remains could likewise be regarded simply as evolved habilines, and B. A. Wood (1978:53–4) has described the major skeletal characteristics of the whole *erectus* group (including the Javanese fossils) as follows: a distinctive cranial shape marked by prominent brow-ridges separated from the rest of the skull by a deep constriction (the postorbital constriction), a low vault with the widest point at the base, very thick cranial bones and strongly marked muscle attachments, a broad large face with large teeth, and an average cranial capacity of about 950 cm^3 (Figs 2.3 and 2.4). Postcranial remains suggest a body size and posture approaching the *sapiens* grade, with the important proviso that the *erectus* grade spans perhaps one million years or more, so considerable temporal and also regional variation can be expected (Howells 1980).

It is with the early *erectus* evolutionary level that Java takes on a major importance, for this small island contains some of the earliest evidence for human radiation out of Africa through the tropical zones of the Old World. According to absolute dates for the hominids of the Jetis fauna in Java, this radiation may have taken place between 1.7 and 1.3 million years ago according to different authorities (see Chapter 1, Section IVB). Although claims for Australopithecine finds in China and Java do appear from time to time, they have not so far survived critical examination (Pope 1977; Woo 1980:184). *Australopithecus* still appears to have been entirely restricted to Africa.

II. *Homo erectus* in Java

The earliest remains of *Homo erectus* in Africa date from between 1.7 and 1.5 million years ago (Wolpoff 1980; Rightmire 1980). The *erectus* teeth and associated stone tools from Yuanmou in Yunnan (China) have been claimed to date to about 1.7 million years ago (Woo 1980:188), but Howells (1977) and Liu and Ding (1983) suggest only a Middle Pleistocene antiquity. For Java (Fig. 2.5) it is not possible to be very specific, but fossils associated with Jetis and Trinil faunas perhaps fall between about 1.7 million (at the earliest) and 500 000 years ago, as discussed in Chapter 1, Section IVB. However, it must be stated firmly that the stratigraphic data from Java are so imprecise with respect to hominid find-spots that no absolute date for hominid appearance can be considered completely reliable at present. For instance, both Matsu'ura (1982) and Pope (1984) favour an initial appearance of hominids at Sangiran between 1.3 and 1.1 million years ago, and Pope (1983) was previously unwilling to extend even as far back as one million years. A date of 1.7 million years may at the moment be considered an uncertain maximum, and given present knowledge of the course of human evolution the Javanese dates can hardly be expected to be older than the African ones for the same early *erectus* grade.

The major find-places for the Javanese fossils have been in the upper Pucangan (Jetis fauna) and Kabuh (Trinil fauna) deposits exposed in the anticlinal dome at Sangiran (see Chapter 1, Section IVB, and Koenigswald

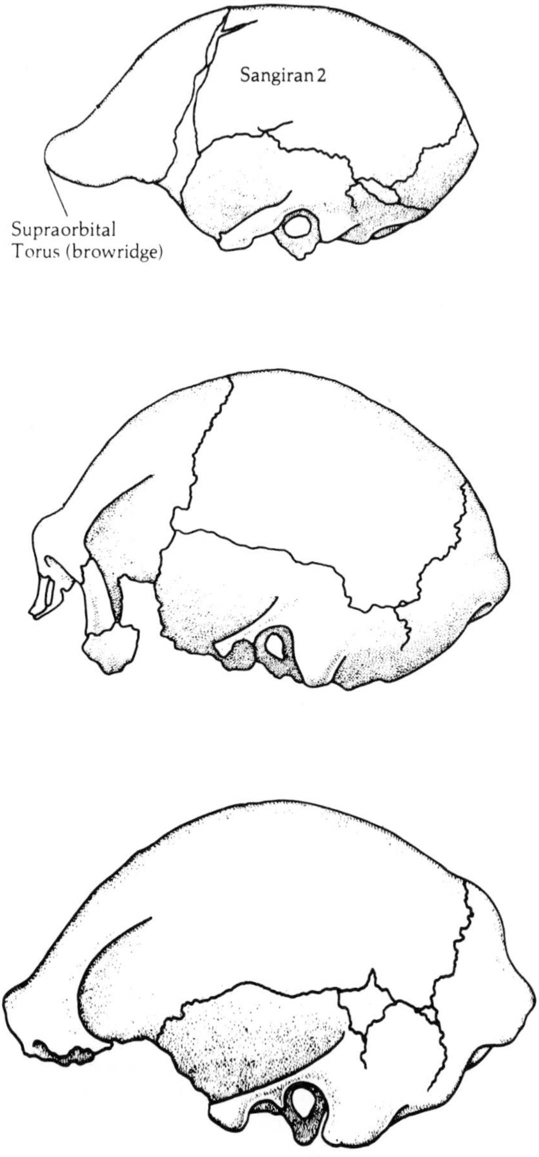

Fig. 2.3. Top to bottom: lateral views of *Homo erectus* crania from Sangiran (Early or Middle Pleistocene), Zhoukoudian (Middle Pleistocene) and Ngandong (Middle or Late Pleistocene). To same scale. From Wolpoff 1980. Courtesy: Alfred A. Knopf, Inc.

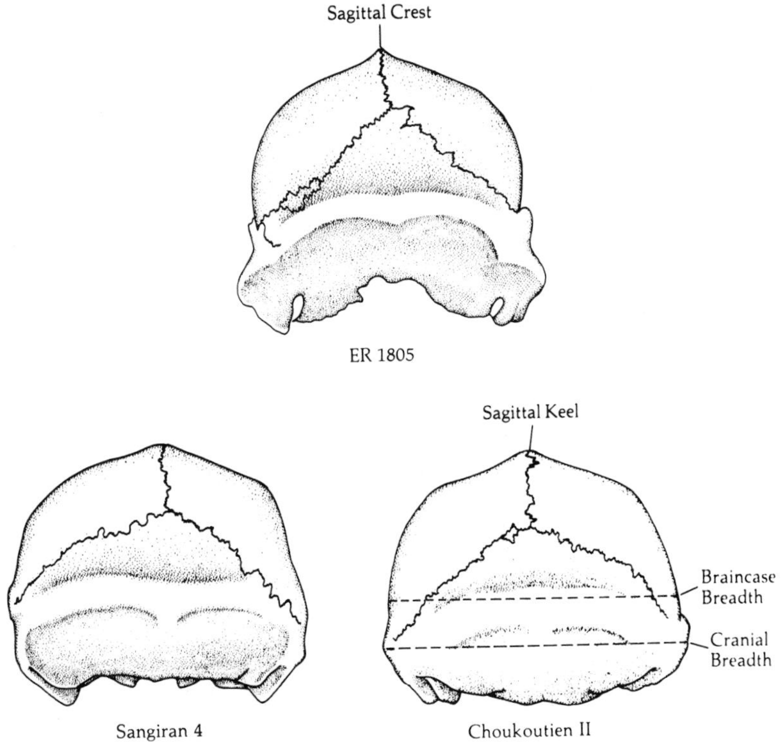

Fig. 2.4. Posterior cranial views of ER 1805, a transitional *habilis–erectus* specimen from Kenya, and later *erectus* crania from Sangiran and Zhoukoudian. To same scale. From Wolpoff 1980. Courtesy: Alfred A. Knopf, Inc.

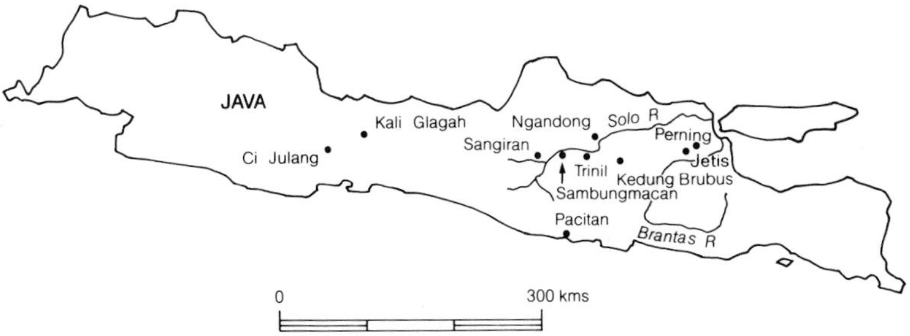

Fig. 2.5. Late Pliocene and Pleistocene sites and localities in Java.

1956 for descriptive accounts). Additional important fossils have also come from possible Kabuh-equivalent beds (Trinil faunal zone) at Trinil itself in central Java, and from Perning near Mojokerto in eastern Java, but both these sites have major dating problems (e.g. Vos *et al.* 1982 for Trinil). At present, all specimens reliably of Jetis faunal age come from Sangiran, and these specimens also appear morphologically to be the oldest in the series. Finally, there is the important cranial series from Ngandong in the Solo Valley, of Ngandong (late Middle or Late Pleistocene) faunal age.

A. The Jetis Hominids

Of the Jetis sample from Sangiran, the most complete specimen, Sangiran 4 (popularly called "Pithecanthropus IV"; Koenigswald and Weidenreich 1939), comprises the posterior part of a braincase and the lower portion of the maxillae (mid-facial region). Both belonged to a heavily-muscled individual with a cranial capacity of about 900 cm^3, with large teeth and particularly large canines (Holloway 1981; Day 1977:294–6). A most unusual feature of the dentition is a gap (diastema) between the upper canines and incisors, into which the lower canines would have fitted to allow the jaw to close. Such diastemata are typically a pongid phenomenon since the great apes have very large canines, and they do not occur in any other *erectus* specimen (with the possible exception of the much later Sangiran 17 skull; Thorne and Wolpoff 1981). The Australopithecines from Laetoli and Afar in East Africa do sometimes show this feature (Johanson 1980:48; Wolpoff 1980:134), but it has recently been suggested that the diastema in the Sangiran specimen could be due to "labial displacement of the maxillary incisors because of vertical collapse after loss of the posterior mandibular teeth" (Zingeser 1979). In this case the feature would be an individual rather than a lineage trait, although the lower jaw of the specimen does not survive to allow direct confirmation.

The Sangiran 4 remains may otherwise be taken as fairly representative of an Early Pleistocene and very robust *Homo erectus* population in Java. They come from a stratigraphically high position in the Pucangan beds, and there are mandible fragments in older deposits which appear to be of the same basic grade. However, the overall picture for the pre-Trinil hominids of Java still eludes simplification. Firstly, there is the problem of too many names for the same group of fossils; such terms as *Pithecanthropus robustus, P. modjokertensis* and *Homo modjokertensis* all refer to what I am calling early *Homo erectus.* Most authors now appear to favour such a single species term, and there is no overwhelming reason why the Javanese fossils should not belong to one single species evolving through a long period of time. This is precisely where the second problem arises — in this case in the form of some massive mandible fragments.

The two most important of these fragments were found at Sangiran in 1941 and 1952, one from the upper Pucangan and the other from the lower Kabuh beds. Clearly hominid, but with massive teeth overlapping in size with those of a gorilla, these specimens were named *Meganthropus palaeojavanicus* by Koenigswald and Weidenreich. Weidenreich (1946) adopted the view that *Meganthropus* was on a direct line of evolution to modern humans, occupying a position between the more massive-toothed *Gigantopithecus* and the smaller *Pithecanthropus (Homo erectus).* This view never became popular and, as the African evidence accumulated, attempts were made to correlate *Meganthropus* with the robust Australopithecines (or *Paranthropus*, Robinson 1968), and with *Homo habilis* (Tobias and Koenigswald 1964). Even today it is still maintained as a genus quite separate from *Homo erectus* by the Indonesian scholars Jacob (e.g. 1978a) and Sartono (1975; see also Orban-Segebarth and Procureur 1983).

So could the *Meganthropus* jaw fragments represent a situation similar to that in East Africa, where robust Australopithecines continued to exist alongside *Homo* in the Early Pleistocene? The answer basically seems to be "no"; Lovejoy (1970) placed *Meganthropus* firmly at the larger end of a considerable range of dental size variation in *Homo erectus*, a view also held by Le Gros Clark (1964), by B. A. Wood (1978:56), and by most recent authors. Furthermore, the *Meganthropus* jaws are contemporary with the other *erectus* remains in Java, and given the fragmentary nature of the material it is clearly most economical to regard them as part of one evolving *erectus* lineage.

Another lesser problem concerning earlier *Homo erectus* from Java relates to the date for an infant cranium recovered from Perning near Mojokerto in 1936. This specimen has always been assumed to be of Jetis faunal affiliation (e.g. Terra 1943), and was for some years associated with a potassium-argon date of 1.9 million years (Jacob 1972b). The species epithet "*modjokertensis*" has long been in use for some of the Jetis hominids (after Koenigswald), and an African specialist has even recently suggested that *Homo habilis* should be subsumed under *Homo modjokertensis* under the rules of zoological nomenclature (Boaz 1979). However, it is indeed fortunate that this tiny and pathetic skull, of a child aged between 2 and 4 years (Riscutia 1975), has never been used for taxonomic description because it is too juvenile; it is now known that the skull is in fact of Middle Pleistocene age (Sartono *et al.* 1981), and even the original potassium-argon date is regarded by Curtis (1981:16) as perhaps inaccurate. It is time to cease using the term *Homo* (or *Pithecanthropus*) *modjokertensis*, before further confusion is created.

B. The Trinil Hominids

From the Trinil faunal zone, perhaps dating between 1.3 million (maximum) and 0.5 million years ago (see Chapter 1, Section IVB), there is a much fuller set of fossil remains. Most specimens again come from Sangiran, and there is also the original find made by Dubois at Trinil itself: the *erectus* calotte (skull-cap) found in the bed of the Solo River during the dry season of 1891. It has recently been claimed (Bartstra 1982a; Vos *et al.* 1982; Vos and Sondaar 1982) that the mammal fauna from Trinil is in fact much older than the fauna *called* Trinil from Sangiran, but the Trinil skull itself does fit morphologically with the Sangiran remains attributed to this period. It may be that the fauna and the skull from Trinil are not contemporary, and it must be admitted that there have always been problems with Dubois' records. For instance, he recovered a number of human femora from the general vicinity of the Trinil skull which have often been used to reconstruct a totally modern body posture for Javanese *Homo erectus.* Fluorine tests (Bergmann and Karsten 1952) appear to support contemporaneity of the skull and femora, even though well authenticated *erectus* femora from Africa and Zhoukoudian are considerably more primitive in appearance. However, Day and Molleson (1973) have recently thrown doubt on the antiquity of the Trinil femora, and certainty is still elusive.

All the other Javanese remains of Trinil age are cranial, and represent a population less robust than the earlier Jetis specimens, but still retaining a high degree of sexual dimorphism. Wolpoff (1980:191) points out that the Java sample has less-projecting brow-ridges than the equivalent African specimens, but more marked facial prognathism, thicker skulls and stronger muscle attachment areas. Cranial capacities range from 813 to 1059 cm^3, with an average of 929 (Holloway 1981). Stature probably ranged up to a maximum of around 160 cm, and weights may have ranged up to 80 kg in the latest populations (Wolpoff 1980:205). It is reasonable to assume that average cranial capacity increased during the time-span of *erectus* evolution, although overall shape varied little until the development of high-vaulted *Homo sapiens* in the Late Pleistocene, and much of the increase in brain size may simply correlate with a slow increase in body size (Bilsborough 1973). Wolpoff (seminar communication) has also suggested that the thick vault and massive teeth of *Homo erectus* may relate to continuing selection imposed by the dangers of a hunting life and the frequent use of teeth as tools; the latter would also select for a massive and prognathous face with very powerful muscle attachments.

C. Broader Perspectives on the Early Pleistocene Javanese Remains

I will now pause and review the Javanese material of the Jetis and Trinil faunal periods, before moving on to the more recent remains. As B. A. Wood (1978:56) states, "the most parsimonious hypothesis is that sequential populations of a single lineage provide the samples at the Javan sites". Thorne and Wolpoff (1981) have further suggested that the Javanese remains all belong to a recognisable and regional morphological lineage within the *Homo erectus* species as a whole, and they also demonstrate that the Javanese fossils show rather less morphological variation than the African remains, an observation which they tie in with their hypothesis that greater variation occurs in the centre of a species range (in this case Africa) than occurs at the edge of the range (in this case Java).

If the single lineage view for Java is accepted, then this island has a sequence parallel to that in China where a single lineage view is now universally held. The major Chinese fossils include the Lantian cranium (probably over 700 000 years old), which compares well with the Javanese material, and the famous Zhoukoudian population, dated to between 500 000 and 230 000 years ago (Wu 1982), and thus later and more evolved than any of the Javanese specimens considered so far. This leads on to the important hypothesis, formulated by scholars such as Weidenreich and Coon (see Chapter 3, Section IIIA), that the Chinese remains lie morphologically in the line of descent of the modern Mongoloids, and the Javanese do likewise for the Australoids. The latter situation has been most recently discussed by Thorne and Wolpoff (1981), who recognise clear morphological continuity, especially in facial prognathism and posterior tooth size, between the Javanese *erectus* population and certain later Australian *sapiens* remains of the terminal Pleistocene.

It will be necessary to return to these opinions in the next chapter, but it should also be noted that the single lineage view is not without challenge. Jacob has developed a very different phylogeny in a number of recent papers (1975, 1976, 1978a, 1979), although he has, perhaps significantly, not committed himself so much in his most recent paper (1980). Basically, the view held by Jacob (1979) is that the Jetis zone hominids (*P. modjokertensis*) lead on via a gracile set of Trinil zone hominids (*P. erectus*) to modern man. Meanwhile, a separate robust line, perhaps also derived from *P. modjokertensis*, leads on to the Late Pleistocene *P. soloensis* population (to be described below), and eventual extinction. Jacob is convinced that he is dealing with true lineage differences, but the fact remains that these views have never been acceptable to the community of palaeoanthropologists at large, despite the possibility that isolation and considerable phenotypic variability between Javanese *erectus* populations may have occurred in the Early Pleistocene (Santa Luca 1980). Perhaps the single lineage hypothesis should be accepted, mainly on the grounds that the Javanese remains are so poorly dated in comparison with remains from elsewhere in the world that B. A. Wood's parsimonious hypothesis should prevail, unless it can conclusively be shown that it is incorrect. At present, it is my suspicion that it cannot.

D. Farewell to *Homo erectus*? The Ngandong Remains

The Javanese remains of *Homo erectus* considered so far appear to span a long period of time prior to 500 000 years ago, with the majority coming from the later part of the time range. The oldest human remains of modern type in the region are not more than 40 000 years old, and betwen these two groups there is only one major fossil population (from Ngandong), plus a number of rather intractable problems.

Between 1931 and 1933, Indonesian field assistants employed by the Geological Survey of Indonesia were given the periodic job of excavating a bone-bearing terrace about 20 m above the dry-season level of the Solo River at Ngandong, a little north of Trinil. The whole terrace deposit was about 3 m thick, and the animal bones (about 25 000 were recovered from a 50 × 100 m excavation) were apparently fairly heavily concentrated in the lower metre of the deposit. From time to time the site was visited by the geologists Ter Haar and Oppenoorth, and also by Koenigswald, and over the two-year period the bone collections eventually yielded no less than 11 crania (all lacking faces) and two tibiae of an advanced population of *Homo erectus* (see Koenigswald 1951, 1956 and Oppenoorth 1932 for eye-witness accounts). It is quite clear that the human skulls were not found together, and Koenigswald noted the unusual circumstance that teeth, mandibles, and other bones apart from the two tibiae were entirely lacking, although such selectivity was not noted amongst the other animal remains. Furthermore, of the 11 skulls only two had parts of their bases surviving, and Koenigswald (1951) thought they had been broken open for purposes of brain-eating, and afterwards used as bowls. The idea of cannibalism has been disputed by Jacob (1967a, 1972a), who points out that the skull base is a fragile area subject to natural breakage, but the observation still remains that the human bone sample is taphonomically unusual.

The Ngandong crania (Fig. 2.6) were described by Weidenreich just before his death in 1948 (Weidenreich 1951), and, like the earlier Javanese remains, have been classified and reclassified so many times that I will merely say that most authors regard them as large-brained (the average of five skulls is 1151 cm^3, Holloway 1980) and late members of *Homo erectus* (Santa Luca 1980). A few, such as Wolpoff (1980:219), regard them as early *sapiens* on the grounds of a broadening of the upper braincase, but I think most would agree that they represent fairly direct descendants of the Trinil hominids. More hominid fragments have apparently been found recently at Ngandong (Jacob 1978b), and another cranium of Ngandong type (perhaps slightly more archaic) has been found in a river terrace deposit of Ngandong age at Sambungmacan, also on the middle Solo River (Sartono 1979c). All are agreed that the "Solo Man" series is post-Trinil, but beyond this major questions exist which fall loosely under the headings of context, environment, and date.

Concerning the context of the Ngandong remains, it is clear from Koenigswald's accounts (1951, 1956) that the skulls were dispersed amongst other animal bones in what must once have been a quiet bank of sand and gravel, perhaps on the inside of a river bend. Perhaps they were washed there after

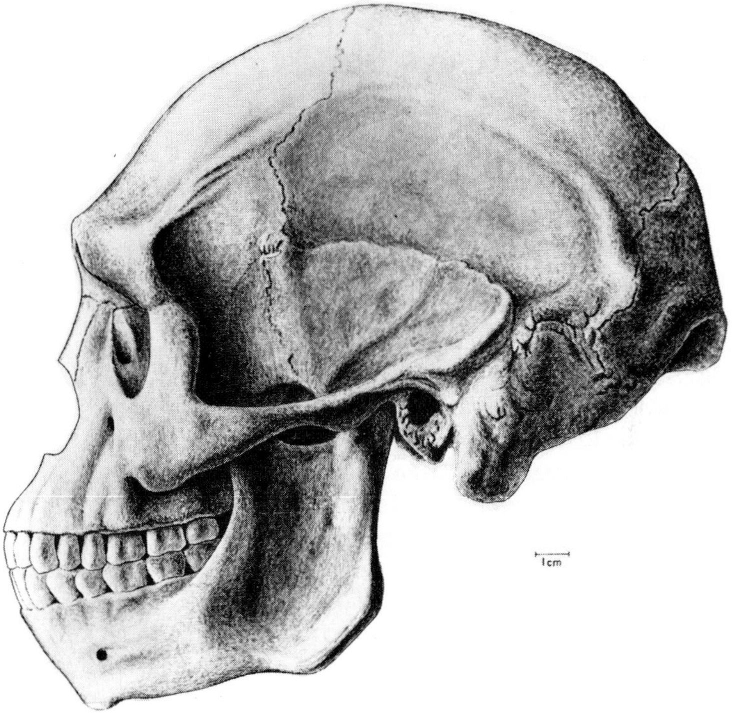

Fig. 2.6. A reconstruction of the Ngandong cranial morphology. From Weidenreich 1951. Courtesy: American Museum of Natural History.

being cannibalised in a nearby hunting camp, and the presence of articulated vertebral columns of cattle could suggest animal butchery in the vicinity. However, if the cannibalism hypothesis is wrong (and there seems to be no very positive way of knowing this), then another idea might explain their predominance. Brain (1978) has noted the predominance of Australopithecine cranial remains over other body parts in the South African site of Swartkrans, and describes for comparative purposes his observations of baboon remains left on the ground after cheetah kills. In these situations crania are left complete, together with some of the long bones, but more fragile items such as the vertebral column are completely destroyed. It could be suggested from this that the Ngandong crania and tibiae are the remains of carnivore kills (Java had a range of tigers, hyenas and other smaller carnivores in this period), and this view would tie in with the total absence of hearths and verified stone tools from the site; these would perhaps be expected if hominids were living close by.

But here another problem arises in that it is very hard to demonstrate that the Ngandong hominids actually made stone tools (I will consider the cultural evidence, such as it is, later on). A totally different suggestion to explain the predominance of skulls has recently been put forward by Santa Luca (1980), who favours the view that the animal bones form a primary deposit, but the skulls were washed out of an older deposit elsewhere and washed into the site, perhaps by river action. However, it is clear that one could go on to ramify hypotheses about the Ngandong remains with no hope of being able to draw any useful conclusions, and I will cease at this point. The answers now will only come from further scientific investigations of sites of the same period, should they exist.

Concerning the environment of the Ngandong region we are on firmer ground. The 25 000 animal bones belong to 17 species (18 if one includes dubious *Macaca*; for lists see Koenigswald 1951; Medway 1972; Sartono 1976). Of these, 12 or 13 are shared with the Trinil fauna, and the major post-Trinil additions appear to be more modern forms of pig and deer. The only wholly extinct genus is *Stegodon.* The fauna as a whole hints at a fairly open landscape, and, as noted by Koenigswald, some of the buffalo had horns up to 2.25 m wide, which would argue against the presence of dense forest. The majority of the bones were of deer and cattle (an ancestral banteng), both animals which are more numerous in open landscapes, although they do also occur in small numbers in the dense forests of Sundaland. In addition, one of Oppenoorth's assistants recovered a bone of a crane (*Grus grus*) from deposits considered to be of Ngandong age at a nearby location called Watualang (Wetmore 1940); this bird winters in southern China today, and the bone's presence in Java could suggest a cooler climate then than now. However, I do not find this small piece of evidence very compelling, and Oppenoorth (1936) placed the Watulang terrace deposits as slightly later in date than those at Ngandong.

It is with the date of the Ngandong remains that the most difficulty occurs. The fauna is always classed loosely as "Late Pleistocene", and the Ngandong terrace deposits certainly post-date the Kabuh beds of central Java (Sartono 1976). However, the fauna is of little help for more precise dating since it is not known when key genera, such as *Stegodon*, became extinct in Java. Although 11 of the species listed by Medway (1972:80) are "extinct", in the sense that they have been given different species names from modern members of their genera, the real situation may simply be that many of the Ngandong species are ancestral to the modern ones. The same problem occurs with animals as with humans: how does one recognise a true chrono-species, how does one divide it for purposes of taxonomy, and how does one recognise situations of true extinction?

If the fauna is of no help for dating, then neither is the geology. There is an often quoted potassium-argon date of 300 000 ± 300 000 years which is claimed to relate to the Ngandong site (Birdsell 1977:152); I know nothing of its context, and its range of possible error is enormous. The recent literature reveals the full extent of the uncertainty. For instance, there are suggested dates for the Ngandong crania of 20 000 years (Campbell 1966:368), 60 000–100 000 years (Jacob 1967a:39), and even an estimate approaching 900 000 years for the Sambungmacan cranium (Jacob 1978b; see also Lestrel 1975). Bartstra (1983:426) mentions a radiometric date of less than 100 000 years for the Ngandong crania, but gives no details.

If the crania are indeed only 20 000 or even 60 000 years old, then the undeniable conclusion must be that they are representatives of an extinct sideline of human evolution. This is the stated view of Jacob (1979) and Birdsell (1972:319), and fits the views of other palaeoanthropologists (e.g. Howells 1973a) who have suggested that modern *Homo sapiens sapiens* evolved in one region of the Old World and spread by replacement radiation into remote regions such as Java. The European Neanderthals, although more evolved than the Ngandong population, are often the major source of data for this hypothesis. If the Ngandong remains represent an extinct sideline, then neither they nor the earlier Javanese hominids can be ancestral to Late Pleistocene Australoids.

However, this is in clear contradiction to the recent view of Thorne and Wolpoff (1981), who regard Javanese *Homo erectus* and some terminal Pleistocene Australoid populations as morphological members of a single lineage — a clear argument for continuity which has had many supporters going back to Weidenreich. Although Santa Luca (1980) has recently stated that such an ancestral-descendant relationship remains merely a logical possibility and cannot be proved, my own view, which is based on more than cranial considerations, favours at least some kind of continuity tempered by the possibility of periodic gene flow from Mainland South-East Asia into the rather peripheral peninsula formed by Java. This means that I regard the Ngandong population as a later Middle Pleistocene intermediary between *Homo erectus* of the Early Pleistocene and at least some of the recent Australoid populations of Indonesia. I will turn to the latter, who belong within the last 40 000 years, in the next chapter.

III. *Homo erectus* in South-East Asia: The Cultural Evidence

It is most unfortunate that all the hominid remains from Java have been found in situations of presumed secondary deposition, devoid of direct cultural context. Stone tools do occur on the island, but never with human fossils, and never in securely-dated contexts; there are no "living floors" of the kind found elsewhere in Africa and western Eurasia. The possibility arises that Javanese *Homo erectus*, unlike contemporary Africans and Chinese, did not make tools of stone. Such a situation would be unusual, to say the least, and the evidence, which at present is very vague, deserves careful consideration.

A. Squeezing Blood from Stones

Firstly, I wish to generalise a little about stone tools, and to examine the data which can, in theory, be extracted from them. As Isaac (1977a) has pointed out, stone tools can be used in many ways — as markers of man's antiquity, as indices of "progress", as symptoms of cultural differentiation in time and place, and as indicators of economic organisation. "However, we need to assess the limits to the amount of blood that can realistically be squeezed from these stones" (Isaac 1977a:5).

In practice, many assemblages of stone tools, particularly from earlier time periods, comprise bewildering arrays of overlapping and rather amorphous forms. Prehistoric artisans were rarely turning out models to blueprints, although it has to be assumed that there is some form and patterning in all assemblages — the major difficulty is to separate the meaningful information from the noise.

Recent attempts have been made to record processes of manufacture and use of stone tools amongst peoples who have used them to recent times, particularly in Australia and New Guinea (e.g. Gould 1977, 1980; Hayden 1977a, 1979). While many of these observations are particularistic they do serve an essential function of bringing a very healthy dose of reality into what was once a field of rambling and incoherent typologising, and similar reality is provided by the rapidly expanding field of edge-damage analysis based on controlled experiments and high-powered microscopy (e.g. Anderson 1980; Keeley 1980). The literatures in both these fields are growing rapidly, and all basic field research on stone-tool bearing sites now has to take account of them. However, the spin-off has so far been restricted, and it works best for new material analysed by aware researchers. New material, in terms of the South-East Asian subject matter which I am about to consider, does not really exist in examinable form.

The aware researcher of the 1980s may present data concerning a stone tool assemblage in a manner which is best outlined in Isaac's useful review (1977a). Technologically defined classes, such as cores, flakes, chips, and retouched and shaped forms will first be identified and quantified. At this level the researcher is merely dealing with worked stone from a technological and stylistic viewpoint. The "tool" concept comes in when considering function; this is where the edge-damage research comes in, and is the level at which tools can best be separated from waste material. The moral here is that a piece of apparent waste may turn out to be a tool when the edge is examined (assuming that one can recognise true use-wear from other forms of edge-damage — a bedevilling problem for all researchers).

After both manufacturing and edge-damage variables have been quantified, the data can be considered as a whole to suggest the most meaningful overall divisions of the material. In the case of the Middle Pleistocene sites at Olorgesailie in Kenya, Isaac (1977b) divided the material into shaped tools, unshaped tools, and unutilised waste. This type of classification, which combines variables of both form and function, cannot be applied easily to any South-East Asian assemblage since the necessary basic information has rarely been recorded, although I will present some rather generalised observations of my own in due course.

The contents of the above diversion will be familiar to readers who have some background knowledge of archaeology, and in my opinion this type of research is of extreme importance, and renders much earlier work on stone tools of very dubious value. This is sadly so when considering East and South-East Asia. Earlier researchers here confused form and function by using such terms as chopper, point, scraper and hand-axe, all of which imply specific activities. In many cases these assumptions may be perfectly right, but the problem is that it is generally impossible to verify whether they are right or wrong. The relevant assemblages were often superficially reported, and are now spread in museums in some very inaccessible parts of the world. Archaeologists are to an extent imprisoned in a network of very imprecise semantic variation; definitions of common terms vary from one writer to another, and for China the non-Chinese reader is forced to rely on second-hand sources written by people who for the most part have not been able to see the relevant material (e.g. Freeman 1977). Available illustrations tend to be of poor quality and naturally very selective.

By now, the reader may feel that I am tending strongly towards a very negative view of the value of stone tools in Pleistocene research in East and South-East Asia. Perhaps I can reinforce the negativism by pointing out that the above paragraphs have only discussed the stone tool assemblage *per se*. When considering problems of date and context the situation becomes even worse; we quickly find ourselves in situations where we are trying to compare one researcher's chopper with the scraper of another, knowing next to nothing of what the tool looks like, how old it is, or the context in which it was found. My own research has told me very clearly that what one researcher calls a Middle Pleistocene chopper could well be a discarded waste core less than 10 000 years old.

But enough, the problems exist (e.g. Hutterer 1977), and it is pointless to lay blame. In this review, I am forced to use much of the terminology and the data as they have been published, although I will use my own experience of some of the material to follow a simple line where complexity is not warranted.

B. Pleistocene Stone Tool Industries of East Asia

The most important Indonesian industries which are *reputed* to be the handiwork of *Homo erectus* come from Sangiran, Ngandong, and from riverine locations in south-central Java (the Pacitanian industry, formerly spelt Patjitanian). Potential but problematic outliers occur in other parts of Sundaland and Malaya, in Sulawesi, in Flores and Timor, and in the Cagayan Valley of northern Luzon in the Philippines. These industries will be described in this chapter. Late Pleistocene industries of more specialised type which postdate 30 000 years ago are discussed separately in Chapter 6.

The Javanese Pacitanian industry belongs to a widespread group of "chopper/chopping-tool industries" which occur widely in South-East Asia, China and India, and which have often been contrasted with the "hand-axe" (Acheulian) industries produced in western Eurasia and Africa during the timespan of *Homo erectus*. This distinction has some statistical validity but it is not absolute; the Pacitanian does have hand-axe forms, as indeed do some Chinese and Korean industries (Yi and Clark 1983).

The South and East Asian industries were first described and compared in a comprehensive way by Movius, in a series of long papers (e.g. 1944, 1948, 1955) which have had a rather fundamental influence on all later work. Movius described a number of tool types made on pebbles, tabular chunks or flakes, and he divided them into bifacial chopping-tools and hand-axes, and unifacial hand-adzes, proto-hand-axes, and choppers and/or scrapers (Fig. 2.7). These definitions were rather intuitive, as Movius was aware, and with the passage of time they have proved too ambiguous for useful comparative purposes. Furthermore, it is clear that many authors have not used these terms as Movius intended, although his definitions were semantically precise (1955:261–2).

My own observations on these classificatory problems stem from my research on later Pleistocene and early Holocene industries, including the Hoabinhian of Malaya and contemporary industries in Borneo and Sulawesi. There seems little doubt that these are the direct but regionally diversified descendants of presumed Pleistocene ancestors such as the Pacitanian and its Mainland South-East Asian allies. I have elsewhere referred to all of these industries as "pebble and flake industries"; in some remote parts of South-East Asia they have continued in production into recent historical times, although new technologies did appear in certain regions during the Late Pleistocene and Holocene.

Despite local idiosyncracies, which probably depend as much on raw material as on varying skills, the Pleistocene pebble and flake industries of South-East Asia and their Holocene survivals all share in common the production of:

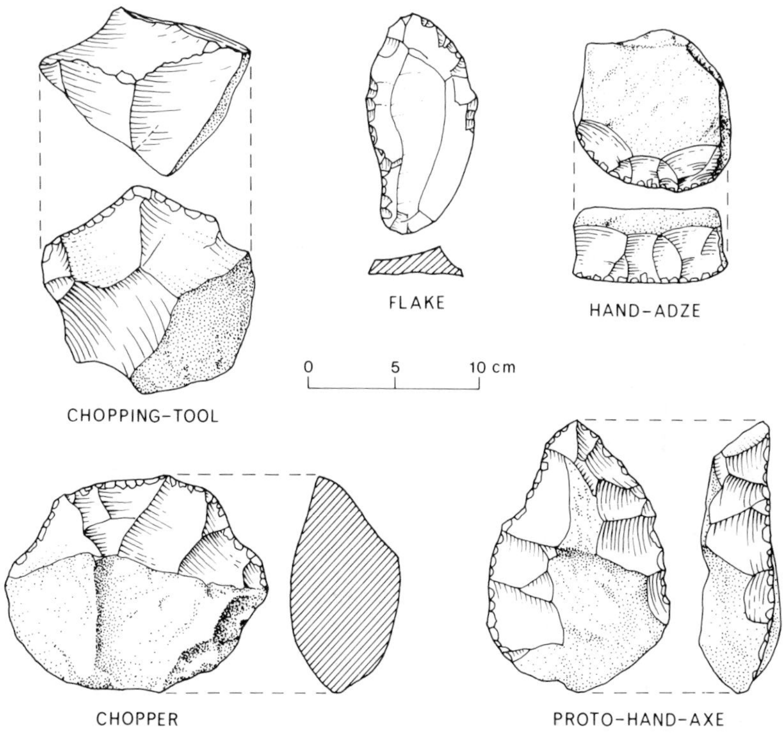

Fig. 2.7. Some major tool-forms of the South-East Asian "chopper/chopping-tool" industries. After Movius 1944; Glover and Glover 1970.

a. Fairly heavy *tools* made by flaking the edges of riverine pebbles, large flakes or quarried nuclei — these are normally called "pebble tools" in popular parlance and include most of Movius' categories. Variables such as edge length, edge position, edge angle, and extent and position of surface flaking and unmodified cortex all intergrade. The distinction between unifacial and bifacial working can often be used with profit, especially to isolate an interesting category of bifacial "hand-axes" in the Javanese Pacitanian (Fig. 2.8a,b). Another useful distinction can perhaps be made with edge angles; the pebble tool forms which Movius defined as choppers, chopping-tools and hand-axes tend to have fairly low edge angles, but his hand-adzes and scrapers seem to belong to a differentiable category of steep-edged, flat-based and thick unifacial tools, usually with edge angles of over 70° (see Fig. 2.7, Fig. 2.8c).

b. Smaller *tools* made on true flakes struck from cores (Fig. 2.8e,f), or sometimes on small chunks of stone. These rarely have specific edge or shape characteristics, and if they do not reveal clear patterns of retouch they can only be separated from purely waste material by edge inspection.
c. Manufacturing *waste*—items not in categories a. and b. because they show no signs of post-manufacture retouch or usage. They include unutilised flakes, chips (that is flake-like pieces lacking bulbs of percussion, caused either by core smashing or flake breakage), shattered cores and chunks, and sometimes true discarded cores. The latter are often hard to recognise as true debitage since the removal of flakes causes edge-shattering which can easily be confused with use-damage. The term "horsehoof core" (Fig. 2.8) is used in Australian archaeology to describe one very characteristic single-platform variant of this class, but there is often confusion as to whether these are to be considered as steep-edged tools or waste items—each example must be examined individually. Other core shapes are less distinctive, but spherical and conical trends in shape can often be observed.

The selection process in these industries is clearly for tool size and edge morphology; overall shape appears to be rather incidental, although shape, edge and size often correlate to some degree. Common sense would suggest that there are at least two major tool classes: heavy tools with axe-like or chopping functions, and tools with scraping and cutting functions. These functional categories do not correspond directly with categories a. and b. above, and any given stone tool could have served several different functions during its life.

C. The Pleistocene Industries of China

Before turning to an examination of the Indo-Malaysian pebble and flake assemblages I will look at the only area of East Asia where the cultural activities of *Homo erectus* are clearly documented. Recent Chinese material is reviewed in a number of selectively illustrated sources (Chang 1977a; Freeman 1977; Aigner 1978a, 1978b, 1981; Atlas 1980; Jia 1980; Yi and Clark 1983), and when these sources are combined it is clear that a lot of potentially detailed evidence is available.

Early Pleistocene sites in China (Fig. 2.9) are surrounded by considerable uncertainty with respect to date and association. The site of Yuanmou, which has produced some rather indeterminate stone tools and a suggestion for the use of fire, now appears to have a Middle rather than an Early Pleistocene antiquity (see Section II). Another assemblage claimed to be of Early

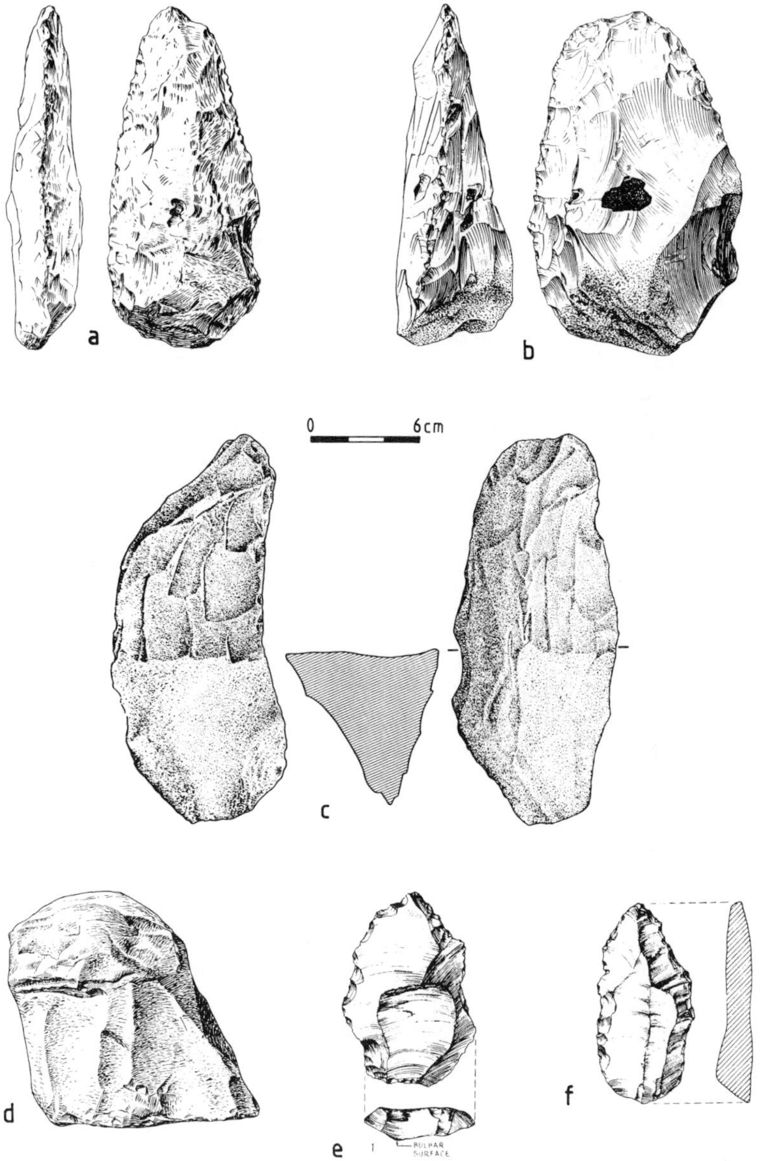

Fig. 2.8. Pacitanian tool forms from Java. (a, b) Hand-axes; (c) steep-edged and flat-based tool; (d) horsehoof core; (e–f) flakes with signs of utilisation. From Bartstra 1976; Movius 1944. Courtesy: G-J. Bartstra (a–d); Peabody Museum (e–f).

Pleistocene age, again with traces of fire (here in the form of burnt bone), comes from Gehe locality 6053 (Xihoudu) in Shanxi, but Aigner (1978b:194; see also Woo 1980:196) disputes the presence of true stone tools. Quite clearly, neither of these sites can be considered as unequivocal evidence for the presence of stone tools during the Early Pleistocene in China.

Better material is reported from the Middle Pleistocene of central China. Charcoal and tools were found in the vicinity of the Lantian skull-cap at Gongwangling in Shaanxi (Jia 1980:16), and other similar assemblages which may run from the Middle into the Late Pleistocene have been recovered from Gehe localities 6054 and 6055 and from Dingcun in Shanxi (Fig. 2.10). The major sites of this period occur in the caves at Zhoukoudian near Peking, where one of the world's most famous populations of *Homo erectus* has been found in direct association with evidence for the use of fire, and the hunting of large mammals such as *Pseudaxis* and *Megaloceros* (both forms of deer), and rhinoceros. Artefacts include a range of possible bone and antler tools (Aigner 1978b:182), and by far the best documented sample of Middle Pleistocene stone tools from any site in eastern Asia (Fig. 2.10). The industry appears to have a predominance of small retouched flake tools, together with larger pebble and core tools (including some bifacially flaked forms), and flaked stone balls ("bolas stones"; Yi and Clark 1983).

In southern China the evidence is not as prolific as that from the Yellow River region further north, but an excellent Middle Pleistocene assemblage of retouched flakes and core tools has been excavated at Guanyindong cave in Guizhou, with animal bones from a fauna with *Stegodon* and *Ailuropoda* which is clearly related to the Jetis and Trinil faunas of Java. Aigner (1978:221) has pointed out that the southern industries mostly utilise flakes, and that the heavy pebble and core elements tend to be lacking. However, when these industries finally emerge into clearer focus as the Hoabinhian of the Late Pleistocene and Holocene, there is little doubt that heavy forms are indeed present, despite their apparent earlier rarity.

D. Stone Industries Possibly Made by *Homo erectus* in the Indo-Malaysian Archipelago

1. The Pacitanian

Tools of this industry (see Fig. 2.8) were first discovered by Koenigswald and Tweedie in 1935 in the bed of the Baksoko River near Pacitan, south-central Java. Further investigations in 1938 by Terra, Chardin and Movius led to characterisation of the finds as part of the chopper/chopping-tool complex of South-East Asia, and to an assumption of a Middle or Late Pleistocene date. Further work was subsequently carried out by Heekeren (1972), who

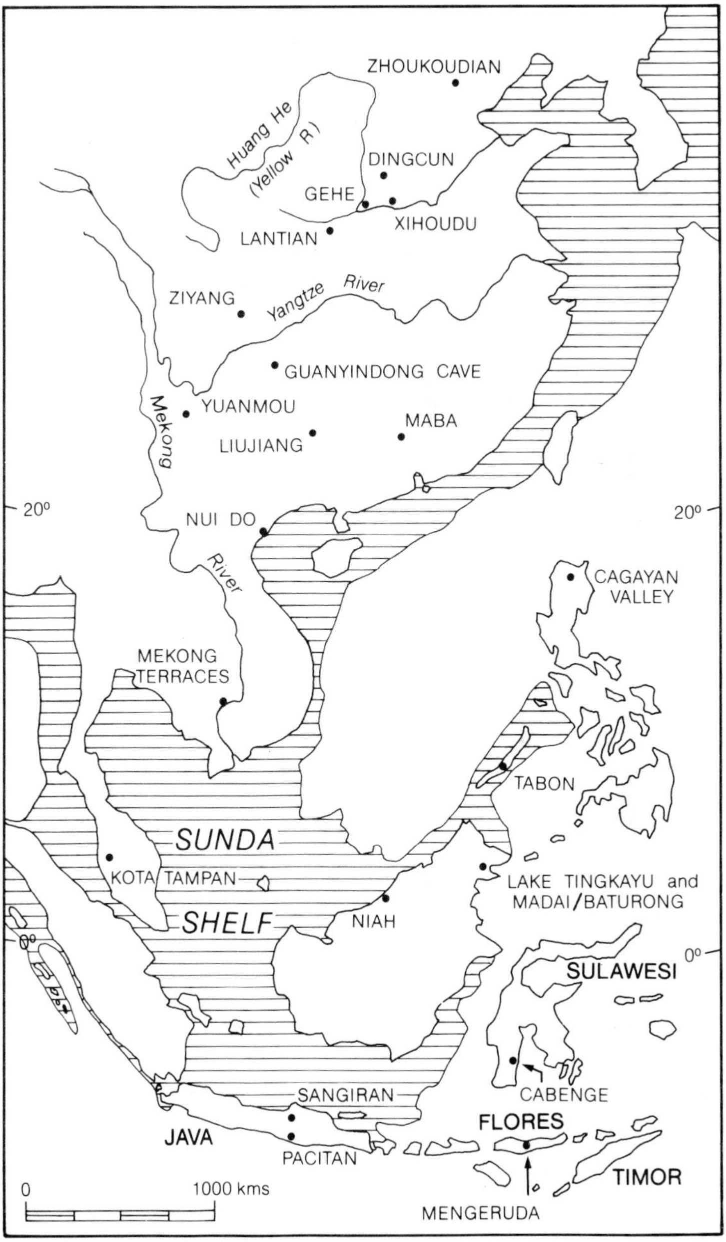

Fig. 2.9. Major fossil and archaeological sites of Pleistocene date in China and South-East Asia.

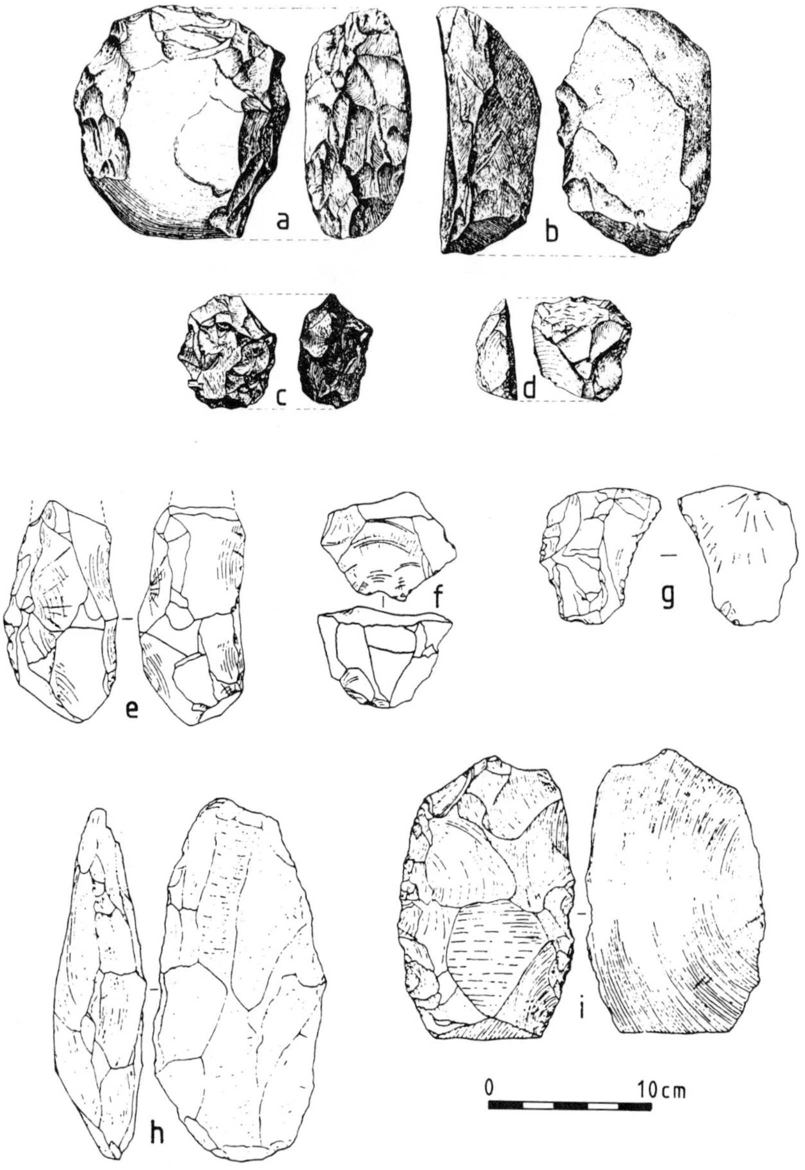

Fig. 2.10. Stone tools from Zhoukoudian (a–d), Gehe (e–g) and Dingcun (h, i). (a) Bifacial pebble tool; (b, d) flat-based steep-edged unifacial tools; (c) core; (e) bifacial core tool; (f) single-platform core; (g) utilised flake; (h) hand-axe; (i) large retouched flake. From Movius 1944; Yi and Clark 1983. Courtesy: Peabody Museum (a–d); University of Chicago Press (e–i).

reclassified the material, reported on finds from adjacent valleys, and suggested that the tools were eroding from four implementiferous terraces in the Sunglon and Baksoko Valleys, with the oldest Baksoko material coming from about 15–20 m above the stream bed. However, the majority of the tools have been found in secondary positions in the modern stream beds, where they have become rolled and mixed with artefacts of apparent Neolithic provenance.

As described, the industry is made on silicified tuff (the best material), silicified limestone and fossil wood, and comprises a range of my category a. tools (see Section IIIB) including bifacial hand-axes and high-backed steep-angled "scrapers", together with numerous flake tools and waste flakes, some of very large size (Mulvaney 1970). It is not essentially different from the Late Pleistocene industries of Borneo, which I will be describing later, but there does appear to be a tendency towards large size. However, this may be due to collection bias; none of the finds represent contemporary and complete assemblages, and it is not clear what the total size range of the material was at any one time.

The most recent work on the Pacitanian has been carried out by Bartstra (1976, 1978a, 1978b). He points out, after exhaustive geomorphological reconnaissance, that alluvial gravels which lack fossils extend up the valley sides to heights of up to 28 m above the stream beds, but due to slumping and colluvial movement it is not possible to correlate terrace remnants or to recognise individual terraces. Tools are occasionally found *in situ* up to high gravel levels, and earliest dates, according to Bartstra, could fall around the Middle–Late Pleistocene boundary. Bartstra's basic view is that the material could cover a very long time span indeed, and he does report finding many small flake tools of a size range which seems to have been ignored by earlier collectors.

2. The Sangiran Flake Industry

In 1934, Koenigswald found some rolled and patinated small flakes of jasper and chalcedony in the Sangiran dome, and started a controversy which still continues today. His claim (stated in Koenigswald and Ghosh 1973) has always been that the tools originally came from the Notopuro beds — a sequence of volcanic breccias and tuffs which overlie and rest unconformably on the Kabuh layers at Sangiran. These volcanic layers are about 20 m thick, and contain in some places a Trinil fauna at the base (including a *Homo erectus* calotte), but otherwise lack animal bones. They do, however, predate the Ngandong terraces and hominids, and in the dating scheme used in this book are undoubtedly Middle Pleistocene.

The main problem, as Koenigswald admitted, is that the tools were all found on the surface or in superficial layers, and the assumption that they originated in the Notopuro beds remains impossible to prove. There has been much disagreement over this in the past. Heekeren (1972:49) claimed that the tools originated from the basal Notopuro, while Terra (1943) claimed that they came from a topmost gravel layer. The most recent opinion, and the one which I find most convincing, is by Bartstra (1974, 1978b) who believes the tools are all from recent colluvial and alluvial deposits and cannot be shown to be from the Notopuro beds at all. Furthermore, Bartstra points out that many of the "tools" are no more than nodules of jasper and chalcedony which occur naturally in the area, although there seems little doubt that the rudiments of a genuine assemblage do exist amongst the collections.

The Sangiran industry as described has some most unusual features, particularly if it is to be associated with *Homo erectus*. The tools are all very small, and well below the average size of the Pacitanian. They comprise small flakes, some with apparent retouch, but little else — the absence of cores and large pebble tools is most unusual. But there are some definite flake tools, including a class of "small bevel-edged flakes" which have been described by Orchiston (1978).

The Sangiran industry therefore falls into the same kind of limbo as the Pacitanian, and it seems likely to occupy this position for some time.

3. The Ngandong Industry

Material associated with the Ngandong fossils, excavated between 1931 and 1933, is sparse and problematical. According to Koenigswald (1951:216), "a few small stone scrapers and some triangular chalcedony flakes were observed, but they have disappeared from our collection". All recent commentators, such as Sartono (1976), Bartstra *et al.* (1976), and Jacob (1978b) seem unwilling to accept that any tools were found in direct association with the fossils at all.

Nevertheless, one of the original investigators, Oppenoorth (1936; see also Stein Callenfels 1936c), was considerably more enthusiastic. He reported worked bone and antler from the general vicinity of the skulls, together with stone balls of andesite apparently similar to those mentioned above from China, and he also found a spine of a marine sting-ray close to skull VI. However, according to a geological section presented by Sartono (1976, after Ter Haar), all these items were found in superficial layers of the terrace, above the skulls, except perhaps for the bone tools which have always remained rather dubious. Oppenoorth did find other tools in terrace deposits in other parts of the Ngandong region — more stone balls at Watualang, a beautiful biserial bone harpoon from Sidorejo, and some chalcedony flakes from the surface at Ngawi (are these the ones mentioned by Koenigswald above?). But none of these items can really be claimed as the handiwork of Ngandong

Homo erectus; all may be very much more recent, particularly the harpoon (which was originally and rather lovingly compared with Magdalenian harpoons from Europe!).

However, this rather sad and confusing story could have a happy ending, given a recent claim by Jacob *et al.* (1978) that two unrolled tools of basaltic andesite — a well-made unifacial pebble "chopper" and a retouched flake — have been found in a late-Middle or Late Pleistocene gravel deposit at Sambungmacan approximately contemporary with the layer which yielded the skull of *Homo erectus* (see Section IID). The tools appear to be genuine, and since the skull is similar to but slightly more archaic than the Ngandong skulls, it may not be unreasonable to claim that the late *erectus* population of Java did make stone tools, even if the history of discovery has only just begun.

4. Other Possible Pleistocene Industries in Western Indonesia

Although stone tools claimed to be of Pacitanian type have turned up as isolated surface finds in Sumatra, Borneo and Bali, none can be regarded as of Early or Middle Pleistocene antiquity on grounds of morphology alone. They will not be considered further.

5. Cabenge, South-western Sulawesi

In Chapter 1, Section IVA, I referred to an important Late Pliocene faunal collection made in the region of Cabenge in the Walanae Valley. From 1947 onwards, stone tools have been found in apparent association with these bones, and several authors (e.g. Heekeren 1972:69) have considered them contemporary. However, recent geological work has disproved this; the tools come from coarse river sediments of presumed but very indeterminate Pleistocene age (Sartono 1979a), and the animal bones which occur in these deposits have probably been washed out from older formations (Bartstra 1978c).

Nevertheless, Bartstra (1978c) does note that the patinated tools found in the highest terrace gravels are rather different from the tools of Toalian type found closer to the river; the latter are of undoubted Holocene date (see Chapter 6, Section IIIB) and the former may be assumed to be older. Heekeren describes them as small thick flakes struck from irregular cores, and refers to a range of scrapers and chopping-tools. Soejono (1982a) also mentions massive core tools, hand-axes and horsehoof cores. However, there remains the problem that the industry has not yet been found in dateable stratified deposits, and there are no grounds as yet for assuming either a Middle Pleistocene antiquity or an association with *Homo erectus.*

6. Flores, Timor and Luzon

In Chapter 1, Section IVA, I discussed the significance of the occurrence of two species of *Stegodon*, one of normal size and one dwarfed, on a number of eastern Indonesian islands including Flores and Timor. Archaeological interest in this situation was aroused in 1970, when Maringer and Verhoeven (1970a and b) published their results of investigations on Flores. In one region called Mengeruda they claimed to have found stone tools in association with *Stegodon* bones in scattered exposures in an area about 3 km long, and described a variety of pebble tools, retouched flakes and one small bifacial hand-axe. Generalised affinities were drawn with the Pacitanian, Sangiran and Cabenge industries, and the suggestion was made that contemporaries of the Ngandong hominids may have been able to venture along the Lesser Sunda chain.

However, even if the tools and *Stegodon* bones are genuinely associated in Flores (no subsequent geological work has been done to check this claim), there remains the problem that it is not known when these proboscids became extinct. It is only known that they are not present in cave deposits in Timor dated to the terminal Pleistocene (Glover 1972a). For the latter island, Glover and Glover (1970) have reported more surface finds of possible Pleistocene tools (see also Maringer and Verschuuren 1981; Azis 1981), but stratigraphic contexts are still lacking. A similar surface industry has recently been reported from Sumbawa (Soejono 1982a).

Similar problems apply to a claimed Middle Pleistocene industry from the Cagayan Valley in northern Luzon, Philippines. A genuinely Early or Middle Pleistocene fauna occurs in deposits exposed in this valley, but as Wasson and Cochrane (1979) note, the stone tools once claimed to be in association with the fauna are probably not so, and they note also that the industry is quite closely paralleled in terminal Pleistocene and Holocene cave deposits in the area. Pebble tools, horsehoof cores and retouched flakes are again the major forms represented.

7. Malaya

I will close this listing of the Indo-Malaysian stone industries having claimed associations with *Homo erectus* by referring briefly to the "Tampanian" tools recovered from gravels in the Perak Valley of Malaya. In the principal report published by Walker and Sieveking (1962) the tools, which have certain affinities with the Pacitanian, were linked to high sea-level alluvial terrace deposits of Early or Middle Pleistocene ("First Interglacial") date. However, a number of widely-held views on the Tampanian were rudely shaken in 1975, when Verstappen (1975:26–7) pointed out that the "terraces" were better regarded as wash and colluvial deposits formed in a tree–savanna landscape during drier glacial periods, and Harrisson (1975a) suggested younger affiliations for the tools by attempting to associate them with an overlying and presumed Late Pleistocene ash-shower. He also disputed human manufacture for many of the items. All this suggests a very difficult situation. I am not convinced that Harrisson's arguments for a late date are correct, but it must be admitted that the weight of recent geomorphic evidence does go against Walker's views about high sea-level river terraces. Good dating evidence for the tools is still entirely elusive.

IV. Some Conclusions on "Early" Industries

None of the Indo-Malaysian industries which I have described occur in dated or even well-stratified contexts. It is also impossible to date them relatively using typological characters; they all belong to a poorly differentiated pebble and flake tradition, and, as recently stressed by Bartstra (1982b; 1983), none of them can be directly associated with *Homo erectus.* We still have no real proof that humans ventured across Huxley's Line before 40 000 years ago, as I noted in 1978. One could in fact take the extreme view that none of these industries are older than 40 000 years and that all could be the handiwork of populations of *Homo sapiens* — the only minor hole in this argument would be the two claimed tools from Sambungmacan in Java. However, stone tools do occur in absolutely certain association with *Homo erectus* from perhaps 800 000 years ago in China, and I still feel it rather unlikely that the Ngandong hominids in Java were not familiar with their use (but see Chapter 3, Section IIID, for an extension of this problem into the Australian fossil record). For the earlier Javanese hominids no more than subjective opinions can be presented, and it has been suggested from dental evidence that they were vegetarians who possibly had no need for stone tools (Puech 1983).

Concerning the tendentious matter of "progress", it must still be admitted that Movius' general view that the South-East Asian pebble and flake industries "cannot be considered as having been in any sense 'progressive' from a cultural point of view" (Movius 1955:538) still holds, despite recent disagreements. One can of course take refuge in the argument that these stone tools fall into a "maintenance" category, that is they were used for making and sharpening a much more task-specific range of tools of organic materials such as bamboo, of which no traces are ever likely to survive in the archaeological record.

The latter argument is one which I have presented myself in the past, but I now find it rather unsatisfactory and negative. In the past few years I have had considerable experience of Late Pleistocene and Early Holocene assemblages from Borneo and Indonesia, and, excepting the more specialised industries to be described in Chapter 6, I am quite happy to agree that the tools appear to be simple, amorphous and undifferentiated to a modern observer with a fairly Eurocentric (or Afrocentric) bias. However, they do have durable and useable edges and I see no reason why they should not have served their intended purposes with a quite acceptable level of efficiency.

Indeed, dangers appear when people make the equation *primitive tools equals primitive people.* South-East Asia has been no less a successful area of human evolution from a present-day vantage point than have Africa and Europe. The very large populations who inhabit the Indo-Malaysian Archipelago today simply must be derived basically from the Pleistocene populations, both *erectus* and *sapiens*, who inhabited the region from central China to Indonesia; a region entirely within the zone of pebble and flake industries. Here I am clearly favouring the argument for considerable *erectus* to modern genetic continuity which I will discuss further in the next chapter, and if this view is correct then the stone tools described must have been made by groups ancestral to modern Australoid and Southern Mongoloid populations. The fact that it cannot be proved at the moment that *Homo erectus* in Indonesia made stone tools does not negate the argument for continuity, since a small in-moving group could have introduced stone-working techniques without any marked genetic effect on the dominant population. What may be more important is that there is no evidence for intensive regional cultural specialisation in stone tool manufacture in South-East Asia, even during the Late Pleistocene. Here there may be good reason to welcome the observation of Service (1970) that being unestablished (that is unspecialised) is an evolutionary privilege from which many historical societies have greatly benefitted in the long term.

3

Indo-Malaysians of the Last 40 000 Years

The raw data required for any discussion of origins, distributions and differentiation amongst recent Indo-Malaysian populations are drawn from two very different and specialised disciplines. One of these disciplines is genetics, and the other is physical anthropology (today increasingly being renamed as biological anthropology). The raw data come in the form of gene frequencies, observations on living phenotypes, and observations on skeletal (especially cranial) phenotypes. In a previous book (Bellwood 1978a: Chapter 2) I presented a review of some of this material from an Oceania-centred viewpoint; now I will move the focus westwards.

The present populations of the region are of course varied, and the variation is expressed, as in all human populations, through a hierarchy of levels; from individuals, through ethnolinguistic groups, geographical zones, and eventually to the level of the major races. The concept of race is clearly very important when considering prehistoric relationships, but it is a concept which tends to evoke a good deal of argument (e.g. Littlefield *et al.* 1982). One extreme view states that there are no races, only clines, while in opposition are the racial pigeon-holing and stratum-mixing theories which prevailed in earlier physical anthropology. For an intelligible narrative of prehistory a concept of race is necessary; it would be unreasonable to claim that there is no geographical patterning to human variation, since this view would force us to consider every small group independently in terms of its place in a whole-world range of variation — clearly an impossible and unnecessary task.

Definitions of race are legionary. I will use one given by Buettner-Janusch (1966:184):

> A race of *Homo sapiens* is a Mendelian population, a reproductive community of individuals sharing a common gene pool. All members of our species belong to one Mendelian population, and its name is *Homo sapiens*. This large species-wide Mendelian population may be divided into smaller Mendelian populations, for all practical purposes an indefinitely large number of them.

Buettner-Janusch's last sentence makes it clear that racial classifications are by nature both hierarchical and diffuse; they are ideal subjects for ramified subdivision. If entering the hierarchy at the top then it can be postulated that the populations of the Indo-Malaysian Archipelago belong to two of the major races of mankind, namely the Australoids (or Australo-Melanesians) and the Mongoloids. This gross splitting is a heuristic device, and I am quite aware that human populations at all times must have shown intergrading or clinal characteristics, just as they do today.

Certain of my colleagues have taken me gently to task for using these terms in a general sense, that is to class Negritos, Melanesians and Australians as Australoids, and Polynesians, Micronesians and East Asians generally as Mongoloids. The grounds for these objections seem to be that, for instance, Negritos are not identical to the Australians for whom the term "Australoid" was originally invented, and the Polynesians likewise are not identical to the Chinese. However, my tendency is to stress classificatory simplicity from an evolutionary viewpoint. Since I consider that Negritos, Melanesians and Australians share a basic common ancestry in Island South-East Asia, despite their present differences, I classify them together as members of one major internally varied Australoid race. Likewise, the Chinese, Malays and Polynesians share a common Mongoloid origin in the subtropical and temperate mainland of eastern Asia.

It is also my belief that the present racial geography of the region is not due entirely to local evolution. It is true that all populations are subject to natural selection, and where breeding groups are small they will be subjected to genetic drift for proportions of specific genetic polymorphisms. These types of *in situ* differentiation amongst relatively or wholly isolated populations have clearly been fundamental to race formation in *Homo sapiens*, but are insufficient to explain the large-scale geographical distributions of the races of mankind prior to AD 1500. Some of these, such as the Southern Mongoloids of the Indo-Malaysian region, have clearly expanded on a very large scale to absorb, replace or surround pre-existing populations.

In already settled areas, major expansions such as this could presumably only have occurred when populations with considerable numerical and technological advantages impinged on less resistant groups. Prior to the development of agriculture and the attendant and rapid growth in population size and technology, it is unlikely that chances for such large-scale expansion would have presented themselves often (Brues 1977:251; Krantz 1980). This, however, is a scale-dependent statement, for small groups of hunters and gatherers could undoubtedly have moved quite large distances during the span of human evolution, even into regions previously but lightly settled. I will discuss one possible example of such an ancient secondary expansion, currently under investigation in Australia, at the end of this chapter. I should also add that I wish to exclude cases of *initial* settlement of previously empty areas, such as Australia, the Pacific Islands and the Americas, from these generalisations — in these cases all a small group needed was the technology and the chance to arrive.

If my views on these matters are generally correct, then the major Old World races of mankind, who occur in often widespread and scattered distributions today, would have been more integrated with respect to geographical distribution in the Pleistocene past. Organised agriculturalists can quickly dominate sparse groups of tropical forest hunters, but those sparse hunters would be much less likely to have such advantages with respect to other hunters with *similar* population densities and technology. During the Pleistocene gentle clines of variation can be expected, while the present pattern, particularly in South-East Asia, often reveals quite sharp interfaces. As I will indicate, the Southern Mongoloids have very clearly expanded southwards at some time in the past.

Before I move on to the Indo-Malaysian evidence in more detail I wish to add some necessary cautions about the use of biological data in reconstructing human prehistory. As noted above, knowledge of the biological intricacies of human evolution through the *sapiens* stage comes from two sources: the skeletal material, often fragmentary and ambiguous, and present-day patterns of genotypic variation (for example blood groups) and phenotypic variation (for example skin colour, cranial shape). As Terrell and Fagan (1975) point out, both sources depend on each other for the production of viable hypotheses about the past, and reasoning from one source alone will give a very biased and probably erroneous view, a sad fact to which the history of physical anthropology often bears witness. Furthermore, even with the best of cooperation between geneticists and palaeoanthropologists there are some very severe limits to the extent to which hypotheses about racial history can ever be decisively proved. To paraphrase Simpson (1947:143), it is possible to disprove hypotheses in the life sciences, but impossible to prove them; "proof" thereby being more the establishment of degrees of confidence rather than certainty.

People are also hard to describe from a purely practical viewpoint. We can usually make quite coherent descriptive statements about ourselves in terms of skin colour or hair form (anthroposcopic traits), stature (an anthropometric trait), and certain internal genetic characteristics such as the blood groups which are inherited through one or a small number of genetic loci. However, we cannot tie important, complex and stable anthroposcopic characters, such as skin colour, to variations at specific genetic loci; the necessary advances in the field of genetics have not yet been made.

These anthroposcopic and blood-based characters vary from person to person and group to group, and they do not vary congruently to provide precise racial boundaries of a clear presence–absence nature, as Krantz (1980) has recently pointed out. For instance, two quite separate populations may have a similar range of skin colour. Thus the recurring debate about African–Melanesian relationships: do the two groups share a common ancestry or is their dark pigmentation the result of independent tropical adaptation? The real answer may be that both views are correct in part, but the derivation of a "real answer" is necessarily a highly intuitive process which takes many diverse factors into account. In this chapter my "real answers" are also intuitive; they can be no more than my assumptions about which hypothesis about the racial history of *Homo sapiens* in South-East Asia provides the best fit for the available facts.

I. The Populations of the Indo-Malaysian Region

The vast majority of the inhabitants of this region today are of Southern Mongoloid type, and the rising population of over 200 million people is exemplified by such important groups as the Malays, Javanese, Balinese and Filipinos. It is obvious that the whole archipelago is now a part of the Mongoloid world of East Asia, which also extends through many of the Pacific islands and right through aboriginal America. But there are other populations who, although small, are of great significance from a historical viewpoint. These comprise the Negritos, and the Melanesians who extend westwards from their own core region into the eastern islands of Indonesia. Following Coon (1966), I define both these populations as being of basically Australoid inheritance.

A. The Negritos

The short-statured Negrito populations (Fig. 3.1) of the region comprise the Malayan Negritos (formerly called "Semang") who inhabit the mountainous region of central Malaya from Pahang north to the Thai border, and the Negritos of the Philippines, who inhabit both coastal and inland localities in pockets of Luzon, northern Palawan, Panay, Negros and Mindanao (for distributions see Chapter 4, Fig. 4.1). The Andamanese, with whom I will not specifically be concerned, are also normally classified with the Negrito group. A similar population may also have survived until recent centuries in Taiwan (Chai 1967:33).

The Negritos of Malaya and the Philippines are traditionally forest and coastline hunters and gatherers, and they differ quite sharply from their Mongoloid neighbours, despite some intermarriage and the presence of a phenotypically intermediate population in the Senoi of central Malaya (Fig. 3.2). Stature is usually very small, averaging around 145–155 cm for males,

Fig. 3.1. Batek Negrito man and forest camp, central Malaya. Photo by Geoffrey Benjamin.

Fig. 3.2. Senoi (Temiar) men on the Nenggiri River, Kelantan, central Malaya (note wild taro growing on the river bank at right).

but there is some overlap here with surrounding Mongoloids, many of whom are of short stature themselves. In appearance, these people are dark, with tightly curled hair (sometimes red or brown), and in facial features they resemble small and gracile Australians or Melanesians. The simplest conclusion concerning them is that they are the small-statured representatives of a once widespread Australoid population which comprises the very varied peoples of Australia and Melanesia today, but which has been absorbed almost entirely into a much more numerous Mongoloid population in South-East Asia.

There are two questions which arise with these Negrito groups: where do they come from originally, and why are they short, whereas most modern Australians and Melanesians are of greater stature? Concerning origins, one view, best presented by Birdsell (1972:497–9), is that the Negritos, Melanesians and some Australian groups (including the now extinct Tasmanians) belong to a distinct Oceanic Negritoid population which is of ultimate African origin. However, there is really no skeletal or genetic evidence to support a view of a recent *sapiens* (as opposed to an ancient *erectus*) dispersal from Africa. Following a recent analysis of genetic polymorphisms amongst the Luzon and Mindanao Negritos Omoto (1981:421) suggests that:

> The African Pygmies and the Asian Negritos have different origins and that similarities ... such as short stature, dark skin colour and kinky hair are probably the reflection of adaptation to similar environmental conditions.

Occurrences of unique alleles further suggest that the Luzon and Mindanao Negritos have probably been separated from each other for at least 10 000 years.

Given this genetic information, it seems much easier to regard all the dark-skinned Australoid populations of South-East Asia and Melanesia as peoples who have undergone similar *in situ* tropical selection pressures over a very long time, just as have the Africans. In this view, which I espouse, the Australoids are the true aborigines of the Indo-Malaysian Archipelago; they represent a specific race of *Homo sapiens* native to that region.

This still leaves the question of short stature, and it should be noted here that there is no skeletal evidence which would give any support to the idea that the peoples of the Indo-Malaysian region were ever *all* short Negritos. That they were once all of generalised Australoid affinity is, however, a much more supportable proposition. The short stature may be simply a localised independent development. For instance, there are similar short peoples in the New Guinea Highlands ("Pygmies") who are not otherwise distinct in appearance from their neighbours, who are Melanesians of normal stature. In this case the explanation is probably natural selection within a small part of the range of a generally taller population; small stature may have great adaptive value in mountainous tropical forest environments with limited nutritional resources (Gajdusek 1970; Howells 1973c:173–4), where a high ratio of strength to body weight is advantageous. Gates (1961) has suggested that the New Guinea Pygmies owe their short stature to a local and recent mutation at perhaps a single genetic locus. This view has not been acceptable to many physical anthropologists (e.g. Birdsell 1967:108), but recent studies of African Pygmies have shown that they are markedly deficient in the production of the insulin-like growth factor IGF-1 (Merimee *et al.* 1981). It is not clear what environmental conditions have promoted this deficiency, but there has presumably been strong selective pressure to favour its survival, and a tendency to short stature in the interiors of other large islands in Melanesia has also been noted.

These views on local adaptation may explain why certain groups have attained short stature, but still do not explain why all the Malayan and Philippine Negritos are small. A possible explanation may be that they were already occupying environments which selected for short stature when Mongoloid dominance in the archipelago began to develop. Their larger-statured neighbours would thus have become absorbed into the present population, while the Negritos, partly through chance and inaccessibility, were mainly left alone until recently.

B. The Varied Populations of Eastern Indonesia

The peoples of the eastern Lesser Sunda and Moluccas Islands to the west of New Guinea clearly present great variation (Fig. 3.3). This is a result of a gradual Southern Mongoloid settlement, much of it historically recent, over the surviving western boundary of Melanesia. The racial picture here is markedly clinal, and there are few sharp boundaries. The eastern Lesser Sundas were described in a dated report by Bijlmer (1929), who reported clines in skin colour, hair form and the frequency of the epicanthic (Mongoloid) eye fold in populations from Sumba eastwards to Timor. Basically, he regarded the Sumbanese in the west as "Proto-Malays", who are gradually replaced eastwards through Flores and Timor by a dominant Melanesian population. Timor and adjacent islands also have interesting juxtapositions of Papuan and Austronesian languages. The same situation occurs on the island of Halmahera in the Moluccas, although here there is another interesting situation in that the Galela of the northern part of the island, who speak a Papuan language, are described by Ishige (1980; see also Wallace 1962:249) as being basically of "Malay stock" with some Papuan admixture. This is clearly a situation where races and languages do not match as might be expected, and it should be noted in this respect that all the Philippine Negritos have adopted Austronesian languages today.

Fig. 3.3. Atoni elders, South Amanuban, western Timor. Photo by James Fox.

The study by Bijlmer was amplified in 1948 by Keers, who also traced the "Proto-Malays" eastwards to western Flores and western Sumba, and claimed that there were traces in present phenotypes of an earlier Negrito population in some of the Lesser Sundas. I doubt whether it is possible to be specific about Negrito rather than more generalised Australoid affinity in this way, but Keers' results can be used to suggest varying degrees of Southern Mongoloid versus Melanesian dominance through the region.

C. The Southern Mongoloid Populations

The Southern Mongoloid populations (Figs 3.4–8), now numerically dominant in the region, are all speakers of Austronesian languages (with the possible exception of some eastern groups such as the Galela mentioned above), and all share considerable physical, cultural and linguistic homogeneity, despite the complex overlays of 2000 years of Hindu–Buddhist, Chinese and Islamic civilisation. Coon (1966:181) describes them succinctly:

> These peoples are mostly short, with a mean stature for males between 157 and 160 centimetres; of medium build; yellowish or brown-skinned; mostly straight

Fig. 3.4. Minahasans of the Lake Tondano region, Northern Sulawesi. Pottery still hot from firing is being given a waterproof resin glaze.

> haired; and with features of a general Mongoloid cast, but without excessive facial flatness. Among most of them the Mongolian eye fold is rare. Like the Australoids, many of them have large teeth . . . They represent a more or less stable mixture between Mongoloid and Australoid elements, with local variations.

A greater degree of Australoid inheritance can perhaps be seen amongst those populations who were once called Proto-Malays (see Section B), as opposed to the Deutero-Malays who are still considered by some authors to represent a second and later migration into the region (e.g. Glinka 1978, 1981). The "Proto-Malays" include many inland peoples of the larger islands of Indonesia and the Philippines, and of course some of the peoples of the clinal region of eastern Indonesia. Since Mongoloid gene flow has been entering Indonesia throughout historical times, it is clear that the so-called "Deutero-Malays", who are basically the populations who inhabit the more accessible areas, have simply had more contact with the Asian Mongoloid world.

Fig. 3.5. A family on Mentawai, off the western coast of Sumatra. The man is tattooed. Photo by Vernon Weitzell.

Fig. 3.6. A Penan family at Lio Matu, upper Baram River, Sarawak (1953). Photo by Hedda Morrison.

Fig. 3.7. A Murut boy, Sabah, photographed in 1910. Courtesy Sabah Museum (G. C. Woolley collection).

Fig. 3.8. Minangkabau women at Payakumbuh, central Sumatra. Photo by Cecilia Ng.

If it is possible to state the situation for Indonesia simply, then it is clear that a Mongoloid phenotype predominates in the west and north, and gradually fades southwards and eastwards (see also Bellwood 1978a:304). In eastern Indonesia, a population which is quite clearly a part of the Melanesian physical and cultural world predominates. A model of Mongoloid expansion into an Australoid sphere, allowing for considerable variation within each group, should suffice to explain the picture. The intricate details may always escape us, for the terms Australoid and Mongoloid themselves are ideal models, and the South-East Asian area may have been a clinal zone between these ideal types for several thousands of years.

D. Skin Pigmentation and the Southern Mongoloids

Anthroposcopic traits are poorly understood in terms of genetic inheritance, but it is believed that many of them have complex polygenic bases, hence they are not subject to rapid phenotypic fluctuations caused by genetic drift. Skin pigmentation is one such trait, and the variations in this must have evolved over long periods owing to the action of natural selection in specific environments. It seems fair to assume that skin colour among members of an undisturbed population in a relatively stable environment will remain stable over very long periods of time, and from known cases of population expansion it can be seen that the processes of natural selection which cause skin pigmentation to vary work at very slow rates. For instance, the tropical American Indians are not reported to be noticeably darker than other Americans after a settlement period of perhaps 15 000 years (Brues 1977:302), and yet it is clear from Old World observations that tropical latitudes have certainly selected for darker skins over much longer timespans. These observations would suggest that human skin colour variation is of great antiquity, and that the geographical variants seen today commenced development in original homeland environments from the beginning of the Old World radiation of *Homo erectus*.

Skin pigmentation is mainly produced in the deepest layer of the epidermis by melanocytes which produce the pigment melanin. The visible colour is also affected by the thickness of the outer skin layer, or stratum corneum, which contains keratin. These factors do not vary congruently; African and Melanesian skins are characterised by deep pigmentation but little keratinisation, Mongoloid skins have a thick stratum corneum packed with keratin but little pigmentation, and European skins lack both pigmentation and keratin. Indeed, human skin colours are formed by the actions of several factors which seem to vary rather independently.

The environmental factors which promote variation in skin pigmentation are still poorly understood. Although most authorities are willing to accept some latitudinal correlation for skin colour (that is dark at the equator, lighter towards the poles), there are many explanatory variations on this theme. For instance, Brace (1964) suggested that the fair skins of higher latitudes developed in part because the wearing of clothing circumvented those selective pressures which constantly promoted the production of protective melanin amongst our universally dark-skinned ancestors. Loomis (1967) adopted another explanation which Brace had rejected, and this concerns the synthesis of vitamin D by sunlight in the skin. Humans need a balanced quantity of this substance, and too much or too little is dangerous. Loomis suggested that human skin is pigmented so that just enough sunlight can penetrate; dark skins protect from too much, light skins protect from too little in high latitudes where sunshine is weaker.

Another viewpoint was adopted by Coon (1966), who regarded dark African and Melanesian skins as adaptations to cloudy and humid forested regions (a view not accepted by Brace), and the light-reflective Mongoloid skin as a protective adaptation to high levels of solar radiation. Brues (1977) has attempted to combine some of these different viewpoints, and she has also stressed the probable importance of camouflage, particularly for dark skins in tropical forests, and yellowish skins in deserts. The most recent view known to me is that of Krantz (1980), who supports a basically simple correlation between intensity of skin pigmentation and latitudinal intensity of solar radiation.

The only conclusion which can be drawn is that skin colour is of complex causation, and factors involved probably include all those listed above, which of course would vary in relative significance from one environment to another. However, the reason I have added this discussion is not to throw any new light on the causes of skin colour variation, but rather to draw attention to the presence of the relatively light-skinned Southern Mongoloid population in the Indo-Malaysian tropics; in a latitudinal belt which, in all other regions of the Old World (Africa, southern India, Melanesia, northern Australia), supports much darker aboriginal populations.

Although Southern Mongoloids are darker than Northern Mongoloids, and there is a clear north–south cline in skin colour which is even visible within South-East Asia, I find it hard to escape the conclusion (as does Brace 1980a) that had the Indo-Malaysian groups evolved entirely within the archipelago then they should be as dark as the latitudinally neighbouring Melanesians and Negritos. There is a clear case here of a pattern which does not meet the demands of long-term local natural selection, just as there is in the American tropics.

II. Genetic Data on the Differentiation of Indo-Malaysian Populations

In this section I will test my generalisations about ultimately separate origin zones (despite the possibility of some geographical overlap) for the Australoid and Southern Mongoloid populations against data on genetically controlled characteristics in blood. A geneticist has described evolution as "a complex flux of shifting dynamic equilibriums" (Clarke 1975), and at all comparative levels from two related individuals to whole populations the human species presents a complex genetic picture of uniqueness, intergradation and identity, depending upon which genetic characters are under study. The most important ones for charting human prehistory are the genetic polymorphisms — systems which can have several states which depend on the occurrence of different alleles at specific genetic loci on the chromosomes.

The best known of these polymorphisms are perhaps the blood groups, which are of simple inheritance based on variation at only one or a few loci. Some years ago it was commonly believed that pooled blood group frequencies could be used to trace ancestries of specific populations, and even major races of mankind. However, it is now known that some blood groups are subject to natural selection over both large and small geographical areas, and amongst small isolated populations they are particularly susceptible to genetic drift, and to a non-random sampling process known as the founder effect (Neel 1967). Selection, drift and the founder effect do of course operate to produce variation in all genetic systems, but some are more resistant to rapid change than others. Those blood groups (such as ABO and Rh) which can change rapidly in frequency in both time and space are of little use in tracing ancient connections between the major racial groups of mankind (Simmons 1962, 1976), and their patterns of frequency around the world do not correlate with the distributions of the modern races (Krantz 1980).

In recent years, however there have been major strides forward in other methods which allow major human populations and races to be "characterised". Perhaps the most important method involves the comparison of populations in terms of their *unique* alleles and allele combinations (haplotypes), many of which are specific to particular geographical races.

A. Evidence from Population-specific Genetic Markers

The genetic systems which are of most use for tracing population origins and ancient connections are those which are not markedly susceptible to natural selection, and which resist local fluctuation through genetic drift. In other words, single alleles or haplotypes in these systems are considered likely to remain in a population through long periods of time and through long migrations, and where they are distinctive to a particular population and do not occur in others they can be of great interest for human prehistory. Genetic systems which are strongly subject to disease-associated natural selection, such as the abnormal haemoglobins, do not have those advantages and are not considered here.

There are now known to be a number of fairly stable genetic polymorphisms, apparently unassociated with disease resistance, which do have population-specific variants. This has been suspected for some years with the Gm immunoglobulin system in eastern Asia (Schanfield and Gerschowitz 1973) and New Guinea. The most recent relevant summaries are by Kirk (1979; 1980a, b; 1982), who demonstrates that Asian and American Mongoloids (including Indo-Malaysian Mongoloids) can be differentiated from Australians and Melanesians on sharp presence–absence occurrences of variants in the Diego red cell antigen system, the transferrin iron-binding serum proteins, the Gm immunoglobulins and the Gc serum protein system. For details on the rather complex genetics of all this I can only refer readers to Kirk's papers, but the evidence does provide very strong support for the view that the Australians and Melanesians are of reasonably close common origin and are quite sharply separated in many characteristics in blood-genetic systems from the Southern Mongoloids.

Evidence for the occurrence of unique genetic markers in populations within the confines of the Indo-Malaysian Archipelago itself is very sparse, however, and few modern studies have been carried out in comparison with Australia and New Guinea (but see Lie-Injo 1976; Sofro 1982). The Negritos of the Philippines do have certain unique alleles (Omoto 1981), but they are not the same as those which characterise Australians and Melanesians. Both the Malayan and the Philippine Negritos have presumably been separated from related Australoid populations further east and south for too long for clear traces of common origin at a purely genetic level to have survived (or, to phrase this observation in another way, to be identifiable with present-day techniques).

B. Evidence from Multivariate Distance Statistics

This evidence comes from two sources — phenotypic measurements (anthropometric and cranial) and gene frequencies — and studies have tended to be at two levels, one stressing major population affinities, and the other being more concerned with microevolutionary patterns of divergence. Anthropometric and cranial distance studies have been confined mainly to the Australian and Oceanic regions (e.g. Howells 1970, 1973b; Pietrusewsky 1977; Kirk 1981), and since the results do not really contradict those from genetic analyses I will not consider them here in detail. However, one recent analysis

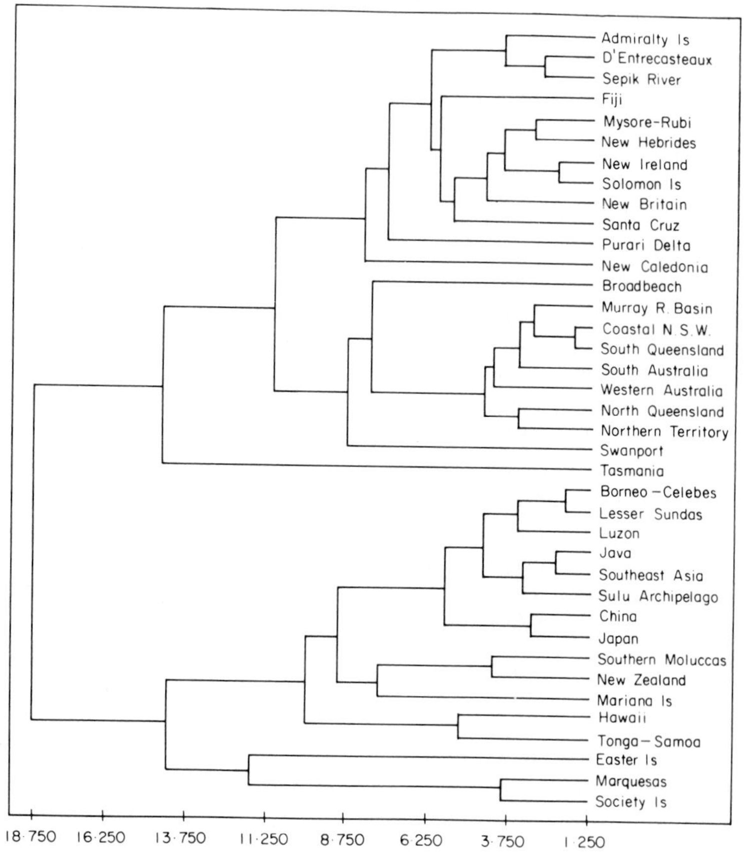

Fig. 3.9. Clustering of distances between 38 Pacific and circum-Pacific male samples (of historical or recent date) using 28 cranial measurements. (Mysore and Rubi are Irian Jaya populations.) From Pietrusewsky 1983. Courtesy: M. Pietrusewsky.

of broad geographical coverage by Pietrusewsky (1983), based on a multivariate analysis of 28 cranial measurements on skeletal populations, does reveal a sharp level of differentiation between Australo-Melanesian and Mongoloid populations (Fig. 3.9).

Distance diagrams for South-East Asian and Pacific populations in terms of genetic systems occurring in blood have been presented with increasing frequency since 1973 (e.g. Schanfield in Howells 1973c:76). Most analyses support the evidence given in the section on unique alleles, but this type of analysis has only very recently been extended into South-East Asia proper. Schanfield (above) reported clear separations between Northern Mongoloids, Southern Mongoloids, and Papuan-speaking Melanesians, but only for five loci. Recent studies have used up to 28 loci, and here the results seem to be in basic agreement; they may be summarised as follows:

a. Australians and Melanesians are always more closely related to each other than either are to Southern Mongoloids (e.g. Piazza *et al.* 1981). Philippine Negritos approach this Australoid grouping (Omoto 1981).
b. Oceanic Mongoloids (Micronesians, Polynesians) group most closely with Southern Mongoloids in Island South-East Asia (for many examples, see Kirk 1979, 1980a, b, 1981; Sofro 1982; Serjeantson, Ryan and Thompson 1983; Serjeantson 1984).
c. Southern Mongoloids as a whole tend to group closer to Northern Mongoloids than to American Indians (Kirk 1979).

These patterns of similarity and difference are clearly unsurprising in the light of the data from the unique genetic markers, and it may be asked what further information can come from this kind of research if the results always seem to replicate themselves within broad limits. Perhaps only the future holds the answer to this question, but both Omoto and Kirk have been experimenting with information concerning rates of genetic mutation over time to see if specific distance measurements between populations can be correlated with times of separation between them. For instance, Omoto (1981) has suggested from inferred rates of mutation that two groups of Philippine Negritos have been separated from each other for over 10 000 years, and Booth and Taylor (1976; see also Kirk 1981:133–4) have attempted to derive time scales by correlating genetic distances with linguistic dates, derived from the technique of glottochronology, for population separations in New Guinea. The results of this work are very hard to evaluate, and the precision of glottochronology itself is not without its critics. Furthermore, none of these methods is independent of other disciplines for the provision of a basic timescale against which to calibrate the genetic distances. However, they may one day be of value in the study of populations for whom other sources of dating are not available, and Omoto's study on Philippine Negritos is a good example of this.

C. Smaller-scale Population Distances

As well as the attempts to characterise major populations, there have been many attempts in recent years to see how small neighbouring populations differ from each other genetically, and to see if these differences vary congruently with linguistic differences, rates of intermarriage, geographical distances, and patterns of variation in anthropometric features. Again, almost all of this work has been done in Australia and Melanesia (together with South America), and the results as presented are clearly of more interest to geneticists and ecologists than to prehistorians (e.g. Friedlaender 1975; Rhoads and Friedlaender 1975; J. Wood 1978; Serjeantson, Kirk and Booth 1983). They are of interest for intensive studies on how genetic variations develop within small isolated populations over time-spans of only a few generations, and they can inform about the true genetic significances of language barriers, patterns of intermarriage, and especially of social structures.

The highly isolated and genetically varied Melanesian gardening populations are of great interest in this regard, and similar patterns of great local variation characterise some isolated groups of hunters and shifting cultivators in South-East Asia (e.g. Polunin and Sneath 1953; Lie-Injo 1976; Fix 1984). These are situations where genetic drift can operate at very rapid rates, but there always seems to be an encompassing anthroposcopic stability, probably maintained by selection, which not even drift can overcome. I would think that the main interest of these studies for a prehistorian comes from the demonstration that rapid genetic microevolution at identifiable genetic loci, over a period of perhaps 5000 years in Melanesian islands and longer in New Guinea, has been insufficient to produce major *in situ* phenotypic differences equal to those which we see in the major Australo-Melanesian and Mongoloid divisions today. Furthermore, the rapid genetic microdifferentiation seen in horticultural Melanesia is not thought to be characteristic of more mobile hunting and gathering groups, and so it is probably not a pattern which is generally characteristic of overall human evolution.

III. Ancient Populations of *Homo sapiens* in the Indo-Malaysian Archipelago

From the genetic information on modern populations presented above it would seem reasonable, to judge from patterns of trait distribution, to hypothesise that the ancestors of the Indo-Malaysian Mongoloids moved southwards into a region previously settled by Australoid populations. The diachronic data from ancient skeletal remains should, in theory, allow evaluation of this hypothesis. In practice, however, skeletal remains tend to be fragmentary, often very poorly dated, and ambiguous in terms of racial correlations. All human populations intergrade, especially in skeletal characteristics, and statements about the affinities of particular crania tend to be probabilistic (older reports often claim more certainty than is now known to be reasonable). While the totality of evidence does suggest to me that the Southern Mongoloid distribution can only be explained by allowing some importance to expansion, the whole story is complex, and we certainly cannot see a clear-cut replacement of populations taking place in the skeletal record. We must allow for intermarriage, local evolution, and also for the important concept that expansion involved more a change in the structure of a Mongoloid–Australoid cline, rather than a migration of uniform and distinct peoples from a remote area such as China.

A. Regional Continuity in Australoid and Mongoloid Evolution

The prevailing opinion amongst palaeoanthropologists today is that the *Homo erectus* populations represented by the skeletal series from China and Java have passed on at least some of their locally-distinctive morphological characteristics to the present Mongoloids and Australoids. This view has a very respectable history of support, and goes back to such influential scholars as Weidenreich (1946) and Coon (1962). According to Coon (1962:ix): "a species which is divided into geographic races can evolve into a daughter species while retaining the same geographical races". Coon did come under serious attack from reviewers for his claim that different geographical races crossed the *sapiens* threshold at different times (Coon 1962:30), but the basic chronology-free idea that geographical racial differences have been maintained through very long periods of human evolution has continued to receive support, for instance by Thorne and Wolpoff (1981) for the Australoids, and by Aigner (1978c), Hughes (1967) and by most recent Chinese authors (e.g. Wu 1982) for the Mongoloids.

The Mongoloids of eastern Asia and the Americas are a very widespread and variable group, but they do have in common a light to medium skin colour, dark eye pigmentation, generally straight black hair, and (especially in northern latitudes) wide, flat faces. The environmental factors which have selected for these features are generally assumed to have operated mainly in China and north-eastern Asia, but all these populations have been adapting for many millennia to the local environments where they are now found; this is particularly true of the Southern Mongoloids, who clearly lack many of the "cold-adapted" features of their more northerly cousins.

Skeletal features which allow one to postulate a fair degree of continuity from *Homo erectus* of Lantian and Zhoukoudian directly to modern Mongoloids are numerous; Coon (1962:459) was able to list 17 (see also Hughes 1967), and the more obvious features include high frequencies for shovelling of the upper incisors, for an absence of the third molar teeth, and for the presence of an accessory Inca bone at the back of the skull. Not all Mongoloids have all these traits, and they do occur in other populations, but there is a statistical tendency for them to be more common in Mongoloid populations.

The line of descent from *erectus* to modern Mongoloids is marked by quite a number of skulls. Following on from the classic *erectus* population of Zhoukoudian there are two important crania of uncertain date from Dali in Shaanxi and Maba in Guangdong. Both straddle the hazy borderline between *erectus* and *sapiens*, and the Maba skull, which comes from a location in the deep south of China, was described by Coon (1962:464) as "mostly if not entirely Mongoloid". Late Pleistocene skulls of more definite *sapiens* affiliation come from Liujiang in Guangxi and Ziyang in Sichuan, as well as from northern Chinese sites such as the Upper Cave at Zhoukoudian (c. 9000 bc, An 1983), and all are claimed to be early representatives of the modern Mongoloid race of *Homo sapiens.* It is a pity that firm dates are not available for the southern finds, and Ziyang could actually be of Holocene date. The Liujiang skull is of great interest, and Coon (1962:469) describes it as Mongoloid with some Australoid features (see also Section IIID), so this may be telling evidence for the existence of an ancient clinal zone through South-East Asia; an area where such a cline may be expected since there are no major latitudinal barriers to gene flow.

For Australoid evolution in the tropical latitudes of eastern Asia the record is less complete than that for China, since no remains fall into the long time-span between the Ngandong *Homo erectus* population and a fairly widely spread scatter of post-40 000 bc remains which, with their expanded brain-cases, are universally agreed to belong to modern populations. This gap has allowed claims to be made that Javanese *erectus* was an extinct sideline (e.g. Macintosh 1972:L), replaced by advanced humans from elsewhere. On the other hand, there is strong evidence, presented most recently by Thorne and Wolpoff (1981; see also Wolpoff *et al.* 1984), for definite regional continuity within a fairly homogeneous morphological lineage from Javanese *Homo erectus* right through to some terminal Pleistocene Australian human remains, particularly those from Kow Swamp in Victoria which have been dated between 7000 and 10 000 bc.

Nevertheless, this idea of continuity should be considered with some care, since it is unlikely that the Sundaland populations evolved entirely without gene flow from other Eurasian populations. It is indeed difficult to believe that the *Homo erectus* lineage of Java became totally extinct, but it is likewise difficult to believe in long-term hermetic sealage of the population. Some of the Indo-Malaysian early *sapiens* remains, and some of the earliest human remains from Australia, may not fit entirely within such a unified locally-evolving series. There is certainly something more complex happening in South-East Asia, in both the Australoid and the Mongoloid arenas. I will examine the latter first since they are the most recent and then work back in time.

B. The Southern Mongoloid Replacement Model for the Indo-Malaysian Archipelago

The idea that the majority of Island South-East Asian peoples belong to a Southern Mongoloid population which has replaced or absorbed an earlier Australoid (or "Australo-Melanesian") population has a respectable pedigree, and is still supported by most recent authors. Perhaps the simplest and clearest statement of this view was published by Barth in 1952; he thought that Late Neolithic and Bronze-Iron Age populations had been pushed southwards out of China by population pressure a little before 500 BC. For some reason he believed that there was a sharp ecological barrier between South China and South-East Asia which Mongoloids were unable to cross until they had developed substantial populations with wet-rice agriculture, and they then dramatically burst over the barrier. Such sharp replacement is not supported by the skeletal record, Barth's dates for initial Mongoloid expansion are far too late, and his view that North China was the ultimate source for all innovations in South-East Asia is now known to be wrong. But the basic need for a hypothesis of replacement, confined mainly to the Neolithic and later periods, still remains.

I will now review some relevant skeletal material, in some cases quite well-dated, for which authoritative opinions have been published. The three most important sites are Niah and Gua Cha in Malaysia, and Tabon Cave in the Philippines, there is also a scatter of important but more poorly dated material from Indonesia (for site locations see Fig. 3.10, Chapter 6, Fig. 6.1).

Niah Cave (the West Mouth) in Sarawak is a major site which will appear frequently in this book; for present purposes it has by far the best series of dated human remains of any site in Island South-East Asia, and these include:

a. The "deep skull" (Fig. 3.11) (Kennedy 1977), generally associated with a carbon date of c. 38 000 bc, although my inclination is to prefer a younger date on the grounds that the skull must have been buried from a higher level (see Chapter 6, Section IIA).
b. A series of flexed, seated and fragmentary burials dating between 12 000 and 1500 bc (Harrisson 1975b; Brooks *et al.* 1977).
c. Extended burials in coffins or mats dating from perhaps as early as 3200 bc (c. 3800 BC) to about 2000 years ago.

The situation with respect to the deep skull has been reviewed recently by Kennedy (1977). The basic analysis of the skull was done by Brothwell (1960), who suggested that it belonged to a young person whose closest morphological affinities were with recent Tasmanians, that is towards the gracile end of the Australoid range of variation. The burial series listed under b. has not

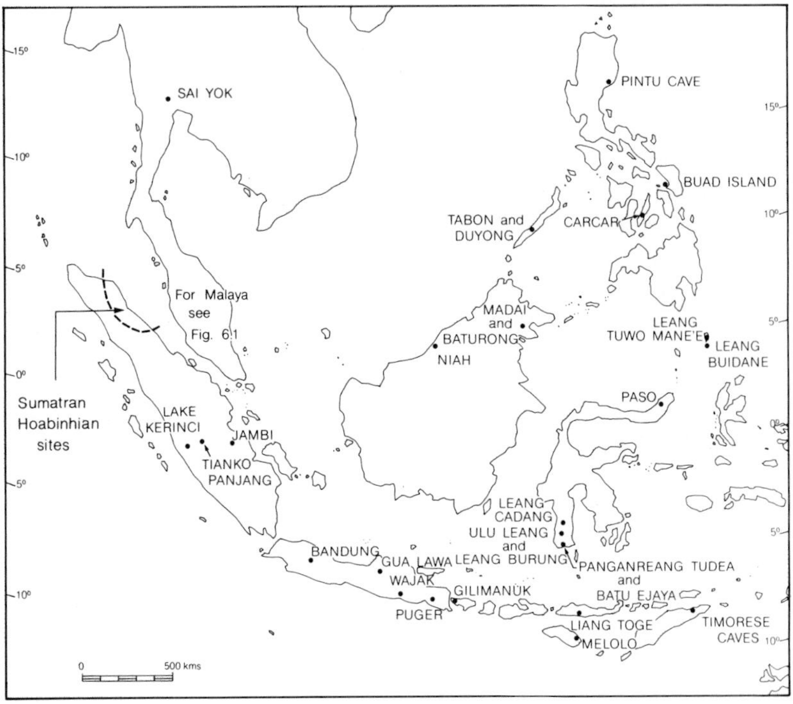

Fig. 3.10. Locations of sites described in Chapters 3 and 6.

been fully described, but Brooks *et al* (1977) provide data on blood groups identified from the bones, and Koenigswald (1958) described the dentitions of the older burials as "Melanesoid" (that is large). Perhaps all that can be said about this group is that its affinities do not appear to be with the recent Southern Mongoloids, who are more probably represented in group c.

From Tabon and nearby caves on Palawan island in the Philippines there are two sets of human remains (Fox 1970):

a. A frontal bone and mandible from Tabon Cave dated to between 20 000 and 22 000 bc (although the relevant deposits are described as disturbed, Fox 1970:40). The mandible is considered close to the Australian range by Macintosh (1978).
b. Jar burial remains in many caves, all postdating 3000 years ago and all Mongoloid in terms of incisor shovelling (Winters 1974).

Thus in both Niah and the Tabon caves there is some evidence, albeit debatable, for postulating that an original Australoid population was being

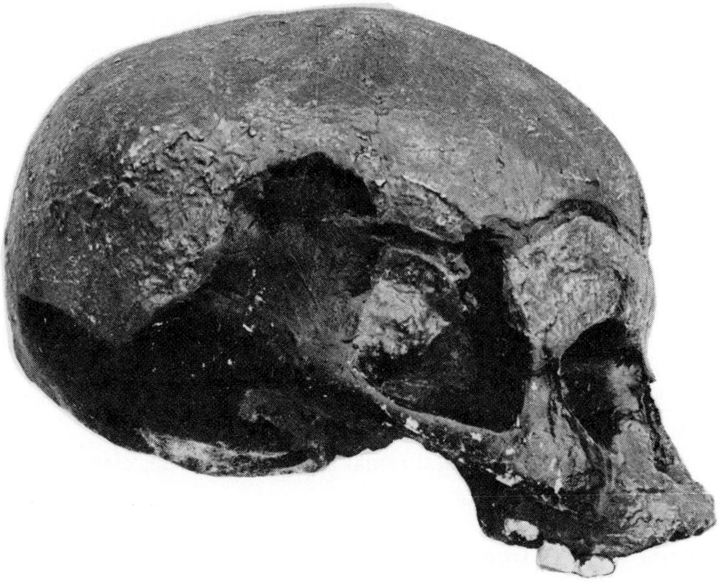

Fig. 3.11. The "deep skull" from the West Mouth at Niah. Courtesy: Sarawak Museum.

replaced by Southern Mongoloids by at least 1000 BC. For Gua Cha the situation is different. This site is a rock-shelter in Kelantan in central Malaya, an area now inhabited by *orang asli* (aboriginal) groups of Negritos and Senoi; both populations of varying but clear Australoid affinity. The 27 burials from Gua Cha date from about 10 000 years ago to perhaps 2000 years ago (Sieveking 1954; see also Chapter 6, Section IA; Chapter 8, Section III), and span both Hoabinhian and Neolithic contexts. Trevor and Brothwell (1962; see also Bulbeck 1982) note that the remains show no change of a racial nature throughout, and have general affinities with Melanesians; they are neither short-statured Negritos nor Mongoloids. Since the Gua Cha remains must be ancestral to some of the present *orang asli* they may represent a population closer to the present Senoi than to the Negritos, and this region was obviously never settled by Southern Mongoloids to any extent until very recently.

To fit the information from these three sites into a coherent pattern we must turn to Indonesia. Most of the important material has been reviewed by Jacob (1967a), but more has been recovered in recent years. First, I will consider the most problematic site; this is Wajak in east-central Java, where two crania were found in 1889 and 1890 (the latter by Dubois) at the base of a limestone cliff in a now destroyed site for which there is no direct evidence for date or context. These crania have been considered Australoid by most authorities (except Pinkley 1935–6), and have large brains and faces; in fact, the face of Wajak 1 is larger in seven of 15 measurable dimensions than the face of a female *Homo erectus* from Zhoukoudian (Coon 1962:445). However, both Coon (1962) and Jacob (1967a) have noted the possible Mongoloid affinities of the large flat faces of the Wajak skulls, although it is not really known how significant these are without a good date. If the skulls are Holocene then they may merely reflect some degree of quite recent Mongoloid gene flow. If they are Pleistocene (and they are well fossilised), then we may have to accept that some skeletal features of a kind normally regarded as Mongoloid actually developed within the Indo-Malaysian Archipelago. This latter view was partly espoused by Jacob (1967a:51–2) who considered the Wajak population as possibly ancestral both to Indonesian Mongoloids and to present Australoids. I will consider the evidence for this view in the next section, since it has been promoted again very recently.

The other Indonesian skeletal remains present a much clearer story, and the material falls into three groups:

a. Skeletal remains from several sites on Flores, all presumed to be of Holocene date, and clearly belonging to the ancestors of the present mainly Melanesian population of the island. One adult female of very small stature from a cave called Liang Toge has been dated to c. 1600 bc (2100 BC) (Jacob 1967a:79).
b. Cranial remains of strong Australoid affinity from regions of northern and western Indonesia which are today inhabited by Southern Mongoloids. The best examples in this group include the large-toothed cranial remains from the cave of Gua Lawa in central Java (Jacob 1967a; Mijsberg 1932), and the skull from the basal levels of Leang Buidane in the Talaud Islands (Bulbeck 1981). Neither of these samples is dated, but both clearly predate the Early Metal phase with its associated Southern Mongoloid populations.
c. Skeletal material, mostly postdating 1000 BC (that is later Neolithic onwards) which is clearly of Southern Mongoloid type, particularly on such criteria as shovelling of the incisor teeth. Material of this type is very widespread; good samples come from Leang Cadang in southern Sulawesi (Jacob 1967a), Gilimanuk in Bali (c. 2000 years old, Jacob 1967b) and Leang Buidane in Talaud (first millennium AD, Bulbeck 1981). In all these cases the populations are clearly ancestral to the present inhabitants of these regions.

Taking this skeletal material at face value, as described in the literature, then the most likely hypothesis is that Southern Mongoloid populations have entered the archipelago from the north, probably via the Philippines, and have been present since perhaps 1000 BC in most areas where they are now found; they have clearly never penetrated in any major way into central Malaya or south-eastern Indonesia. Again accepting old reports at face value, the presumed clinal effects of this expansion in such post-1000 BC populations as those from Melolo in Sumba (Snell 1948) and Puger in eastern Java (Snell 1938) can also be seen.

Let me expand this hypothesis further by describing how it fares at the hands of authoritative supporters, and how it may relate to historical trends and events. Coon's basic view (1962, 1966) was that Indonesia and adjacent parts of the South-East Asian mainland formed the Australoid homeland, and he wrote of a "great rush" of Mongoloid expansion southwards, commencing by at least the Neolithic, and culminating in historical times within the past 2000 years. Coon (1962) also reviewed the early Holocene skeletal material from Mainland South-East Asian Hoabinhian sites, and there are indications here of a confusing array of Mongoloid and Australoid features stretching from northern Vietnam (e.g. Duy and Quyen 1966 for Quynh Van, c. 4000 BC) down to Malaya (e.g. Jacob 1967a for Guar Kepah). My own tendency is to regard this pre-Neolithic material as basically clinal between present Australoid and Mongoloid norms, and the Malayan Negritos in the south represent an Australoid population still in existence. There are also reports of extant Negritos from Cambodia (Olivier 1956:142–3), but data are scarce and no recent investigations have been carried out. For the mainland north of Malaya it is not really known when the ancestors of the present Mongoloid populations first began to establish themselves, and in the northern part of the region and southern China they may always have been predominantly Mongoloid. For more southerly regions it is probable that Southern Mongoloid expansion was taking place during the Neolithic and Early Metal phases, and linguistic and historical sources suggest that considerable expansion of such Mongoloid groups as the Thais, Vietnamese and Malays has affected vast areas of the mainland since 3000 years ago, and this process has continued with Chinese expansion to the present day (e.g. Fitzgerald 1972).

A more recent variation of Coon's basic viewpoint has been presented by Howells (1973c, 1976, 1977), and some details of this are given in Fig. 3.12. Howells (1973c) defines a Late Pleistocene province of "Old Melanesia", comprising continental Sundaland, Wallacea, and continental Sahulland. Populations ancestral to modern Australians and Melanesians have inhabited the Indo-Malaysian part of this region since at least 50 000 years ago (as represented by the remains from Niah, Wajak and Tabon), and the present Australians and Melanesians now represent the differentiated descendants of Old Melanesian ancestors. For the present day Howells (1973c:192) defines

Fig. 3.12. "Old Melanesia" and "Hoabinhia", according to W. W. Howells (1973c). Courtesy: W. W. Howells.

a province of "New Melanesia", now flanked by the Southern Mongoloid populations who have settled Indonesia, Polynesia and Micronesia, and regards all these expanding Mongoloids as Austronesian speakers of post-3000 BC southern Chinese origin.

Another recent viewpoint in support of the postulated Southern Mongoloid expansion is that of Brace (1976, 1980a) and Brace and Hinton (1981). In the first two articles, Brace developed the hypothesis that a reduction of overall tooth size occurred with the development of agriculture, and suggested that the Austronesian-speaking Southern Mongoloids (fairly small-toothed) had expanded into Indonesia, via the Philippines, where they replaced a larger-toothed population still represented by the Australians and

Melanesians. Basic gradients in tooth size through the region, with the smallest in southern China and the largest in Australia and New Guinea, support this view. In the later article the hypothesis was expanded to take in the Pacific Islands, and Brace and Hinton stress the importance of soft food preparation in containers such as pottery as a factor which could relax selection pressures favouring large teeth; pottery is absent in the New Guinea Highlands, although horticulture is of high antiquity there, and tooth sizes have remained large. Again, we are presented with a hypothesis that small-toothed Southern Mongoloids of southern Chinese origin (Austronesian-speakers) have replaced a more macrodont population in Indonesia and the Philippines.

There is, however, a very recent view which relates to the model of Mongoloid expansion with which I am inclined to disagree. This view is the reconstruction by Krantz (1980:148) of South-East Asian racial distributions at 10 000 years ago. He postulates a Negrito population right through South-East Asia to New Guinea, and an Ainu population to the north in what is now China, with Mongoloids restricted to central and northern Asia. This reconstruction is based purely on assumptions about natural trends imposed by climatic selection on unmoving populations, and it seems to me that all the fossil evidence suggests that it is incorrect. Small-statured Negrito-type skeletons do occur in prehistoric South-East Asia, but they are not universal (Mijsberg 1940). Furthermore, Krantz' basic view (which I tend to share) is that major racial expansions into pre-settled areas have generally occurred with large agricultural populations. It is therefore surprising that he has Ainu, not Mongoloids, as the inhabitants of the very regions of China where early East Asian cereal agriculture first began; to follow Krantz' own logic, virtually all East Asians should now be Ainu, they clearly are not.

The views of Coon, Howells and Brace outlined above are all generally in accord with my own, and I have taken ideas from all three before (Bellwood 1978a). However, not all authorities present this same viewpoint of recent Mongoloid expansion and replacement, and it is now time to turn to another view which may be correct in part and which may necessitate modification of basic replacement theories. This view is that many aspects of the present Southern Mongoloid phenotype have actually evolved within South-East Asia from the Late Pleistocene onwards. No one would dispute that intense Mongoloid gene flow into the area has taken place in historic or even prehistoric times, but it may be that all the populations of eastern Asia were undergoing similar trends in terms of modernisation of skull and facial form throughout the Late Pleistocene and into the Holocene. Hence the postulated Southern Mongoloid migrants may have been settling amongst populations who were also evolving in similar ways, and who may have contributed more to the present dental and cranial phenotypes of the region than is usually allowed.

C. The Indo-Malaysian Continuity Model

This model, presented in its most recent form by Bulbeck (1981, 1982), switches the emphasis strongly away from migration. The model has a respectable pedigree; it was foreshadowed by Weidenreich in 1945 when he pointed out that brachycephalisation (a trend towards an increasing broadness of the skull) could have evolved locally in different populations; an important observation at a time when long skulls and broad skulls were thought to identify different migrating races. Hooijer (1950b, 1952) also pointed out that large teeth *alone* could not, as others had assumed, be used in the prehistoric South-East Asian context to identify "Melanesoid" populations. This was not an attempt to discount migrations (see Koenigswald 1952 for a spirited rejoinder based on a misunderstanding about this), and Hooijer was merely disputing theories based on teeth in isolation; he was able to show that reduction in tooth size *could* be a local development, and need not necessarily imply a migration from outside by a separate small-toothed population.

In recent years this view of local evolution has become more positive. Turner and Swindler (1978; see also Turner 1983) have suggested that Late Pleistocene Sundaland was occupied by a population with widely-shared dental characteristics which they term "Sundadont". The present Southern Mongoloids are thought to have retained a Sundadont dentition from this ancestral Proto-Mongoloid population, and hence to have developed *in situ* within Sundaland and adjacent parts of Mainland South-East Asia. Polynesian and Micronesian dentitions are also within the Sundadont range, thus attesting to their Island South-East Asian and Proto-Mongoloid origins. The "Sinodont" teeth of north-eastern Asia and the Americas are also thought to have evolved from an original and more widespread Sundadont-like ancestral form. Melanesian teeth, which are placed in a separate class by Turner and Swindler because of their simplified crown morphologies and low percentages of incisor shovelling, are derived from the same Pleistocene populations which gave rise to the Sundadonts, but have evolved their own local form within Melanesia. Thus, this view suggests that Southern Mongoloids are indigenous to South-East Asia, and share a Late Pleistocene common ancestry there with the Melanesians.

But can we really argue in such detail from teeth alone? Perhaps we are back with the objections made by Hooijer (1950b, 1952), but from the other side of the fence. To counter this possibility, Bulbeck (1981, 1982) has recently considered the whole question of local evolution within South-East Asia in great detail. He sees the main problem as how to explain the obvious modernisation which has taken place within South-East Asian populations; are these changes due to *clade* (lineage) changes (that is to a Southern

Mongoloid migration replacing an Australoid population) or are they due to *grade* changes (that is modernisation within a single *in situ* population)? To approach this problem Bulbeck has examined a large amount of cranial material from the Late Pleistocene through to recent Southern Mongoloid, and has documented what appear to be continuous and unbroken trends throughout: occurrence of the Sundadont dentition; size reductions in teeth, faces and palates; and a reduction of facial prognathism. On the other hand, there has been a recent increase in the occurrence of upper incisor shovelling, and this is of course a feature most developed in Mainland Asian Mongoloid populations.

In his conclusions, Bulbeck stresses that there is nothing in the evolutionary record of recent South-East Asians which demands a migration of Southern Mongoloids from the north, and in the absence of a rigidly-defined chronology for the remains it is clear that the documented changes could be due to changes in clade, in grade, or in both. In terms of teeth, his conclusions parallel those of Turner and Swindler (1978), and suggest that local evolution is at least as good a hypothesis as migration. But it must not be forgotten that these conclusions are drawn only from cranial and dental characteristics; in these areas alone it may be possible to regard Southern Mongoloids as the results of *in situ* modernisation. However, I think there is evidence from other sources, not always considered by physical anthropologists concerned with skeletal remains, which must be considered. I have already mentioned such phenotypic traits as skin colour, but in addition, linguistic evidence indicates that Austronesian-speakers with agriculture have expanded throughout the Indo-Malaysian Archipelago and the Pacific Islands within the past 5000 years; the modern Austronesians must to some degree be descendants of original founder populations who expanded from southern China, even if local genetic input has been considerable.

In this latter regard I think that Bulbeck has made a very important point, and we must not expect to find a time in prehistory when Mongoloids replaced a population identical to present Australians or Melanesians. The ancient Indo-Malaysian Australoids who remained in the archipelago as "cousins" to the descendants of those groups who settled Australia and New Guinea clearly evolved independently on the western side of the Wallacean sea barriers, and many of the changes which they underwent were probably shared to an extent with more northerly Asian Mongoloid populations. In fact, there may have been continuously intergrading populations from southern China right into continental Sundaland — a clinal Mongoloid-Australoid zone evolving as one rather than two separate populations, but still spanning a sufficiently broad latitudinal zone for natural selection to have very different results at either end.

My own suspicions are therefore as follows:

a. Australia and New Guinea were *initially* (see Section D) settled from the Indo-Malaysian Archipelago, presumably the Wallacean end of it, by at least 40 000 years ago.
b. Australians and New Guineans have since undergone independent differentiation, but still retain clear traces of their common origin.
c. The Indo-Malaysian populations "left behind" after Australia and New Guinea were initially settled continued to diversify, and underwent certain trends in facial and cranial gracilisation in common with adjacent Mainland South-East Asian populations. Some of these changes may have taken place as a result of Pleistocene gene flow from more northerly (ancestral Mongoloid?) populations (not a possibility to be dismissed lightly, see Section D), but I suspect that changes in local selective pressures, perhaps via undocumented cultural changes, may also have been important. These groups remained phenotypically as Australoids, in some cases to the present (the Negritos and eastern Indonesians).
d. From 3000 BC onwards the Indo-Malaysian region was settled from the north by linguistically-related and expanding populations of Southern Mongoloids — the Austronesian-speaking populations. The chronology of this expansion can best be reconstructed from archaeology and linguistics, and it was clearly underway by about 4000 BC in Taiwan, by 2500 BC in the Philippines and eastern Indonesia generally (with Micronesians and Polynesians hiving off by 1500 BC), and by perhaps 1000 BC or later in western Indonesia. This presumed (but unproven) late date for western Indonesia could be of great importance, and it might suggest that densely populated islands such as Java were still occupied by bands of small and gracile Australoid hunters and collectors into the first millennium BC — at present there is no very powerful evidence for or against this view. It should, of course, be remembered that all the evidence suggests that many of the present Southern Mongoloid populations of Indonesia and Malaysia have a high degree of Australoid genetic heritage.

D. The Australian Window

From this region there are further implications which involve the Indo-Malaysian Australoids. The most simple view of Australian origins postulates that only one founder population ever reached the continent, and that the patterns of variation in the ethnographic population are due to local selection, plus perhaps some minor later arrivals. This view tells little about past variation in Island South-East Asia, but it does find favour with a number of recent authorities (e.g. Macintosh and Larnach 1976; Howells 1976; Wolpoff 1980).

A very different view has been espoused for many years by Birdsell (1949, 1967, 1972, 1977), and involves three separate migrations which could be each of great potential significance for the Indonesian region, were they to receive support. First came Negritos from an ultimate African source, and this group has had a lasting impact in Melanesia; second the Murrayians, from a possible Ainu source; and finally the Carpentarians of northern Australia, from a possible southern Indian source. In his latest article, Birdsell (1977) has dropped references to the Carpentarians, and clearly favours as more likely an Indonesian Wajak-like source for the Murrayians; he has retained his views on the Negritos. The problem here, as Birdsell is aware, is that there is little skeletal evidence from either Indonesia or Australia to support widespread and separate Pleistocene populations of Murrayian Australoids and Negritos, and these ideas have never found favour with other Australian specialists. But Birdsell's belief that Australian variation does not derive from one single founder population alone has recently come back into favour, even if opinions are couched in very different terms.

For instance, a recent view suggested by Brace (1980b) is that Australia was settled first by a large-toothed population, of whom ethnographic descendants survived in the southern part of the continent and in Tasmania. But the population of the central and northern regions (Birdsell's original Carpentarians?) have smaller teeth, and these groups are thought to descend from migrants who entered Australia later. Brace's view has a certain appeal, for it suggests that Australia was reached by successive Australoid groups from Indonesia, who, as noted above, were developing smaller teeth and faces through time. However, as Birdsell (1977:163) has asked, and as I have asked above, how can one or more small groups of migrant hunters impose their phenotypes on an already settled continent?

The answer to this question, which may apply to an isolated land mass such as Australia, could be that the newcomers were better equipped in terms of stone tool technology and perhaps evolutionary grade than their predecessors. The Australian Pleistocene fossil evidence now takes on a very specific relevance, because for some years it has been observed that two rather different populations are represented. The first is a fairly gracile group, best known from Lake Mungo in western New South Wales, where stone tools and associated dates of over 30 000 years ago have been obtained. The second group has a much heavier facial and cranial skeleton, with large teeth and faces which overlap in size with those of later *Homo erectus*, and it lacks any very coherent association with a stone tool industry (Wright 1975). This second group is known to date to between 9000 and 12 000 years ago at Kow Swamp in Victoria, although the morphology suggests that its ancestors arrived in Australia long before that.

According to Thorne (1980a, b), these two groups represent well-defined skeletal populations of quite different origins; we are now getting into the realms of positive prehistoric population identification, rather than assumptions made on a single criterion such as tooth size. Thorne's positiveness here is recent, and in his earlier papers (e.g. 1977) he was much more hesitant about the one- or two-population question. Howells had in fact favoured such a two-population theory in 1973, but had later dropped it for a single-founder model. However, Thorne's most recent statements (1980a, b) have very clear-cut implications for Australoid differentiation within the Indo-Malaysian Archipelago.

Thorne's theory is that the Kow Swamp population, plus other "rugged" skulls from various parts of Australia, represent an initial settlement by an Indonesian population derived from a line which leads back directly to the *Homo erectus* population of Ngandong in Java. As noted in Chapter 2, Section IIID, the evidence for stone tool use by this lineage is distinctly sparse. The other more gracile group, which is represented by the Niah, Wajak and Tabon remains in South-East Asia, is thought to represent a second and probably later migration of more competent toolmakers from at least Indonesia, with the possibility of an ultimate Chinese source. As Thorne has stated (1980a:100):

> Remains from sites in China, particularly at Liu-Kiang (Liujiang) and Choukoutien (Zhoukoudian), suggest the possibility that the ultimate source of the gracile people of Australia and Indonesia is to be found there.

The implications of Thorne's views for the Indo-Malaysian archipelago as well as for Australia are considerable, for if he is correct about a "Chinese connection" 30 000 years ago, then it may be unwarranted to regard the Southern Mongoloids of the Indonesian region as entirely the descendants of a population expansion confined only to the Neolithic and later periods (that is confined to the period of Austronesian expansion). Seen in this light, Thorne's view may come partly into line with the reconstructions favoured by Turner and Bulbeck.

E. Some Further Observations

I will finally turn back to my views expressed earlier concerning cultural capacity to support a major population expansion. Small groups of hunters and gatherers might be expected to expand very slowly under favourable circumstances, but major and rapid migrations into territories previously settled by groups with equivalent grades of technological and economic organisation would be unlikely. The Australian case just described may be a very significant and unusual exception, but in overall support of the generalisation it should be noted that studies in the 1950s on resettled

Malayan *orang asli* groups of forest collectors and recently acculturated shifting cultivators showed fairly clear evidence for decreasing nutritional health and increasing disease (Polunin 1953). Groups such as these which have been adapting to highly specific local environments for millennia do not take kindly to upheaval.

On the other hand, it is clear that groups longer adapted to a horticultural lifestyle focussed on the partial creation of artificial environments can adapt to movement more easily; the ancestral Polynesians and Micronesians were clearly well adjusted to this strategy. But were the earlier Austronesian-speakers in Island South-East Asia? I suspect the answer here to be partly "yes", but prefer a model of fairly slow expansion along the coasts of the major islands of the region to one stressing a long-distance kind of migration. The Polynesians clearly adapted themselves well to the latter strategy, but as representatives of the supertramp distributional strategy of Diamond (1977) I am inclined to regard them as chronologically recent and specialised. I am not inclined to accept the *orang laut* sea nomads of Island South-East Asia as representatives of an original Austronesian dispersal strategy, but more of these later.

In conclusion, I regard the earlier millennia of Southern Mongoloid and Austronesian-speaking expansion, prior to the long Polynesian and Micronesian migrations, as being based on fairly slow population growth and expansion through horticulture. Concerning any pre-Austronesian expansions of mainland Asian populations into the Indo-Malaysian Archipelago, such as that which might have been involved in an early but secondary colonisation of Australia, one can only surmise. Research still has a long way to go in this region, and many of the answers will always be elusive. But while it may be unwise to equate entirely the Southern Mongoloid phenotype now present in the archipelago with the linguistic evidence for the past expansion of the Austronesian speakers, I am prepared to state my belief that the correlation must be at a very high level.

4

Recent Indo-Malaysian Prehistory: According to the Languages

Once they had split up each group forgot the past customs they had enjoyed together and developed different languages because some had short tongues and others long tongues. Each group found a new name for itself. (From a story related by a Penan headman, Sarawak; Arnold 1958).

The modern traveller who has the good fortune to wander at will through the Indo-Malaysian region will quickly observe that there are many varieties of culture and economy, and this remains true even if the tremendous impact of modern urbanisation and industrialisation is ignored. Furthermore, there are great variations in language, although these are often not noticed by outsiders owing to the increasing strengths of the national languages Malay and Bahasa Indonesia (these are actually the same language, that is Malay, with small dialect differences). It stands to reason that in order to construct a prehistory of the present Indo-Malaysians one cannot work purely from the archaeological data, which often limit themselves rather baldly to stone tools and potsherds.

There are in fact many very important observations to be made from comparative and historically-oriented studies in the fields of linguistics and anthropology. Linguists in particular have developed very precise techniques for drawing inferences about the history of a language family, and I consider that any general statements concerning the prehistory of the region within the past 5000 years must take the linguistic evidence seriously into account. This is especially true for any discussion of recent human population expansion.

I. Language Families in South-East Asia and the Western Pacific

Virtually all the peoples of Indo-Malaysia speak languages termed Austronesian (Wurm and Hattori 1983). There are two small exceptions: the *orang asli* of interior Malaya who speak languages (called Aslian) in the Austro-Asiatic family; and some peoples of eastern Indonesia who speak Papuan languages, a group of diverse families centred on New Guinea. When looking at Austronesian linguistic prehistory, and the relationships of Austronesian to outside families, research cannot be restricted to Indonesia and Malaysia alone. I will paint a broad picture to begin with (Fig. 4.1), and then focus in detail on more localised questions.

Estimates of the number of Austronesian languages generally vary from 500 upwards, and Blust (personal communication) has informed me that the true total is certainly in excess of 700[1]. Over half of these languages are spoken in Oceania, from New Guinea eastwards. Present Austronesian speakers are roughly distributed as follows: Indonesia 160 million, Malaysia 14 million, Philippines 50 million, Taiwan 250 000, interior Vietnam 630 000, Madagascar 10 million, and Oceania about 1 million — most of the dispersed languages in this vast latter region clearly have very small speech communities.

The Austronesian languages therefore have a geographical distribution which is relatively unbroken, except for the outliers in Madagascar and southern Vietnam, the latter having been isolated by recent Vietnamese expansion. There are three language families which abut directly on to the Austronesian sphere of distribution. The first is the Papuan complex of families of New Guinea, western island Melanesia and a few islands of eastern Indonesia, which has about 740 languages (Wurm 1982). The second is the Austro-Asiatic family of Mainland South-East Asia, a scattered group of about 150 languages (Diffloth 1974, 1979) which includes Aslian of Malaya, Mon-Khmer, Vietnamese, and outliers in the Nicobar Islands, Assam and north-eastern peninsular India. The third comprises the Thai (or Tai) family (Thai, Lao and related languages) of the central and northern mainland, extending up into southern China (Lebar *et al.* 1964).

When considering geographical distribution alone the extent of the Austronesian languages is impressive — over half way around the world in

[1]Terrell (1981:225) quotes a total of 940. Such great variation in what might appear to be no more than a job of simple counting seems to be due to conflicts over differentiating dialects from separate languages (see Wurm and Laycock 1961 who document this problem for New Guinea). Dyen (1965a) classified speech systems as dialects of one language if they share 70% or over of basic vocabulary, and gave a figure of under 500 separate languages for Austronesian. Most other linguists use a figure of 80% for the division.

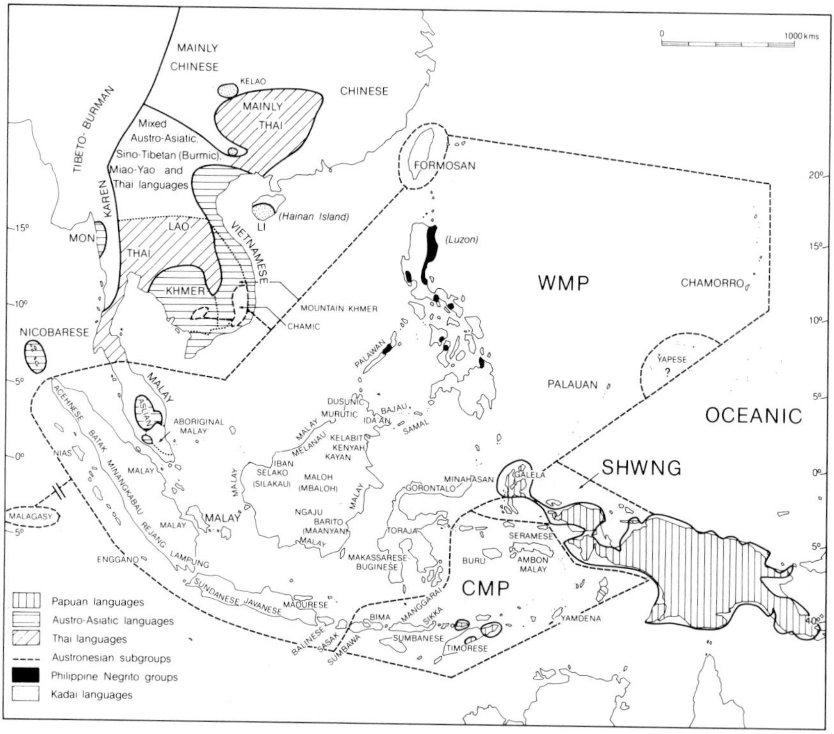

Fig. 4.1. Languages, major subgroups and language families in South-East Asia.

tropical latitudes. It is my view that the expansion of this family has involved an actual expansion of Austronesian-speaking founder communities through this vast area. This may seem self-evident (especially for Oceania), although the possibilities of adoption of Austronesian languages by members of unrelated linguistic groups cannot be entirely disregarded, especially for western Melanesia. If this expansion has occurred, then it would appear to have reduced the area of prior distribution of the Papuan and Austro-Asiatic languages (with the exception of Vietnamese). The questions for Austronesian expansion are when, how, and why?

II. Some Linguistic Concepts

According to Swadesh (1964:575), a linguist who has made great contributions to prehistory:

> There are three main ways in which linguistics can illuminate prehistory: (a) by establishing facts concerning the common origin and subsequent divergence of languages, implying the earlier unity and subsequent separations of peoples; (b) by discovering diffused features (of phonetics, structure and vocabulary) among languages which bear evidence of prehistoric culture contact; and (c) by reconstructing the vocabulary of old stages of languages so as to bring out suggestions of the physical environment and content of prehistoric cultures.

A number of terms which linguists use in their deliberations now require a brief introduction. *Dialects* of a language share sufficient basic vocabulary in common, usually over 80%, so that they remain mutually intelligible. If they diverge so as to become no longer mutually intelligible they become separate languages. This separation is of course gradual since intelligibility does not come or go with one percentage point, and the development of two separate daughter languages from one parent can take a millennium or more, especially if contacts continue.

Languages considered to be related are grouped into *families*, such as Austronesian or Indo-European. All languages are probably related in the final resort, since the roots of language must go back with increasing convergence through all levels of human evolution. But for comparative purposes relationship has to be observable in phonology, structure and vocabulary, and when languages have been evolving apart for something over 10 000 years it seems that such observations can no longer be made with confidence.

Languages in a family can be ordered into *subgroups* with ordered implications for time depth; closely related languages (closely related, that is, in terms of shared innovations) must clearly have more recent common ancestries than those more distantly related. Hence subgroups are hierarchical in terms of geographical space and time depth. A subgroup can be defined as "any group of languages which have passed through a period of common development exclusive of the other languages of the same family, and during which period some linguistic change has occurred" (Grace 1959). Members of a subgroup also share a common *proto-language*, an entity reconstructed by identifying *cognates* found in daughter languages; the more widespread the cognate, the further back the proto-language for which it can be reconstructed. A cognate is a word deemed through correspondences in sound and meaning to have been inherited by two or more languages from a common ancestor, rather than *borrowed* from an outside language.

Like subgroups, proto-languages are also hierarchical in space and time, each one corresponding to the base of a branch in the family tree. Minor proto-languages on the "outer branches" of Austronesian (for example Proto-Polynesian, Green 1981) can be shown to have been single languages or dialect chains in many cases, but when moving towards the main trunk and back in time the picture becomes more diffuse and complex. An entity such as Proto-Austronesian (Table 4.1), which existed perhaps 5000 years ago, may or may not have been a single language — it is possible that we will never know for certain.

I must also emphasise that the entity reconstructed as Proto-Austronesian is in no real sense a "beginning" for Austronesian; what the concept refers to is that point at which the language or chain of languages ancestral to all modern Austronesian languages underwent an initial split to form two diverging subgroups, whose descendant languages have survived apart to the present. Proto-Austronesian is preceded by a phase which I will call Initial Austronesian, which in turn goes back to when the ancestral language for the whole Austronesian family split off from its contemporary sister languages. The latter have either developed along different lines to become other modern language families (Thai may have this kind of relationship with Austronesian, see below), or some might have become extinct; if they were never written we may never know about this second possibility, but language termination is a very common event in linguistic history.

The ancestry of Austronesian thus goes well back beyond the proto-stage, and the family may be visualised as a very large and multi-branched limb on the total linguistic tree of mankind. Where the limb departs from another bigger limb (which will in turn join back through others to the ultimate trunk), it is convenient to place the label "Initial Austronesian". We can only get back beyond the start of this limb by comparing Austronesian languages with those in other families, and many linguists have claimed significant results from such comparisons.

Lexical cognates are also utilised in the subdiscipline of *lexicostatistics*, which subgroups languages hierarchically in terms of percentages of cognates between pairs. Innovated shared cognates of restricted geographical occurrence help to define subgroups, while those which occur within and beyond a particular subgroup are defined as shared inheritances (not innovations), and as such refer to a deeper level of subgrouping. I will return below to the assumptions of lexicostatistics and its chronological offshoot (glottochronology) when I come to consider the crucial question of the rate of linguistic change. I should, however, make it clear that languages are not subgrouped purely by comparing words. Our basic knowledge of Austronesian linguistic prehistory comes from much deeper comparisons in the complex fields of phonology and grammar (for example word order in sentences, occurrences of prefixes and suffixes, pronoun forms), and in what may be called word structure — many Oceanic languages, for instance, have lost final consonants from older Austronesian forms. Lexicostatistics alone can in fact lead to a quite erroneous view of Austronesian linguistic prehistory. This is because

Table 4.1. Some Proto-Austronesian terms and their related forms in several modern languages
After Pawley 1974. Courtesy: Encyclopaedia Britannica.

	Proto-Austronesian	Tagalog	Malay	Fijian	Samoan
two	* Duwa	dalawa	dua	rua	lua
four	* e(m)pat	apat	empat	vā	fā
five	* lima	lima	lima	lima	lima
six	* enem	anim	enam	ono	ono
bird	* manuk	manok	manu	manu-manu	manu
eye	* mata	mata	mata	mata	mata
road	* Zalan	daan	jalan	sala	ala
pandanus	* panDan	pandan	pandan	vadra	fala
coconut	* niuR	niyog	nior	niu	niu

* Form that is not actually found in any document or living dialect; it is a reconstructed, hypothetical form.

great lexical diversity alone does not automatically correspond with great time-depth, although there is certainly much truth in the view that great *overall* linguistic diversity does (Dyen 1975).

III. The Major Subgroups of Austronesian

Comparative linguists are now in general agreement about the basic shape of the Austronesian family tree, although names given to particular subgroups have changed over the last decade. In my last major review of Austronesian linguistic prehistory (Bellwood 1978a: Chapter 5), I used a basic classification which recognised three major subgroups, namely Atayalic in Taiwan, Western Austronesian, and Eastern Austronesian (Halmahera and Oceania). This classification was drawn from sources available at the time (e.g. Grace 1964; Haudricourt 1965; Dahl 1973; Blust 1974; Pawley 1974; Shutler and Marck 1975; Blust 1976), but the resulting family tree contained a number of question marks and problems, especially with respect to Taiwan and Western Austronesian. The validity of the Oceanic subgroup together with an adjacent subgroup in South Halmahera and West New Guinea (joined as Eastern Austronesian by Blust in 1974, and since re-named by him as Eastern Malayo-Polynesian) seemed quite firm, and this remains the case today. However, new work, particularly by Blust, requires some rethinking of the situation in the Western and Taiwan (Formosan) divisions.

In several recent papers, Blust (1977, 1978, 1980, 1982a) has developed a more coherent subgrouping for Austronesian based on shared innovations in pronoun forms together with other considerations of grammar and phonology (cf. Dyen 1965b and Harvey 1982 for support regarding the

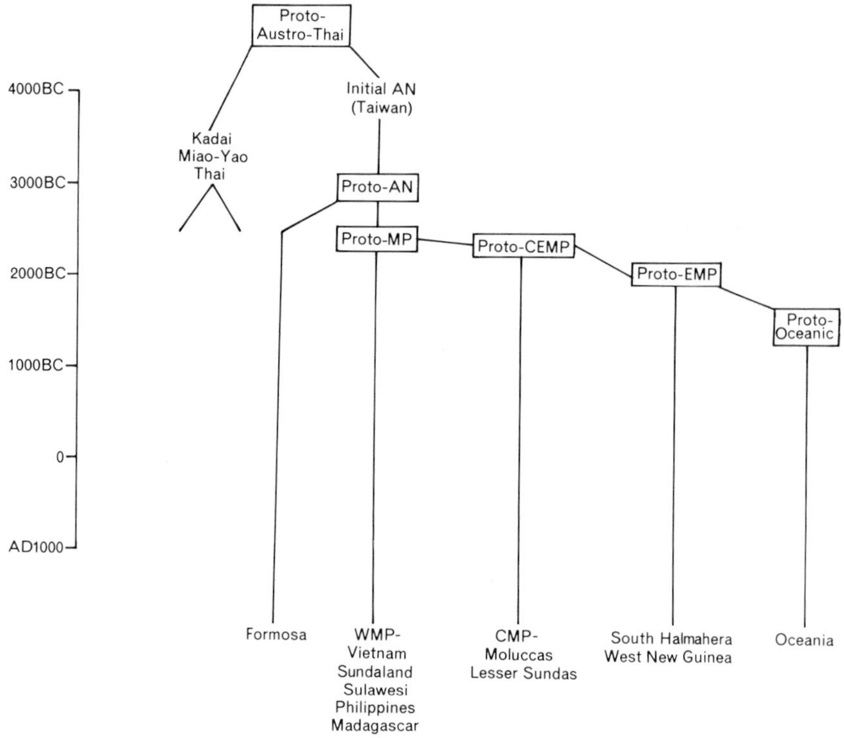

Fig. 4.2. A family "tree" (here shown inverted) for the Austronesian languages. AN = Austronesian, MP = Malayo-Polynesian, WMP = Western Malayo-Polynesian, CEMP = Central-Eastern Malayo-Polynesian.

position of Formosan). I find that this schema fits well with considerations about Austronesian prehistory from other disciplines, Fig. 4.2.

The major subgroups shown are as follows[2]:

1.1. Formosan (three presumably coordinate branches)[3].

1.2. Malayo-Polynesian (all Extra-Formosan languages according to Blust (1982a), although Reid (1982) excludes some Northern Philippine languages from Malayo-Polynesian and places them in a separate subgroup intermediate between 1.1 and 1.2).

2.1. Western Malayo-Polynesian (Philippines, Vietnam, Madagascar, Malaya, Sumatra, Java, Borneo, Sulawesi, Bali, Lombok, western Sumbawa) and two languages (Palauan and Chamorro) of western Micronesia.

2.2. Central-Eastern Malayo-Polynesian (3.1 plus 3.2).
3.1. Central Malayo-Polynesian (Lesser Sundas from eastern Sumbawa eastwards, Moluccas except Halmahera).
3.2. Eastern Malayo-Polynesian (South Halmahera and all the Pacific Island Austronesian languages; Melanesia, Micronesia and Polynesia).
4.1. South Halmahera — West New Guinea.
4.2. Oceanic (all Eastern Malayo-Polynesian languages except 4.1.).

By translating this family tree into an account of the expansion of the Austronesian speakers, the following founder moves can be listed in chronological order:

1. Initial Austronesian and Proto-Austronesian are located in Taiwan. The founders of Malayo-Polynesian then move into the Philippines via Luzon.
2. Founders move south through the Philippines, then perhaps into Borneo and Sulawesi, and later towards Java, Sumatra, Malaya and Vietnam — Western Malayo-Polynesian.
3. Other founders move south into the Moluccas — Central-Eastern Malayo-Polynesian.
4. Further founder movements give rise to Central Malayo-Polynesian and Eastern Malayo-Polynesian (via Halmahera and New Guinea).

The subgrouping of Blust, in so far as it concerns the Indo-Malaysian region, is given some support by a recent analysis of verb forms by Sirk (1978). He divides the Formosan and Western Malayo-Polynesian languages (the latter not claimed to be a unified subgroup) into two major groups: Philippine and South Sunda. The first includes Formosa, the Philippines,

---

[2] I have not discussed older subgrouping arrangements, such as that by Capell (1962) which divides the Western Austronesian (or "Indonesian") languages into Western, Northern and Eastern groups (see also Lopez 1967), since all have been modified since their appearances, and so they are of historical interest only.

[3] In a recent paper Blust (1982a:233) divides Formosan into the Atayalic, Tsouic and Paiwanic branches proposed by Ferrell (1969) and Dyen (1971b). Both the latter authors raised the possibility that there might have been more than one Austronesian immigration into Taiwan, and in 1978 I attempted to equate this possibility with the archaeological evidence from the island (Bellwood 1978a:206–7). Today, there seems to be tacit agreement that all the Formosan languages stand apart from the rest of Austronesian (Foley 1980; Harvey 1982; and also Blust 1982a), and the idea of two or more immigrations is no longer necessary. Furthermore, Ferrell (1980) has since refuted the above subgrouping on phonological grounds, so I have chosen to indicate Formosan as one primary subgroup since disputes about internal Formosan classification are not here of especial concern.

western Micronesia, northern Sulawesi and northern Borneo. The second includes western Indonesia and the rest of Sulawesi. Certain regions, such as Aceh (north Sumatra), Vietnam, interior Borneo and south-eastern Indonesia are excluded by Sirk from these two groups. Superficially, his verbal classification resembles the general classification of Capell (1962), and it does obviously cross-cut Blust's subgroups. But it provides important support for the view that Austronesian languages have been developing longest in Taiwan and the Philippines, and the "shape" of Austronesian expansion derived from Sirk's analysis is similar to that derived from Blust; an initial north–south expansion from Taiwan, and then a split in the vicinity of Borneo and Sulawesi into westerly and easterly expanding branches (see also Foley 1980).

A. The Location of Proto-Austronesian

I have already made it clear that the island of Taiwan is central to the question of the location of Proto-Austronesian. This conclusion has been reached with increasing frequency in recent years, for instance by Dahl (1973), Shutler and Marck (1975), Foley (1980), Harvey (1982), and Reid (1985). Many earlier authors, using the results of traditional comparative linguistics, had concluded that the location of Proto-Austronesian would have to lie somewhere in or close to the western region of the Austronesian distribution (excluding Madagascar). For instance, Kern (1889/1917) favoured the Vietnamese coastal region, Haudricourt (1954) favoured the coastal region between Hainan and Taiwan, and Benedict (1975) has for the past 40 years been strongly in favour of linking Austronesian through Taiwan with the Thai and Kadai languages of southern China. Blust (1982a) has recently shown that words for placental mammal species (pangolin, bovids, monkeys) reconstructed for the Proto-Austronesian vocabulary make a location west of Huxley's Line, that is in Taiwan or Sundaland, a virtual certainty. Taking all these views into account and noting recent trends, there now seems little reason to doubt Taiwan as by far the most likely location.

The most important arguments against Taiwan in recent years have been those by Dyen, whose lexicostatistical classification of the Austronesian languages (Dyen 1962, 1965a) showed that lexical (but not structural) diversity was higher in western Melanesia than in any other Austronesian region (Fig. 4.3). Dyen's theories on diversity and migration patterns led him to suggest western Melanesia (particularly the Bismarck Archipelago) as the location of Proto-Austronesian; a claim supported by Murdock (1964), but seen by most authors (including myself) to be totally impossible for reasons not connected with linguistics alone (Bellwood 1978a:131–2). I will be returning to Dyen and the question of Melanesia later, but it should be noted that he, as a linguist of broad and respected knowledge, has long been

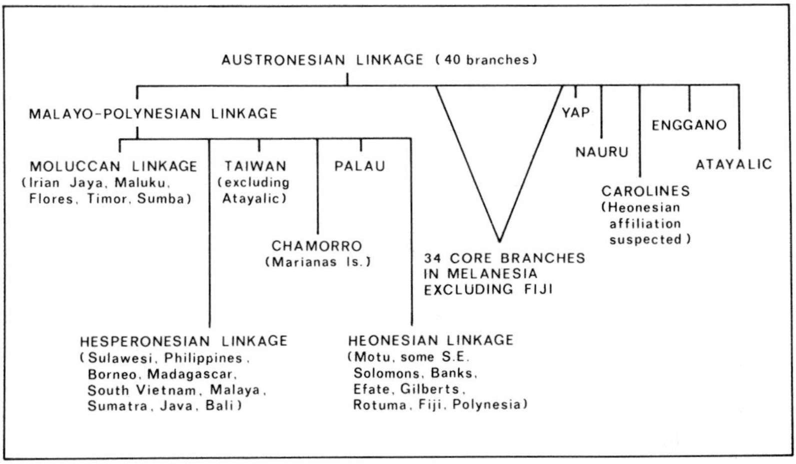

Fig. 4.3. Dyen's family tree for the Austronesian languages. From Bellwood 1978a.

ambivalent about the Formosan languages and has frequently admitted their qualifications to represent a primary subgroup of Austronesian (e.g. Dyen 1965b). However, he has also suggested (Dyen 1971a, b) that Taiwan would have been too cold to be the location for Proto-Austronesian in terms of the reconstructed vocabulary for tropical plants, but I will counter this suggestion below. Most recently, Dyen (1975:19) has suggested that Proto-Austronesian might have been located in the east Indonesia–west New Guinea region rather than further east towards the Bismarck Archipelago, and Pawley (1974) has also supported this view, but the main argument in its favour turns on lexical diversity, and this is not sufficient to convince all linguists today.

In coming down strongly on the side of Taiwan as the location of Proto-Austronesian I should make it clear that I do not regard this small island as the "homeland" of the Austronesians. It is simply the place where Initial Austronesian was established and where the first split from reconstructed Proto-Austronesian occurred. The true homeland of the ancestral Austronesians (before the Initial stage) was most probably on the mainland of southern China.

B. The Material Culture of the Proto-Austronesians

Words and meanings can only be reconstructed for Proto-Austronesian if cognates are found in at least two languages which are known to have descended entirely independently from Proto-Austronesian. The catch here, of course, is that the shape of the family tree must be known in order to reconstruct the proto-language, and as I have indicated above there are still disagreements about this, although I have chosen the version suggested by Blust (1982a:233) as the most satisfactory. Nevertheless, despite disagreements, it is generally accepted that words which have cognates in at least one language in the Formosan, Western Malayo-Polynesian and Eastern Malayo-Polynesian major subgroups are almost certain candidates for Proto-Austronesian (see Table 4.1), so long as borrowing can be ruled out (as it can for most widely-spread cases).

Two discussions of the Proto-Austronesian vocabulary which deal with general matters of cultural history are those by Pawley and Green (1975) and Blust (1976). Blust makes his reconstruction procedures very explicit, and attributes a word to Proto-Austronesian if it is found in at least two of the three major subgroups. However, a moment's thought will suggest that words reconstructed from Western and Eastern Malayo-Polynesian alone without Formosan cognates (there are many of these in Blust's list) cannot automatically be considered as Proto-Austronesian if Taiwan was the location of the latter. They can only truly be regarded as Proto-Malayo-Polynesian, and since I will try to establish in due course that Proto-Austronesian and Proto-Malayo-Polynesian may be separated by half a millennium in time and a subtropical versus a tropical latitude I believe this distinction to be very significant.

Indeed, it leads straight back to Dyen's (1971a, b) claim that Taiwan was too cold to have been the location of Proto-Austronesian in terms of the reconstructed vocabulary for plants. But words for true tropical plants such as sago and breadfruit can only be reconstructed for Proto-Malayo-Polynesian, exactly as expected. Words for colder climate species such as rice, millet, and sugarcane go back to Proto-Austronesian, and so these clearly were grown in Taiwan. Dyen has therefore been using a vocabulary for Proto-Austronesian which is in fact a conflation of a much greater entity.

The major point to be made is that the vocabulary listed in Table 4.2 does not refer specifically to Proto-Austronesian communities located just in Taiwan, but to communities from Proto-Austronesian to Proto-Malayo-Polynesian times located, almost certainly, in both subtropical Taiwan and the tropical Philippines. The fact that there is quite an expanse of latitude here across an important zone of change in world climate clearly makes interpretation at the level of the individual community rather hard. I will try to make it easier by giving Blust's reconstructions, Table 4.2, according to the code N (north) = Formosan; W (west) = Western Malayo-Polynesian; E (east) = Eastern Malayo-Polynesian. Items marked NWE or NW are potentially Proto-Austronesian (NE never occurs), and items marked WE are potentially Proto-Malayo-Polynesian and only possibly Proto-Austronesian. To simplify matters I have not added the Proto-Austronesian reconstructions themselves (they are given in Blust's paper), and I will leave reconstructions of aspects of society for discussion in the next chapter.

It will be noted from Table 4.2 that most reconstructions are defined as WE, and few have cognates in Formosan. This no doubt reflects the limited information available on some of the Formosan languages, but another reason may be that Austronesian cultures underwent marked change as they moved southwards into tropical regions, as I will demonstrate later. This becomes rather obvious when one examines the garden and field section. Still another possibility is that the Formosan languages became cut off very early from the rest of the Austronesian family, and since Proto-Austronesian is older than Proto-Malayo-Polynesian the Formosan languages have had longer in their relative isolation to innovate new words.

I will be making further observations on this list in due course, but it should be noted that the domesticated animals do not include any herbivores (cattle, sheep, goats). In addition, the word for wild pig, as expected, does not occur in New Guinea or Oceania. Another point, made by Pawley (1981) and by Blust (1976), is that sound correspondences suggest very strongly that material culture traditions (potting, agriculture, fishing and so forth) were continuous, that is they were never lost by any widespread groups of Austronesians and later regained. This is particularly important for any consideration of the prehistory of pottery, especially in western Melanesia.

C. The Antecedents of Proto-Austronesian

The cultural relationships of the Initial Austronesians who crossed from mainland China to Taiwan are universally agreed to be with the mainland, rather than with island areas to the south, which at this early date were settled by hunters and gatherers who presumably spoke non-Austronesian languages now extinct. Only the Philippine Negritos survive from this early phase in the islands directly south of Taiwan, and they have now universally adopted Austronesian languages very similar to those of their Filipino neighbours.

The most persuasive proponent of Austronesian links with mainland languages has been Benedict (1942), who first suggested that Austronesian, Thai, and a small group of isolated languages in Hainan and southern China (which he called Kadai) can be classified into one large family. The Thai and Kadai languages and all other Mainland South-East Asian languages apart from Malay are now monosyllabic and tonal, but it has long been recognised that this is a development from original polysyllabic and non-tonal languages, as most Austronesian languages are today (Holmer 1968).

Table 4.2. Terms for material culture reconstructed for early Austronesian societies*. After Blust 1976.

Class of material culture	Reconstruction code	Terms
House and contents	NWE	house/family dwelling
	WE	ridgepole, rafter, thatch, house-post, storage rack above hearth, notched log ladder, hearth, public building
Tools, utensils, weapons	NWE	bow, shoot an arrow, rope/cord
	WE	putty/caulking substance, comb, conch shell trumpet, cooking pot, nail, pillow/wooden headrest, digging stick, bamboo trail- or pitfall-spikes, torch, hew/plane
Arts and crafts	NWE	needle
	NW	loom (early Western Malayo-Polynesian only?)
	WE	plait/weave, draw, whet/sharpen, sew
Adornment	NW	tattoo
Refreshment	NW	drunk (adjective)
	WE	lime for betel quid, betel nut
Hunting and fishing	NW	hunt, go hunting
	WE	bait, bamboo basket trap for fish, kind of fishnet, fishhook, fish drive, dragnet, derris root fish poison, bird lime, snare

The canoe	NW	canoe/boat
	WE	canoe, canoe paddle, outrigger, rollers for beaching a canoe, sail, canoe bailer, to paddle, rudder/steer, raft, cross-seat in a boat, punting pole.
Domesticated animals	NWE	domesticated pig, dog
	WE	cock/rooster
Garden and field	NWE	rice (E cognates not beyond west New Guinea), pestle, garden/cultivated field, sugarcane
	NW	husked rice, mortar, cooked rice, winnow, rice straw, millet
	WE	to weed, *Alocasia* sp. (an aroid), breadfruit, ginger, citrus fruit, banana, yam, sago, taro, fallow land, to plant, melon
Food preparation	NWE	to smoke meat or fish
	NW	salt

N (north) = Formosan; W (west) = Western Malayo-Polynesian; E (east) = Eastern Malayo-Polynesian.

* Although Blust reconstructed a knowledge of iron and writing for Proto-Austronesian, and iron was also favoured by Kern (1889/1917), I have ignored these in the table since both go totally against all archaeological information. Rice also presents problems, since it was never grown in Oceania (except possibly in the Mariana Islands), and many authors have assumed a late introduction into Indo-Malaysian economies, after an assumed root-crop stage (e.g. Shutler and Marck 1975). For archaeological reasons it is now clear that rice was grown by Proto-Austronesians, as I will show later. It is not my purpose here to discuss the construction of Proto-Austronesian canoes and navigational techniques, but for possibilities see Doran 1981.

Since 1942, Benedict has added the scattered Miao and Yao languages of southern China and northern Mainland South-East Asia to the Thai-Kadai-Austronesian family, and has coined the term "Austro-Thai" to refer to the whole group (Benedict 1975). He has also reconstructed a large Proto-Austro-Thai vocabulary, which includes terms for field, wet field (for rice or taro), garden, plough, rice, sugarcane, the betel nut complex, cattle, water buffalo, bow and arrow, axe and canoe. Some of these terms are also found in Proto-Austronesian, while others, such as cattle and water buffalo, are not, although this may simply mean that these animals were not taken off the mainland during the early period of Austronesian expansion. If Benedict is right, then these reconstructions apply to Neolithic societies in southern China, whose archaeological remains will be described later. They seem to me to be quite reasonable, and Benedict's general views are supported in part by other linguists, such as Dahl (1973) and Reid (1985).

Benedict has also made two other proposals, one being that early Austro-Asiatic languages on the mainland borrowed a number of terms from an ancient and extinct Austro-Thai language (Benedict 1976), and the other being that a very broad range of terms, including agricultural and metallurgical vocabulary items, have been borrowed by early Chinese from an Austro-Thai source. This second hypothesis takes us rather beyond the confines of this book, and is especially controversial. Benedict placed some faith in archaeological dates for early bronze metallurgy in northern Thailand which are now believed to have been too early (that is post 2500 rather than 3500 BC), and he had difficulties in explaining how his Austro-Thai loans were transmitted from southern China into the homeland of Chinese civilisation in the Yellow River Valley (Benedict 1975:124–5). The whole question clearly requires further modern examination.

IV. Dating the Austronesian Family Tree

Before commencing a closer look at linguistic prehistory within Indonesia and Malaysia, I want to digress into the very important question of linguistic dating. In theory, if the lists of basic vocabulary items (that is words for non-cultural terms such as man, woman, sky, usually compared in lists of 100 or 200 meanings) used for lexicostatistical classifications can be shown to change at a known and constant rate through time, then proto-languages can be dated by a mathematical comparison of the shared cognate percentages between selected pairs of their daughter languages. Thus, in theory, all the major splits in the Austronesian family tree could be dated — a feat of no small importance for prehistory.

But do such constant rates really exist? Let us start with some simple assumptions about how dialects start to diverge. For instance, it may be assumed that people of one ethnic group who live contiguously and interact freely with each other will maintain a single language over time, regardless of the size of the group or of changes which occur within the language as a result of the passage of time or borrowing. If a few families move off to a new area and maintain only diminished contact with the main group they will slowly develop a different dialect, but as long as mutual intelligibility continues to be required the new group will tend not to drift across the boundary into a separate language (as defined by lack of mutual intelligibility), unless they become effectively cut off. In a sense, this process of becoming "cut off" may be regarded as optative and as reflecting social structure; in atomising tribal polities one may expect it to be more frequent than in large integrated civilisations. It may also be assumed that the rate of divergence between two communities speaking an initial common language will be much faster if they are totally separated than if they maintain contact. Hence the family tree concept, which suggests sharp breaks where branches diverge, does not represent true reality for all situations and is no more than a convenient model.

In tribal situations where communication is slowed by distance or difficult terrain but not broken, a sufficiency of time will often produce a dialect chain. In such situations dialects at distant ends of the chain can often be mutually unintelligible (and thus actually different languages), but the differences will only be very gradual as one moves along the chain, unless it is broken up by expansion of groups within it or by the moving in of unrelated language groups. The existence of such chains does not stop linguistic change, but it may well act to slow it down since linguistic innovations will tend to be widely shared, rather than localised and concentrated in one community. Many tribal regions of South-East Asia and Oceania exhibit chains of this kind (e.g. McFarland 1981).

We may conclude from this discussion that the rate of linguistic change following the expansion or splitting of a language community will depend very much on rates of subsequent communication, as well as on individual sociolinguistic situations. Such variables, undocumented for prehistoric communities, can cause problems with chronological calculations. Lexicostatistical studies *per se*, such as the major Austronesian study by Dyen (1965) already referred to, do not concern themselves directly with time, but only with classification and subgrouping. However, the time factor is central to an offshoot of lexicostatistics called glottochronology (Gudschinsky 1964). Analyses of languages (mostly Indo-European and west Asian) with long written histories have led to suggestions that basic vocabularies will change at constant rates: 19.5% per millennium for a standard 200-word list, and 14% for a 100-word list (see Blust 1981a for a description and critique). Hence simple glottochronological formulae can be derived for calculating how long ago the common ancestor of two or more related languages was in existence.

Two basic assumptions of glottochronology are that the basic vocabularies of all languages change at the same rate, and basic vocabularies in turn are more stable than "cultural" vocabularies and more resistant to borrowing. Certain basic vocabulary items (such as the words for two, five, eye and louse in the Austronesian languages) can be shown to be more resistant to change than others (Dyen 1975: Chapter 11; see also Grace 1967), but taken as a whole the rate of overall basic vocabulary change is stated to be constant.

The idea of such a constant rate, quite apart from the stability of individual vocabulary items, has of course long been challenged (e.g. Teeter 1963; Bergsland and Vogt 1962), and some languages, such as Icelandic, can be shown to have been extremely conservative, while others, as in Melanesia, can be shown to have changed their vocabularies very rapidly. Although there exists an insufficient written record for Austronesian languages from which variant rates can be demonstrated directly[4], it is possible to throw light on this matter by using another method. Theoretically, all daughter languages of a proto-language should be equally different in basic vocabulary from the proto-language if the rate of change is a constant.

A detailed study using this reasoning has recently been carried out by Blust (1981a), who has compared 62 Austronesian languages outside Taiwan with a reconstructed 200-word list for Proto-Malayo-Polynesian. The results are quite dramatic; Western Malayo-Polynesian languages retain an average of 41% of cognates with Proto-Malayo-Polynesian (for example Malay 59%, Minangkabau 50%, Tagalog 46%, Makassarese 38%, Sundanese 35%), while Oceanic languages retain only 25% on average (for example Motu 37%, but most other New Guinea languages retain only 16–30%). These differences are significant, although there is much overlap, with some Western languages having low percentages (for example Yogyakarta Javanese 30%) and some Oceanic languages having moderately high percentages (for example Fijian and Motu 37%). Nevertheless, one can hardly escape the conclusion that Western Malayo-Polynesian languages have changed, on the average, much more slowly than Oceanic.

Are there any observations which can be made to throw light on this situation? Perhaps I can extend this discussion a little further by looking at some of the social factors internal to specific communities which might cause rates of change to vary from one language to another (regardless of those separation factors influencing the time needed to reach a cut off point, which I have already discussed above). For instance, it has been claimed that certain languages, such as Atayal of Taiwan and Enggano of western Sumatra, have

[4]Old Malay (from the seventh century) and Old Javanese (from the ninth century) do occur on inscriptions in Sumatra and Java (earlier inscriptions are all in Sanskrit), but these are too limited to assist in more than purely local reconstructions. The Cham language of Vietnam also occurs in inscriptions back to the fourth century (Marrisson 1975).

been subjected to rapid changes due to "word taboos" (that is certain sounds, such as those which occur in the name of a dead chief, may acquire a taboo against further utterance; Dyen 1965a:53; Kahler 1978). Other languages, especially in the more stratified Austronesian societies, have different vocabularies for use by or when addressing persons of high status. Others, such as Atayal again, have slightly different vocabularies for male and female speakers (P. J–K. Li 1983). But all these customs are restricted in occurrence, and can hardly explain the overall picture. They are individual idiosyncracies.

Clearly, there are other more fundamental sociolinguistic factors which are likely to affect rates of linguistic change. Such variables as the size of the speech community, its internal integrity (that is the quantity of dialect variation), and, most importantly, the external relationships between speakers of a given language and other communities with varying degrees of linguistic relationship are all sure to be important. Different rates for large urban communities, mobile hunter-gatherers, and small groups of tribal gardeners may perhaps be expected, and there are reasons for suggesting that the latter, particularly when they are atomised into small independent groups and have occasion for interaction with speakers of quite different languages, can have very rapid rates of vocabulary change.

We have now reached a point where further generalisations will serve little purpose. I have tried to show that the rate of linguistic change will be affected by the degree of communication maintained between related language communities, and by various sociolinguistic factors. Small independent populations of tribal horticulturalists, especially if they inhabit a region of existing linguistic diversity, will tend to develop a fast rate of change. Large integrated civilisations should change more slowly. The time has now come to look at some of the more detailed relationships of the western Austronesian languages, and to suggest some archaeological correlations (which will be expanded in later chapters) for time-depth. I will then do the same for the Austronesian languages of Melanesia, since the comparative scene is an important one. I will not be able to raise glottochronology to the status of a reliable and useful tool, but I will try to give some understanding of the linguistic history of the two regions, and to suggest why different rates of linguistic change have occurred.

V. Indo-Malaysian Linguistic Prehistory: Some Possibilities

There is no coherent information about the linguistic situation in Indonesia and Malaysia prior to Austronesian expansion, simply because this expansion was so successful and so complete in all but the more remote corners of the archipelago. It can only be assumed that before the break-up of Proto-Austronesian and the expansion of its daughter subgroups southwards, the unknown languages of the archipelago were flanked to the west (on the South-East Asian mainland) by ancestral Austro-Asiatic languages, and to the east (in eastern Indonesia and New Guinea) by ancestral Papuan languages. The intervening languages may have shared relationships with either or both of these families, and there are hints of such a situation in the claim made by Greenberg (1971) that the Papuan and Andamanese languages may be distantly related, and in the possibility of a Mon-Khmer substratum in Acehnese of northern Sumatra. Beyond this little can be said.

Turning now to Austronesian languages, I have already made it clear that the location of Proto-Austronesian is best placed in Taiwan. Internal relationships of Formosan languages need not be of concern here (but see Footnote 3), and the archaeological evidence from Taiwan suggests a date between 4500 and 4000 BC for Initial Austronesian settlement. My reasoning here is simply that pottery, a known cultural and linguistic marker of early Austronesian communities, first appears in Taiwan at about this time—perhaps 1000 years before its appearance in any of the islands to the south.

As I have noted, however, the date of Proto-Austronesian does not correlate with the date of Initial Austronesian settlement in Taiwan. Instead, it correlates with the point at which the Initial Austronesian communities of the island, whether speaking one language or several, split irrevocably in such a way that two subgroups were formed, both of which have survived separately to the present day. These subgroups are of course Formosan and Malayo-Polynesian (or Extra-Formosan), and since languages of the latter subgroup do not occur in Taiwan it may be assumed that the break-up of Proto-Austronesian involved a migration into isolation to islands to the south—presumably the northern Philippines. In the same way, Proto-Malayo-Polynesian correlates with a split into the separate ancestors of the Western and Central-Eastern Malayo-Polynesian subgroups, presumably as a result of slow expansion through the southern Philippines towards Borneo, Sulawesi and the Moluccas. Each proto-language is thus founded on a prior stage of linguistic development which originates from the break-up of a previous proto-language.

Let me now try to clarify what was happening in the early Austronesian world by tying down the linguistic prehistory with date-estimates from archaeology (Fig. 4.4). Taiwan was settled by Initial Austronesians around or before 4000 BC, and their descendants remained predominantly confined to this island for about a millennium. At about 3000 BC some Austronesians sailed south towards Luzon, and Proto-Austronesian underwent its first and only split (taking Formosan as one primary subgroup and Malayo-Polynesian as the other). Malayo-Polynesian speakers then spread through

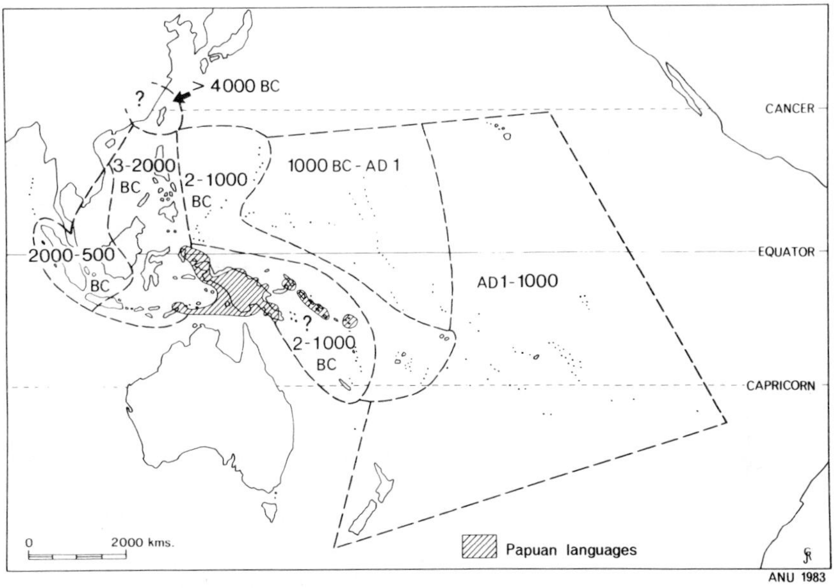

Fig. 4.4. The expansion of Austronesian settlement.

the Philippines until perhaps 2500 BC, when migrants presumably moved into relative isolation in the Moluccas and founded the Central-Eastern Malayo-Polynesian subgroup. The populations who "stayed behind" in the Philippines, and their descendants who expanded into Sulawesi and along the geographically much less fragmented route via Palawan into Sundaland, continued to speak languages ancestral to those we now term Western Malayo-Polynesian. All the radiocarbon-dated cave and rock-shelter sequences which document the Neolithic in these regions of the archipelago seem to support these dates, and it must of course be remembered that the cultures themselves were adapting as they expanded, hence the variant proto-language vocabularies to which I referred above.

At this point, I will return again to the observations made by Blust (1981a) on varying retention rates in the Malayo-Polynesian languages. If the average Oceanic retention figure (25%) is used to calculate a date for Proto-Malayo-Polynesian by using the standard formula of glottochronology (80.5% retention per language per millennium), then the answer will be around 4000–5000 BC. If the much higher average Western Malayo-Polynesian retention figure (41%) is used, then the answer will be about 2000 BC. Such a difference is no small matter and cannot be ignored. So which rate reflects overall Austronesian reality in the most satisfactory way?

The answer is clearly the Western rate, since a date of 2000 BC for the break-up of Proto-Malayo-Polynesian is closer to the date of 2500 BC which I am suggesting on archaeological grounds. It is of course slightly conservative, but this may be due to the integrating effects of the civilisations of the past 1500 years in the western islands. Furthermore, the standard retention rate of glottochronology is not, as I have already demonstrated, correct in any absolute sense, although it apparently corresponds to reality more closely for Western Malayo-Polynesian than for Oceanic. The Oceanic retention rate is obviously highly depressed, and may be considered unrepresentative of the general Austronesian situation. I will look again at the the Melanesian languages in due course.

A. After Proto-Malayo-Polynesian

The dates I am suggesting for the Philippines indicate an Austronesian colonisation between 3000 and 2500 BC, followed by movements to Borneo and Sulawesi by about 2500 BC. Whether these movements took place before the Philippines were wholly settled we may never know. The archipelago is highly fragmented, and settlement of remote parts may have continued long after other Austronesian settlers had expanded southwards. If this did happen there may be a lesser linguistic diversity and time-depth for some parts of the Philippines than expected, as already suggested by Grace (1964:367). This is just an example of a possible complication in what may otherwise appear to be a simple story.

We now come to the two major subgroups termed Western Malayo-Polynesian and Central-Eastern Malayo-Polynesian. The former has never been established as a true subgroup with rigour, but most of its members share quite high cognate percentages between themselves (over 38% according to Dyen 1965a, who termed this subgroup the Hesperonesian linkage), and also high retention rates from Proto-Malayo-Polynesian. Many languages have large numbers of speakers (possibly over 60 million in the case of Javanese) and are spoken over large areas. It is also evident that the major languages of the region, such as Javanese, Malay and Sundanese (western Java), have had long histories of civilisation.

The Western Malayo-Polynesian "subgroup" does present some problems. Its overall internal relationships are unclear, and, as Blust (1981a) has pointed out, the lexicostatistical clustering of these languages (as, for instance, into the Hesperonesian linkage of Dyen 1965) may be more an artefact of high retention rates than of a true subgrouping relationship. In this sense, Western Malayo-Polynesian may be a kind of residuum of Austronesian languages which cannot be pigeonholed into Formosan or Central-Eastern Malayo-Polynesian. For our purposes, however, this may be a small point, since the

Western Malayo-Polynesian area is clearly quite unified geographically, and there is no good reason to doubt that all its languages are fairly closely related, even if an overall subgrouping analysis utilising the principle of shared innovation has not been carried out. Furthermore, many of the major languages of these civilisations have borrowed from each other so intensively that true shared innovations are often very hard to detect.

Within Western Malayo-Polynesian a number of localised subgroups can be detected. Thomas and Healey (1962) have subgrouped the Philippine languages into a Philippine "stock". This excludes some languages of southern Mindanao, but they do incorporate these into a Philippine "superstock", in which they also tentatively include Chamic and Malay. However, even if the Philippine languages do ultimately form one subgroup (and Reid 1982 disputes this), it is clearly unlikely that their closest outside relatives will be Chamic and Malay to the exclusion of the geographically much closer languages of northern Borneo. The latter (Prentice 1970), plus those of northern Sulawesi (Sneddon 1978), have in fact long been stated to have generalised Philippine characteristics (e.g. Capell 1962; Uhlenbeck 1971), although they cannot be placed entirely within a Philippine subgroup (Blust 1982b).

Another important subgroup, proposed by Dyen (1965) and examined in detail by Nothofer (1975) under the name Malayo-Javanic, includes Javanese, Sundanese, Madurese, Malay, Minangkabau and Kerinci of Sumatra (both very closely related to Malay), Acehnese of northern Sumatra, and Lampung of southern Sumatra. This subgroup clearly occupies a huge geographical area, and since the languages all share quite high cognate percentages they give the impression of a recent major expansion, perhaps during the first millenium BC, although archaeological correlations are almost non-existent for most of this region. This impression of recency could be tempered by high retention rates and undetected borrowings, but I think we can hardly escape the working hypothesis that the Austronesian languages of Sumatra, Malaya and Vietnam (and possibly Java?) were not established prior to 1000 BC, or perhaps even later in some areas.

The internal details of Nothofer's classification have been challenged by Blust (1981b), who doubts the close relationship of Javanese and Madurese with Malay, but who does support a close relationship for Malay, Minangkabau and Kerinci with the Iban, Maloh and Selako languages of western Borneo (see also Hudson 1970), and with Sundanese, Chamic and Acehnese. As Blust points out, these languages have never been completely separated and have borrowed intensively from each other, so the application of the family tree model with its implied sharp divisions to this region may be unrealistic. For present purposes it need only be noted that all the languages of Sundaland are closely related in terms of the total range of Austronesian diversity, with the exception of the languages of northern Borneo, and certain other minor languages with low retention rates such as Enggano off western Sumatra. One is viewing, in essence, a relatively unified period of culture history which may have a time-depth of only 3000 years.

The Chamic languages of Vietnam, characterised by their adoption of a monosyllabic word form, are very closely related internally. Observations on their closest outside relationships point to Malay (Dyen 1971c), and this link is strengthened by comparisons of written forms of Old Malay and Old Cham which have survived in inscriptions from the first millennium AD (Marrisson 1975). There seems little reason to doubt that both these mainland groups have a very closely related if not immediate common origin, and it may be concluded that the Chamic languages have a Sundaland origin, with perhaps Borneo or Malaya as a most immediate homeland. A direct Philippine origin is most unlikely linguistically, despite the apparently close arrchaeological relationship between the two regions (see Chapter 9, Section II). Furthermore, and most importantly, the Malay and Chamic languages of the mainland are without doubt the results of movements *from* Sundaland. The old idea, so often repeated in popular works today, that the Austronesians migrated from the Asian mainland through the Malay Peninsula or Vietnam, is absolutely wrong.

Many of the linguistic expansions on the western fringes of Western Malayo-Polynesian probably date well into the Christian era. Malay is of course still gaining ground in the archipelago today, and has gained most impressively since its adoption as a widespread trade language during the period of the Islamic sultanates from the 15th century onwards. The Chamic languages may only have spread into the Vietnamese highlands during the first millennium AD (Thomas 1964), and the languages of Madagascar provide us with the most interesting example of a late expansion. The fairly uniform languages here probably originated from a settlement of Austronesians from southern Borneo, where the most closely related languages are Maanyan and Ngaju (Dahl 1951; Dyen 1971d). According to Dahl, the presence of certain key Sanskrit loans in the languages of both Madagascar and southern Borneo suggest that the migration postdates AD 400, which is when the first evidence for the influence of Sanskrit on the Western Malayo-Polynesian languages appears. A date during the mid or late first millennium AD seems likely, and it should not be forgotten that Austronesians also reached New Zealand, on the opposite side of the world, at about the same time.

On turning to the languages of the Central Malayo-Polynesian subgroup we move into a very different linguistic situation from that of most of Sundaland. This region has a very large number of languages, about 100 according to Pawley (1974), and most of them have small numbers of speakers and occupy only small geographical areas. Yet Blust's analyses do indicate that the Central Malayo-Polynesian languages have a higher average retention rate (about 36%) from Proto-Malayo-Polynesian than do the Oceanic languages. Thus, while many of these societies are of a similar small-scale tribal nature to those of Melanesia, it may be that the higher retention rate reflects a much weaker influence from the pre-Austronesian inhabitants of the region.

To date, rather little can be said about internal relationships within Central Malayo-Polynesian, but it is apparent from archaeology that Austronesian settlers had reached Timor well before the end of the third millennium BC, and soon after 2000 BC the Oceanic languages underwent their first expansion into Melanesia from an immediate homeland in the region of Halmahera and western New Guinea. Within Melanesia the descendant languages of Proto-Oceanic underwent a very rapid process of diversification owing to geographical fragmentation and the presence of very strong social and linguistic influences from the speakers of the Papuan languages. I would now like to review this matter briefly, to give a clearer perspective on the prehistory of the Indo-Malaysian languages themselves.

B. The Oceanic Languages of Western Melanesia

The Oceanic languages of Melanesia, Polynesia and Micronesia all share one common origin in Proto-Oceanic, as established by Dempwolff, Milke, and other more recent authors such as Grace and Pawley (see Pawley 1981). In New Guinea and adjacent parts of eastern Indonesia and western Melanesia the Oceanic speakers were preceded by long-established settlements of Papuan speakers, who may well have had agriculture and quite sizeable populations before Austronesians first arrived. The immediate origins of the Proto-Oceanic speakers should on linguistic grounds be in the south Halmahera and west New Guinea region.

As I have noted above, proto-language reconstructions indicate that the Oceanic speakers, and the Austronesians as a whole, have had an unbroken potting tradition, except on atolls or in the unusual late Polynesian situation (the last 1500–2000 years) where the craft of potting was lost. According to the linguists Oceanic speakers in Melanesia must always have maintained potting traditions, and their arrival can therefore only be tied in with the Lapita archaeological culture, with its decorated pottery, which spread through Melanesia around and after 1600 BC (Bellwood 1978a: Chapter 9). Many years of intensive archaeological research have failed to produce older pottery traditions in Melanesia, and although I have in the past played with the idea of an early aceramic Austronesian settlement there, I now believe this view to be incorrect.

I am here dating Proto-Oceanic much later than I and most of my colleagues have suggested previously on grounds of glottochronology and to my mind erroneous archaeological assumptions. For instance, Pawley and Green in 1975 suggested a date before 3000 BC for the break-up of Proto-Oceanic. However, in a more recent paper, Pawley (1981; see also Pawley and Green 1984) has suggested a more likely date of 2000 BC, and a rapid sea-borne dispersal of Proto-Oceanic speakers, as the Lapita evidence suggests, would fit well with Pawley's observations on the shape of the Oceanic family tree.

I have made this digression in order to make the point that the Oceanic languages cannot have a time-depth of over 4000 years. Yet the lexicostatistical study of Dyen (1965) showed tremendous lexical diversity in the Oceanic languages of Melanesia — so much, in fact, that his reasoning forced him to deny the existence of an Oceanic subgroup against all the phonological and structural evidence, and to suggest western Melanesia as the location for Proto-Austronesian (see Fig. 4.3) — a suggestion which is known to be quite impossible from the linguistic evidence as a whole. What Dyen's study in fact indicates is that the Melanesian languages have changed very greatly in lexicon in terms of their antiquity, while the older language subgroups to the west have changed less — much less in Malay and some western Indonesian cases. So why have the Melanesian languages changed so quickly?

The answer may be that they have been influenced very intensively by the unrelated Papuan languages of the New Guinea region — a region where the pre-existing population was perhaps very much denser than it was in the Indonesian islands to the west. This borrowing theory (often called "pidginisation" in the past) has not always been well-received by linguists, partly because some of its earlier proponents incorporated ideas of multiple movements from Indonesia which do not accord with present linguistic hypotheses about the region. But the idea of heavy influence, two-way and not just from Papuan into Austronesian, is acceptable to the majority of modern linguists (e.g. Chretien 1956; Cowan 1965; Capell 1969; Benedict 1975; Wurm 1978; and most recently given explicit support by Lynch 1982).

Pawley (1981) has recently presented another viewpoint, which does not at face value depend on Papuan influence, and this view is that the Austronesian languages of Melanesia remained relatively unified for a long time, and then rapidly atomised after shared cognate percentages dropped below the level of mutual intelligibility. There is some archaeological evidence in support of this view, which suggests an early (Lapita) unity and later cultural fragmentation. But the basic reasons for such fragmentation may still have much to do with the long-term influences of the linguistically diverse Papuan societies on the scattered Austronesian communities, and Pawley's view does not really contradict the view in favour of heavy linguistic and cultural borrowing between Papuans and Austronesians. As Benedict has stated (1975:137):

> The divergence in the Melanesia-New Guinea area is on a superficial level, manifestly the product of the attenuation of AN [Austronesian] lexical material at the edges of an expanding AN area as it gradually encroached upon non-AN areas.

Grace (1981) has also recently presented a sociolinguistic argument, a little too complex to reproduce here, for the high lexical diversity in New Caledonia — an island without Papuan languages, but one where bilingualism breaks down the concept of regular language change and allows situations of massive borrowing and linguistic instability.

Melanesia may be regarded as an area where small independent and relatively egalitarian communities, in frequent contact with a large array of different linguistic communities and practising bilingualism as a major method of communication for trade and social interaction, have become subjected to very high rates of lexical diversification. The same situation does not hold for Sundaland and may never have done so, although the relative homogeneity seen there now may be partly due to the integrating effects of 1500 years of civilisation. Those islands which were little affected by these civilisations, such as Sulawesi, the Philippines and the islands of eastern Indonesia, do show much more linguistic diversity, both in terms of the large numbers of languages with small numbers of speakers, and the degrees of difference between them.

VI. The Papuan Languages and their Relationships with Indonesia

Within Indonesia (excluding Irian Jaya) the Papuan languages are spoken in central and eastern Timor, Alor, Pantar, and on Morotai and the northern half of Halmahera (see Fig. 4.1). Elsewhere in the Moluccas and Lesser Sundas all the languages are Austronesian. A superficial glance at a map might suggest that these Papuan enclaves are simply remnants of an earlier and larger distribution overrun by Austronesian speakers, but recent research on the Papuan languages as a whole may make such a view rather simplistic. I am not here concerned with the bulk of the Papuan languages in their New Guinea and western Melanesian centres of distribution, but I do want to look at an overall view of their prehistory, especially that espoused in a number of recent papers by Wurm (1978, 1982, 1983).

The main documented phases of expansion in the prehistory of the Papuan languages, according to Wurm, are as follows (and here I am simplifying what Wurm presents as a rather more complex story):

1. New Guinea was first settled about 60 000 years ago (according to inference based partly on Australian archaeological dates), but no present-day Papuan languages descend directly from this early linguistic phase.
2. About 15 000 and 10 000 years ago the first Papuan-speakers, possibly in two separate groups according to pronoun forms, settled the New Guinea region, including the eastern Indonesian islands mentioned above. The dates may be regarded as little more than guesses. The languages of Halmahera and Morotai, which are classified in the West Papuan Phylum, descend directly from one of these two periods of linguistic expansion.
3. About 3000 BC a major expansion of the Trans New Guinea Phylum of languages took place. This expansion began west of New Guinea according to Wurm, and occurred after Austronesians had already arrived in the general region according to the evidence of loan-words (this perhaps makes the suggested date of 3000 BC a little too old). The Trans New Guinea Phylum languages spread mainly along the northern coast of New Guinea, and also expanded to Timor, Alor and Pantar, where they replaced the earlier West Papuan languages.
4. Since 1500 BC the Trans New Guinea Phylum languages, strongly influenced by Austronesian loan-words acquired in the vicinity of the Markham Valley, have expanded in the highlands of New Guinea. The Phylum now contains about 500 languages and covers about four-fifths of the Papuan linguistic area. It is an excellent example of how a successful linguistic expansion can wipe out traces of earlier diversity (is there a moral here for the historical interpretation of the Sundaland Austronesian languages?)

The basic conclusions which can be drawn from Wurm's accounts are clear. Halmahera was settled by Papuan speakers long before any Austronesian presence in the area. Timor, Alor and Pantar might have been settled by two separate groups, one long before and the other contemporary with an Austronesian presence. New Guinea has a far more complex history.

However, there are aspects of Wurm's reconstruction which I think need some comment. For one thing, he derives all his strata of migration from Indonesia at separate times. It would seem to me that most of them should represent expansions from within the large pool of population supported by the large size and varied resources of New Guinea, and there is now some excellent evidence which indicates that New Guinea Highlanders did develop their own localised form of horticulture long before Austronesians could have arrived on the New Guinea coasts. This would be sufficient to support a considerable increase of population over that possible with a hunting and gathering economy, and it would be sufficient to explain the expansionary success of the Trans New Guinea Phylum, and also the remarkable resilience which the Papuan languages have shown in holding their domination of the New Guinea region despite Austronesian settlement. The main problem with my view is that it goes against the direction of expansion of the Trans New Guinea Phylum as postulated by Wurm, and it also does not account for the claimed presence of Austronesian loans in Trans New Guinea Phylum language from the beginning of its expansion. Since I make no claims to professional linguistic expertise I will not pursue this argument further, except to suggest that linguists might take it into consideration.

So far, most of the linguistic opinions I have presented in this chapter have been what I term "standard"; despite quibbles over details, they are all generally acceptable to the majority of linguists. One exception to this generalisation is of course the hypothesis of Dyen that the Austronesian languages developed in and spread from Melanesia. The past 20 years of research in linguistics and archaeology leave little hope for a hypothesis which was originally so clearly presented and yet can now be shown to be incorrect. It was therefore with some surprise that I recently read an article by Terrell (1981) which seems to be harking back to Dyen's viewpoint, albeit from a totally different theoretical perspective. Terrell in fact suggests that both the Papuan and the Austronesian language families in Melanesia could have a common origin, and that the divergences between them have evolved within Melanesia with the passage of time and a fast rate of linguistic change[5]. As Terrell (1981:251) states: "In short, in the interests of parsimony, do not invoke migrations beyond necessity".

The point I wish to make to close this chapter is that I believe the linguistic reconstruction I have presented fits the available facts in the most convincing way. Terrell clearly adopts a totally different stance; one which is reasoned and logical, but which (in my view) is heavily dependent on one rather peripheral region of the Austronesian world (western Oceania) for its facts and theories. We may never know which answer, if any, is correct, but I do feel that there is a point where the recent trend towards using rather abstract models, as exemplified by Terrell's article, will have to face a much broader field of reality.

[5]Some Melanesian languages, such as those of the Santa Cruz region, have such a "mixed" appearance that even professional linguists disagree as to whether they should be classified as Papuan or Austronesian (Lincoln 1978; Wurm 1978). This could, on the surface, provide some highly localised support for Terrell's arguments, although I would ascribe the situation to the operation of rapid change and heavy inter-language influence.

5
The Patterns of History and Ethnography

It is not possible to give an exact figure for the number of different ethnic groups in the Indo-Malaysian Archipelago, simply because of problems of definition and boundary-recognition very similar to those discussed for languages. However, the major Human Relations Area Files compilations (Lebar *et al.* 1964; Lebar 1972) describe about 100 groups for whom there are good literatures, and H. Geertz (1963) has given a total figure of 300 for Indonesia (some of the more important are shown in Chapter 4, Fig. 4.1 and Chapter 8, Fig. 8.16). As one would expect, there is considerable cultural variation which is due in part to differences which developed between Austronesian societies in prehistoric times, and in part to the varying influences of Indian, Islamic and European traditions during the past 1500 years.

I should perhaps explain here my basic stance on the background to cultural variation in the tribal societies of the archipelago. Many ethnologists in the past adopted a view that observable variations reflected the successive migrations into the region of different cultures and their associated racial groups (e.g. Loeb 1935; Kennedy 1937; Cole 1945). I am sometimes disagreeably surprised at how often these "waves" of Veddoids, Proto-Malays and Deutero-Malays, together with their cultural idiosyncracies, are repeated without question in modern books on the history and peoples of the region, but this is a matter which I will not pursue. My own view is simple; the Negritos and their hunting and gathering traditional lifestyle must be considered as autochthonous to the Indo-Malaysian Archipelago, whereas the agricultural lifestyle of the Austronesian speakers is to a great (but not total) extent the result of an original expansion from more northerly latitudes. The explanations for the present variations in the latter group require not mixing between clearly differentiable and successive races and cultures, but the slow expansion and adaptation of a relatively unified ethnolinguistic population, combined with inter-group contact and the successive influences of external civilisations.

The ethnolinguistic complexity of the Indo-Malaysian region makes the process of prehistoric reconstruction much more difficult than for an area of relative cultural homogeneity such as Polynesia. Furthermore, in Indonesia and Malaysia the boundaries between cultures were perhaps more diffuse in prehistoric times than now, and much of the ethnic consciousness which characterises the region today may have become sharpened in recent centuries as groups have symbolised their different identities in response to degrees of incorporation in state and colonial systems (Keesing 1981:119; Fried 1983). Conversely, small groups can often "pool" their separate identities in unison against outside pressures, as Nicolaisen (1977–8) has described for small groups in Sarawak in the face of Iban and Kayan expansion.

The last millennium of intensive contact between the outside world and the archipelago has therefore probably witnessed an increase in the degree of conscious visibility of different ethnic groups, and also an increase in the rates of boundary fluctuation and assimilation of fringe groups. But one cannot of course generalise very usefully about this, since every region has followed a different course of development. Large-scale assimilatory societies such as those of the Javanese and the widespread Malays have undoubtedly expanded over a great deal of earlier diversity, while on the other hand the Aslian peoples of Malaya have stressed their ethnic identities in order to resist such assimilation (Benjamin 1976, 1980). Each region now presents an ethnic "picture" which reflects its settlement and cultural history and its degree of incorporation into a native state or colonial polity, and each must therefore be considered on its own merits.

On looking at the societies of the region in broad terms, that is with respect to descent, political systems, influences from Indian and Islamic civilisations and so forth, it is apparent that there are three major groupings, defined most clearly by H. Geertz (1963). These are: (1) the partly Indianised wet rice-growing cultures centred on Java (now Muslim) and Bali; (2) the coastal Islamic societies which have become very widespread through the archipelago as a result of the trade and commerce focussed on the Islamic sultanates since the 15th century; and (3) the tribal, still partially "pagan", and mainly interior or remote island populations. In the pages which follow I will concentrate attention on some of the tribal societies in the third category, describing their systems of descent and inheritance, and their systems of status and political integration. The cosmopolitan societies of the first two categories, such as present-day Javanese and Malay, will only be mentioned in certain historical contexts. Furthermore, most of the tribal groups have undergone at least some change as a result of contact with modern civilisation, and my descriptions will clearly favour traditional customs and behaviour as described in historical or ethnographic records.

In terms of descent, the most commonly used terminology divides the tribal societies of the region into unilineal (patrilineal or matrilineal) and cognatic categories (Murdock 1960a, 1960b). This terminology is now enshrined in the literature, and it does of course refer to differences in descent reckoning which are undoubtedly of social significance. But this does not necessarily mean that all Austronesian societies can be placed unequivocally in distinct unilineal and cognatic categories, or that such categories imply totally separate evolutionary trajectories. Indeed, the differences could reflect in part the presence or absence of corporate descent groups, as I will discuss later. Furthermore, the dichotomy does not really reflect Indo-Malaysian reality, since in practice most societies follow both unilineal and cognatic principles depending upon context. Examples of the real-life multitude of cross-cutting context include affiliation to a corporate group, location of post-marital residence, inheritance of swidden land or of wet rice fields, inheritance of status, and membership in burial or irrigation associations.

My line of approach will be to introduce the surviving hunting and gathering societies, whom I believe do demand separate consideration, and then document the arrival and distribution of Indian and Islamic influences, before turning to the main discussion of the tribal agricultural populations of Indonesia and Malaysia.

I. The Hunters and Gatherers

The equatorial rainforests of the region shelter a number of hunting and collecting societies which have either survived assimilation by, or have adapted out of, the expanding Austronesian agricultural economy. Some of these groups, such as the Negritos of Malaya, are undoubtedly "pristine" hunters and gatherers who have long resisted acculturation by surrounding cultivators. Others, such as the Austronesian-speaking hunters and gatherers of interior Sumatra and Borneo, have probably adopted this way of life as a result of change from an agricultural ancestry.

The Negrito peoples of the Andaman Islands, Malaya and the Philippines are of course of great significance in any discussion of the overall prehistory of the archipelago. Although all the Philippine Negritos have now adopted Austronesian languages, and some groups have become partly acculturated to a lifestyle of shifting cultivation (for example the Pinatubo of western Luzon, Fox 1953), there can be no doubt that the Negrito population as a whole has a local ancestry which long predates that of the Southern Mongoloid Indonesians, Filipinos and Malaysians.

Superficially, the Negrito lifestyle is simple; small bands of families with rather fluid membership and informal leadership move in a nomadic fashion through the forest, sleeping in camps of lean-tos and shelters. Cultural simplicity is expressed partly through an absence of many features characteristic of the surrounding cultivators. Some of these, such as the absence of headhunting, land tenure, pottery (except in the Andamans), weaving and alcoholic beverages (Cooper 1941), are no more than one would expect given the nature of Negrito society and economy. Other features, such as the practices of body scarification amongst the Philippine Aeta, face painting and the wearing of porcupine quills through the nose by the Malayan Negritos (Carey 1976), and the general absence of ear ornaments, tattooing and dental mutilation, all serve to set these groups apart from surrounding Austronesian cultivators.

While there is not space here to list the many details reported about Negrito hunting and gathering lifestyles, I do wish to question the old view that the Negritos represent a direct and totally static window on the Pleistocene past, as implied by Cooper (1941), and as stated rather derogatively by Burkill in 1951: "the Andamanese and the Semang are Negritos. There is no future for such; and their past has been millennial stagnation". It is true that the hunting and collecting economy and the associated band forms of social organisation are of great antiquity, but the Negritos have been in contact with outsiders for several millennia, and those who survive today, especially in Malaya and the Philippines, have done so by adapting to changing circumstances and pressures. Peterson (1978) has described how the Aeta of north-eastern Luzon have come to terms with pressure from Filipino cultivators by forming trading and labour relationships with the latter; the Aeta provide hunted meat and labour in return for cultivated produce. Here we can see one case of adaptation in order to survive under pressure, and other Philippine Negrito groups have actually adopted cultivation practices as their hunting territories and resources have shrunk. It is true that many such adaptations have occurred only very recently, but the important fact that all the Philippine Negritos now speak Austronesian languages does indicate very strongly that pressures for change have been acting on these groups for a long time.

In central Malaya the pressures have not been as great, and the Negritos here (often called "Semang"; see Endicott 1979a, b; Rambo 1979, for recent descriptions) have been able to continue their forest lifestyle through a conscious emphasis of differences between their culture and those of adjacent Malay and Senoi cultivators. This is a conclusion recently drawn by Benjamin (1976, 1980, 1983), who shows how certain features of Negrito social life, such as avoidance practices and prohibitions which promote marriage outside the group, wide social contact and freedom of movement, help to ensure the mobility which these people need for survival. The Negritos have no corporate descent groups, and the independent nuclear families are thus allowed to move and make new camp relationships freely.

The hunters and gatherers of the Indonesian islands are in a very different category from the Negritos, since both physically and linguistically they are undifferentiated from their Austronesian-speaking and plant-cultivating neighbours. They dwell mostly in the inland forests of Borneo and Sumatra, but their general avoidance of cultivation is not a good reason for assuming that they represent an ancient stratum of Austronesian-speaking hunters and gatherers. For all cases I would suggest a recent penetration of forested regions where a gathering lifestyle clearly became more economical for the very small groups involved (see also Bronson 1976; Hutterer and Macdonald 1982:7).

The most well-known groups of these Indonesian hunters and gatherers include the Kubu of the lowland swamps of Sumatra (who speak dialects of Malay; Loeb 1935), the Penan of interior Borneo, the Togutil (Papuan-speakers) of northern Halmahera, and the Tasaday of interior southern Mindanao. I will restrict my comments to the Penan and Tasaday since they are adequately described in the recent literature. The Penan (sometimes called Punan; Needham 1954 reviews the confusion) occupy many forested areas of inland Sarawak and Kalimantan and dwell in temporary camps (Fig. 5.1) of a few families, hunting with blowpipes, exploiting stands of wild sago (*Eugeissona utilis*), and collecting the fruits of wild rambutan, durian and mangosteen trees (Hose and McDougall 1912; Kedit 1978). Linguistically there is no apparent unity, and most groups seem to be related more closely to surrounding cultivators than they are to other Penan as a whole, an important point stressed by Hoffman (1981). Many groups collect forest items such as beeswax, birds' nests, camphor and rattan for trade purposes, and this has often led to close relationships with surrounding agriculturalists such as the Kayan. Indeed, such close relationships may have led to many apparent signs of acculturation in some Penan societies, such as the practice of horticulture (Nicolaisen 1976), ironworking, and systems of ranked headmanship (Arnold 1958). However, it is my own belief that these features need not in totality be the result of acculturation, but may simply reflect the fact that the Penan have always straddled the boundary between settled horticulture and forest hunting and gathering, with only some groups shifting entirely towards the latter economic mode. If the linguistic reconstructions of early Austronesian society described in the previous chapter have any merit at all, then clearly there is little scope for any widespread and ancient Austronesian hunting and gathering adaptation in Indonesia.

This conclusion can be stressed even more forcefully with respect to the Tasaday of Mindanao in the Philippines, a group who achieved media prominence through their "discovery" in 1970 (Fernandez and Lynch 1972; Nance 1975; Yen and Nance 1976). The Tasaday band was living in a cave in the interior rainforest at an altitude of about 1300 m above sea-level, and had clearly had no regular contact with outsiders for a very long time. In 1972 it comprised 13 adults and 14 children (12 boys and 2 girls), and having lost contact with its traditional source of wives — another band called the Tasafang who may have succumbed to pressure from expanding cultivators and

Fig. 5.1. A Penan camp in Sarawak. Photo by Hedda Morrison.

loggers — it was clearly facing problems with respect to its future demographic viability. The culture of this group was simple in the extreme; a number of widespread Austronesian customs such as tattooing, betel chewing and tooth filing were practised, but the people did not hunt, had no baskets or carrying devices, lacked the bow and used only flaked or edge-ground stone tools. The food supply came mainly from fruits, wild yams (the tops of which were replanted after harvest), grubs, and hand-caught fish and frogs.

Since their discovery the Tasaday have been regarded by some as the unacculturated remnants of a very ancient lifestyle. Yet linguistically this cannot be true — they speak a dialect of the Manobo languages of the nearby cultivators, and they have at least one Sanskrit loan-word. A separation at around 600–700 years ago seems most plausible (Molony and Tuan 1976), and thus it must be assumed that the ancestors of the Tasaday abandoned a previous cultivating lifestyle through choice, hostility, or, according to their own belief, due to an epidemic. Whatever the real answer, this group serves as a warning that not all cultural change has to be in the direction of greater complexity.

A. The *Orang Laut*

Other Austronesian groups who once practised a rather unusual economy on the cultural fringes of the Indo-Malaysian world are the *orang laut* (sea-people), who are concentrated in two separate regions along the coasts of the Strait of Malacca and in the Riau Archipelago, and on the north-eastern coast of Borneo and in neighbouring Sulu (Sopher 1965). Smaller groups also live down the eastern side of Sulawesi and in pockets in the Lesser Sundas. Favoured habitats are protected mangrove or coral reef coasts, especially where there are many small islands, as in Riau and Sulu. Traditionally, each family lived permanently at sea in a houseboat complete with a cabin, sleeping facilities and a cooking place. The Bajaus of Sulu and eastern Borneo still lived wholly in boats until around 1930, but most groups throughout the archipelago have become settled on land in recent decades.

Traditional Bajau houseboat anchorages comprised a number of independent nuclear families with a very fluid bilaterial organization. Large groups of families sometimes combined for major fishing operations, and some groups shared the usage of small islands for burial. But Bajau houseboat families generally lived independent lives fishing and trading with land-based Samal and Taosug communities (Nimmo 1972; Sather 1978). The *orang laut* of the Riau–Lingga Islands were rather heavily influenced and controlled by the Malay sultanates of the region, and maintained a mobile trading lifestyle until the turn of this century. However, in all regions the pressures to settle down on land are now so strong that the true houseboat lifestyle probably will not survive intact for much longer.

The *orang laut* lifestyle appears to have developed locally in more than one region. The western groups speak dialects of Malay, and the Bajau language is closely related to the Samal language spoken by many settled agricultural people in the Sulu Archipelago. Hence Sopher's view that the Bajau migrated in Islamic times from the Malacca Strait region cannot be entirely correct (Nimmo 1967, 1968). However, the real antiquity of the mobile houseboat adaptation is unknown, and may always remain so since such groups will obviously leave no recognisable archaeological remains. In the Lesser Sundas the spread of the Bajaus occurred mostly in the 18th and 19th centuries, and as traders in Makassan or their own praus some Bajau sailors actually reached Australia (Fox 1977b). In the core regions of Sulu and the Malacca Strait there were certainly *orang laut* communities reported in the 16th century (Sopher 1965), but here the records stop. I tend to agree with Sopher that the adaptation is not an ancient one in Austronesian terms, and I do not see this lifestyle as having been significant in early Austronesian expansion. I suspect that it has developed as a specialised economic adaptation within the exchange and trade networks which have been focussed on the Strait of

Malacca and (to a lesser extent) the southern Philippines within the last 1500 years.

II. The Influences of India and Islam

I will approach my main discussion of the tribal and agricultural societies of the archipelago by first outlining the transformations which have affected many of the western and the more accessible eastern regions during the past 1500 years. The phenomena of "Indianisation" and "Islamisation" in South-East Asia have long been major fields of historical study (for general surveys see Vlekke 1945; Hall 1968; Coedes 1975), and here I will only touch on some of the major points.

Indian trading enterprise into South-East Asia, and complementary Austronesian sailing to India (and ultimately on to Madagascar), appear to have commenced in the first few centuries AD (Wolters 1967). By the fifth century some trade routes may also have linked the archipelago directly with China, but the actual evidence for any Chinese presence in South-East Asia outside Vietnam before the Song dynasty (960–1279) is really very slight.

This initial Indian contact appears to have stimulated the development in some western regions of apparently native trading states from the second century AD onwards (see Chapter 9, Fig. 9.5) — states such as Champa in central Vietnam, Funan around the Gulf of Siam, several small states in the narrow isthmus of southern Thailand, and the rather hazy Ko-ying in Sumatra or western Java (Wheatley 1961; Wolters 1967, 1979; Whitmore 1977; Mabbett 1977). However, a widespread and early settlement of Indian traders in the archipelago is most unlikely to have occurred according to the linguistic evidence, for the Indian loan-words in Austronesian languages are almost all from Sanskrit — a language which would not have been in everyday use amongst Indian traders at the time. As Gonda (1973) has noted, there are no Prakrit loans and no trade pidgins in evidence, both of which would be expected had heavy colonisation taken place.

The major religious and political processes of Indianisation at the court level are now agreed by many authorities (e.g. Reed 1976; Christie 1979a; Hall 1982) to have developed some centuries after this initial period of trade. The first indications that the native rulers of these Indo-Malaysian trading states were beginning to model themselves on the Pallava kings of Tamil Nadu and their contemporaries appear around the fifth century, when inscriptions in Sanskrit and in the Pallava script record kings with the Pallava name-ending -varman in eastern Borneo and western Java (Kumar 1974; Casparis 1975; Meer 1979).

By the seventh century, the sources of the Indian influences seem to have shifted towards northern India and the Pala kingdom of Bengal (Bernet Kempers 1959), and it is now, for the first time, that really tangible Indianised kingdoms with divine rulers and magnificent Hindu or Buddhist monuments begin to appear in the archipelago. The Sumatran trading state of Srivijaya, founded about 670 (Wolters 1967; Hall 1976), was probably the focus of an interlocked group of trading towns in eastern Sumatra and the Malay Peninsula, although this kingdom, despite its historical promise, has not left any very coherent archaeological record (Bronson and Wisseman 1976; Bronson 1979a). The Javanese kingdoms are in fact much better known owing to their superb monuments; the great Buddhist stupa termed the Borobudur was constructed by the Sailendras in the eighth or early ninth century, and splendid Hindu temples were constructed slightly later in the region of Prambanan (Fig. 5.2). After 930 the political focus of Javanese civilisation shifted to eastern Java, and culminated in the Majapahit kingdom of the 14th century, which was eventually to decline under the pressure of Islam.

The Hindu and Buddhist beliefs on which these kingdoms were founded were almost certainly brought into the archipelago by Hindu Brahmans and learned Buddhists. The former may well have been invited by native rulers to bolster their authorities with the rituals and architecture of a major world civilisation, but Buddhism seems to have had only a very brief period of popularity in Indonesia. The role of the Brahmans in the process of Indianisation is generally agreed to have been crucial, and far in excess of that attributable to traders (Bosch 1961; Leur 1967; Gonda 1973). It was perhaps through them that the majority of the Sanskrit loan-words, which fall mainly into the intellectual and administrative categories, were introduced into Austronesian languages. As might be expected, the languages with the most Sanskrit loans are those associated with long-lived civilisations, such as Chamic and Javanese. Malay also acquired many loans through the kingdom of Srivijaya, which has bequeathed to posterity a small number of seventh century inscriptions in Old Malay. Malay has also been the medium for the more recent spread of Sanskrit loans to many non-Indianised parts of Indonesia, and even as far as Irian Jaya (Gonda 1973).

The geographical impact of Indian influence in the archipelago was always focussed heavily on the lands around the Strait of Malacca and the Java Sea. Hence it was of maximum strength in eastern Sumatra, the western Malay Peninsula, Java and Bali, but it rapidly dwindled in parts of highland Sumatra (for example amongst the Batak) and was almost non-existent in Nias and Mentawai. In eastern Borneo the Kutei kingdom of the fifth century seems to have left few descendants, and in general this island, plus Sulawesi, the Lesser Sundas and the Moluccas were only affected by Indian civilisation in a most superficial way. Traditions that the 14th century Javanese kingdom

Fig. 5.2. Hindu influence in Java: the 9th century Candi Kalasan near Prambanan, central Java.

of Majapahit once controlled the whole of the archipelago are hard to evaluate; Naerssen (1977) has suggested that it claimed tribute from the whole of Island South-East Asia except for northern Sulawesi and the Philippines, but this may be a substantial exaggeration (Rausa-Gomez 1967; Hall 1968:87). In the Philippines some Sanskrit loans appear to have spread as a result of Malay enterprise after the tenth century (Francisco 1965; Scott 1968), and this period also saw the commencement of extensive trade with China through which the Philippines were drawn increasingly into the wider Indo-Malaysian world.

Some caution is clearly necessary in interpreting the real significance of Indian influence. The great strength and tenacity of Austronesian cultural tradition is evident throughout the whole period, whether in ancient inscriptions in Old Malay or Old Javanese, in the terraced design of the Borobudur, or in certain cosmological concepts (Alkire 1972). The everyday life of the Javanese peasant was probably little changed by the far-off existence of a Hinduised court, and of course one major feature of Hindu society in India, the caste system, has had only a limited impact in South-East Asia. A view that the Austronesian societies allowed in the Indian influences by select invitation only is not without attraction.

Today, the only ethnic group in South-East Asia to have maintained a coherent, even if highly modified, Hindu tradition is the Balinese. Prior to Dutch government this island was divided into a number of rajahships, with rulers and nobles belonging to widespread high-ranking and intermarrying patrilineages. Commoner kin groups have always tended to be localised to individual villages, but commoners also belong to corporate organisations such as temple groups and irrigation societies (*subaks*; Geertz 1972; Meer 1979) which cross-cut lineage and village boundaries. There is also a priesthood of Brahman derivation, but any visitor to Bali will quickly observe that the picturesque and ubiquitous temples owe little to Indian styles of architecture; there are even indications that some of them preserve aspects of a more ancient "megalithic" tradition (Sutaba 1976) which is widespread throughout the Austronesian world, and which received one of its most coherent expressions in late prehistoric Polynesia.

Apart from Hinduism and Buddhism, the only other major religion to affect the archipelago in pre-European times was Islam, and this today has become the national religion of Indonesia and Malaysia. Its spread has been much more recent than that of the Indian religions, and as a result it has a much more coherent history. The major sultanates only preceded the Portuguese by less than a century.

By the eighth century, communities of Arab and Persian Muslims were already settled as traders in Guangzhou (Canton) and other southern Chinese cities (Leslie 1981). However, the spread of Islam in Indonesia occurred several centuries later, and linguistic evidence suggests that the Arabic and Persian loans in Austronesian languages came for the most part directly from India (Gonda 1973; Hall 1977). How the religion came to spread so quickly through the archipelago is not clear, but a combination of trading enterprise, missionary conversion, and the acuity of native rulers who sought power through alliances with well-connected outsiders probably suffices as an explanation (Kumar 1979). By the 14th century a trade network, mainly in Javanese and Malay hands, had been set up to bring spices such as cloves, nutmeg and camphor from the Moluccas (Reid 1980). This, plus the well-established trade network from China through the Philippines and around Borneo, undoubtedly provided an excellent channel for the propagation and spread of Islam. By the late 13th century Islamic influence was well established in northern Sumatra, and a Muslim tombstone found on the north-western coast of this island is believed to date from 1206 (Ambary 1981). During the 14th century a number of Islamic sultanates developed in this region (Miksic 1979), and from 1400 through to the growth of Portuguese power in the early 16th century the spread of Islam took place with great rapidity. Sultanates and trading ports developed in Malacca (Melaka), along the northern coast of Java, all around the Borneo coast (with very important states in Brunei and Banjarmasin), on the island of Jolo in Sulu, and on the islands of Ternate and Tidore off Halmahera. In the early 17th century two more very important trading states were developed by the Makassarese and Buginese of southern Sulawesi (Macknight 1973), but after this the increasing control by European colonial powers seems to have slowed the spread of Islam, until the period of national independence in this century.

The importance of Islam in Indo-Malaysian societies today is clearly not just the result of a single-minded missionary activity, but a reflection of much more fundamental economic changes. During the earlier Indianising period there were certain coastal states which specialised in trading, mainly in Sumatra and Malaya, and which kept the archipelago in contact with the outside world. The archaeological record suggests that these small states were not of great importance (some have a decidedly mythical aspect), and the Javanese civilisations, despite their far more impressive remains, were generally agrarian-based and more concerned with royal prestige than long-distance trade.

The early centuries of the second millennium witnessed some very major transformations in terms of outside interest in the islands of South-East Asia. For one thing, the sheer volume of ceramics imported from China during the Song and later dynasties contrasts starkly with the virtual absence (at least in any quantity) of such material during the first millennium. The trade in spices and "forest products", which earlier was perhaps a rather sporadic affair, also spread to encompass virtually the whole archipelago. The islands were thus rapidly brought into contact with many groups of outsiders — not just Muslims, but with other groups such as Chinese and Thais. There are even some slight hints that ethnic Chinese may have settled in some places as craftsmen prior to the spread of Islam (e.g. Manning *et al.* 1980 for Kota Cina in Sumatra; Cheng 1969 for Sarawak).

The point I wish to make here is that virtually the whole archipelago became connected to the greater Asian world between the tenth and 15th centuries to an extent far greater than in the earlier Indianising period. The spread of Islam was one major reflection of this, and this of course helped to speed up the process during the 14th and early 15th centuries. By 1521 trans-archipelagic trading was established on a frequent and formal basis, as can be seen from the presence of special port officials (*shahbandars*) in Malacca to handle trade from regions as far apart as the Moluccas, Java, Luzon, Banjarmasin and Palembang (Pelras 1981; Andaya and Andaya 1982).

One of the major effects of all this intensified trade and contact was that certain groups were able to take advantage of newly-emerging options in order to expand widely through the archipelago. The Bugis and Makassarese of southern Sulawesi have been the most important of such groups in recent history, but the Malays have had the greatest impact of all, as they had the advantage of a westerly location around the trade highway of the Strait of Malacca which enabled them to make their moves very early. Indeed, the whole phenomenon of the spread of the Islamic sultanates is very much tied in with the spread of Malay language and culture. This does not mean that all the Malay communities of the archipelago result entirely from migrations out of the Malay peninsula; the process has been far more complex and assimilatory than this.

Today, coastal Islamic populations who speak dialects of Malay and who identify themselves as Malays with localised epithets (e.g Brunei Malays, Banjar Malays) form a homogeneous belt of peoples around most of the coastal regions of Borneo, eastern Sumatra and the Malay Peninsula. Had the Javanese not had such highly developed earlier civilisations this island would also have supported many such coastal groups, but the two-way interaction between Javanese and Malay cultures has been so intense here that no such division is really visible. The modern Malay language perhaps descends from a lingua franca which developed along the shore of the Strait of Malacca, especially in the old Srivijayan heartland of south-eastern Sumatra, in southern Malaya, and in the Riau and Lingga Islands. This development cannot be dated with precision, but it must have been underway by at least the time of the foundation of the important sultanate of Malacca in 1414. From this period onwards the Malay language has spread rapidly through the coastal regions of the western archipelago, and both the language and the culture have taken on some decidedly assimilatory characteristics; at the present time people can "enter" Malay culture (*masok Melayu*) by converting to Islam and speaking the Malay language. Hence most of the coastal Malays of Borneo are almost certainly of local origin in a genetic sense (Harrisson 1970b), although ruling classes do often have traditions of foundation marriages with Johor or Malaccan noble families.

The structures of the Moslem sultanates present intricate details which I can hardly hope to summarise here, but I will close this section with a pocket view of Brunei, one of the most important of these trading states (Brown 1970, 1978). During the Song dynasty Brunei was apparently known to the Chinese as P'o-ni, and long before the arrival of Islam it seems to have been developing size and renown, partly on the rich pickings from the trade routes linking southern China and the Strait of Malacca (Bellwood 1978b; Bellwood and Omar 1980; Omar 1981). By 1515 the ruler had converted to Islam (Nicholl 1975), and the rather elaborate ruling bureaucracy, which dominated northern Borneo (in spite of Spanish hostility) until the eventual reduction of its territory by the Brookes of Sarawak in the 19th century, appears to have acquired great wealth from the taxation of riverine districts all the way from Pontianak in western Borneo to the southern Philippines. In 1521 the sultan's court was described by Antonio Pigafetta, a survivor of

Magellan's expedition, in terms which give an impression of considerable wealth and splendour. The Brunei nobles and commoners of today belong to an ethnic category which has been called Brunei Malay since at least sometime in the 19th century, while of a lower social status are the native (non Brunei Malay) populations, some being Muslim and Malay-speaking (the Kedayans), while others are of more varied religious and linguistic affiliation (Bajau, Melanau, Dusun and Murut). The Brunei Malay commoners themselves, who live in and around the riverine town of Bandar Seri Begawan, most probably have an origin through the assimilation of local populations into the high status Malay lifestyle from the early years of the Sultanate.

It will be apparent by now that the bulk of the present-day population of the archipelago, excluding the tribal agricultural groups who are still to be considered, lives a way of life which obviously no longer has much connection with the prehistoric Austronesian past. Furthermore, there is one very important aspect of the past century which must not be overlooked. The population of Indonesia is now over 160 million, of whom about 100 million live in crowded and agriculturally-intensified Java. But the 15th century population of Java was only about 4 million (Sudjoko 1981:3), and in 1815 the Raffles census reported it as 4.6 million; it then increased to 29 million in 1900 (McDonald 1980). The total population of the archipelago between the 16th century and 1820 probably fluctuated around 8 million (C. Geertz 1963; Reid 1980), indicating a level of demographic stability which is certainly not present any more.

III. The Indo-Malaysian Tribal and Agricultural Societies

I will now consider the tribal and small-scale agricultural societies in the third category defined by H. Geertz in 1963 (see beginning of this chapter). In terms of descent ideology, the societies of Sumatra and the Lesser Sundas tend towards unilineal norms (as do the Chams of Vietnam), while those of Malaya, Borneo, Sulawesi and the Philippines are basically cognatic (mainly bilateral, but occasionally with ambilineal descent reckoning). These distinctions are by no means as clear or necessarily as historically significant as some of the pre-1950s writers suggested, and the unilineal–bilateral "dichotomy" may be simply a reflection of other more fundamental differences in social structure. For instance, unilineal (and also ambilineal) kinship reckoning can only be expressed within a framework of corporate descent groups which have a membership greater than that of the individual nuclear or stem family. Societies which do not have such corporate descent groups, such as the hunter–gatherers and some of the horticultural societies of Borneo and the Philippines, are necessarily bilateral.

These observations reflect little more than the logic of descent ideology, and could lead into a discussion of correlations between different aspects of social structure which I am rather unwilling to undertake. Perhaps I can suggest that, amongst the tribal societies, there are correlations for both unilineality and ambilineality with the existence of corporate descent groups, stability of land use and tenure, and relatively high population densities. Conversely, there are apparent correlations between bilateral kinship reckoning and the absence of corporate descent groups, mobility in land use, and relatively low population densities. As far as kinship reckoning is concerned the significant differences may thus be between societies (both unilineal and cognatic) which have corporate land-holding descent groups, and the purely bilateral societies which do not. I will return to this matter briefly at the end of this chapter, although I should add that social anthropologists have not to date been concerned with the study of such correlations on a pan-Austronesian or even a pan-Indo-Malaysian scale, and there may be a great deal of historically significant information in this field which still awaits exposure.

A. The Unilineal Societies

In Sumatra, societies with strong patrilineal tendencies are found in the northern highlands (Aceh, Gayo, Batak), in the south of the island (Rejang), and in the isolated island of Nias off the western coast (Loeb 1935; Lebar 1972). In eastern Indonesia they are found, intermixed with small matrilineal enclaves, from Flores eastwards and in the Moluccas (Loeb and Broek 1947). Examples of this kind of organisation have been described for many groups; for instance, the Bataks of northern Sumatra inhabit villages, formerly defended by embankments, of large patrilineage houses with mat partitions for individual families (Loeb 1935). The island of Nias has a similar system. Originally, each new settlement would perhaps have been founded by members of one patrilineage, but as settlements grow they become more complex; Cunningham (1967) describes a village in Timor which has 78 lineages represented in its population (although six of them form a definite majority). Lineages always become dispersed through processes of growth and fission over time, and many groups, such as the Batak, still call the localised lineages and the larger clans by the same name (*marga*).

Societies with strong matrilineal tendencies include the upland Chams of Vietnam, the Minangkabau of Sumatra and the Minangkabau-derived population of Negri Sembilan in Malaya, and a number of groups amongst the mainly patrilineal societies of the Lesser Sundas and Seram. The best-known group is undoubtedly the Minangkabau of Sumatra, whose village sections are focussed on land- and house-owning matrilineages with uxorilocal residence. Traditionally these matrilineages were grouped into four

Minangkabau-wide clans, and further into two moieties (Loeb 1935). However, status positions are inherited by males, and noble lineages have a very strong tendency towards patrilineal descent.

One interesting feature of matrilineality amongst the Minangkabau of Sumatra and Negri Sembilan has been its survival in the face of Indian and Islamic cultural traditions within which patrilineality has always been stressed. The Minangkabau are not a remote and isolated population; in Sumatra they had Indianised rulers by the 14th century and they have been under the influence of Islam for the last 300 years (H. Geertz 1963; Kumar 1979). In Negri Sembilan the matrilineal system has survived as an enclave within Islamic Malay society since at least the 16th century, and here some aspects of a matrilineal ideology appear to have spread into neighbouring tribal societies such as the Temuan and the Semelai (Carey 1976). Hence the Minangkabau represent a situation where matrilineal descent within corporate land-holding lineages has obviously been very stable in the recent past. But, as with the unilineal–bilateral distinction, it is difficult to show that patrilineal and matrilineal ideologies are always permanent, opposed and non-overlapping.

For instance, most patrilineal societies have a system whereby the groom's family pays brideprice to the family of the bride, and the bride is then "released" by her family to live virilocally. But poorer families often cannot afford to pay brideprice, and then the husband lives uxorilocally, often in a position of low status (e.g. Cunningham 1967 for Timor). Even if brideprice is paid, initial post-marital residence will normally be uxorilocal for a year or so, and this custom also occurs amongst the cognatic societies of Borneo and Sulawesi. In matrilineal societies such as the Minangkabau there is no brideprice, and here the bride's family sometimes pays a dowry to that of the groom, who will live uxorilocally.

Amongst the patrilineal societies it is clear that the ideal of virilocal residence is not always practised, either because brideprice is not paid or because females and their lineages hold important rights to land (as in Mentawai where women own and inherit rice and taro plots). It can be seen, therefore, that in decisions about post-marital residence and child affiliation to one or other parental lineage there will often be a strong tendency towards ambilineality in real life (e.g. Ellen 1978 for the Nuaulu of Seram). So it may come as no surprise to find that the Rejang of Sumatra turned from a patrilineal and virilocal ideology towards matrilineality around 1930 after brideprice payments were eliminated owing to economic circumstances and pressure from Islam (Lebar 1972:32, quoting Jaspan). In western Timor and eastern Flores there are also situations where very closely related ethnic groups can have either patrilineal or matrilineal tendencies (Schulte Nordholt 1971; Metzner 1982).

It is apparent from this that fluctuation from one norm towards the other can occur quite rapidly in some circumstances, although I hesitate to theorise about general causes or to postulate whether the role of brideprice is generally one of cause or effect. But it is necessary to warn against a view that the patrilineal and matrilineal ideologies represent ancient and long-lasting differences between different Austronesian societies.

B. The Cognatic Societies

Cognatic societies which practise shifting cultivation with low population densities are found throughout large parts of Borneo, Sulawesi, the Philippines and Malaya. Many of the Borneo societies still inhabit distinctive raised longhouses with adjoined family living quarters linked by a common verandah, although this tradition is rapidly disappearing today. In the egalitarian and truly bilateral societies without descent groups, such as the Dusun of Sabah (Appell 1978) and the Iban of Sarawak (Freeman 1960, 1981), the individual two or three generation families form independent corporate groups who can make alliances with other families for decisions concerning residence and land use. Amongst the Iban the land- and property-owning family is called a *bilek*, and it survives from generation to generation as new members are born or join through marriage. Iban longhouses can hold up to 50 *bilek* families living in side-by-side dwelling apartments facing on to a shared verandah — the whole structure being up to 200 m long. Families can move from one longhouse to another if they wish; some villages consist of just one such structure, others of two or more.

The Iban do, however, represent one pole of Borneo variation, since cognatic land-holding descent groups of greater generational depth are sometimes found in other societies; for instance among the Maanyan of Kalimantan (Hudson and Hudson 1978) and the longhouse-dwelling Selako (Schneider 1978). From the available ethnographies it seems that a variable patterning of independent family units and larger descent groups also occurs in Sulawesi, although here there is a tendency for related families to share multi-family houses, rather than to build independent units in longhouses (Downs 1956; H. Geertz 1963; Lebar 1972). Basically, the rather fluid cognatic social structures characteristic of societies such as the Dusun and the Iban seem to be well adapted to situations where land and labour are not in short supply (Frake 1956), and it is interesting to note that larger corporate descent groups can develop in societies of this type in modern situations of cash-cropping, especially of rubber, where land rights become more permanent and where a larger pool of labour is required (Miles 1972).

C. Political Integration and Ranking

The Indo-Malaysian tribal societies exhibit relatively small-scale systems of political integration and ranking. Many are basically alliances between egalitarian and independent villages, others are focussed on ranked lineage systems which encompass one or more villages, or a territorial unit such as a river valley. There is no indication that true states with specialised bureaucracies and the powers to maintain allegiance by force developed anywhere in the region before the Indian and Islamic periods. However, prior to such contacts it is possible that Indo-Malaysian societies evolved in some places (Java?) into small-scale ranked chiefdoms or "domains" similar to those of Micronesia and Polynesia (although perhaps lacking some of the more extreme expressions of chiefly divinity and power frequently recorded in 18th century Polynesia).

Ranking in Indo-Malysian tribal societies is based on a number of principles, the main one being that the descendants of the group which founded a settlement and first cleared the land will tend to preserve high status. So we have a kind of "founder principle" which can be applied to the ranking of lineages, whether unilineal or ambilineal, but this ranking is also normally open to constant rearrangement through individual cleverness and the manipulation of wealth. Rank can therefore be both inherited and achieved in a great many societies.

High-ranking founder lineages provide the incumbents for positions of secular and religious power in many societies — such persons have an important say in village affairs, are entitled to occasional prestations of food and labour from their "subjects", and normally control decisions about land use within the group territory. These lineages generally display their status through the ownership of wealth items — Chinese jars, ancient beads, megalithic monuments, fine weapons or drums, and so forth. Another kind of wealth is expressed through success in agriculture and the raising of livestock, the products of which can be used in prestige feasting. A powerful lineage can also reinforce its position through intermarriage with members of high-ranking lineages in other regions; this procedure has the double function of setting nobles apart from commoners and of expanding valuable alliances. Brideprice also often increases in value with rank; this can reinforce tendencies towards high-rank endogamy, and it can enable powerful lineages to increase their manpower by requiring males unable to meet the necessary payments to reside uxorilocally (e.g. Forth 1981 for eastern Sumba).

Such processes of rank enhancement might give the impression that a successful lineage, if it wished, could expand its power almost indefinitely. This is most certainly not the case. Lineage affiliations in real life are notoriously complex, oral genealogies can be manipulated, families wax and wane in terms of wealth and size, and, more importantly, as soon as one lineage leader shows signs of increasing power in an unpopular way there will either be fission or a revolt (as discussed in detail by Leach, 1954, for societies of a similar level of organisation in Burma). A state cannot develop from a tribal society unless the emerging leaders can monopolise power and convert the network of military and economic alliances between tribal sections into a centripetal flow towards themselves. This never happened anywhere in the Austronesian world until the period of the Indianised states of the middle and late first millennium AD.

Turning now to look at the expressions of rank and class and their supporting ideologies throughout the tribal regions of the archipelago, one finds that societies tend to be fairly egalitarian in central Malaya and parts of Borneo, Sulawesi and the Philippines, where population densities are low and where there is a dependence on shifting cultivation with bilateral organisation and considerable family mobility. Villages are normally independent of each other, and leadership is frequently by election rather than by inheritance within a separate class of nobles. As groups come to depend more on permanent land-holdings for wet rice or tree crops (as in the Sunda islands) the separation of noble and commoner classes becomes more marked, and this is especially true for those societies which have had close associations with the Islamic sultanates and the networks of international trade. The latter of course have provided many of the prestigious wealth items which so frequently provide material support for rank. In general (see beginning of this section), it is apparent that the existence of rank and class divisions in the tribal societies tends to correlate with the existence of corporate descent groups of unilineal or ambilineal type, since it is between such groups that differential statuses are displayed. However, it is not true to assume that all bilateral societies necessarily have no class structure; ranking can be maintained within a society with no corporate group structure beyond the level of the single household, as amongst the Kayan of central Borneo (Rousseau 1978).

Amongst the relatively egalitarian societies with their autonomous village structures there is considerable local variation. The Austro-Asiatic-speaking Senoi of Malaya dwell in villages which are led mainly by councils of influential elders or by elected headmen (Leber *et al.* 1964; Dentan 1968), as do the Malay-speaking Jakun and Temuan (Carey 1976), although in the latter groups there are now district headmen as a result of Islamic Malay influence. Many groups in Sulawesi and Borneo have elected headmen and other non-hereditable leadership positions at the village level, and one group in this category is the Iban of Sarawak.

The Iban have attracted much interest owing to their phenomenal rate of expansion from the Kapuas Basin of western Kalimantan through vast areas of Sarawak within the past 400 years. By 1850 they had expanded to settle most of the Rejang Basin (St John 1974), and during the late 19th century they continued onwards to encroach upon the borders of Brunei. Their expansion involved the clearance for shifting rice cultivation of enormous areas of virgin equatorial rainforest, and Freeman (1955:25) reports the case of one *bilek* family which moved over 300 km in one lifetime. McKinley (1978) and King (1976) have suggested that this expansion was not simply due to population pressure or shortage of land, and King believes that the values and beliefs connected with the need to acquire human heads to increase health, prosperity and status may also have been significant.

Yet, despite the Iban successes in colonisation and in assimilating other groups, they never had permanent leaders until they came firmly under the control of the Brooke government after 1841 (Brown 1978; Freeman 1981). Their society was basically classless and egalitarian; according to Freeman (1981) each longhouse had non-hereditary guardians or leaders for a number of specific spheres of activity, including *adat* law, warfare, and the opening up of new lands. Men achieved these statuses through individual prowess and charisma, and through success in agriculture and the getting of heads. War captives were generally adopted into *bilek* families, rather than condemned to a slave class as amongst other more stratified Borneo societies such as the Kayan.

Let us turn now to examine some of the more stratified tribal societies of the region. I have already noted the very widespread principle that descendants of founder lineages tend to be of high rank and to control many of the important decision-making positions. Some groups in Sumatra use titles of Indian origin for high-ranking persons (for example the Singa Maharaja of some Batak groups), but such occurrences do not alter the basic observation that systems of rank and class are very widespread in Austronesian societies (particularly in Oceania), and they must in some form be of great antiquity.

In the unilineal societies of Sumatra and the Lesser Sundas the district and village leaders are drawn from high-ranking lineages, and they are often entitled to labour services from commoners as well as food shares (e.g. Loeb 1935 for the Bataks). If there are district titles then their occupants are generally drawn from lineages which have attained very high rank and which are not localised to particular villages. High-rank endogamy has often developed, and many ethnographic societies had noble, commoner and slave (war captive and debtor) classes (e.g. Cunningham 1967 for the Atoni of Timor, Forth 1981 for eastern Sumba). Fox (1977a) has described the numerous small states (or "petty feuding domains") of the past few centuries on Roti and Savu; the hierarchies here were based on ranked patrilineages, and on Roti 12 of these small states were in existence in 1690 — during the 19th century the number increased to 18. The Savu states were linked by the sharing of island-wide lunar rituals, and their leaders had heavily ritualised functions; on Roti there appears to have been less integration between the units. However, both Fox (1977a) and Forman (1977) have stressed that these localised hierarchies and their supporting tribute-collecting arrangements have probably been intensified by Portuguese and Dutch trade and colonial interference.

One society which does present an interesting and presumably indigenous system of ranking is that of southern Nias, off the western coast of Sumatra (Loeb 1935; Suzuki 1959; Schnitger 1964). Village chiefs here held hereditary titles controlled by noble patrilineages, and there was also an important hereditary male priesthood. The massive chiefs' houses and the unique megalithic monuments of Nias have long been famous as material creations of this intensely ranked society, and it appears that Nias chiefs were considered as semi-divine, like some of their Polynesian counterparts. They became powerful spirits after their deaths, and only they were allowed to wear gold ornaments and to hold inter-village feasts. Chiefly status for the living and the dead was the motivation behind the creation of the spectacular stone structures, and chiefs were also able to keep slaves.

The competitive feasting which bolstered chiefly status on Nias involved great prestations of wealth, especially of pigs, of which up to 1500 were killed in reported cases. Similar periodic and massive pig slaughters are also characteristic of many societies in the New Guinea Highlands and they may once have been more common in Indonesia; the Islamic prohibitions against eating pork, which never reached Nias, have of course had a great impact elsewhere in this region. Nias chiefs could also accumulate and loan wealth with similar profit motives (see Suzuki 1959:40–1) to those found in Melanesia, and I suspect that this type of competitive achievement imposed on a basic system of hereditary ranking was once characteristic of many ancient Austronesian societies.

Some of the cognatic societies of Borneo also have class systems and aristocracies based on inheritance, family alliances and the ownership of highly-valued objects. Most traditional forms of leadership operate at the longhouse or village rather than the district level, but amongst some groups, such as the Kenyah, the Kayan and the Maloh, strong ruling classes emerged in the past which were able to demand labour, impose fines on commoners and restrict their movements, and to hold slaves (Hose and McDougall 1912; Lebar 1972; King 1978). The Kayan in particular, despite their low population density, maintained three or four social strata from nobles to slaves (Rousseau 1978), and the chiefs retained much of their status through intermarriage with chiefly families in other villages, while commoners tended to be village-endogamous. Slave sacrifice on the death of a chief (as in Nias) is also reported to have occurred amongst the Kayan and the Melanau of Sarawak (St John 1974).

IV. Other Features of Austronesian Tribal Societies

It is not my purpose here to list all the material correlations of the traditional tribal societies in the archipelago, but some features drawn from the ethnographic record are of obvious interest for prehistory. Settlements, for instance, are normally focussed on village-type nucleations for social reasons and (in the past) for defence. Houses (Figs 5.3–6) are almost universally rectangular, with the great longhouses of Borneo at the upper end of the size range — up to 200 m long and sometimes raised 10 m off the ground. The Minangkabau, Batak and Toraja have particularly fine multi-family houses with some superb artwork, but in most coastal areas where outside influences have been strong much smaller nuclear or extended-family houses are the norm. Circular houses are not common, but they are constructed in Enggano, western Flores, and by the Atoni of Timor.

Most tribal villages in the archipelago also had in the past one or more special houses in which sacred paraphernalia such as hunted heads, ancestor relics, and lineage symbols and valuables were kept. Sacred storage houses of this kind often served also as temples and as foci for meetings; the small god houses described for the Simalungun Bataks of Sumatra by Bartlett (1934) were inside fenced enclosures which were also used for the growing of sacred plants and for assemblies — functions rather like those of the *marae* of Polynesia. Bartlett, incidentally, regarded these Batak sacred houses as pre-Islamic survivals, and the widespread distribution of such structures in the Indo-Malaysian Archipelago and in Oceania argues for their great antiquity.

Amongst items of portable material culture it should be noted that most ethnographic communities either made or had trade-access to pottery (see Ellen and Glover 1974 for the Moluccas) and iron (Marschall 1968). The clothing of early Austronesian societies was of barkcloth, beaten from the

Fig. 5.3. An Iban longhouse at Simanggang on the Batang Lupar, Sarawak. Photo by Hedda Morrison.

Fig. 5.4. Batak houses near Lake Toba, northern Sumatra.

inner bark of a number of local trees such as Manila hemp, paper mulberry, and breadfruit, but use of the backstrap loom for weaving has spread through most parts of the archipelago and into parts of western Oceania since at least Proto-Western-Malayo-Polynesian times (see Chapter 4, Section IIIB). Bows and arrows and spears are of at least proto-Austronesian antiquity, but the blowpipe is probably more recent. This device, used with poisoned darts or clay pellets, was developed in or around Borneo according to Jett (1970). It was used throughout the archipelago and taken, presumably by the initial Austronesian settlers, to Madagascar (Fig. 5.7). The blowpipe has also been adopted by the Austro-Asiatic speaking Negritos and Senoi of Malaya, although the Philippine Negritos have retained the bow. To my knowledge the pellet bow of India and Mainland South-East Asia has never been used in the South-East Asian islands.

Tattooing is a fairly universal trait in the Austronesian world (see Chapter 3, Fig. 3.5); it has spread to the Senoi of Malaya (who have also preserved a more ancient tradition of body painting), and has even been retained by the isolated Tasaday of Mindanao. Murut men in northern Borneo traditionally tattooed stars on their shoulders to denote captured heads (Rutter 1929). Deformation of the skulls of infants has not been widely reported, but the Melanau of Sarawak depressed the foreheads of young girls, the people of Minahasa (north Sulawesi) practised cradleboarding (Hickson 1889:213),

Fig. 5.5. Circular Atoni house, South Amanuban, western Timor. Photo by James Fox.

Fig. 5.6. Toraja houses decorated with buffalo carvings and horns, Palawan village, central Sulawesi. Photo by Hedda Morrison.

and Maceda (1974) reports cases of fairly recent head deformation and trepanation from the Philippines. The practice of headhunting was widespread in the larger islands (it would clearly have been impractical on the smallest ones), and I have already mentioned its association with status and expansion amongst the Iban. Downs (1955) reports that the Bare'e Toraja of Sulawesi used to form raiding parties of 10 to 20 men to take heads for the rituals associated with mourning ceremonies, to consecrate sacred houses, and to prove bravery. Mourning rituals were also a major stimulus for headhunting in Borneo.

Most groups in the archipelago who have not been influenced heavily by Indian, Islamic or Christian traditions practise secondary forms of burial, in which the defleshed bones are eventually stored in a receptacle of some kind. Interesting ethnographic examples of such receptacles include: the stone sarcophagi and stone urns of the Bataks of Sumatra and the Minahasans of

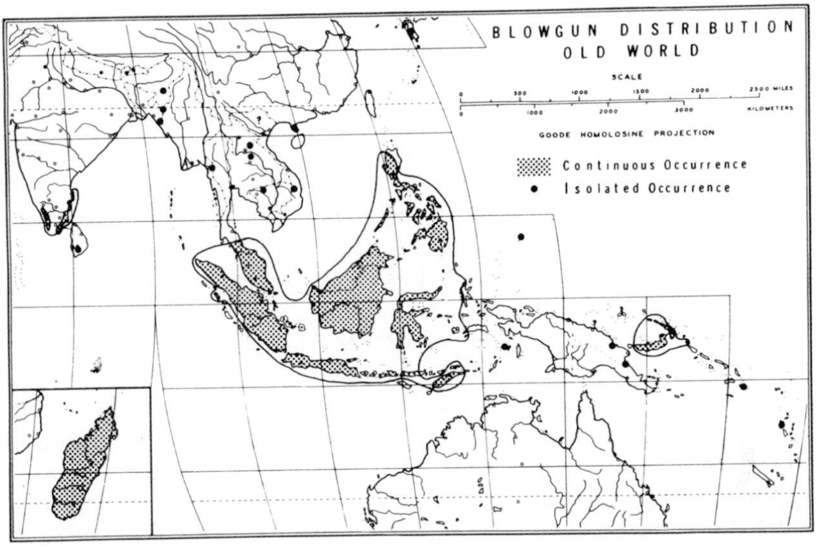

Fig. 5.7. The distribution of the blowgun. From Jett 1970. Courtesy: Association of American Geographers; S. C. Jett.

northern Sulawesi (Bellwood 1978a: Figure 8.24; Dalrymple 1984); the common use of large stoneware jars, often cut open to take crouched primary burials, in Borneo (e.g. Harrisson 1962 for the Kelabits; Massing 1981 for the Benuaq of Kalimantan; Evans 1923); the use of log coffins in Borneo (Hose and McDougall 1912; Hose 1926) and by the Toraja (Downs 1956); and the common use of megalithic structures, particularly in Borneo and the Lesser Sundas (Perry 1918; Schneeberger 1979). The total range of variation here is of course absolutely enormous, despite the very common occurrence of a two-stage (secondary) burial ritual. Even in Java there are indications that "charnel houses" raised on posts were used for secondary burial prior to the period of Indianisation (Stutterheim 1956).

A. The Comparative Reconstruction of Early Austronesian Society

In the final section of this chapter I will present observations from comparative ethnology to supplement the list of features reconstructed linguistically for early Austronesian society in Chapter 4. The problem can be approached in two ways — either by broad pan-Austronesian comparisons, or by trying to find isolated societies which might have preserved earlier cultural patterns. I will examine the second approach first, if only to reject it totally. I have already shown that isolated hunter–gatherer groups such as the Tasaday and

Penan are not valid candidates for ancient reconstructions, and neither are the presumably long-isolated societies of Mentawai and Enggano off the western coast of Sumatra. Traditionally, the Mentawaians lacked betel chewing, pottery, metal, rice and the blowpipe, and the now virtually extinct people of Enggano had a similar list of absences which also included weaving and cattle. Both groups used stone tools and depended on taro cultivation until recent times (Loeb 1935; Lebar 1972). Yet one has only to examine the linguistic list of early Austronesian reconstructions (see Chapter 4, Table 4.2) to see straight away that while metals, the blowpipe, cattle and possibly weaving are relatively recent in the archipelago, three of the items (pottery, betel chewing and rice) are of at least Proto-Malayo-Polynesian antiquity. So these cultures have presumably lost these three items during their ancestry and cannot be fossilised pre-pottery or pre-rice survivals. They clearly reflect local adaptation and some loss of cultural items rather than a totally pristine and conservative ancient stratum.

Broader comparative reconstructions are of more value, but there are pitfalls. For instance, simple observations that pile houses, headhunting and megaliths are widespread are of little assistance in indicating antiquity without linguistic support, and when such entities are studied in isolation they can give peculiar results. I need hardly stress the impracticability of Perry's view (1918) that megalithic monuments in Indonesia were introduced by sun-worshipping "stone-using immigrants".

However, when turning to concepts and customs in the religious and social spheres, where simple trait-diffusion is perhaps less likely, we can make some headway. In the realm of religion it is clear that beliefs centred on spirit animism and ancestor cults are so widespread and deep-seated that they must be of great antiquity. Shamans (that is inspirational priests or mediums who are able to converse with spirits through trances) are particularly widespread in Austronesian societies, although this custom has apparently disappeared in some of the Lesser Sundas (Kennedy 1937). A dualism of male sky (for example Nias *Lowalangi*, Maori *Rangi*) and female earth deities, concepts of supernatural and mystical power (*mana* in Polynesia, *semangat* in Malay; Winstedt 1953:19) and taboo (*tabu* in Polynesia, *rebu* in Batak; Loeb 1935:94–5) are also virtually pan-Austronesian. Blust (1981c) has recently presented a linguistic reconstruction for a Proto-Austronesian term referring to supernatural punishment for offending ancestors or superior persons (that is breaking a taboo), and he has also traced other ritual activities to possible ancient borrowing from Negrito societies.

On the matter of status positions in early Austronesian society, Blust (1980) has reconstructed a Proto-Malayo-Polynesian term *datu* for a lineage official, and Pawley (1981) has suggested that Proto-Oceanic society was stratified with terms for hereditary chief, firstborn son of a chief and a person of low status. Historical evidence from Java shows that the term *raku* or *datu* (*raka* in the Kalasan inscription of AD 778) was applied to a head of a district grouping of several villages (Naerssen 1977; see also Meer 1979; Wisseman 1977). The implication of this is that central Javanese society in the immediate pre-Sailendra period was ordered into a number of embryonic small states or chiefdoms, although this is perhaps no more than would be expected at this period given subsequent developments in this region.

I will turn finally to the reconstruction of aspects of Proto-Austronesian social organisation. Goodenough (1955) has compared societies in the Philippines and Oceania to reconstruct a cognatic type of society for this early phase, possibly with land-holding ambilineal descent groups. More recently, Blust (1980) has presented a totally different reconstruction based on the Lesser Sunda evidence as interpreted by Wouden (1968). The details of this are complex, but basically he thinks that early Austronesian societies were organised around a double unilineal descent system, with each person belonging to a separate exogamous matrilineal and patrilineal lineage. Each society would have had four maximal lineages — two matrilineal and two patrilineal — which would have been paired (one of each) into two exogamous moieties.

Both these reconstructions are in obvious opposition, and it is not easy to select one or the other as being most plausible. I tend to favour Goodenough's reconstruction since most Austronesian societies, outside the region of unilineal tendency in the Lesser Sundas, Melanesia and Micronesia, are predominantly cognatic today. Furthermore, most commentators on Blust's article in *Current Anthropology* (1980) were clearly unwilling to adopt a strongly unilineal reconstruction. In fact, it is quite possible that the earliest Austronesian societies used both cognatic and unilineal ideologies in different contexts, as do many tribal Austronesian societies and even more cosmopolitan groups such as the Balinese today. Tendencies towards unilineal and ambilineal descent reckoning may therefore have developed in those societies which evolved ranked corporate groups under situations of high population density and permanency of land use. Since I have already discussed such correlations in this chapter I will not pursue them further, but I think it should be stressed that proto-Austronesian society, whatever its precise nature, must have held the seeds of all the traditional and non-outsider imposed variations which are evident today (see also Fox 1985).

Another final possibility which may be significant for eastern Indonesia (and also Melanesia) is that the unilineal tendencies amongst Austronesian societies could reflect very strong influences from the pre-Austronesian populations of the region. These were presumably related to the ancestors of the present Papuan-speaking and predominantly unilineal populations of New Guinea and western Melanesia. Close relationships between some aspects of the societies of eastern Indonesia and New Guinea have also been pointed out by Lebar (1972:124) and Kennedy (1937). However, the issue is complex and may never be fully resolved; I can only present here my own rather intuitive views on the matter.

6
The Hoabinhians and their Island Contemporaries

I will now turn to the archaeological record of the Late Pleistocene and early Holocene periods in the Indo-Malaysian Archipelago. In this time-span there are a number of long-occupied, radiocarbon-dated and stratified sites (for locations see Chapter 3, Fig. 3.10 and Fig. 6.1), and all associated human remains are of modern physical type. Prior to about 5000 years ago all industries in the region comprised exclusively flaked and not ground stone tools (although Niah in Sarawak may be an exception, see below), and the rather limited economic evidence at present available suggests a universal economy of hunting and gathering. During the Holocene the stone tool industries became more varied, and after 3000 BC new items, of which pottery and fully ground stone adzes are the most visible, spread through the region. As I have shown in Chapter 4 the linguistic evidence clearly attests a slow expansion of Austronesian-speaking agricultural groups during the last five millennia, but as I have stressed before this expansion was not a geographically unified process of replacement. The hunting and gathering lifestyle has been progressively eroded but it has certainly never disappeared entirely, and flaked stone tools continued to be used by both hunting and gathering and agricultural groups until the recent past in some areas. Hence in recent millennia different technologies and economies could and did occur in neighbouring and contemporary sites in a mosaic-like fashion (Hutterer 1976). The archaeological record has to be considered partly in terms of synchronic regional variation, and not totally in terms of pan-archipelagic technological and economic phases.

Before going further, it is necessary to give a brief recapitulation of the palaeoenvironmental evidence from the archipelago, particularly that which pertains to the last 20 000 years within which the great bulk of the dated sites lie (see Chapter 1, Section IVD). The most dramatic environmental changes would undoubtedly have been caused, particularly in the Sundaland region, by the rise in sea-level of perhaps 130 m between approximately 15 000 and

Fig. 6.1. Major archaeological sites in Peninsular Malaya.

8000 years ago. Apart from drowning an unknown number of coastal archaeological sites, to the obvious detriment of modern prehistoric studies, this change carved the Sundaland continent into the islands which exist today, and in the presumed absence at this time of a developed voyaging technology it would have produced a number of separate pools of human population. Economically the change would have had certain benefits, since it certainly increased the length and environmental variety of coastline, but there might also have been less favourable changes, particularly through the expansion of rainforest with the prevailing warmer and wetter climate.

Although the post-glacial climatic amelioration perhaps had little effect in the core regions of the equatorial rainforest, it would presumably have had more impact on the fringing areas of seasonal climate, where monsoon forest or parkland vegetation may have been more extensive during the last glacial period. An increasing density of vegetation in these areas would have affected hunting populations through a diminution in mammal biomass, which decreases dramatically as one moves from optimal savanna conditions, through parkland, towards rainforest. For instance, modern densities of wild banteng cattle range from about 10–15 animals per ha in Javan savanna grasslands down to only 1–2 animals per ha in rainforests (Pfeffer 1974). Rainforest faunas present additional problems in that animals rarely herd together and many species are arboreal, and so are more difficult to hunt. This atomistic pattern also characterises rainforest vegetation, with many species mixed in a mosaic of small numbers of individuals, rather than in large stands. Such patterns tend to promote non-specialised economies and low population densities amongst hunting and gathering populations, and if the archaeological record is taken at face value it suggests strongly that rainforest occupation is very much a Holocene adaptation, perhaps as a result of increasing population pressure in the more favourable but shrinking monsoon forest and parkland regions, and perhaps also owing to the development of new methods of trapping and subsistence.

This may not mean that the equatorial rainforests were entirely unoccupied during the Pleistocene. However, there are some interesting lacunae in the archaeological evidence from these regions, and I suspect that modern Indo-Malaysian hunters and gatherers, who have survived in the more densely forested equatorial parts of the archipelago, are not entirely representative of the bulk of the hunting societies who would have been concentrated more in the regions of seasonal climate in the Late Pleistocene. Perhaps it is no coincidence that most of the flaked stone assemblages come from such seasonally dry regions as central Java, southern Sulawesi, the Lesser Sundas and parts of the Philippines. In Borneo there clearly was last glacial occupation (perhaps under drier climatic conditions) in near-coastal caves and around at least one near-coastal lake (see below), but I am inclined to doubt that the densely forested interior was inhabited very much, if at all, prior to Austronesian settlement — there are no physical or cultural traces of earlier peoples, and so far no Pleistocene archaeological assemblages in the deep interior regions of the island (e.g. Harrisson 1970a:21; Hanbury-Tenison 1980). A similar situation applies in Sumatra and Malaya, although the inland forests of Malaya were settled widely by Hoabinhians from the beginning of the Holocene.

I. Malaya and Mainland South-East Asia: The Hoabinhian

Prior to Austronesian settlement the Malay Peninsula and the adjacent coasts of north-eastern Sumatra belonged culturally to the mainland of South-East Asia, rather than to the islands. From about 10 000 years ago Hoabinhian assemblages appeared throughout this region, and there seems little reason to doubt that in Malaya they were made by populations ancestral to the present Austro-Asiatic-speaking *orang asli* (Negritos and Senoi, Solheim 1980). These groups ceased to make flaked stone tools long before recorded history, but the Negritos have preserved a hunting and gathering way of life which may be regarded as a modified descendant of the inland Hoabinhian economy.

The term "Hoabinhian" has been in use since the 1920s to refer to a stone tool industry characterised by distinctive pebble tools. Hoabinhian sites are found all over the mainland of South-East Asia, westwards to Burma and northwards to the southern provinces of China and perhaps Taiwan. So far, all radiocarbon-dated Hoabinhian assemblages fall between 14 000 and 3000 years ago, and it is possible that some Hoabinhian tool manufacture continued into even more recent times in some regions. Unfortunately, the Late Pleistocene ancestry of the Hoabinhian remains obscure, except in northern Vietnam where an antecedent pebble tool industry termed the Sonviian has been dated back to about 23 000 bc (Ha Van Tan 1978, 1980, 1985a). Another ancestral industry may occur in the undated lower levels of the cave of Sai Yok in western Thailand (Heekeren and Knuth 1967).

The Hoabinhian is therefore very much a terminal Pleistocene and Holocene phenomenon, and while its ultimate ancestry may be vague there seems little reason to doubt that it is indigenously South-East Asian. In Malaya and Sumatra the Hoabinhian does not appear to extend back in time for more than 10 000 years, and the prehistoric record prior to this date is virtually a complete blank. Again the question arises of whether the rainforests of this region were settled before this time, or were people living only along the now drowned coastlines?

Hoabinhian sites are found mostly in rock-shelters, but there are a few coastal shell middens in Sumatra, Malaya and northern Vietnam which seem to belong to the present period of sea-level (that is post 6000 BC). In addition, some inland non-midden open sites have been reported from Sumatra, eastern Malaya and northern Thailand. However, the excavation record is highly skewed towards inland shelters, and the coastal middens in Malaya and Sumatra have never been satisfactorily investigated; most have now been destroyed for lime-kilns.

The characteristic tool types of the Hoabinhian are unifacially or bifacially flaked flat river pebbles of an approximate fist size, often with cutting edges all around their peripheries (Fig. 6.2). They come in a variety of shapes from

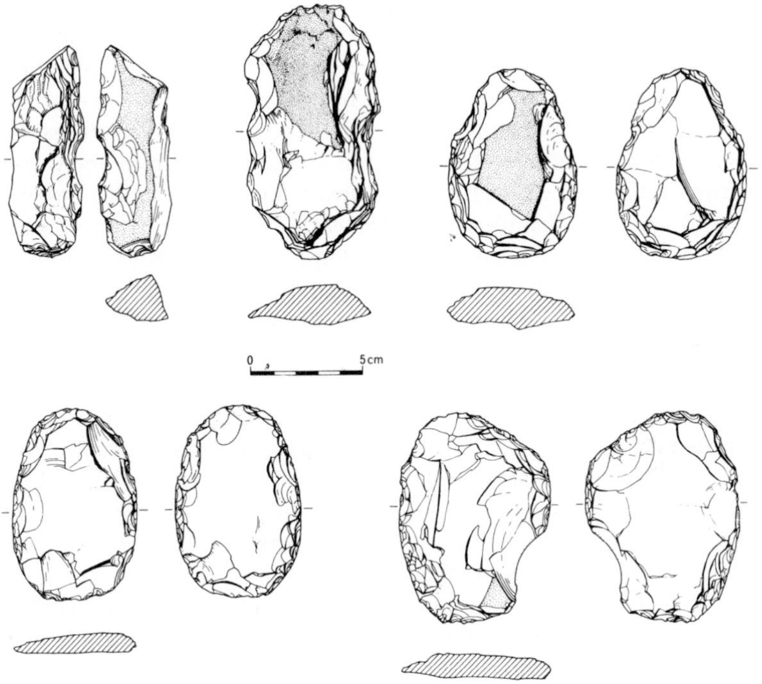

Fig. 6.2. Hoabinhian tools from Gua Cha. Note the incipient waisting on some.

oval through rectangular to triangular, and some occasionally have waisted forms. Bifacially worked tools appear to predominate in some Malayan sites, but unifacial forms, according to the rather inadequate reports available, predominate elsewhere. The industry (or technocomplex, after Gorman 1971) has been excavated most prolifically in the limestone massifs of northern Vietnam, where it is associated with flake tools, bone points and spatulae, stone mortars and pounders of various sizes, and flexed burials often dusted with hematite. In Vietnam there is considerable industrial variation within the Hoabinhian time-span, and many sites also have edge-ground tools and pottery in their upper layers. These present some problems in interpretation, and it is possible that many major cases of stratigraphic disturbance have gone unrecorded (Matthews 1965), particularly in the older excavations. However, taking the published record at face value, it must be accepted that edge-ground tools and pottery did appear in late Hoabinhian contexts prior to the appearance of the more formal polished adze and pottery associations which most South-East Asian archaeologists, including myself, term "Neolithic".

Let me illustrate this in more detail. In Vietnam, a large number of recent radiocarbon dates, mostly from freshwater shells, indicate that the Hoabinhian falls between about 10 000 and 5000 bc (Meacham 1976–8; Bayard 1980; Ha Van Tan 1980). Overlapping with this is a related industry known as the Bacsonian, which is in reality little more than an aspect of the Hoabinhian with an occurrence of edge-ground tools, and this dates from about 9000 bc onwards. In Vietnam edge-grinding is clearly an early Holocene innovation, and I will return to the question of the early distribution of this technique later. Pottery (mostly plain or vine/mat impressed rather than cord-marked) was also widespread in Vietnam by at least 4000 BC, but at present there is no good evidence to suggest how far back it goes into the Hoabinhian–Bacsonian matrix.

Another major question concerns the role of the Hoabinhian in the development of agriculture in South-East Asia. It should be noted that the Hoabinhian technocomplex covered a vast area, extending virtually from the equator in Sumatra to beyond the Tropic of Cancer in southern China. In the far southern regions I remain fairly convinced that it had no agricultural status, but there can be less certainty for northern Vietnam and northern Thailand. On this question there are still only the results of Gorman's excavations in Spirit Cave in north-western Thailand (Gorman 1970, 1971; Glover 1977b:11–17), where remains of a number of edible but not necessarily cultivated fruits and legumes appeared in terminal Pleistocene Hoabinhian levels. Furthermore, an important Neolithic assemblage of cord-marked pottery, polished adzes, and slate knives was added to the continuing Hoabinhian tools during the seventh millennium BC. Gorman and Charoenwongsa (in press) have tentatively suggested that the cultivation of annual rice may have been associated with this later transitional phase of the northern Hoabinhian, and there may be a hint here of a very important stage in South-East Asian prehistory — a stage of initial cereal cultivation which attained its most coherent archaeological expression amongst the Neolithic cultures of southern China, south of the Yangtze River.

A. Malaya

Having given this contextual introduction to the Hoabinhian, I will now turn to its most southerly expressions in Malaya (see Fig. 6.1) and Sumatra. In Malaya a number of inland Hoabinhian caves and shelters have been excavated in the many limestone massifs scattered through the northern states of Perlis, Kedah, Perak, Pahang and Kelantan, and coastal shell middens once existed in the north-western states of Pinang and Perak. The majority of sites were excavated during the 1920s and 1930s, and the reports can only be described as brief. However, the very important site of Gua Cha

Fig. 6.3. The rock-shelter of Gua Cha, Kelantan, during excavations in 1979. Courtesy: National Museum, Kuala Lumpur.

in Kelantan, excavated in 1954 and more recently by a Malaysian National Museum team in 1979, has produced a firm record.

This massive limestone rock-shelter (Fig. 6.3) lies in a remote inland region of equatorial rainforest on the bank of the Nenggiri River, a tributary of the Kelantan River which flows into the sea at Kota Bharu. In 1954 three large trenches were excavated in the shelter by Sieveking, who published a detailed report on the contents of the Neolithic layers (Sieveking 1954), but gave only stratigraphical observations on the underlying Hoabinhian. In order to throw light on a number of questions concerning the Hoabinhian the shelter was excavated on a small scale again in 1979, by Adi Taha of the Malaysian National Museum, who at that time was doing postgraduate research under my supervision at the Australian National University (Adi 1981; Bellwood and Adi 1981). I will combine the results of both excavations here.

The Hoabinhian layers at Gua Cha are up to 170 cm thick, and rest on sterile alluvial deposits. According to sediment analyses by Philip Hughes the Hoabinhian deposit itself is also of alluvial origin, and was clearly formed by occasional flooding of the shelter by the neighbouring river (Adi 1981: Appendix). The industry is a surprisingly homogeneous collection of bifacially flaked flat river pebbles (see Fig. 6.2), and it has a minority component of cruder pebble tools together with a few utilised and waste flakes, and a number of river pebbles which may have served for crushing and pounding — some have hematite stains. Bone tools were absent, despite their occurrence

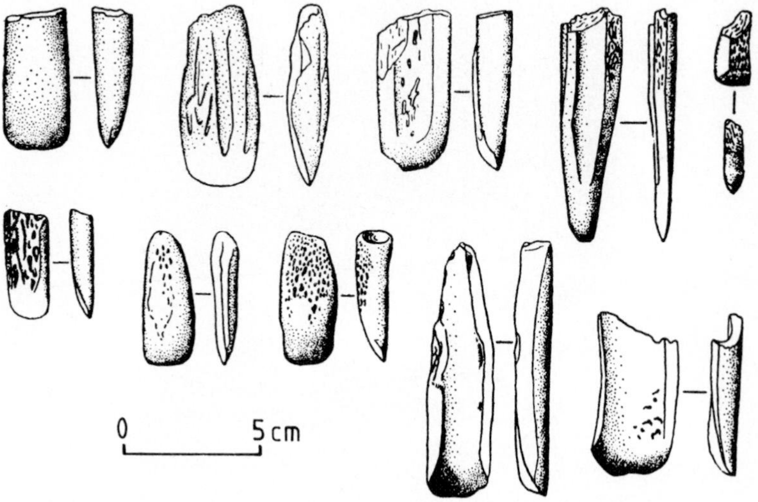

Fig. 6.4. Spatulate bone tools from Gua Bintong, Perlis. From Collings 1937a. Courtesy: National Museum of Singapore.

at other Malayan sites such as Gua Bintong in Perlis (Fig. 6.4). The homogeneity and emphasis on bifacial working of the Gua Cha industry are both quite striking, and radiocarbon dates indicate a commencement soon after 10 000 years ago, and a fairly decisive termination a little before 1000 BC. A number of primary flexed or secondary burials had been placed in the Hoabinhian deposits; none contained certain grave goods, but one flexed young male excavated in 1979 (Fig. 6.5) had a stone-slab pillow and a body cover of tufa chunks dusted with hematite, and another unexcavated burial lay beneath two limestone slabs.

The diet and economy of the Gua Cha Hoabinhians was investigated from three angles. Firstly, an examination by Bulbeck (1982) of the occurrence of caries in the teeth of the burials excavated in 1979 suggested considerable consumption of sweet foods such as fruits and honey. Secondly, flotation of the deposits produced a large quantity of charcoal but unfortunately no recognisable plant-food remains, and in this regard it is important to note that a large quantity of carbonised rice was found in an upper layer of the site dated to about 900 years ago, so this cereal would have been detected had it been present earlier. Therefore there is no evidence to suggest cereal cultivation at Gua Cha, either Hoabinhian or Neolithic. Finally, large numbers of animal bones (identified by Groves and Weitzel, see Adi 1981:Appendix) were found throughout the Hoabinhian layers; pigs (*Sus*

Fig. 6.5. Flexed burial of a young male with a stone pillow excavated at Gua Cha in 1979. Probably c. 2000 BC. Courtesy: National Museum, Kuala Lumpur.

scrofa and the bearded pig *Sus barbatus*) were the most commonly killed animals, and it is possible that large numbers of pigs were killed during mass river crossings, as described by Hislop (1954) for Malaya, and by St John (1974, I:138) for northern Borneo. Sieveking (1954) found about 25 small heaps of jaws and skull fragments of juvenile pigs in one sector of the Hoabinhian deposits, and young animals seem to have been favoured as prey in other species too. The latter included deer of several species, Malayan bear, monkeys and gibbons, rats, squirrels, flying foxes, and (more rarely) rhinoceros and cattle. This species list is very similar to that found in Hoabinhian sites as a whole (Gorman 1971: Table 2). In one of my earlier papers (Bellwood 1976a:162–3) I suggested very tentatively that the predominance of juvenile pig bones at Gua Cha could suggest some form of domestication, but this statement was made before I was able to work at the site and I now consider an explanation of simple hunting to be more likely. It is also worth noting that small quantities of fresh-water shellfish were found in the site, but marine shells were absent.

Within the South-East Asian Hoabinhian in general, the question of overlap with Neolithic assemblages characterised by pottery and fully-ground stone adzes has always been a particularly vexed one, partly because the necessary stratigraphic details were simply not recorded in the earlier excavations. At Spirit Cave, as noted above, Hoabinhian tools were stated by Gorman (1970) to overlap quite definitely with the Neolithic assemblage of potsherds and stone adzes, and in northern Vietnam there are indications that similar situations prevailed. So in these northern regions it is quite possible that the Hoabinhian did grade slowly into a fairly coherent and presumably agricultural array of Neolithic cultures. However, in Malaya the situation appears to be different. According to Sieveking (1954), the Hoabinhian at Gua Cha was separated by a gap from the overlying Neolithic occupation, which commenced with a working-floor for quadrangular cross-sectioned adzes like those in the top layer of Spirit Cave, and later continued with a series of burials which I will describe in Chapter 8. The 1979 work at Gua Cha tended to support Sieveking, although there can be no doubt that a few Hoabinhian tools do occur in the pottery-bearing upper layer from which the Neolithic burials were cut, despite their absence in the adze working-floor. My own inclination here is to regard these tools as having been brought to the Neolithic surface during the course of intensive grave digging, and then either reused or simply thrown away. They certainly do not occur amongst the Neolithic burial goods themselves, which do include several fully-ground stone adzes.

It seems, however, that Sieveking may have overemphasised his concept of a gap between the Hoabinhian and the Neolithic; a more likely explanation is that rapid cultural change took place in the region of the site, and that this change, according to the skeletal evidence reviewed in Chapter 3, Section IIIB, involved no replacement of population. I strongly suspect that the whole of the Gua Cha sequence belongs to ancestral *orang asli* populations who, as I will document later, were brought fairly rapidly into the Neolithic world of the Thai-Malayan peninsula at about 1000 BC.

Some of the complexity of the overall Malayan situation for the Hoabinhian can be estimated from a brief review of other sites. At the cave of Gua Kechil in Pahang, Dunn (1964, 1966) found Hoabinhian tools together with cord-marked and plain pottery in a lower occupation layer about 40 cm thick. This was overlain by a layer with polished adzes and pottery similar to that of the main Neolithic layer at Gua Cha, dated rather surprisingly by radio-

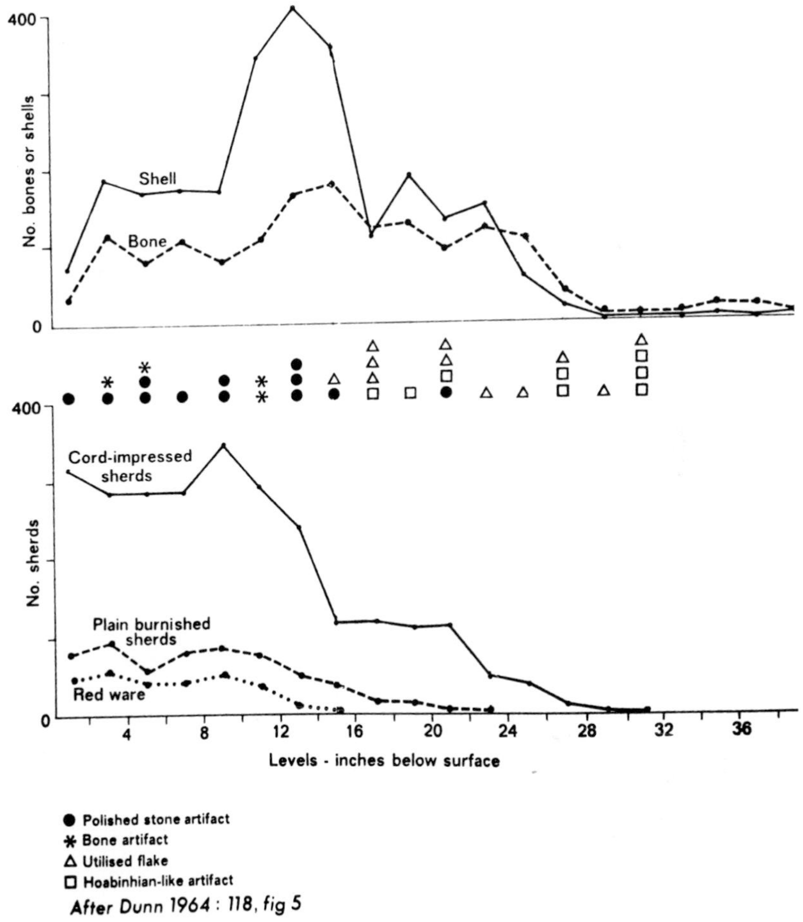

Fig. 6.6. The overlap situation between Hoabinhian tools and pottery at Gua Kechil, Pahang. From Peacock 1971. Courtesy: University of Sydney; B. A. V. Peacock.

carbon to the earlier fourth millennium BC. Hoabinhian tools were absent in this upper layer, but the situation beneath suggests an overlap situation of Hoabinhian tools and pottery (Fig. 6.6) which can certainly not be recognised in the sequence from Gua Cha.

A less certain case of overlap is illustrated by Peacock (1971) for the unpublished excavations at Kota Tongkat, another shelter in Pahang. The Hoabinhian levels here have high quantities of occupation materials such as animal bones and shells, and there does appear to be some slight overlap

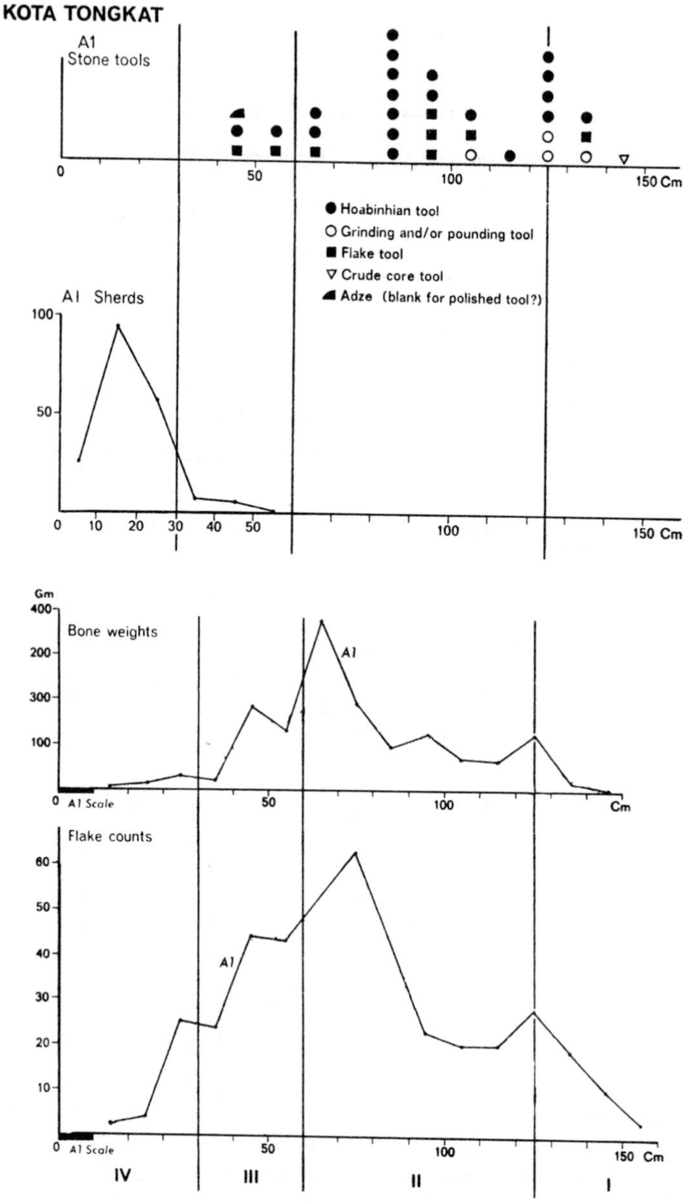

Fig. 6.7. Distributions of Hoabinhian tools, pottery, bone and stone flakes by depth at Kota Tongkat, Pahang. From Peacock 1971. Courtesy: University of Sydney; B. A. V. Peacock.

between the Hoabinhian tools and an upper level characterized mainly by pottery and apparently little else. However, I must confess from Peacock's illustrations (here shown as Fig. 6.7) that I can see little real difference in the overall sequences of Gua Cha and Kota Tongkat, and it may in fact be the overlap situation at Gua Kechil which is unusual in the Malayan context — unfortunately the necessary data for a firm assessment are not available.

It may also be recalled that edge-ground tools are very characteristic of later stages of the Hoabinhian (that is the Bacsonian) in Vietnam, yet such tools are to my knowledge quite absent from the three Malayan sites which I have just described. However, they have been reported from old excavations at Gua Madu in Kelantan (Tweedie 1940), and from Gua Baik (Gol Ba'it, Stein Callenfels and Noone 1940) and Gua Kerbau (Stein Callenfels and Evans 1928) in Perak. At the last two sites they were reported as occurring down to the bases of the deposits, but I am inclined to accept this with considerable reservation, especially since the Gua Kerbau deposit was excavated in 75 cm thick spits and was apparently riddled with animal holes, and Gua Baik produced only one specimen.

The Malayan shell middens now tell rather a sorry tale of destruction, although Adi (1983:53) has recently reported a new discovery at Seberang Perak near Telok Anson in Perak. It has also been known since 1860 that large middens of marine bivalves (formerly published as *Meretrix* and *Arca*, but I believe more probably *Batissa* and *Anadara* in modern classification) once occurred on old beach ridges in the mainland portion of Pinang state (formerly Province Wellesley). These have now been destroyed apart from small remnants, but the remains of three were excavated long ago by Stein Callenfels at a location about three miles inland called Guar Kepah (Stein Callenfels 1936a, the sites were then called Guak Kepah).

According to Stein Callenfels these middens, which were originally up to 5 m thick, contained hearths, secondary burials dusted with hematite (one jaw was classified as "Palae-Melanesian" by Mijsberg 1940; see Chapter 3, Section IIIB), pig and estuarine fish bones, Hoabinhian tools, necked and apparently hammer-dressed axes, and small quantities of cord-marked and incised pottery (Fig. 6.8). No stratigraphic order for these items was clearly established, but Tweedie (1953:69) thought that the pottery may have post-dated the Hoabinhian tools. It appears that the Hoabinhian tools and the necked axes (often described as "ground", but I suspect from illustrations that they were simply hammer-dressed) did belong together with the midden deposits, which presumably date from the present phase of sea-level, and thus somewhere within the Holocene. These sites clearly pose a number of unresolved problems; they appear to represent a coastal Hoabinhian adaptation and thus an aspect of Hoabinhian life which cannot be found in the inland shelters, but which may now be virtually lost as a result of the terminal Pleistocene rise in sea-level and the activities of lime burners.

Fig. 6.8. Top: **basal section (about 60 cm thick) of Guar Kepah midden A**, resting on clay. From Stein Callenfels 1936a. Courtesy: **National Museum** of Singapore. Bottom: hammer-dressed and necked axes from Guar Kepah. From Tweedie 1953. Courtesy: Malaysian Branch of the Royal Asiatic Society.

Fig. 6.9. Hoabinhian shell-midden being quarried for lime manufacture at Sukajadi near Medan, northern Sumatra. Photo by Ian Glover.

B. Sumatra

The only Hoabinhian sites found within the modern political boundaries of Indonesia lie inland from the north-eastern coast of Sumatra between Lhokseumawe and Medan (Witkamp 1920; Kupper 1930; Heekeren 1972:85–92; Brandt 1976; Glover 1978b). Many of the sites are large shell middens up to 30 m in diameter and 5 m deep (Fig. 6.9), with interstratified lenses of shells, soil and ash. They appear to be located at approximately present sea-level on an early Holocene strandline which now lies between 10 and 15 km inland, and most have been buried under sediments deposited along this rapidly aggrading coast during the past few millennia. None have been systematically excavated or dated, although a radiocarbon date within the sixth millennium BC has recently been obtained from the remnants of a midden at Sukajadi, unfortunately mostly quarried away for lime burning (Bronson, in press). Like the Pinang middens of Malaya, the Sumatran middens must be of Holocene date and may have been occupied at any time between 10 000 and perhaps as recently as 3000 years ago. The region has no caves or shelters, but other non-midden Hoabinhian sites have been reported from inland terraces and flat limestone rises to about 150 m above sea-level.

It appears that virtually all of the shell middens have now been destroyed for lime manufacture, but many archaeological collections have been made from them and these are described by Heekeren (1972). The majority of the tools appear to be unifacially flaked oval or elongated pebbles, often flaked all over one surface. Bifacial tools and edge-ground tools appear to be rather rare, as are retouched flakes, and this industry gives the impression of being technologically simpler than that of the Malayan sites as a whole. Grindstones, mortars, hematite and human burials also occur in the middens, and faunal remains include elephant, rhinoceros, bear, deer, and presumably many smaller species. The shellfish illustrated by Heekeren (1972: Plate 36) appear to belong to the genera *Batissa, Anadara* and *Telescopium*; the same estuarine species which once formed the Pinang middens. Pottery appears to be universally absent, at least in confirmed association with the Hoabinhian deposits.

C. Further Comments on the Hoabinhian

As reported from Malaya and Sumatra the Hoabinhian seems to have had a coastal and inland hunting and gathering mode of economic orientation, and I feel it is pushing the evidence too far to suggest a local development of agriculture in these regions. As I have stated, the Hoabinhian of the intermediate tropical zone in northern Thailand, northern Vietnam and southern China may hold more significant evidence in this regard, although a lot more material needs to be excavated if this possibility is to be substantiated. The edge-grinding of stone tools and the making of pottery may be innovations from within a Hoabinhian cultural matrix, but again I think the evidence is at present inconclusive, partly because shelter deposits are so prone to those types of hidden stratigraphic disturbance which will always perhaps cloud the issue.

Hoabinhian sites do not occur in the Indo-Malaysian islands outside north-eastern Sumatra. I suspect they are present in Taiwan, perhaps in the so-called "Changpinian" of the eastern coast (Sung 1979), and also perhaps in some aceramic assemblages of "chipped hoes" reported by Koyama (1977) from the western coast. In the Philippines, assemblages termed "Hoabinhian" have been reported by Kress (1977a, b) for Palawan and by Peterson (1974) for the Pintu shelter in northern Luzon, but the illustrations provided by Peterson (1974: Plate 1) do not convince me that the tools from this site are really any different from the contemporary pebble and flake industries characteristic of many of the other Indo-Malaysian islands. Naturally, signs of a gradation from the classic mainland Hoabinhian into the very different stone tool expressions found in the islands might be expected, and it is possible that the Philippines and Sumatra are in such gradation areas. But my own experience from handling Malayan and Sumatran Hoabinhian stone tools is that they represent a dominance of pebble tools as opposed to flake tools which sets them well apart from contemporary industries in all the island regions, including the Philippines.

II. Island South-East Asia: The Later Pebble and Flake Industries, with Variations

In the Philippines, East Malaysia and Indonesia the record of flaked stone tool production goes back about 40 000 radiocarbon years — considerably longer than in the Hoabinhian region (this is, of course, ignoring the undated but possibly much older Tampanian industry described in Chapter 2, Section IIID7). Basically, it comprises a widespread pebble and flake technocomplex which was also, on present evidence, carried by at least one of the first populations to settle in Australia and New Guinea. The technocomplex includes the majority of Indo-Malaysian flaked stone assemblages, and in its most basic form is characterised by varying proportions of simple pebble tools, cores and flakes with non-standardised shapes. As I have noted, the Hoabinhian tendency towards a dominance of pebble tools with regular bifacial or all-over unifacial working is not present, and while this circumstance may reflect important cultural differences I suspect there may also be some geological reasons behind it. For instance, the blocky cherts and obsidians used more commonly in the island regions may have been more amenable to a flake technology than the flat coarse-grained pebbles which occur in Malayan rivers, although this is only a subjective opinion drawn from my own rather limited geological observations.

The best way to visualise the prehistoric record of flaked stone tools within the last 40 000 years in the Indo-Malaysian islands is in terms of periodic and normally highly localised accretions on to the basic pebble and flake technocomplex, which in its basic form underwent very little change over this period. Thus, sporadic and short-lived occurrences of prepared core, bifacial lanceolate, edge-grinding and blade technologies occur, each in a restricted region and over a different period of time. The final stage is of course the widespread appearance of fully-ground adzes and axes together with pottery after 3000 BC, and I will return to this in the following chapter. However, it should be noted that the older flaked stone technologies continued with no obvious changes until they finally faded in the face of metal tools from the late first millennium BC onwards. The flaked stone traditions do not in themselves record the spread of an agricultural lifestyle in the region.

In organising this chapter I have decided to proceed along geographical lines from Borneo through to eastern Indonesia. However, the industries with a blade or "microlithic" component, all dating to within the last 7000 years, are described separately in the final section.

A. The West Mouth, Niah, Sarawak

The huge West Mouth of the Niah Caves in Sarawak (Fig. 6.10) contains the longest stratified record of human occupation in Island South-East Asia. The caves themselves form a network of high and awe-inspiring passages, with an area of about 10.5 ha, inside the Gunung Subis limestone massif near Niah in northern Sarawak. The system has many outlets, of which the West Mouth is the largest, being about 250 m across and 60 m high. Most of the system is floored with continuously-deposited wet guano, but an area high and dry at the northern end of the West Mouth was used for habitation and burial from about 40 000 until perhaps 2000 years ago or later. This area was excavated on a fairly massive scale by the late Tom Harrisson between 1954 and 1967.

Harrisson produced many impressionistic articles and a few detailed typological studies based on his research at Niah, but no proper plans or stratigraphic drawings were ever made. Since most of the site was destroyed by the excavations it is now too late to make full amends, although Majid (1982) has recently attempted to piece together some of the information which can be gleaned from the earlier records. In addition, other publications since 1967 by Barbara Harrisson, Lord Medway (the Earl of Cranbrook) and by biological anthropologists (see below) have filled in many lacunae in the records of animal faunas and human burials.

Harrisson's reconstructions of the cultural sequence at Niah were based partly on the idea that depths and ages could be correlated regularly across the site. However, the site has an uneven surface, and arbitrary levels of excavation up to 24 inches thick, plus a set of partially contradictory radiocarbon dates recorded only by depths below surface, clearly do not encourage much confidence in the finer details of the "Niah area phaseology" which he published and revised from time to time. His last version appeared in his 1970a paper, in which he favoured a basal flake industry with pebble tools appearing intermittently, and becoming edge-ground after about 10 000 bc. I will consider the Neolithic tools and the pottery (the latter comes in at about 2500 BC) in a later section, but wish now to examine the preceramic West Mouth sequence in terms of artefacts, faunas and human burials.

1. Artefacts at Niah

Since Niah has no sources of fine-grained stone such as chert or obsidian in its vicinity, the tools were made mainly on various types of sandstone which

Fig. 6.10. The West Mouth, Niah. Harrisson's excavation area is at top right, and the poles to the roof are for bird's-nest collection.

had to be smashed rather than flaked to give sharp-edged pieces. Hence the industry comprises mainly an unretouched array of chunks and chips, without coherent core forms and with few conchoidal flakes. There is little systematic retouch. Pebble tools also occur, but apparently not in the oldest levels. Bone spatulae and points do apparently occur to the base of the site, some made on pig tusks or mammal longbones (Harrisson and Medway 1962; Majid 1982:Appendix 3). Stone mortars and edge-ground pebble axes appear later in the sequence; dates unfortunately are not clear, but Majid suggests that both could have appeared somewhere between 20 000 and 10 000 years ago, although Harrisson preferred the latter date for the edge-ground axes.

The edge-grinding of pebble axes is of course a significant technological development (Hayden 1977b). It occurs from the end of the Pleistocene in Vietnam, from dates in excess of 20 000 years ago in northern Australia (Schrire 1982), from about 30 000 years ago in Japan (Ikawa-Smith 1979; Serizawa 1982), and possibly before 14 500 years ago in the New Guinea Highlands (Mountain 1983:94–5). Hence, if Niah is included, there are four separate Late Pleistocene occurrences, to which may be added a possibly early Holocene appearance on Palawan in the Philippines (Kress 1977a; see also Peterson *et al.* 1979 for Luzon). The technique clearly precedes the devlopment of blade technologies, even in Japan where blades appear by perhaps 26 000 years ago, and it occurs in similar pebble- and flake-based industrial backgrounds in each region. At Niah it was probably adopted because of the difficulty of finding good stone for flaking, and it is totally absent in many contemporary or later Indo-Malaysian industries where good cherts were available (for instance, in neighbouring Sabah). Hence there are two rather contradictory aspects of distribution — on the one hand a widespread distribution of the edge-grinding technique in Late Pleistocene times around the eastern fringes of the Old World, but on the other hand a very spotty occurrence within this territory (within Australia, for instance, it remained strangely restricted to the region of Arnhem Land until about 5000 years ago). It thus seems that equal cases can be made for multiple independent development of the technique or for its diffusion from one source, and the real answer may combine both processes.

2. The Niah Economy

The animal bones from the West Mouth indicate fairly eclectic hunting patterns. Medway (1977a) lists 58 species of mammals found in the cave, and apart from the bats, which may have fallen naturally into the deposits, there are numerous species of rodents and insectivores, seven species of primates, eleven carnivores (excluding the Neolithic dog and a tooth of the non-native tiger from the top of the site), and ten other large native mammals. Wild pigs (*Sus barbatus*; Medway 1978) were the most popular prey throughout, together with porcupines at depth but with an increasing emphasis on monkeys in higher levels. Other large mammals from the oldest levels include giant pangolin (now extinct), Malay pangolin, Malayan tapir, orang utan, deer, and perhaps bovids (Hooijer 1963; Medway 1977a). The Sumatran rhinoceros (Medway 1965) and the Malayan bear also make rare appearances at higher levels. Apart from the mammals, fish, birds, monitor lizards, snakes and crocodiles were also brought into the cave.

In Chapter 1, Section IVE, I discussed some of the faunal evidence which suggests that the Niah region may have had a drier and more seasonal climate during the period of the last glacial maximum. Some of the larger mammals such as rhinoceros and bear seem to have been more common at this time, and during the early Holocene a number of species (such as orang utan, rhinoceros, monkeys, and rats; Medway 1978) commenced a slight decline in size. The Malayan tapir also declined into local extinction, and Medway (1977a) attributes these Holocene changes to the spread of dense forest and its non-clearance by human agency. Estuarine shellfish also increased in numbers in both the West Mouth and neighbouring Lobang Angus as a result of the rise in sea-level. Majid (1982) has reported a few plant remains from early levels, particularly of the large edible nuts (toxic until soaked in water) of the forest tree *Pangium edule*.

3. Human Burials

The possible racial affinities of the Niah human remains have been discussed in Chapter 3, Section IIIB, and I will only add cultural details here. The single "deep skull" (see Chapter 3, Fig. 3.11), associated by Tom Harrisson (1975b:161) with a radiocarbon age of about 40 000 years, was found together with some longbones under a large stone. No stratigraphic details have ever been published, but Barbara Harrisson (1967:143) has stated that the dated charcoal was taken from directly above the skull. Nevertheless, the fact that it lies some 125 cm below all other human remains in the site must at least suggest burial from a higher level and consequent mixing of deposits of different ages. The problem cannot really be solved since all deposits surrounding the skull have now been excavated away.

The other burials from the preceramic levels comprised flexed, sitting, and disturbed fragmentary remains. A number of radiocarbon dates on bone collagen have now been published (Harrisson 1975b; Brooks *et al.* 1977) and these suggest that the burials in a sitting ("Buddha-like") posture date between 12 000 bc and 6000 BC, while the flexed ones (Fig. 6.11) run from perhaps 9000 bc onwards. Several of the flexed burials occurred in later levels with pottery, so this mode is not of course a guarantee of an early date. Hematite powder and traces of burning occured on several burials (Harrisson 1967), and goods included an edge-ground pebble (unfortunately not with a dated burial), a rhinoceros femur pillow, a bone point and an estuarine shell with hematite. It should be noted that the only burial dated twice, number 147, has one published collagen determination of 7020±135 bp (Brooks *et al.* (1977), and another very contradictory determination of 13 600±130 bp (Harrisson 1975b).

The task of summarising 35 000 years of pre-agricultural life around the Niah Caves is a difficult one — the flaked stone tool tradition has a stunted appearance due to the poverty of raw material, and there are insufficient data to study trends in economy within these 35 long millennia in any very useful way. The sequence clearly lacks the specialised flaking technologies which appeared in other nearby regions, yet the early adoption of edge-grinding suggests for Niah a fairly innovative prehistory somewhat unique to itself.

B. Sites in Eastern Sabah (Northern Borneo)

Since 1980, an excavation project carried out in eastern Sabah under the aegis of the Sabah Museum in Kota Kinabalu has documented a number of cave and open sites with deposits extending back for perhaps 30 000 years (Bellwood 1984). The situation of these sites is shown in Fig. 6.12; the caves and shelters are found in the Madai and Baturong limestone massifs, both of

Fig. 6.11. Flexed burial (undated) from a preceramic level at the West Mouth, Niah. Courtesy Sarawak Museum.

which contain networks of solution tunnels, some of which emerge into the open air as dry habitable locations (as in the Niah Caves). Baturong is in turn surrounded by a large area of water-laid deposits which are presumed to have been laid down in the bed of an extinct lake, formed by the damming of an old course of the Tingkayu River by a lava flow extruded from the flanks of nearby Mount Mostyn (Fig. 6.13). Although these sites are near the coast now, the low sea-level conditions of the Late Pleistocene may have placed them up to 150 km inland.

In Fig. 6.12 I have shown the approximate boundaries of the old Tingkayu lake as identified by previous soil and geological surveys, and by fieldwork undertaken in 1981 with Philip Hughes. The lake covered perhaps 100 km^2 before it drained away as the outlet for the present Tingkayu River was downcut into a gorge just north of Tingkayu village. The date of formation of the lake is probably indicated by a radiocarbon determination of 28 300$\pm$750 bp from charcoal sealed beneath the end of the lava flow, which outcrops into the side of the exit gorge near Tingkayu village, and active research to verify this surprising antiquity is currently underway. In addition, very weathered water-laid sediments at the base of the Hagop Bilo shelter in the Baturong massif were exposed to subaerial weathering as a result of draining of the lake some considerable time before 17 000 years ago (John

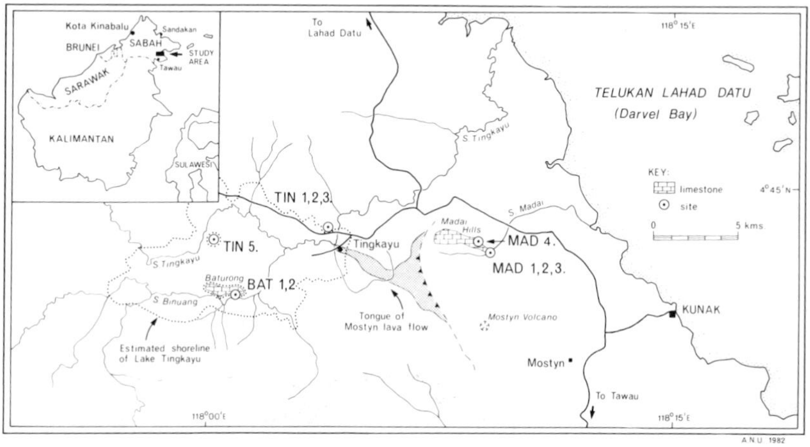

Fig. 6.12. The locations of the Tingkayu, Baturong and Madai sites in eastern Sabah. See text for explanation of abbreviations.

Fig. 6.13. The old Tingkayu lake bed (now under oil palm plantations), with the Baturong limestone massif just right of centre.

Magee, personal communication). These dates are highly significant because a number of open sites lie directly on the shoreline of the old lake, and on locational grounds they may be considered as contemporary with the lake-full stage, and thus between 28 000 and 17 000 years old.

The major lake-edge sites, labelled TIN 1–3 in Fig. 6.12, lie close together on a small promontory which juts into the old bed close to the lake outlet. Another site, TIN 5, lies on top of what must have been a small island — today it is a hill amongst the oil palm plantations which occupy the western half of the old lake bed. TIN 1 has been mostly destroyed by the bulldozing which led to initial discovery of the site, but TIN 2, excavated in 1980 and 1984, contained a discrete manufacturing floor for the bifacial tools which characterise the Tingkayu industry. Unfortunately, the acid forest soil in which these sites lie has left no traces of bone, although it is hoped that charcoal fragments from the stone tool layer in TIN 2 can be dated in the near future.

The Tingkayu stone industry (Fig. 6.14) shows a unique level of skill for its time period in South-East Asia, and the tools are mostly made on a locally quarried tabular chert (the precise source is not known, and may no longer exist, or it may be buried somewhere in the vicinity of the site), together with a few riverine pebbles of chert. The basic aspects of the industry are not exceptional, and comprise a range of large pebble tools, multi- and single-platform (horsehoof) cores, and utilised flakes. However, many of the tabular blanks were worked into large bifaces, and into smaller and quite remarkable lanceolate knives. Only one of the latter has been found complete (in TIN 1, see Fig. 6.14), and it has very fine surface flaking, but broken segments and points with varying degrees of finish are common. In TIN 2 several broken lanceolates (one example being 17.5 cm long) and other bifaces have been excavated together with their manufacturing debris. The use-wear which occurs on a few of the lanceolates from TIN 1 suggests utilisation of mainly the side edges, despite the overall pointed shapes. Hence, they could have served combined functions as projectile points and knives. The majority of the tools were found in the bulldozer-disturbed area of TIN 1, but the stratigraphic evidence from TIN 2 strongly suggests a single unified industry.

At the present time this bifacial industry is quite unique in the whole of South-East Asia, except for one apparent lanceolate found years ago in a tin mine in Kedah in Malaya (Stein Callenfels 1936b), and although similar forms do occur in northern Australia they all seem to postdate 4000 BC. It seems likely to me that this tradition was developed locally, perhaps to meet a specific need in this rather unusual lacustrine environment. In north-eastern Asia there are remote parallels for the lanceolates in the Late Pleistocene Diuktai tradition of north-eastern Siberia (Chard 1974; Ikawa-Smith 1982), and in several regions of Japan after about 18 000 years ago (Ikawa-Smith

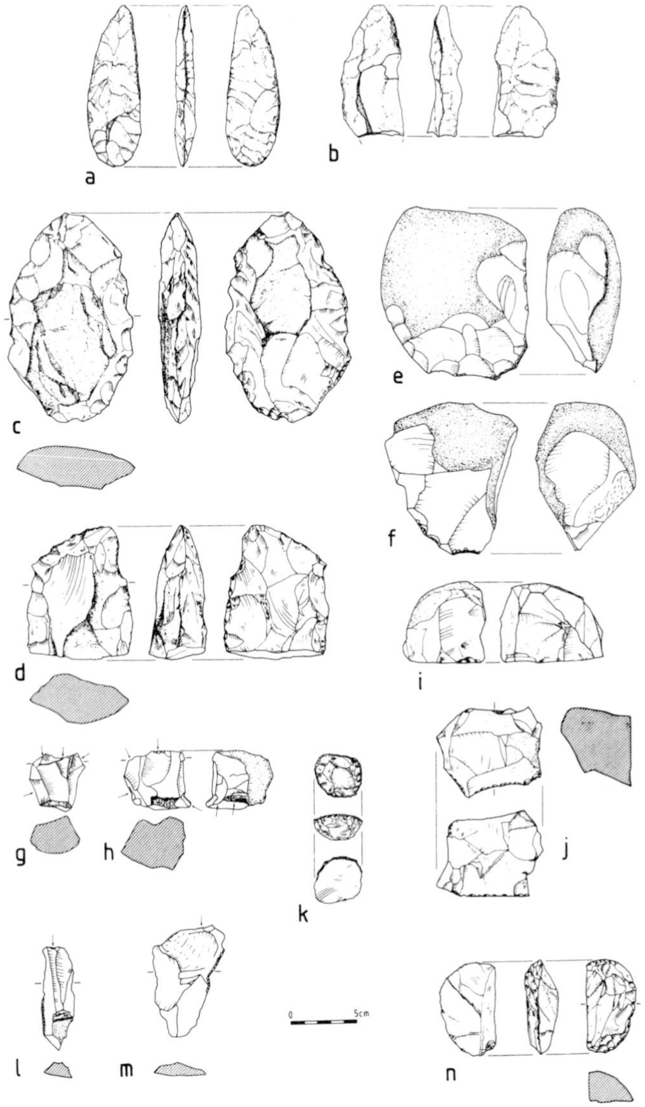

Fig. 6.14. The Tingkayu industry (all from TIN 1). (a, b) Bifacial lanceolates; (c, d) large tabular bifaces; (e, f) pebble tools; (g, h) cores; (i, j) single-platform "horsehoof" cores; (k) small "thumbnail scraper"; (l, m) utilised flakes; (n) small tabular uniface. Drawn by Lakim Kassim.

1979; Aikens and Higuchi 1981), but these occurrences are so distant that they can be no more than noted at the present time.

During the lake period the Baturong massif formed a towering limestone island, and the rock-shelters along the base of its southern cliff were all drowned. After the lake drained away the open sites were abandoned, and an occupation hiatus, which may have lasted for about 10 000 years, now intervenes in the sequence. In the shelter of Hagop Bilo (BAT 1 in Fig. 6.12) the basal and culturally-sterile lake sediments were overlain, after a long break characterised by considerable weathering, by midden deposits in riverine alluvium dating between about 15 000 and 10 000 bc. These midden layers contain mainly three species of lacustrine gastropods in the genera *Balanocochlis, Sulcospira* and *Brotia*, and marine shells are absent. The animal faunas, provisionally identified by the Earl of Cranbrook, include pig, sambhur deer, mouse deer, porcupine, monkey, rat, snake, tortoise, monitor lizard, birds, and probably other small unidentified species. The stone tools of this period lack the bifaces, and comprise a fairly typical Indo-Malaysian pebble and flake industry with single- and multi-platform cores, utilised flakes, and flat-based and steep-edged domed scraper-like tools, all made on chert. Characteristics of some interest include a class of long blade-like knives (Fig. 6.15), perhaps functional descendants of the Tingkayu lanceolates, and also the presence of an opal phytolith gloss on some tool working edges. This gloss is widely reported from other sites of this period and later in South-East Asia, but was absent in the Tingkayu industry where open situations may not have been conducive to its survival, had it once existed. Another tool of interest from Hagop Bilo is a large bone spatula, similar to those from Niah, and pieces of scratched hematite were also recovered.

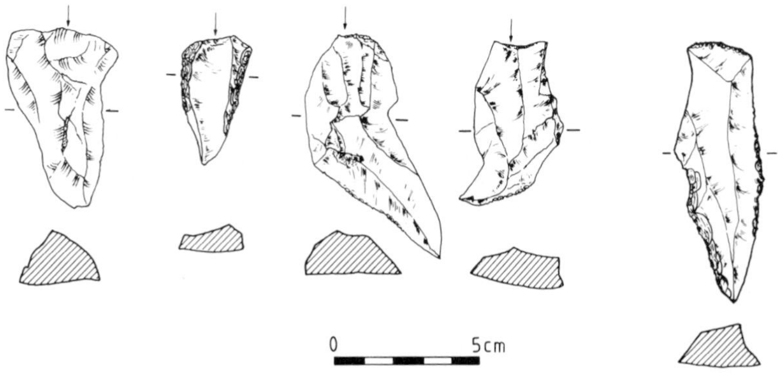

Fig. 6.15. Elongated blade-like flakes from Hagop Bilo.

Soon after 10 000 bc the Hagop Bilo shelter was in turn abandoned. The absence of marine shells in the deposits suggests that its inhabitants were mainly inland dwellers, and with the shoreline originally perhaps 100–150 km away this interpretation is clearly sensible. However, by 9000 bc the Madai Caves (Fig. 6.16) may have been coming within easy reach of the approaching coastal resources, and the cave users apparently moved seawards from Baturong to Madai at this time. The largest of the Madai Caves, Agop Atas (MAD 1; see Harrisson T. and B. 1971 for earlier excavations here), today contains a substantial Idahan village occupied seasonally for bird's-nest collection. Above MAD 1 lies the smaller Agop Sarapad (MAD 2); both these caves were intensively inhabited by hunters during the early Holocene, between about 9000 and 5000 bc.

Fig. 6.16. The Madai Caves; Agop Atas (MAD 1) lies just behind and above the village (which extends into the cave), and Agop Sarapad (MAD 2) is the upper opening to the left.

The early Holocene human deposits in MAD 1 lie in a very acidic guano deposit, and, as at Tingkayu, only stone tools survive with some charcoal, all animal bones having totally dissolved. But the MAD 2 cave has much better conditions, for here the people deposited a large shell midden which has created and maintained its own alkaline environment; bone survives in quite good condition, although both caves are too damp for any plant organic matter to have survived. The MAD 2 midden thus tells the best story, and has yielded thousands of stone tools of local river pebble chert, of an industry similar to that from Hagop Bilo but lacking the blade-like knives (Fig. 6.17). There is a heavy emphasis on pebble tools, large steep-edged tools, multi-platform and horsehoof (single-platform) cores, and utilised flakes, many of which have glossed edges. A number of large pitted anvils or grindstones occur, some coated with red ochre, and hammerstones are also common, either for stone tool making or for food or ochre preparation on the anvils.

The food remains in the midden include many shells of the estuarine mangrove shellfish *Batissa* and *Anadara*, and clearly the inhabitants were visiting the encroaching coast frequently. Most shells, however, are of the three same riverine shellfish species which were eaten earlier at Hagop Bilo. The animals hunted were also similar, with the addition of larger creatures such as the orang utan, cattle and rhinoceros; these appear to have been absent at Hagop Bilo, but the small sample size and the provisional nature of the identifications makes this uncertain. Remains of Javan rhinoceros have also been identified from Agop Sarapad by Cranbrook (in press a); this is the only report of this animal from Borneo, and it evidently survived in parts of Sabah until the early Holocene.

After 7000 years ago the two Madai caves were abandoned, and I am unable to see any clear explanation for this, except to suggest that the inhabitants may have moved to a coastal location, or perhaps dwelt elsewhere in an unexcavated part of the cave system. However, the sweet waters of the Madai stream flow directly through the lower cave at Madai (Agop Alag, MAD 3), and I have seen no other caves suitable for long-term habitation in the massif; this implies strongly that the population did move away. For about 4000 years the caves remained unoccupied, and then a new and totally different cultural assemblage makes its appearance; I will describe this in the next chapter.

C. The South-western Arm of Sulawesi

The south-western arm of spider-like Sulawesi has produced one of the best preceramic sequences of Late Pleistocene and Holocene stone tool working in the whole Indo-Malaysian Archipelago. This region is the homeland of the Makassarese and Buginese peoples who have played such major roles in the

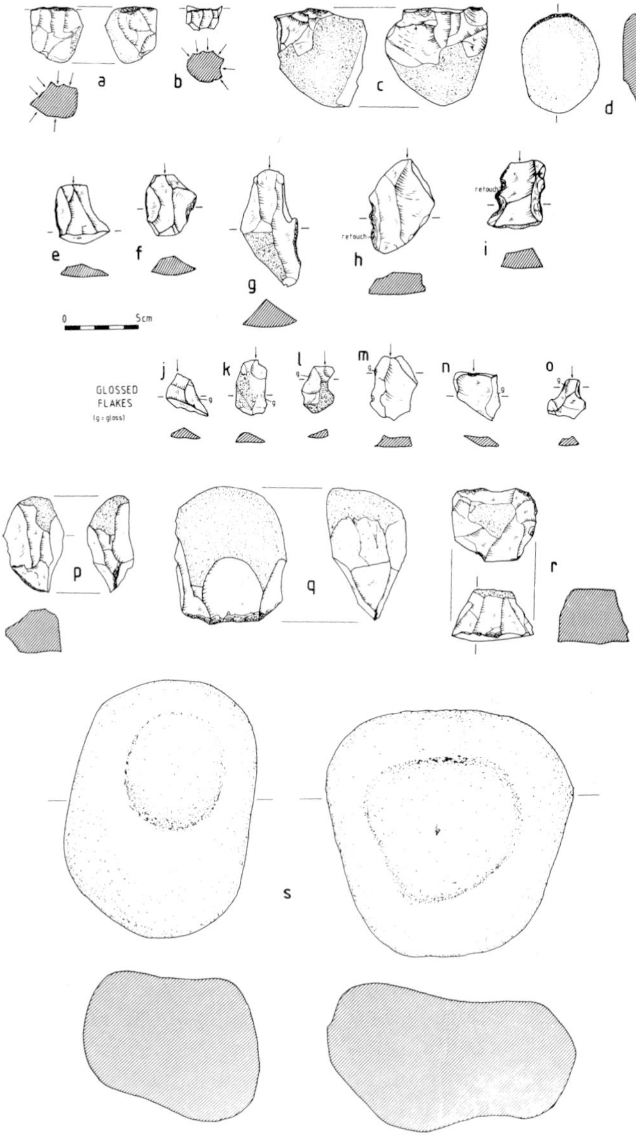

Fig. 6.17. The Agop Sarapad (MAD 2) industry. (a–c) Single-platform cores; (d) hammerstone; (e–i) utilised flakes; (j–o) glossed flakes; (p, q) pebble tools; (r) flat-based steep-edged tool; (s) pitted anvils or grindstones. Drawn by Lakim Kassim.

recent history of Indonesia, and archaeologically I have already looked at the rather enigmatic open-site industry of the region around Cabenge (Chapter 2, Section IIID5). Archaeological excavations have also been carried out since early this century in caves and shelters in the tower-like karst topography which is particularly well-developed in the Maros region inland from Ujungpandang (Makassar), and many sites have now produced assemblages belonging to the industry of backed flakes and microliths known as the Toalian, which I will describe in the next section. The Toalian postdates 7000 years ago and overlaps with the appearance of pottery in the region. However, earlier assemblages are now known as a result of several seasons of fieldwork by Glover, and these come from the shelters of Leang Burung 2 and Ulu Leang in the Maros limestone.

The shelter of Leang Burung 2 (Presland 1980; Glover 1981) is the most important site, and has produced an industry characterised by unretouched flakes and small multi-platform cores of chert from levels dated between 29 000 and 17 000 bc from radiocarbon determinations on freshwater shell. Some flakes have the typical opal phytolith edge-gloss which is found so widely in this region, and Glover suggests that it may result here from the working of matting or basketry, possibly of palm leaves (see also Kamminga 1979). In addition, there are at least four elongated blade-like flakes with facetted striking platforms (Fig. 6.18a, b), which Glover regards as similar to those of the Levalloisian prepared-core technology associated with the late Acheulian and Mousterian technocomplexes of the northern and western territories of Eurasia (generally prior to about 30 000 years ago). These tools are significant because they do indicate a degree of conscious core preparation prior to flake removal which is not otherwise found in any other South-East Asian industry, although rather strangely it does appear again, perhaps quite independently, as recently as 4000 years ago in the north-western parts of Australia (Dortch 1977; Dortch and Bordes 1977). However, there are no recognisable Levalloisian cores in Leang Burung 2, and the technique seems here to have played quite a minor role. Its invention may have been independent of occurrences elsewhere, and it does not appear to continue on into the Holocene period in the Sulawesi sites.

Also found in Leang Burung 2 are pieces of the ubiquitous hematite, but bone points are absent, as are fishbones and marine shells since the sea was presumably very far from the site at this time. The industry seems to continue (after a possible gap) into the lower levels of the shelter of Ulu Leang (Glover 1976) which date from the early Holocene, and here there is a distinctive range of steep-edged domed tools and horsehoof-shaped cores of white chert, very similar to the Agop Sarapad industry of the same date from Sabah (Fig. 6.18c, d, e). Bone spatulae also appear in basal Ulu Leang, and this bone tool tradition is elaborated in the succeeding Toalian industry.

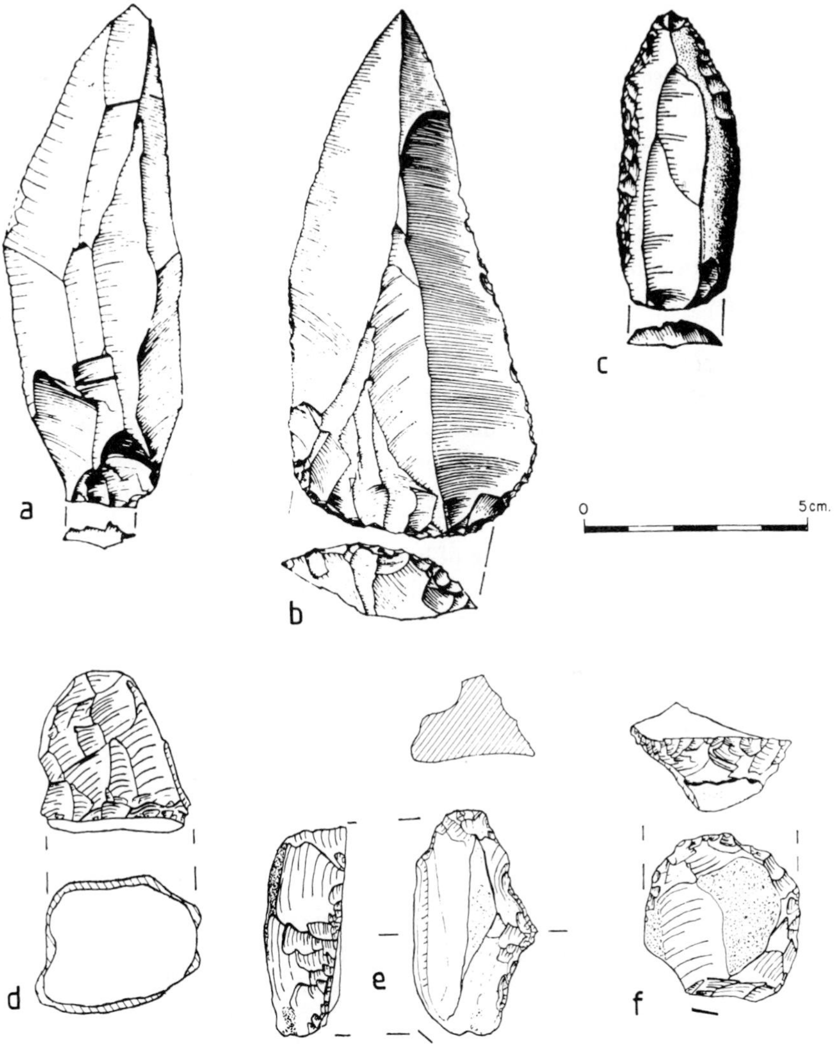

Fig. 6.18. Top: stone blades with prepared striking platforms (a, b) and a retouched blade (c) from Leang Burung 2. Bottom: "horsehoof core" (d) and flat-based steep-edged tools (e, f) from Ulu Leang lower layers. From Glover 1977a. Courtesy: I. C. Glover.

D. The Northern Arm of Sulawesi: The Paso Midden

The Paso shell midden (Bellwood 1976b) lies close to the shoreline of Lake Tondano, in the inland volcanic terrain of the Minahasa Peninsula. The midden is about 30 m in diameter and averages 1 m in depth, and consists of lenses of loose lacustrine shell interstratified with occupation layers (Fig. 6.19). The latter contain an obsidian flake industry, bone points, hematite, and prolific faunal remains. The site is radiocarbon dated to about 6500 BC.

The obsidian, collected locally, is vesicular and coarse, and lumps were mostly smashed to obtain sharp chips and chunks, although flakes were struck individually from multi-platform cores as well. There are no pebble tools (one would perhaps not expect them in a raw material of this type), and no edge-gloss has been observed, perhaps due to low visibility rather than total absence. A few chunks and flakes were retouched, often into steep-edged and high backed forms like those of Agop Sarapad and basal Ulu Leang.

The faunal remains from Paso and from the contemporary (Pre-Toalian) layers at Ulu Leang have been identified by Clason (1980; in press). Pigs (*Sus celebensis*, not babirusa) were most popular in both sites, and occurred with anoa, monkeys, rodents and the two Sulawesi species of marsupial cuscus (*Phalanger celebensis* and *P. ursinus*). The lake-edge situation of Paso allowed for considerable hunting of birds, while the karst-riverine situation of Ulu Leang led to more frequent catches of tortoises, snakes and occasional fish. In neither assemblage are there indications of animal domestication.

E. Eastern Timor and Flores

From four caves in eastern (formerly Portuguese) Timor, Glover (1971, 1972a, 1977a) has excavated an industry with basal dates of about 13 000

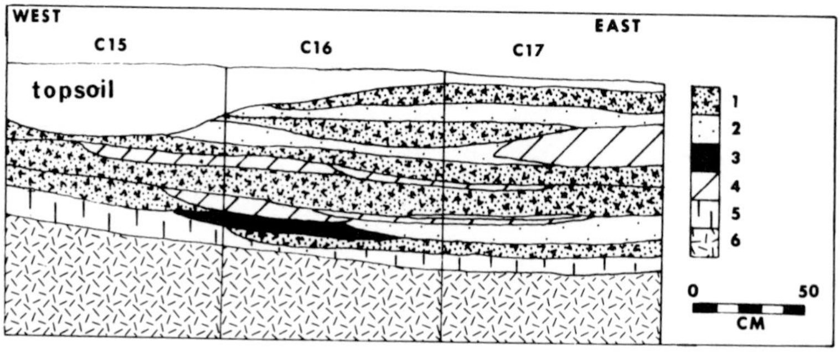

Fig. 6.19. The structure of a part of the Paso midden. 1, Loose shell; 2, broken shell, black soil and charcoal; 3, charcoal; 4, ash; 5, old topsoil; 6, light grey lacustrine sand. From Bellwood 1976b.

years ago, which continued with little change into the ceramic period which began here during the third millennium BC. The tools are primarily chert flakes (there is also a little obsidian) and the retouched forms are mainly steep-edged scrapers. A number of the unretouched flakes have an edge-gloss and there are also a few long thick blades (Fig. 6.20).

The fauna of the period prior to 3000 BC is dominated by several species of extinct giant rats which survived until about 2000 years ago, together with fruit bats, snakes, reptiles, fish and shellfish (other placental mammal species such as pigs and deer were all introduced into Timor after 3000 BC). Remains of gathered plants in the early levels included seeds or fragments of the perennial cereal Job's tears, betel vine and *Areca* nut (the ingredients of betel chewing), and candlenut (*Aleurites*) (Glover 1977b:18). Basically, this Timorese industry has much in common with those just described from Sabah and Sulawesi, but it does seem to be a little distinctive in its minor predilection for long blade-like artefacts.

An undated industry from several open sites on Flores may be related to the Timor material, and I have already referred to these industries in Chapter 2, Section IIID6, since some components may be of considerable antiquity, possibly contemporary with extinct species of *Stegodon*. However, none of this material is dated, and with scattered surface finds of this type it is quite possible that the collections cover an enormous timespan.

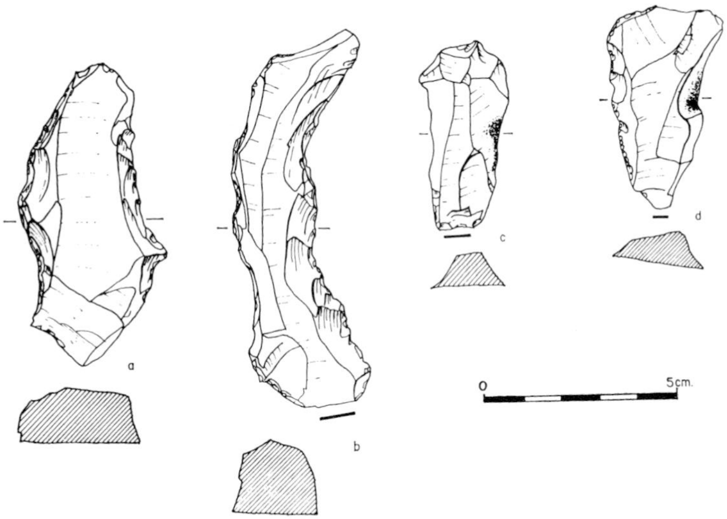

Fig. 6.20. Principal stone tool types of East Timor. (a, b) Blade-like flakes with steep retouch; (c, d) flakes with silica gloss. From the cave of Uai Bobo 2, 4th–3rd millennia BC. From Glover 1977a. Courtesy: I. C. Glover.

F. Comments

I should first add to the above list the only dated industry from Sumatra, which comes from the cave of Tianko Panjang in the Sumatran highlands near Lake Kerinci (Bronson and Asmar 1975), and which comprises unretouched obsidian flakes and chips which date from about 9000 bc onwards. Many other scattered industries of this kind have been found across Indonesia, particularly in Sumatra and Java (e.g. Franssen 1941; Heekeren 1972:137–9) and eastern Indonesia, and they have continued in production almost into the ethnographic present amongst the Tasaday (here with some edge-grinding; Fox 1976), and in the New Guinea Highlands and central Australia. The long industrial sequence from the Tabon Caves on Palawan (Fox 1970, 1978) also fits well within the Indo-Malaysian pebble and flake repertoire.

All the chert and obsidian-based industries I have looked at (that is excluding the more intractable raw materials used at Niah) are characterised by flake production with stone hammers from multi- or single-platform cores. Retouch is often steep, and high-domed "scraper" forms are quite common, as is the edge-gloss on retouched flakes. In some sites core smashing appears to have been as important as systematic flaking (especially with obsidian), and this has been emphasised by Coutts and Wesson (1980) for the Philippines, where they refer rather colourfully to a category of "smash and grab" industries. Although flakes often have blade-like proportions, there is no sign of any systematic attempt at blade production until after 6000 BC.

The basic core, flake and pebble characteristics of these Late Pleistocene and Holocene island industries are on a similar technological level to some of the Mousterian or Middle Palaeolithic industries of northern Asia (including Japan) and India, and they find fairly close parallels in the "core tool and scraper tradition" (Bowler *et al.* 1970) of Australia and New Guinea, both of which were first settled from Indonesia before or around 40 000 years ago. These similarities are not surprising, and the localised variations which relate to raw materials and chance are often overstressed by prehistorians with purely local concerns. It is true that unusual variants do occur, and apart from those at Leang Burung 2 and lake Tingkayu there is also the unusual significance of large waisted axe-like tools ("waisted blades") in the New Guinea Highlands and parts of Australia. These latter items do not occur in the Indo-Malaysian islands, but they appear occasionally and perhaps independently in some Hoabinhian sites (see Fig. 6.2).

III. The Flake and Blade Technocomplex of the Mid-Holocene

In parts of the Philippines, Sulawesi and Java there are a number of assemblages dated to after 6000 BC which demonstrate regionally-varied emphases on the production of small blades, and sometimes on other specialised tools such as "microliths" with blunted backs and small projectile points. In all cases these new technologies appear as accretions on to the old and continuing tradition of unprepared flake production.

In a previous book (Bellwood 1978a:71) I quoted a definition by Morlan (1971:143) of blades as "elongate parallel-sided flakes with parallel arrises or parallel-sided facets on their dorsal faces. Blades are struck (by indirect percussion) from prepared, polyhedral cores . . .". The Upper Palaeolithic industries of much of the Old World were focussed on the production of blades of this type, and in Japan, northern China and north-western India it is now clear that they were widespread by at least 20 000 years ago. However, in Island South-East Asia and Australia blades form only a small minority component of most assemblages in which they occur, and true cylindrical or conical blade cores are generally very rare. Many of the "blades" found in this region fall into Morlan's category of blade-like flakes, which are less symmetrical than true blades and which lack the parallel ridges. Nevertheless, since cores of a subprismatic shape do occur in small numbers, and since I believe that both blades and blade-like flakes were produced intentionally in some sites, I will refer to the industries described in this section as the "flake and blade technocomplex".

At present there appear to be two kinds of industry within the flake and blade technocomplex; the unretouched blade industries of the Philippines and the Talaud Islands of north-eastern Indonesia, and the backed flake-blade and microlithic industry, termed the Toalian, in south-western Sulawesi. At the end of this section I will also consider some undated industries, perhaps related to the Toalian, which have been found on Java. The Philippines, Sulawesi, Java, Australia, and possibly southern Sumatra encompass the distribution of industries in this technocomplex, and they seem to be completely absent from Borneo, eastern Indonesia and New Guinea (although Timor does have a later Neolithic industry of tanged blade-like points, see Chapter 7, Fig. 7.13).

A. The Philippines and Talaud

Industries in which a component of small unretouched blades is added to a continuing flake tradition occur in the Philippines, and in the Talaud Islands south of Mindanao. In Duyong Cave, near Tabon Cave on Palawan, Fox (1970) has excavated an industry with small blade-like flakes struck from what he originally termed "prepared cores", although he has since stated that such cores were not present (Fox 1979:236). The tools occurred in a midden of marine and estuarine shell dated to the sixth millennium BC. Possibly similar industries have been described from Cebu by Tenazas (1985), and from a small island called Buad off the western coast of Samar by Cherry (1978). No clear chronologies are available for these sites, and both late preceramic and Neolithic associations seem likely. Blades account for up to 50% of the Buad collections and some pieces have glossed edges or traces of a mastic used in hafting.

The most detailed information on an industry of this type comes from the rock-shelter of Leang Tuwo Mane'e on Karakellang Island in the Talaud group (Bellwood 1976b). This shelter was originally cut by the sea into a cliff of coral limestone, and was then uplifted to a habitable level by about 4000 BC. The basal deposits produced an industry comprising blades and blade-like flakes (about 50% of all flaked stone), together with some rather rudimentary prismatic cores, made on a grey chert (Fig. 6.21). Retouch is virtually absent, but some edge-gloss occurs. Around 2500 BC pottery appeared in the site, and at this time there was a surprising and unexplained change away from the grey chert towards a nodular brown chert which was used for the production of a much less refined flake industry, which continued on into the upper layers of the site. The blade industry is thus restricted mainly to the preceramic levels, and the date of its actual appearance in Talaud cannot be determined from this site. Both preceramic and ceramic layers contained large numbers of shellfish of no less than 94 species from a wide range of reef and mudflat habitats (Heffernan 1980), but apart from pig in the ceramic layers no mammal bones were present; the Talaud Islands had only a limited native fauna of rats, bats and a species of *Phalanger*.

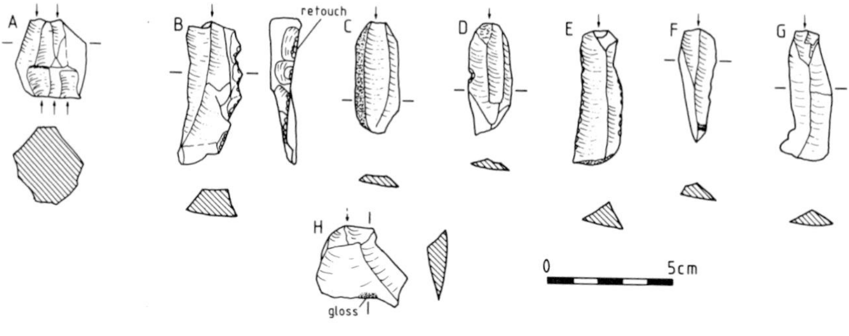

Fig. 6.21. Blades and blade-like flakes from Leang Tuwo Mane'e, c. 4th millennium BC. (A) Sub-prismatic core; (H) glossed flake.

B. The Toalian

The most important industry of the flake and blade technocomplex is undoubtedly the Toalian of south-western Sulawesi, which commenced about 6000 BC with an array of microliths (small backed flakes and geometrics) of types seemingly unique in the Indo-Malaysian Archipelago. Toalian assemblages have been excavated since 1902 from caves and shelters scattered across the southern half of the south-western peninsula of Sulawesi, and during the 1930s and 1940s some rudimentary typological successions were established by Stein Callenfels (1938) and Heekeren (1949). In Heekeren's last major summary (1972), by which time about 20 sites had been excavated, he felt justified in supporting a three-phase sequence commencing with plain blades, followed by a second phase with backed flakes and blades and geometric (crescentic and trapezoidal) microliths, and culminating finally in a third phase with bone points, serrated and hollow-based stone points, and pottery.

As a result of two recent excavations there is now much more information on the Toalian. Both sites are located in the Maros limestone region north of Ujungpandang; one is called Leang Burung 1 (Mulvaney and Soejono 1970, 1971; Chapman 1981) and the other, Ulu Leang, has received detailed treatment over several seasons by a team led by Glover (1976, 1977a, 1978a; Glover and Presland 1985). The latter site has the most complete sequence.

I have already considered the basal industry of flakes and steep-edged tools at Ulu Leang, dated to between 8000 and 6000 bc (see Section IIC). The Toalian tool types (Fig. 6.22) appear in higher levels dated from about 6000 BC within a continuing basic industry of flake tools and bone points, although the steep-edged tools fade in importance. The most important new tool type is a small flake or blade with straight or oblique blunting down one side and often around the butt (that is similar to a "backed blade" in Australian terminology), and some of these backed forms have distinctly crescentic or trapezoidal shapes (geometric microliths). The present trend (Chapman 1981; Glover and Presland 1985) is to refer to all these new Toalian forms as "microliths". Sometime after 4200 BC another type of microlith, the "Maros" serrated and hollow-based point, appeared in the sequence, perhaps as a result of local innovation. Other artefacts which occur throughout the Ulu Leang sequence include glossed flakes, small bipolar cores, bone points, and bivalve shell scrapers (Willems 1939).

The site of Leang Burung 1 (Fig. 6.23) is later than Ulu Leang, and the deposits appear to date within the last two millennia BC and have pottery throughout. Hence there is no long sequence here, but the microliths and Maros points are still present and Chapman (1981) stresses the importance of the edge-gloss (on 24% of used tools), and also notes the absence of steep-edged tools, pebble tools and edge-ground tools (the latter, to my knowledge,

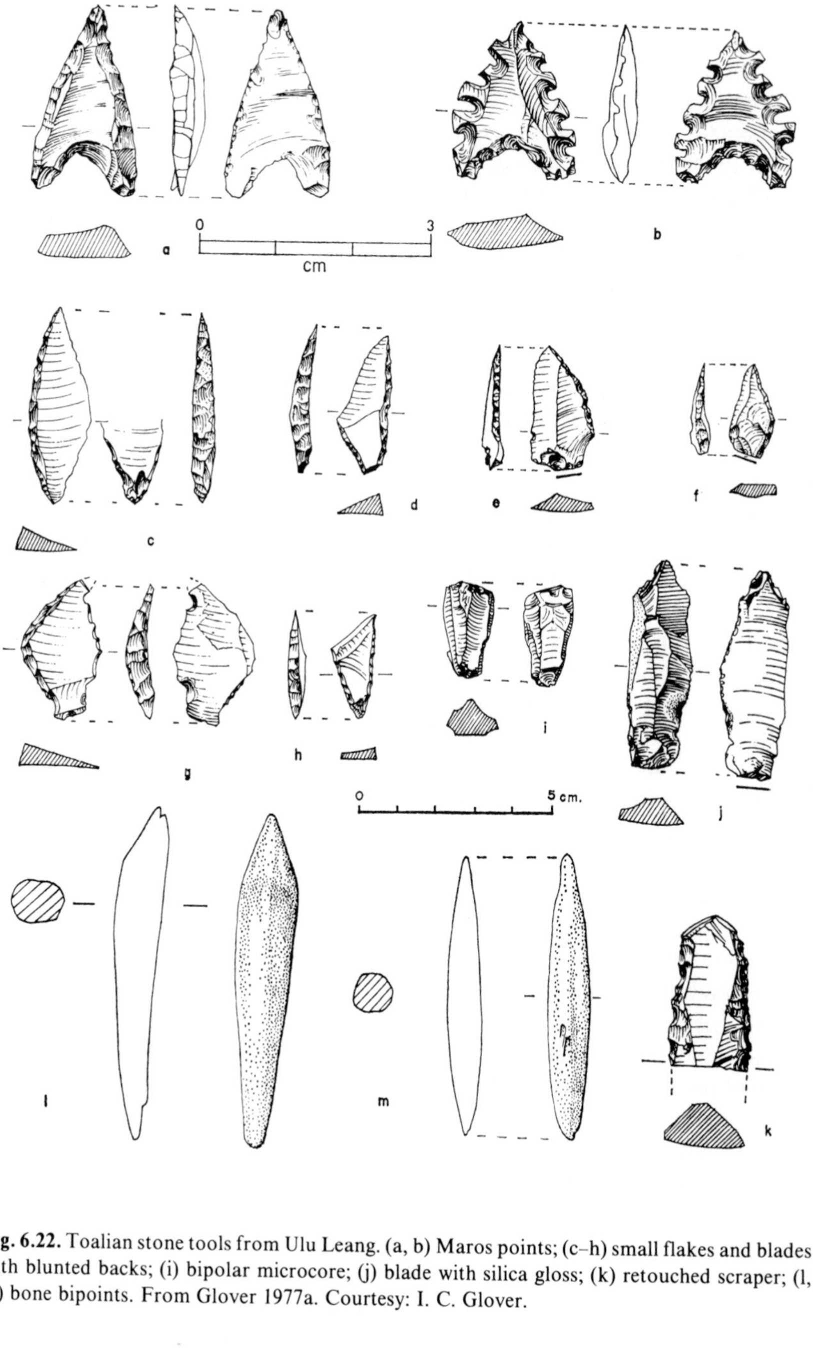

Fig. 6.22. Toalian stone tools from Ulu Leang. (a, b) Maros points; (c–h) small flakes and blades with blunted backs; (i) bipolar microcore; (j) blade with silica gloss; (k) retouched scraper; (l, m) bone bipoints. From Glover 1977a. Courtesy: I. C. Glover.

Fig. 6.23. Excavations at Leang Burung 1 in 1969. Photo by John Mulvaney.

appear to be absent in all Toalian sites). At Leang Burung 1 the microliths (including Maros points) comprise about 35% of all retouched tools, which in turn comprise only 6% of the total of stone artefacts, and at Ulu Leang the corresponding percentages are 20% and 6%.

The Ulu Leang sequence generally supports the essentials of Heekeren's second and third phases (that is backed microliths succeeded by Maros points), but the site has no earlier phase with plain blades. This need not mean that this earlier phase does not exist in all other Toalian sequences, and as I have shown it is present without later typological elaboration in the Talaud Islands. The question of intentional blade production in the Toalian is in fact a difficult one. Chapman feels that it was practised at Leang Burung 1, and about 10% of flakes here had blade proportions, although no prismatic cores were found. Heekeren (1972: Plate 63b) also illustrates a series of blades from the site of Panganreang Tudea (near the southern tip of the peninsula) which remind me closely of the blades from Talaud. However, Glover and Presland (1985) deny the existence of a blade technology at Ulu Leang, although Glover has often used the term "blade" in his published discussions of the site. After analysing the stone tools from the much older site of Leang Burung 2 (see Section IIC), together with those from Ulu Leang, Presland (1980) concluded that a blade technology was not evident in these particular Maros sites, although flakes did become smaller by about 20% in average size over the whole period (over 20 000 years). However, no one has challenged the significance of the sudden appearance of the new microlithic forms after 6000 BC. These raise the question of outside parallels, which I will consider later.

The Toalian industry continues on well into the pottery phase at most excavated sites, and in itself it reveals no clear evidence for the agricultural economy which must surely have been developing in some parts of Sulawesi after 2500 BC. Even as late as AD 1000 the retouched and glossed flakes still occur at Batu Ejaya near the southern end of the peninsula (Chapman 1981), although most of the microliths have by now disappeared and the serrated Maros points appear to have been replaced by plainer round-based forms. The late survival of the Toalian here may document a continuing tradition of hunting and gathering, perhaps amongst indigenous non-Austronesian speakers contemporary with cultivators elsewhere, or perhaps as a sporadic activity by village-based agriculturalists.

The economic evidence from the Toalian sites includes a range of hunted and gathered resources. Riverine shellfish are very common, and Glover (1977b:52) found remains of wild seeds and nuts at Ulu Leang, although carbonised rice grains only appeared in the site after AD 500 (Glover 1985). In Section IIE I described the animal remains from the lower levels of Ulu Leang, and the faunas from other Toalian sites (Hooijer 1950a) were drawn from a similar range of Sulawesi mammals; the two species of *Phalanger*, macaque monkey, civet cat, anoa, *Sus celebensis* and babirusa. A small quantity of art found on the limestone walls of Toalian sites has been described by Heekeren (1950b, 1972:119–20), although none can be dated. Hand stencils and wild pigs were depicted in red hematite, and the former are of great interest because of the world-wide occurrence and great antiquity of this motif. Some of the hand stencils, interestingly, lack one or more digits.

C. The Sampung Industry of Eastern Java

This industry (Fig. 6.24), called the "Sampung bone industry" by Heekeren (1972:92), is best known from a cave called Gua Lawa near the village of Sampung, between the Lawu and Liman volcanoes in central Java. The site

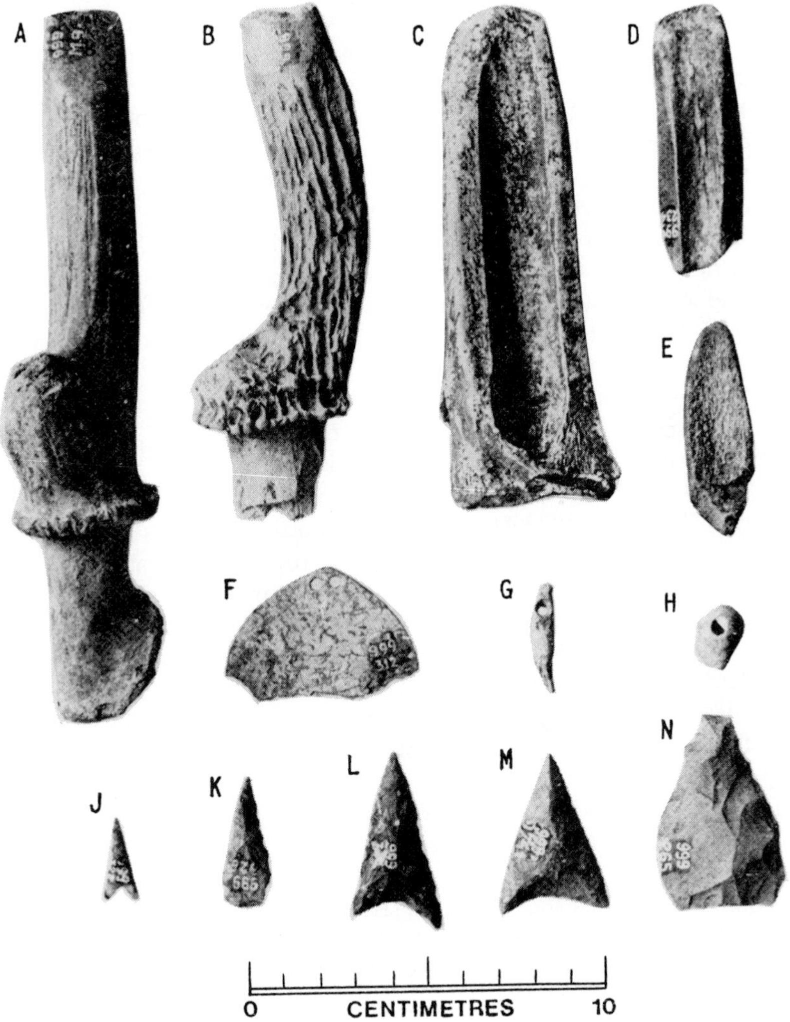

Fig. 6.24. Tools from Gua Lawa Cave, Java. (A–E) Bone and antler tools; (F–H) perforated shell and tooth pendants; (J–N) stone points. From Heekeren 1972. Courtesy: Martinus Nijhoff.

was excavated by Stein Callenfels in 1931, and although the methods were rather crude and the site obviously disturbed, he did provide a section drawing in his report (1932) which shows the vertical distribution of all the artefacts found within a 2 m thick occupation deposit. The lowest of three apparent levels of occupation produced a number of stone projectile points with hollow or round bases, but without the serrated edges characteristic of Maros points. Hollowed stone grindstones and spherical rubbing stones with traces of hematite also appeared in this layer, but no records were made of the basic flaked stone industry which was also present.

Above the lowest level, and apparently extending over about half of the excavated area within the cave, Stein Callenfels found a lens of bone and antler points and spatulae with more stone mortars, and a few possibly downwards-disturbed potsherds and a polished adze. Pottery, metal, and a general mixture of other material then occurred in the top layer, with four bone fishhooks. Flexed burials, at least one under a stone slab and including one child with a shell necklace, were indicated as stratified within the middle layer with the bone tools; all have been classified as Australoid or Melanesian (see Chapter 3, Section IIIB).

At face value (and there is no other way to interpret this site now) the Gua Lawa sequence indicates a definitely preceramic industry of bone tools and stone arrowheads very similar to the non-serrated Toalian types, together with "flakes and blades without secondary working and many retouched shell scrapers" (Heekeren 1972:94). In a previous account of this site (Bellwood 1978a:76) I included the bone tools with the top pottery-bearing layer, but I am now inclined to regard the latter as little more than a surface skin and to regard the bone tools as basically preceramic. The fauna, apparently mainly from the middle layer with the bone tools (Dammerman, Annexe I in Callenfels 1932), comprised a broad range of big mammals such as banteng cattle, deer, pig (*Sus vittatus*), monkeys, Indian elephant, buffalo, and several large felines (see also Chapter 1, Table 1.1). Monitor lizards were especially frequent.

This type of industry is known from sites scattered all over the eastern end of Java, but all from very old excavations. South of Gua Lawa a rock-shelter in Gunung Cantalan has produced round-based stone points and many facial, masklike parts of macaque monkeys (Heekeren 1972:99). Other sites occur to the north around Bojonegoro and inland from Tuban. Heekeren (1935–6; 1937) also excavated three caves, called Petpuruh, Sodong and Marjan near Puger in south-eastern Java, about 200 km east of Gua Lawa. These caves produced the same preceramic assemblage of round-based stone points, bone tools, shell scrapers and rings, and flexed burials. Pebble tools and flakes of quartz, chert and obsidian also occurred, together with hammerstones and grindstones. Heekeren seemed to favour Hoabinhian affinities for these industries, but I find this most unlikely and would rather stress their close similarities with the Toalian, except for the obvious absences in eastern Java of the backed flakes and geometrics. A similar mid-Holocene date also seems very likely.

D. Other Flake and Blade Industries in Java

A large number of sites in western Java, especially on the Bandung Plateau, have produced an undated but presumably preceramic industry of obsidian (Bandi 1951; Heekeren 1972:133–7; Anggraeni 1976). The sites still await detailed archaeological investigation, and the existence of a definite blade element seems to be rather uncertain. However, the available illustrations leave no doubt that backed flakes, round-based and unifacially retouched projectile points, and a few crescentic and trapezoidal geometrics are present (Fig. 6.25). The sites may in fact be mixtures of several time periods, for a number of more archaic domed and steep-edged tools also occur, but the overall impression is of an industry which may be fairly similar to the Toalian. Some surface collected obsidians from sites around Lake Kerinci and Jambi in south-central Sumatra (Hoop 1940) may also contain points and microliths, and Glover and Presland (1985) report backed crescents from some of these sites, although such forms were absent in the excavated Tianko Panjang cave.

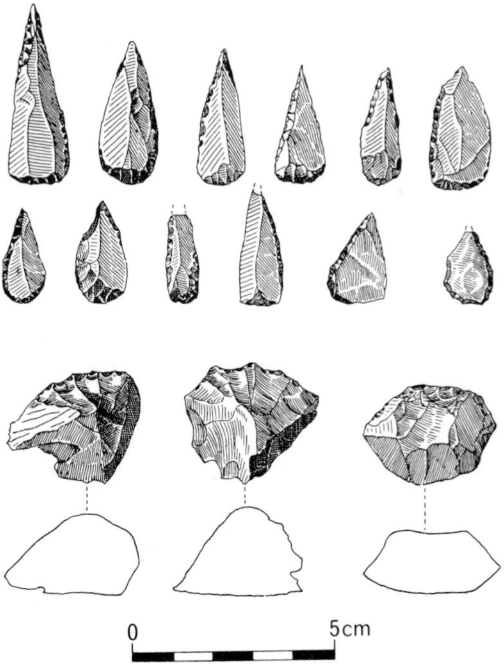

Fig. 6.25. Obsidian backed points, geometrics and steep-edged tools from the Bandung Plateau. From Bandi 1951. Courtesy: Museum für Völkerkunde, Basel.

E. Comments

Reasons for the appearances of these new flake and blade technologies, both in the Indo-Malaysian region and in Australia, are topics which cause considerable dispute amongst prehistorians. One important fact which should be noted is that in Island South-East Asia and Australia these new technologies are always grafted on to old ones — there are no wholesale replacements of flake industries by blade industries, and no good reasons from the stone tool evidence to invoke large-scale human expansions into the region prior to that of the agricultural Austronesians. Nevertheless, it is difficult to decide for individual regions whether the new technologies developed independently or whether they were adopted from an outside source, and in some cases the answer may be a combination of both processes. In company with Glover and Presland (1985) and Dortch (1977) I feel that some significance must be allocated to diffusion, although it should not be forgotten that the ability to produce elongated blade-like flakes was present at the sites of Leang Burung 1 and Hagop Bilo well before the end of the Pleistocene. Indeed, many Australian prehistorians today regard the "small tool industries" of Holocene Australia as local developments quite unrelated to anything in Indonesia (e.g. Hallam 1977; White and O'Connell 1982).

I rather doubt that these questions of independence versus diffusion will ever be resolved, since stone tools of this kind, with the possible exception of the Maros points, do not carry a large component of cultural as opposed to purely functional information. However, the simple fact of coincidence in dates can hardly be overlooked, and the points, backed blades and geometrics so characteristic of later Australian prehistory do appear there from about 4000 BC onwards (Schrire 1982; Mulvaney 1985). Possibly Heekeren (1972:125) was correct when he suggested that these tool types actually diffused to Sulawesi from Australia. Radiocarbon dates as known at present do not in my opinion provide much support for this view, but it should not be dismissed entirely.

Perhaps the most likely region of outside influence on the islands of South-East Asia in terms of these flake and blade industries is Japan. India is only a remote possibility, since the intervening Hoabinhian industries show no signs of any of the developments under consideration. However, during the Initial, Early and Middle Jomon periods of Holocene Japan (c. 7500 bc onwards) there is a range of hollow-based projectile points and blade tools which look a little like some of the South-East Asian examples, although geometric microliths of the Toalian types are to my knowledge not found there. An undated but presumably Holocene industry with some blades has recently been reported from a site near Guangzhou (Canton) in Guangdong province in southern China (Huang *et al.* 1982), but there seems to be no material of this type from Taiwan or the Ryukyu Islands. Nevertheless, Japan does provide a number of interesting but vague possibilities, and no prehistorian with competence in both South-East Asia and Japan has ever really looked into this matter in any detail. As with the appearance of edge-grinding, a development obviously quite unrelated to the appearance of the flake and blade industries, there are a lot of question marks when looking at questions of origin.

7
The Archaeological Record of Early Austronesian Communities

The ethnolinguistic prehistory of the Austronesian-speaking populations who now inhabit virtually all of the Indo-Malaysian Archipelago must be written, at grass roots level, from the linguistic evidence. This is because languages are crucial witnesses to past and present ethnic identity, certainly more so than the items of material culture which are likely to survive in tropical archaeological sites. As I demonstrated in Chapter 4, the reconstructions of the comparative linguists indicate very strongly that the earliest Austronesians expanded from southern China, through Taiwan, and then southwards into the Philippines, Indonesia and Oceania. They had an economy based firmly on agriculture and some domesticated animals, and a technology which included pottery, sailing canoes, and well-constructed wooden houses. The linguistic evidence can also tell a great deal about the geographical patterning of Austronesian expansion, and about certain adaptations which took place in the Austronesian lifestyle. It cannot, however, tell very much about absolute chronology, or many essential details of the changing regional patterns of material culture and economy.

The provision of information in the latter categories is of course very much the domain of archaeology, as the bulk of the next three chapters will show. This discipline can also provide some information which can be equated with the record of ethnic prehistory as derived from linguistics, although the archaeological record from the long-settled Indo-Malaysian Archipelago is naturally more ambiguous and circumstantial in terms of ethnolinguistic affiliation than it is in the island groups of Fiji and Polynesia, where settlement was relatively recent and Austronesians found no prior inhabitants. For instance, I believe that the documented spread of pottery after 3000

BC through parts of Island South-East Asia is a result of Austronesian settlement, but this is naturally impossible to prove in any absolute sense since pots cannot talk. Neither can stone adzes — but both have dates, typological characteristics and distributions which we can attempt to interpret.

It will soon be apparent, however, that the reconstruction of ethnolinguistic prehistory is by no means the only concern of the modern prehistorian. In dealing with this in the Austronesian context I have chosen to focus on a linguistic model, and to use the data from archaeology and biological anthropology in supportive roles. But, as I will show there is much more to the Austronesians and their archaeological record than the documentation of founder expansions.

To anticipate the following sections I will set out here a brief version of my overall model for the later stages of Indo-Malaysian prehistory:

1. The Austronesian-speakers who expanded into the Indo-Malaysian Archipelago carried a fully agricultural economy initially focussed on cereals, and introduced pottery and a new repertoire of uni-bevelled stone adzes.
2. The pre-Austronesian inhabitants of the archipelago may occasionally have used edge-ground axes (as at Niah), but they did not use pottery. While they undoubtedly exploited many tubers and fruit trees, later of major importance as domesticates, they did not systematically cultivate these species. Had they done so, the present ethnic record of non-Austronesian and non-Mongoloid populations in the major islands of South-East Asia would be much fuller than it is.
3. Non-Austronesian hunters and gatherers survived in ever-diminishing numbers throughout the millennia of Austronesian expansion, but an agricultural economy may have developed independently in some parts of New Guinea before this expansion took place.
4. During the millennia of expansion southwards and into Oceania, the economies of Austronesian societies underwent a number of latitudinal and more localised ecological adaptations, and cereals were gradually replaced by tubers and tree fruits.
5. During the millennium between 500 BC and AD 500 the archipelago was incorporated into wider South and East Asian spheres of interaction — major introductions or developments of this period include metals and probably domesticated cattle and buffalo, together with a postulated significant increase in land areas committed to terraced and irrigated rice cultivation.

I. The Origins of Agriculture in Southern China and South-East Asia

It is my belief that there is enough botanical, linguistic and archaeological evidence to allow a partial reconstruction of the early stages of agricultural prehistory in China and South-East Asia. This has not always been the case, and until a few years ago it was fairly commonplace for geographers and botanists to offer purely hypothetical reconstructions which were always plausible but never testable. Hence the well-known theory of Sauer (1952) that agriculture arose with the vegetative planting of tubers and other useful plants in the monsoonal regions of Mainland South-East Asia, especially in resource-rich coastal and riverine situations where many useful plant species were available for many purposes as well as food.

The literature which has grown up around Sauer's theory is too extensive to review here, but I do want in this chapter to challenge two widely-accepted corollaries of his views. One is that cultivation based on the vegetative planting of trees and tubers long preceded the cultivation of cereals in South-East Asia, and the other is that agriculture began in "affluent forager" conditions of leisure and plenty.

As far as the first corollary is concerned I accept Gorman's suggestion (1977) that rice was one of the earliest plants to be domesticated in southern China and the northern parts of Mainland South-East Asia, and archaeological evidence which supports this observation will be reviewed below. The simple observation that Oceanic populations did not grow cereals in prehistoric times is insufficient evidence to support a model of their secondary domestication in the South-East Asian region as a whole. Furthermore, a world-wide perspective on the archaeological record which pertains to the origins of agriculture indicates that cereals, rather than tubers and fruits, were the major food resources behind the earliest developments of sedentary village-based lifestyles and the resulting cultural changes towards complex societies. It is true that certain regions, such as New Guinea and parts of South America, may have witnessed independent developments of agriculture which were not based on cereals, but as far as China and South-East Asia are concerned I think it most likely from the evidence now available that rice and the millets were of primary and fundamental significance.

The second corollary has recently been revived by Chang (1981) for southern China, but it seems to me that the affluent forager viewpoint is now at loggerheads with the majority of published opinions, which virtually always regard the origins of agriculture as a reaction to stress, whether due to direct demographic pressures on resources (Boserup 1965; 1980; Cohen 1977) or to less specific environmental and social perturbations affecting resource availability (e.g. Bronson 1977; Rindos 1980; Hayden 1981). One very common assumption is that hunter–gatherers will not turn to cultivation, which requires intermittent higher inputs of labour and forward planning for land clearance, weeding and harvesting, unless they are forced to do so by a growing imbalance between population size and/or social demands, and available food.

This general view has always seemed to me to be very plausible, but alone it can hardly explain why agriculture should have developed, apparently independently, in a number of hearth regions in the Old and New Worlds early in the Holocene period of rapid climatic amelioration. This is not a question which I am able to answer, but I do believe that the record from south-western Asia, which is the most detailed in the world for an early transition to agriculture, holds important information about this climatic amelioration and its impact on humans and cereals. Since the cultivated rices and millets are annual cereal grasses like wheat and barley a comparative perspective on this region may be informative.

In general, Late Pleistocene environments in south-western Asia seem to have been cold, relatively treeless, and perhaps too dry for large-grained annual grasses to have flourished; those species which were later brought under cultivation as domesticated cereals were therefore probably restricted to refuge areas at this time, or they could have been predominantly perennial. A major environmental change then commenced with the spread of a warmer climate, apparently with a more dependable winter wet season, after about 12 000 bc (Wright 1977; 1983; Bottema and Zeist 1981). The result of this was a spread of annual grasses adapted to winter rains and summer drought which allowed some groups, such as the Natufians of the Levant, to inhabit small but fairly permanent villages supported by the reaping of these wild cereals and the storage of grain for lean seasons (Hassan 1977; Henry 1983).

According to modern studies on recently settled hunter–gatherers, the resulting decrease in Natufian population mobility should have allowed more frequent births, and an increasing dependence on cereal gruel for infant food might also have allowed a reduction in the average duration of contraceptive-linked breast feeding (Cohen 1980; Lee 1980; Anderson 1983). The result would have been a slow but inexorable rise in population. This in itself might have been sufficient to encourage groups to increase their grain yields by systematic cultivation, and a postulated shift back to a cooler and drier climate in the Levant after 8000 bc may have provided an extra stimulus (Henry *et al.* 1981; Davis 1982). If this scenario is correct (and it is possible to complicate matters with an enormous range of additional social and ecological variables), then the late Natufians were probably the first people in the world to cultivate grains, and we may almost know why.

It is impossible to apply such a model directly to eastern Asia, since we know nothing about Chinese or Mainland South-East Asian agriculture until it appears well-developed with quantities of millet or rice in large and presumably sedentary Neolithic villages, all of which postdate 6000 BC. No truly incipient agricultural phase has been discovered here so far. Such may of course exist, but until the evidence appears we can only make informed guesses. According to Whyte (1972, 1975, 1983), the annual rices and millets ancestral to the present cultivated species radiated from perennial ancestors around the eastern fringes of the Himalayas under conditions of increasing warmth and seasonality of rainfall distribution at the end of the Pleistocene. In its basic form this radiation parallels to some extent that proposed for the annual wheats and barleys in south-western Asia, and if the proposal is correct then it may be expected that such events occurred several times during the Pleistocene, although during previous interglacial ameliorations there is no evidence that humans took advantage of them.

In the early Holocene the advantage clearly was taken, and annual millets (especially foxtail millet, *Setaria italica*) were being cultivated in the Yellow River Basin by perhaps 6000 BC, and annual rice in the lower Yangtze Valley by at least 5000 BC — in both cases on a fairly large and certainly not incipient scale. According to Oka (1975) and Chang (1976a, 1976b, 1983; see also Glover 1985), the wild annual ancestor of modern cultivated rice (termed *Oryza nivara* by Chang) was first domesticated somewhere in a zone from north-eastern India, across northern South-East Asia, and into southern China (Figs 7.1 and 7.2). The ecological preferences of the wild annual rices today are alluvial backswamps or swampy areas with a seasonal abundance of water for growth; during the dry season the grains remain dormant in the ground. Most modern authors clearly believe that initial cultivation of rice took place in such seasonally wet habitats, perhaps under conditions of natural inundation with little onerous field preparation being required (Barrau 1968, 1974; Condominas 1980; Chang 1985; Gorman and Charoenwongsa, in press). Such conditions would have existed in the vicinities of those sites in the Gangetic plain, northern Thailand and the lower Yangtze where the earliest cultivated rices occur.

The lower Yangtze sites, which lie in Zhejiang and Jiangsu provinces (Fig. 7.3), are sufficiently early in date (see below) to make it likely that they represent a localised and independent centre of rice domestication. It is simply not known at present whether the Thai and Indian sites can be similarly regarded, and I do not wish to consider this problem here. However, the location of the lower Yangtze region may be very significant, because although it lies beyond the northern limit of wild annual rice distribution today (Chang 1976a; Matsuo 1975), it is possible that the early Holocene climate in this region was warmer and more suited to wild rice than at present (Chekiang 1978). There is thus a slight possibility that the development of cultivation here followed a similar course to that which now seems likely for

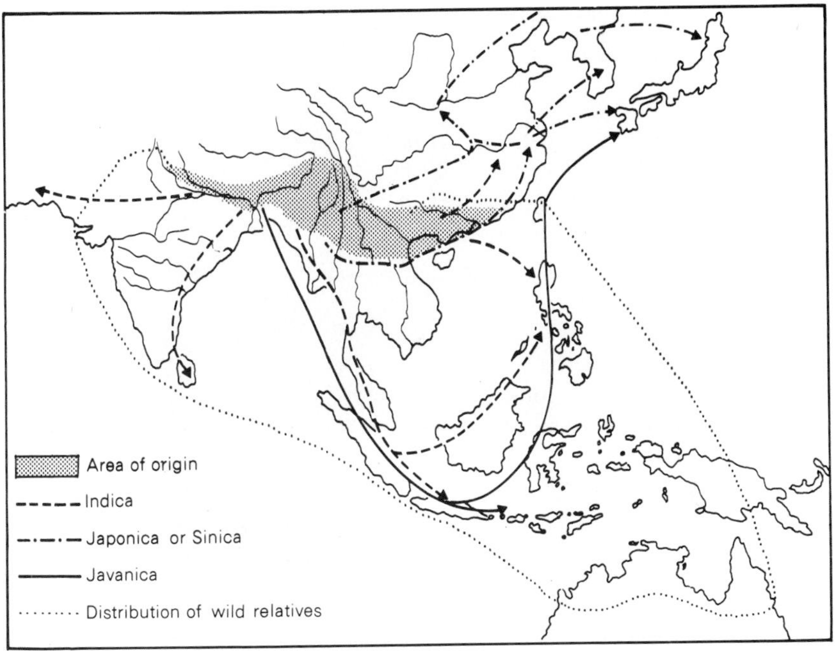

Fig. 7.1. The present distribution of wild relatives and the spread of geographic races of *Oryza sativa* in South-East Asia, after T. T. Chang 1976a. The northern limit of the wild rices may have been closer to the Yangtze in early Holocene times (see text). (The arrows on this map do not clearly reflect the prehistoric developments proposed in this chapter.) Courtesy: T. T. Chang.

south-western Asia; a sedentary lifestyle based on the harvesting of wild annual rice developed at the beginning of the Holocene, and then harvesting became transformed into systematic cultivation as a response to some kind of stress — perhaps climatic, or perhaps some more subtle enemy of the balance between human population and available wild food resources. I need hardly add that this is no more than a conceivable model at the moment, but in terms of dated archaeological evidence it is clear that rice, still morphologically close to wild forms, was being systematically cultivated in Zhejiang by 5000 BC.

The early stages of rice cultivation probably involved some fairly vigorous selection, whether intentional or not, towards a gene pool characterised by a non-shattering habit, a reduced duration of dormancy, more synchronous ripening of planted stands, and increased grain size and numbers on each panicle. Such changes do not happen overnight, and in northern Thailand, well within the homeland region of wild annual rice, it appears that they were

Fig. 7.2. (a) A possible evolutionary sequence for cultivated rice: right, the wild perennial *Oryza rufipogon*; centre, the wild annual *Oryza nivara*; left, cultivated *Oryza sativa*. Photo by Colin Totterdell, CSIRO, Canberra. (b) Cultivated rice (*Oryza sativa*) being harvested with a metal finger-knife. Iban, Sarawak. Photo by Hedda Morrison.

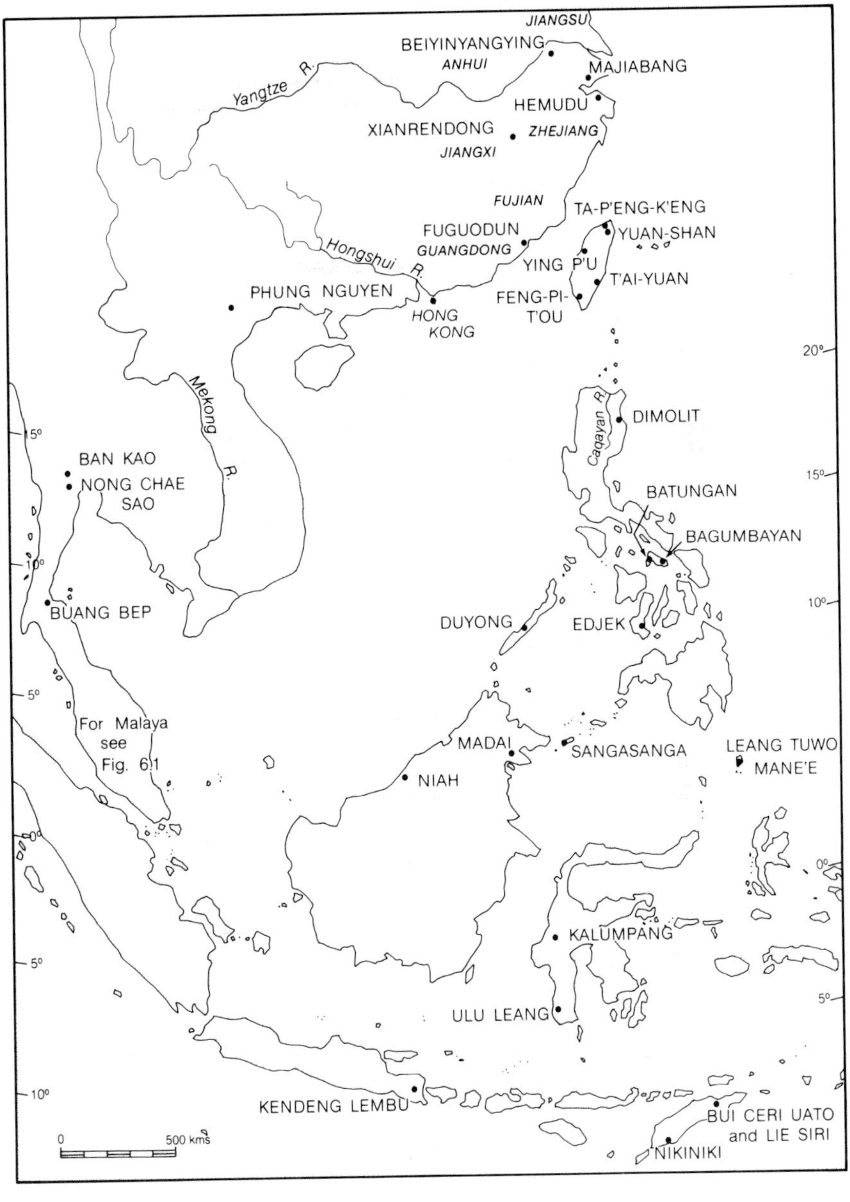

Fig. 7.3. Locations of sites described in Chapters 7 and 8.

very slow to develop (Yen 1977). In the lower Yangtze region, on the other hand, genetic changes appear to have been more rapid. Hence, I accept Chang's viewpoint (1983) that:

> The true domestication process (of rice) undoubtedly first took place in China because the cooler weather and shorter crop season there exerted great selection pressure on the early cultivars and made them more dependent on human care for perpetuation than were their tropical counterparts.

However, I should stress that this only implies that the process of genetic domestication of rice occurred more rapidly in southern China than in other regions, and races developed there were most probably the ones introduced by early Austronesians into Island South-East Asia. It does not necessarily mean that the total agricultural complex originated in China and spread into other adjacent areas such as northern Thailand, since a separate process of cultivating a stable and basically wild rice may have developed here quite independently of regions to the north. The possibility of a separate Gangetic centre of rice domestication far to the west must also be recognised, but this is not of direct relevance here.

II. The Beginnings of Austronesian Prehistory

I now wish to move straight into a review of the modern archaeological evidence; it is not my purpose here to review the outdated but historically interesting theories about stone adze types and waves of migration into the archipelago, readers will find these details in my previous book (Bellwood 1978a:170–5; 207). Adzes are interesting objects and I will describe them as necesary, but my views about Austronesian and South-East Asian prehistory do not depend upon them. I have also recently read with interest a series of articles by my colleague Solheim (1975a, b, 1979a, b, 1981a), in which he develops a theory of Austronesian origins amongst mobile trading sea peoples in eastern Indonesia, with secondary movements up to the south Chinese coast, and then eventual back movements of Malays and Chams from south China into the archipelago. These theories do differ from my own in several fundamental respects as this chapter will indicate, although I will refer to many of Solheim's other publications in due course.

A. The Prehistory of Taiwan*

Prior to the Neolithic, the island of Taiwan has only a limited record of flaked stone assemblages, probably related to the Hoabinhian, which survived in at

* Wade-Giles placename spellings have been retained in this section.

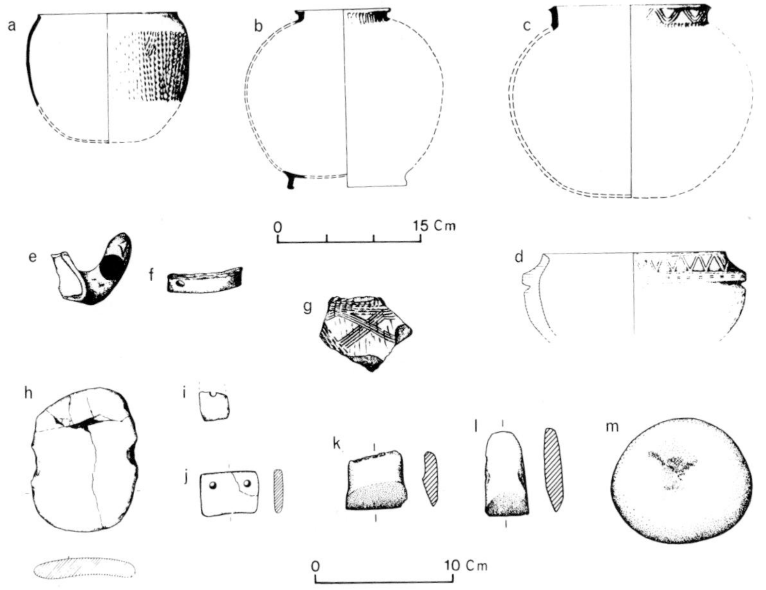

Fig. 7.4. Artefacts of the Ta-p'en-k'eng culture. (a–g) Cord-marked and incised pottery, including a lug (e) and a perforated ring-foot (f); (h) waisted "net sinker"; (i) perforated slate projectile point; (j) clay pendant (?); (k) stepped adze; (l) adze; (m) pitted pebble anvil. From Chang 1969a. Courtesy: Yale University, Department of Anthropology.

least one east coast cave to about 3500 BC (Chang 1969b; Sung 1979). The oldest Neolithic assemblages belong to a culture with cord-marked pottery, termed the Ta-p'en-k'eng culture by Chang (1972, 1977a, 1981), recorded from sites down the western coast of the island (for details see Chang 1969a, 1970, Chang *et al.* 1974; Dewar 1977). One of these sites (at Pa-chia-ts'un near T'ainan) is dated to about 4300 BC, and the culture appears to have continued in existence in western Taiwan until about 2500 BC. Characteristic artefacts (Fig. 7.4) include cord-marked globular pots with incised everted rims and occasional lug handles or ring feet (some with perforations), stone adzes with quadrangular cross-sections and occasionally with hafting steps, polished slate points, stone net sinkers, and possibly a stone barkcloth beater. The whole culture gives the appearance of having been introduced into the island, and the only likely "Hoabinhian" carry over is a form of stone hoe.

The economy of the Ta-p'en-k'eng culture has been a matter of some obscurity since cereal remains have not yet (to my knowledge) been reported from the major excavated sites. Nevertheless, given the importance of rice cultivation in the mainland province of Zhejiang at least a millennium before the Taiwanese Neolithic commenced (see below), I would be most surprised if it was totally absent on the island before 2500 BC. Most authorities on

Taiwanese prehistory have hitherto suggested that cereals were not introduced into the island until after 2500 BC, when stone reaping knives became common in the western region. However, the pollen diagram from the Sun–Moon Lake in the mountainous centre of Taiwan indicates a marked increase in grass pollen around 2800 BC (Tsukada 1966), and since this region must have been one of the last subjected to clearance on the island then agriculture (if this is what the core records) must have appeared long before this date in the western lowlands. More significantly, actual rice remains have now been reported from the Chih-shan-yen site in Taipei (c. 1500–2000 BC, Wang 1984) and rice impressions in pottery from the K'en-ting site on the Heng-ch'un Peninsula in the far south of the island (c. 3000 BC; Li 1983), so it may be that a new era of discovery is about to commence.

By the late third millennium BC the Ta-p'en-k'eng culture had apparently differentiated into two separate archaeological complexes — the Yüan-shan in the north and east, and the "Lungshanoid" (Chang 1969a) cultures of mainland Chinese type in the west and south. The Lungshanoid cultures are best known from Chang's excavations at Feng-pi-t'ou, and from the Choshui and Tatu river sites in the west-centre of the island (Chang *et al.* 1974; Dewar 1977; Stamps 1977). Dates run from about 2500 to 500 BC, and assemblages include cord-marked and painted pottery with a considerable elaboration of form, represented by tripods, high perforated ring feet, bottle forms and the use of a slow wheel (Fig. 7.5). In addition there are clay spindle whorls, bone points, large numbers of ground slate reaping knives and projectile points of coastal Chinese types, and stone hoes and adzes (untanged and shouldered). The postholes of part of a rectangular house were excavated at Feng-pi-t'ou, together with a Mongoloid burial.

The Lungshanoid cultures of western Taiwan do not appear to be of direct significance for the settlement of the Philippine and Indonesian islands to the south. However, I think the situation may be different with the Yüan-shan culture of northern and eastern Taiwan, which was derived, according to all authorities, by local development from the preceding Ta-p'en-k'eng culture (possibly via the newly-described Chih-shan-yen culture in the Taipei region, Wang 1984). Dates for Yüan-shan and Chih-shan-yen assemblages range from 2500 BC into the first millennium BC, and the Yüan-shan pottery is characterised by globular vessels with ring feet and strap handles, decorated with some incision or punctation and occasional red or brown slips (Fig. 7.6). Cord-marking and tripods are absent, and this is very significant since the oldest pottery assemblages in the Philippines and Indonesia also lack these features. In addition, the slate reaping knives are absent in the Yüan-shan culture, as they are again in the later sites to the south. So if rice cultivation continued, and there is little reason to suspect that it did not in the case of Taiwan, then people may have turned to bamboo knives (as used today for millet in highland Taiwan) or hand stripping for harvesting.

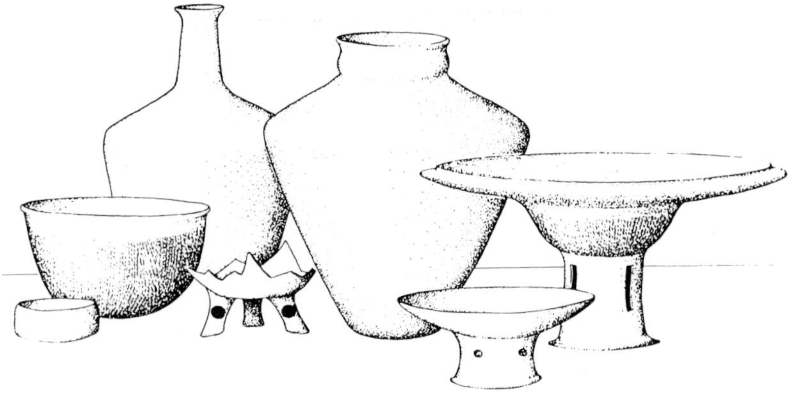

Fig. 7.5. "Fine red ware" from Feng-pi-t'ou, c. 2000 BC. From Chang 1969a. Courtesy: Yale University, Department of Anthropology.

Fig. 7.6. Incised and stamped pottery from Ta-p'en-k'eng (Yüan-shan culture). Scale in cm. From Chang 1969a. Courtesy: Yale University, Department of Anthropology.

Other Yüan-shan items include untanged, shouldered and stepped quadrangular adzes, slate projectile points, chipped stone hoes, stone barkcloth beaters, and spindle whorls of clay (Fig. 7.7). The latter are of interest since they also occur in the Lungshanoid sites of the western coast and in the Yangtze Neolithic cultures (see below), and they suggest that a knowledge of weaving, perhaps using hemp fibres on a backstrap loom, was present. Domestic dogs are also claimed from some Yüan-shan sites. Down the eastern coast of Taiwan, Pearson (1968, 1969, 1970) has investigated sites of the related T'ai-yuan culture; these are generally undated but they seem to be associated with stone slab-graves and uprights, together with Yüan-shan pottery with the characteristic ring feet and loop handles. Very little is known about the prehistory of eastern Taiwan, but there is as yet no evidence from here to force one to look elsewhere for a source of early Austronesian settlement in the Philippines.

Looking at Taiwanese prehistory from an Indo-Malaysian perspective it is obviously the cultural phase prior to about 2500 BC which is of most interest, since it is clear that Austronesian settlers had already moved well into the Philippines and Indonesia by this time. Hence the Ta-p'en-k'eng culture is of enormous importance as a potential record of the oldest stage of Austronesian society which can be identified on linguistic grounds (that is Initial Austonesian). Not only does this culture have clear mainland origins, but it also has what I believe are clear successors in the Yüan-shan culture and the earliest Neolithic cultures of the Philippines and Indonesia. I have presented a case for rice cultivation as at least one driving force within this cultural sequence, for although most highland Austronesians of Taiwan grow hardier millets today (*Setaria, Panicum* and the more recent Indian *Sorghum* and *Eleusine*, Chen 1968; Fogg 1983), it must be remembered that the warmer western lowlands where the oldest Neolithic sites occur are now entirely settled by Chinese. Other aboriginally-cultivated plants in Taiwan include sugarcane and gourd, and it is highly likely that these were grown, with *Setaria* millet, by Ta-p'en-k'eng societies as well; all are of at least Proto-Austronesian antiquity. However, although coconuts and breadfruit grow in south-eastern Taiwan today, it seems more than likely that these two tropical species were introduced later into the warmer parts of the island from the Philippines.

B. The Southern Chinese Background

The immediate origins of the Ta-p'en-k'eng culture clearly lie on the Chinese mainland. Corded pottery occurs in association with bone and antler tools and a presumed Hoabinhian or Bacsonian industry in the cave of Xianrendong in north-eastern Jiangxi (Aigner 1979; Meacham 1983), but the dates

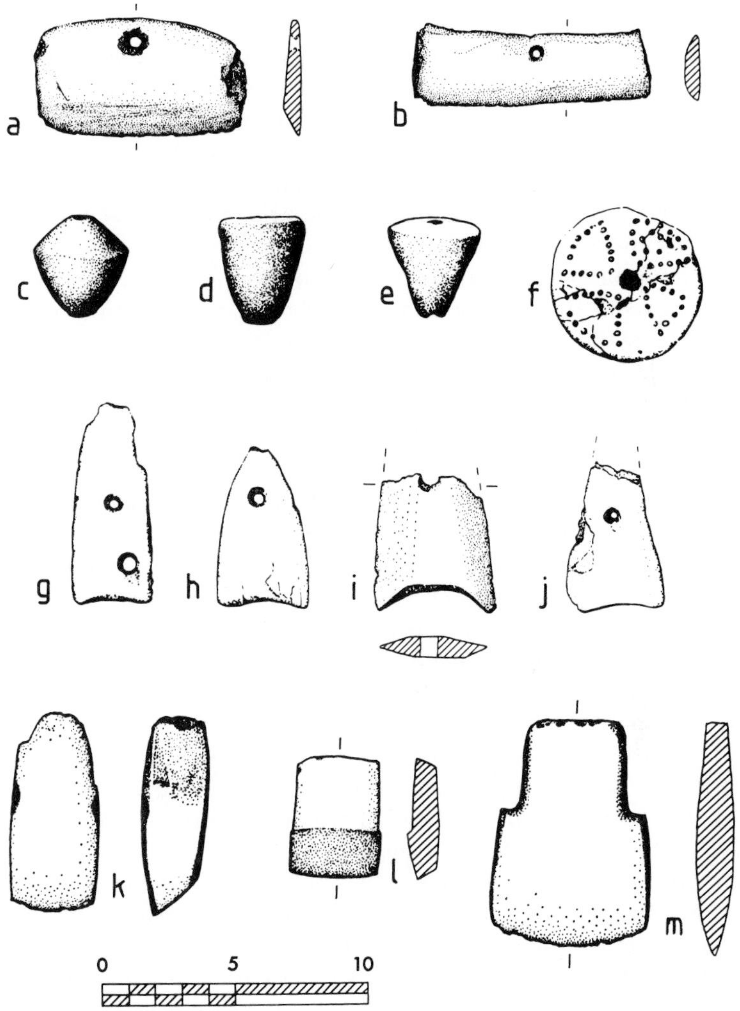

Fig. 7.7. Top two rows. Artefacts from Feng-pi-t'ou ("Lungshanoid" culture). (a, b) Stone knives; (c–e) baked clay spindle whorls; (f) clay disc (compare Fig. 7.8a). Bottom two rows. Artefacts from Ta-p'en-k'eng (Yüan-shan culture). (g–j) Perforated stone points; (k) untanged adze; (l) stepped adze; (m) shouldered adze. Scale in cm. From Chang 1969a. Courtesy: Yale University, Department of Anthropology.

from here are highly contradictory (between 9000 and 6500 bc from the same layer, Barnard 1980:52). Chang (1977b) has drawn attention to Ta-p'en-k'eng ceramic parallels with the shellmound site of Fuguodun in nearby Fujian, dated to between 5200 and 4200 BC, and from here there are potsherds decorated with incised lines, impressed rows of semi-circles, and zoned patterns made by dentate stamping with the toothed edge of an *Anadara* shell. This decorative repertoire is by no means identical to that of the Ta-p'en-k'eng culture (for instance, there is little cord-marking) and the site has apparently yielded no evidence of an agricultural nature, but it may represent a part of the ancestral cultural matrix from which the Initial Austronesian settlers of Taiwan were derived.

More information on southern Chinese developments has been excavated in recent years in Hong Kong, and while I believe this area to be rather too far south to be directly connected with Taiwanese prehistory, a brief review will add more perspective to the whole region. The oldest Neolithic sites here date from the late fifth millennium BC, after the sea had reached its present level, and they include Chung Hom Wan (Bard 1975), Tung Kwu (Meacham 1975), Hai Dei Wan (Williams 1979), and the very important site of Sham Wan on Lamma Island (Meacham 1978, 1980). The assemblages from all these sites, which have a number of dates between 4000 and 2500 BC, include round-based corded vessels (dominant in numbers) and a range of more complex forms, often in a chalky white ware, with incised and stamped circle decoration, some red painting, and occasional perforated ring feet. Adzes include untanged and shouldered quadrangular forms, and there is a Hoabinhian-like industry of pebble picks and choppers. Sham Wan has also yielded pig and deer bones. In a higher level at this site, dated to after 2000 BC, the earlier assemblage is enriched with items apparently new to this region which include stepped adzes, stone projectile points, stone reaping knives, and geometrically-stamped pottery of the characteristic southern Chinese Late Neolithic and Bronze Age type.

In recent syntheses, Meacham (1977, 1983) has related a number of southern Chinese and Vietnamese sites (that is basal Sham Wan, Phung Nguyen in Vietnam, and certain sites in Guangdong, Maglioni 1952), to a cultural complex which he terms the Yüeh Coastal Neolithic. He regards these Neolithic cultures as indigenous to the south and not derived from an expansion from the Yangtze region, as many Chinese archaeologists have in the past assumed, and I am in full agreement with this viewpoint. However, in the case of the oldest Taiwanese Neolithic assemblages I think the possibility of an expansion of rice cultivation and its associated technology from the Yangtze region through Zhejiang and Fujian must be accepted. This is simply because I regard rice cultivation as an important component of the economy behind early Austronesian expansion, and because the Yangtze sites do have an impressive chronological priority for rice cultivation in terms of present knowledge. Should evidence for rice cultivation prior to 3500 BC eventually be found in Vietnam, Hong Kong and Guangdong then I would perhaps change this view.

There can be no doubt that the most important site excavated in recent years with respect to rice cultivation is Hemudu, which lies on a flat alluvial plain about 25 km to the south of Hangzhou Bay in north-eastern Zhejiang (Chekiang 1978; Chang 1977a:523–4; An 1981). The bottom waterlogged layer of this site dates to between 5200 and perhaps 4900 BC (Barnard 1980:86), and belonged to a village of rectangular timber houses (one being 7 m wide by over 23 m long) constructed with skillful mortice and tenon techniques, and raised on rows of small timber piles. Large quantities of rice husks, similar to *indica* varieties but with some wild characteristics (Chang 1983) were found as temper in the sherds, and in one area of the excavation a solid mass of rice husks, grains, straw and leaves formed a layer with an average thickness of 40–50 cm. This rice was presumably cultivated in the alluvial soils around the site, possibly with a range of aquatic plants in low-lying swamps (H-L. Li 1983). Pigs accounted for 90% of all animal bones and it is assumed that they were domesticated, together with dogs and possibly water buffalo. A range of birds and mammals were hunted including deer, rhinoceros, elephant and monkey. An interesting occurrence amongst the plant remains is the gourd (*Lagenaria siceraria*), a plant of widespread importance in South-East Asia and Oceania. Pollen of species found today only in Guangdong and Taiwan suggest that the climate may have been a little warmer then than now.

The material culture of Hemudu (Fig. 7.8) is particularly impressive, and includes hoes made from animal scapulae, bone tools and whistles, jade penannular earrings, and stone adzes with oval or quadrangular cross-sections, some resembling the stepped form of the Ta-p'en-k'eng culture. Knee-shaped adze hafts were found, of a shape which occurs in Initial Jomon Japan and almost universally amongst the Austronesian peoples of Oceania, and there are also some detachable wooden spade blades.Pottery items include spindle whorls, and a range of round or flat-based cord-marked vessels, the former often having carinated bodies and incised rims (Fig. 7.9). Potstands, animal figurines, footed dishes and lids also occur, and there are a few painted sherds. While this pottery tradition clearly has more variation in form than the Ta-p'en-k'eng and Yüan-shan cultures in Taiwan, it shows that the totality of potting knowledge found in the early island cultures was already present in this region a millennium before the beginnings of Austronesian expansion.

By about 4200 BC or before, Hemudu and many other sites in Zhejiang and southern Jiangsu had entered a new cultural phase termed the Majiabang.

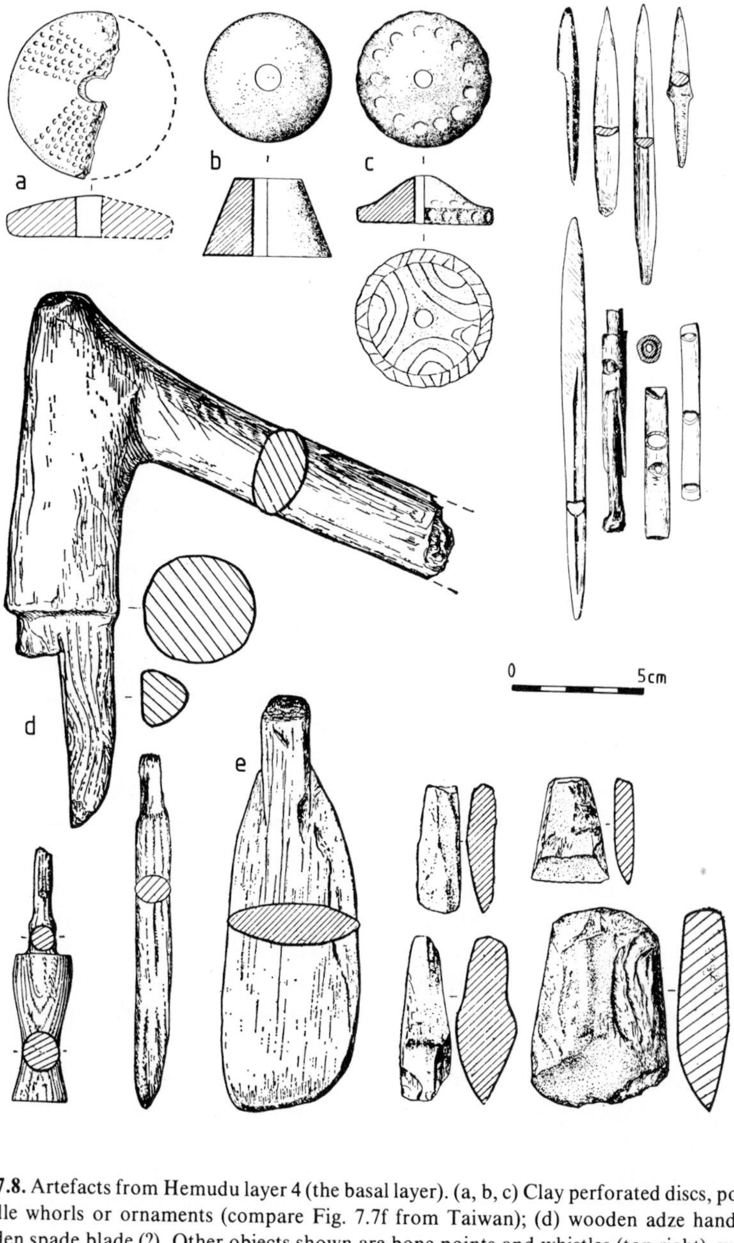

Fig. 7.8. Artefacts from Hemudu layer 4 (the basal layer). (a, b, c) Clay perforated discs, possibly spindle whorls or ornaments (compare Fig. 7.7f from Taiwan); (d) wooden adze handle; (e) wooden spade blade (?). Other objects shown are bone points and whistles (top right), wooden objects (bottom left), and adzes, including one with an incipient step (bottom right). From Chekiang 1978.

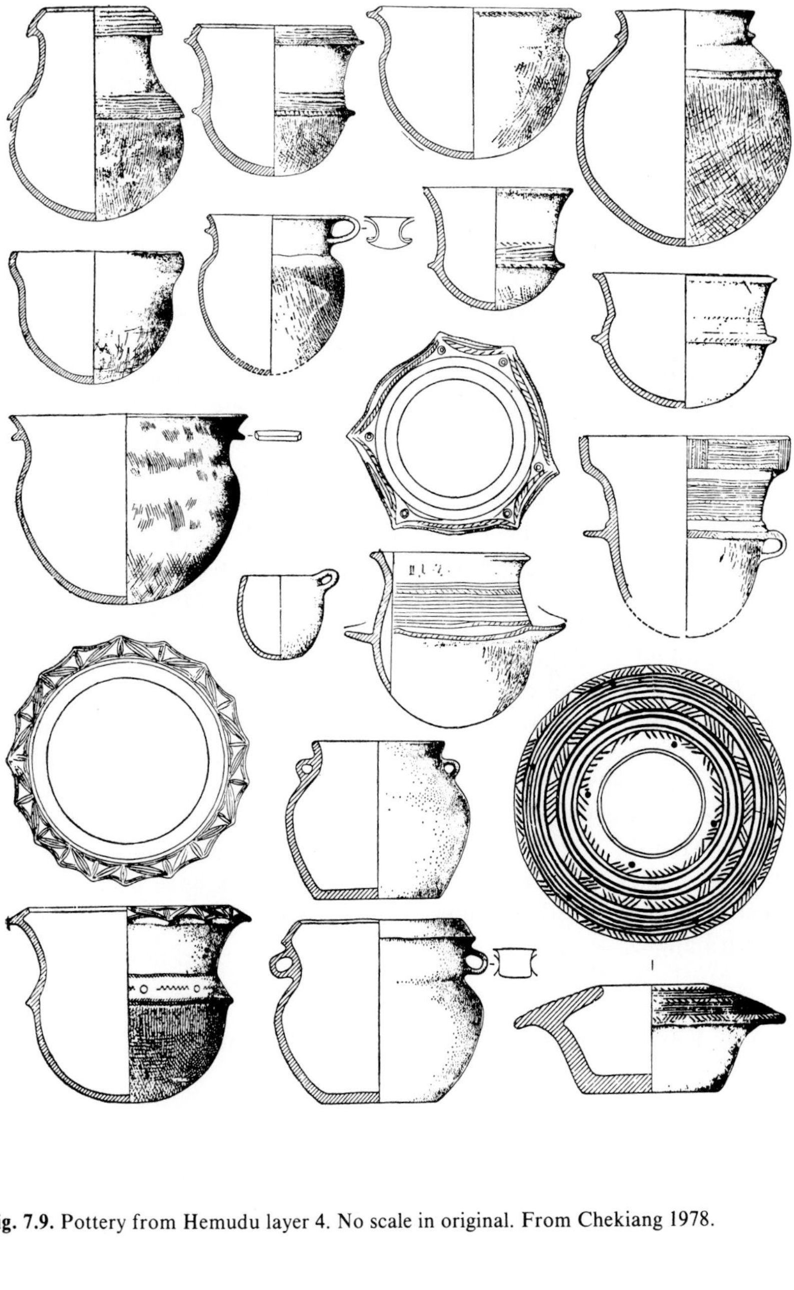

Fig. 7.9. Pottery from Hemudu layer 4. No scale in original. From Chekiang 1978.

The settlement pattern of rectangular houses in riverine or lake edge situations with ample evidence for rice cultivation continued, and new pottery variations, of importance for Taiwan and the early island cultures, include a surface red slip and occasional cutouts in ring feet (both occur in the Yüanshan culture, for instance). Stone reaping knives appeared in the succeeding Beiyinyangying phase (Pearson and Lo 1983), perhaps around 3700 BC. These are generally more common north of the Yangtze, and may have originated amongst peoples who cultivated millet.

Without going into further detail on these Yangtze sites, I think it is important to emphasise the high economic and technological levels attained by societies in this region before 3500 BC. No good evidence has survived to indicate the presence of any marked level of social stratification at this time, but Pearson (1981) has suggested from burial evidence that it was emerging further to the north in the Dawenkou culture of Shandong, perhaps during the third millennium BC. The rice cultivation upon which these Yangtze cultures were founded suggests that they can no longer be derived simply from the millet-cultivating Yangshao Neolithic culture of the Yellow River region; millet can only be assumed to have been present but of minor importance in the lower Yangtze cultures, and legumes were probably of little significance (Li 1970; Ho 1977). Pigs and water buffalo appear to have been domesticated, presumably for meat, and domestic dog and possibly the chicken were also present. Wild jungle fowls (*Gallus gallus*) are native to southern China and Mainland South-East Asia (Ball 1933), and their bones have been found in inland sites of this period in Henan and Hebei (Rodwell 1984). Of other material culture we have the pottery types, spindle whorls, stone adzes, bone and stone points, reaping knives, and the details of Hemudu carpentry. All of these items overlap most convincingly with the range reconstructed for Proto-Austro-Thai and Proto-Austronesian by linguistic means (see Chapter 4, Table 4.2), and for the early Taiwanese Neolithic from the archaeological record. If the phenomenon of Austronesian expansion commenced anywhere, it surely must have been from the southern Chinese coastline, somewhere between the Yangtze delta and southern Fujian.

III. The Early Neolithic Phase in Island South-East Asia

I will now consider the archaeological evidence for early Neolithic assemblages in the Philippines and Indonesia, and will later expand this evidence into a larger picture of economic change and adaptation. However, I should first go back again to the Neolithic cultures of Taiwan between 3500 and 2500

BC and note the material items present. These include quadrangular cross-sectioned adzes, bone and slate projectile points, and a pottery tradition which trends from a predominance of cord-marking towards an emphasis on plain or slipped bodies (in the case of the Yüan-shan culture), with the continuing presence of incised, stamped circle and punctate decoration and perforated ring feet. Other items include stone net weights, hoes, and possibly bones of domesticated pigs and dogs. Reaping knives and spindle whorls are not clearly present until after 2500 BC.

Although the presence of cereal cultivation on Taiwan at the very onset of Neolithic settlement cannot yet be demonstrated, I feel, from the mainland Chinese evidence already given, that either rice or millet (or both) were almost certainly present. It is my belief that a major cause of Initial Austronesian expansion into Taiwan, and possibly onwards into the northern Philippines, involved the development of shifting cultivation of rice, as well as the continuation of the original and less extensive swamp and alluvial bottom-land types of cultivation. Shifting cultivation of cereals is quite demanding in terms of soil nutrients and the quantity of land required to support a viable cropping and fallow system (Harris 1977), and it can also promote soil erosion and the spread of uncultivable grasslands if fallows are too short. Hence societies who practiced shifting cultivation would have had a strong tendency to expand if they were not constrained by surrounding populations, and I suspect they were not in this region at the time under consideration.

In the Philippines, the Talaud Islands and northern Borneo there is some evidence for a reasonably well-defined Early Neolithic phase characterised by simple pottery forms with plain or red-slipped surfaces. This phase has no very clear internal divisions at present, and I hesitate to refer to it as a "culture". The main sites date between about 3000 and 500 BC, although incised and stamped pottery assemblages which I will refer to in the next chapter as Late Neolithic do appear in some areas (central Philippines, Timor, island Melanesia) prior to the latter date. I am therefore unwilling to commit myself to a strict delineation of a time-span for the Early Neolithic — it clearly survived in terms of the pottery types by which I define it much later in some areas than in others. The most varied assemblages of this early phase occur in the northern Philippines, which is what could be expected given their closeness to Taiwan, and the more southerly sites in Borneo, Talaud, Sulawesi and Timor show a marked attenuation of material culture. Java is unclear in this respect, since no presumed Neolithic sites here have been dated.

In northern Luzon, an important open site called Dimolit has been excavated by Peterson (1974) on Palanan Bay in Isabela Province. The lower occupation level here has three rather widely-spread radiocarbon dates, but was probably occupied between 2500 and 1500 BC. Post-hole settings for two

3 × 3 m square houses were found, each with double walls, the outer post row being set in a slot (Fig. 7.10). The pottery is plain or red-slipped, and comprises globular or carinated vessels and dishes, some on ring feet with clustered small perforations. Two other sites in northern Luzon, both in a tributary of the Cagayan Valley called the Piñacanauan de Tuguegarao, have yielded similar types of pottery (Thiel 1981a, b). The first, Musang Cave, produced a basal flake industry dated to between 12 000 and 9000 bc, and then, after a gap in occupation, an Early Neolithic assemblage dated to sometime after 3500 BC. This contained plain and red-slipped pottery with some ring feet, a pottery earring, and large numbers of wild pig bones. A second cave called Arku produced a burial assemblage dated to between 1500 BC and 0, with pottery similar to that from Musang. Other items from this site, many clearly paralleled in Taiwanese Neolithic sites, include shell and stone beads, shell bracelets, earrings of stone, shell or pottery, a stone barkcloth beater, pottery spindle whorls, barbed bone points, and stone adzes. The burials were apparently primary or secondary, and sometimes dusted with ochre or placed in jars. One jar burial has been radiocarbon dated to about 500 BC, and it is clear that this assemblage continued on to overlap with a major Indo-Malaysian jar-burial tradition which I will describe in Chapter 9.

Other artefacts with Taiwanese parallels, such as slate projectile points, have been found in surface collections in Luzon, and it is apparent that excavations on this island are well on the way to demonstrating a significant Taiwan–northern Philippine axis of Neolithic continuity (see Chapter 8, Footnote 1). This conclusion is reinforced by the recent discovery of a site called Sunget on Batan Islan, between Taiwan and Luzon. Although Sunget has not yet been excavated or dated the preliminary survey report (Kumamoto 1983:55–61) refers to discoveries of red-slipped pottery with ring feet and lug handles, perforated slate points, and stepped and shouldered adzes; all items closely paralleled in the Yüan-shan repertoire. I suspect that this site may produce a very striking record of Yüan-shan expansion beyond the confines of Taiwan, although it need not of course bear any relevance to the question of earliest Austronesian expansion into the Philippines; the possibility of continuing contact throughout later prehistory need not be surprising.

Moving southwards from Luzon the material becomes sparser. In Duyong Cave on Palawan (Fox 1970) a flexed and face-down burial of a male included a stone quadrangular adze, four *Tridacna* shell adzes, two ear discs and a breast pendant made from perforated *Conus* shells (Fig. 7.11), and six *Anadara* shells which may have been used as lime containers for betel chewing (the skeleton also had betel-stained teeth). Charcoal from the burial pit was dated to about 3000 BC, and similar shell implements also occurred

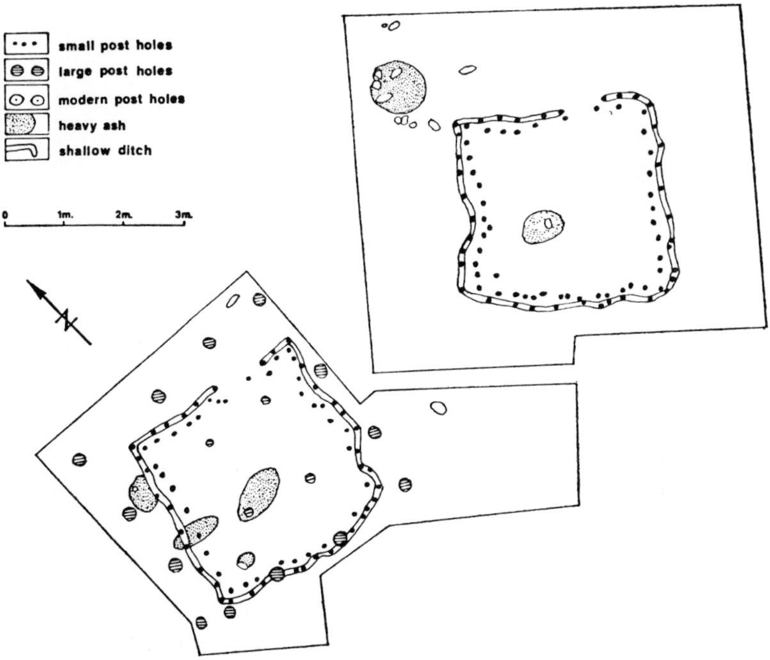

Fig. 7.10. House plans from Dimolit, northern Luzon. From Peterson 1974. Courtesy: University of Sydney.

in a level in the cave deposits dated to about 4300 BC. This site is unusual in having no pottery, and its early date suggests that the stone adze may have been traded from agricultural populations situated elsewhere into an indigenous hunting and gathering community. The shell tools may indicate a local tradition, of which other possible traces have been recently reported from southern Mindanao (Solheim *et al.* 1979:116–7).

Elsewhere in the Philippines, plain pottery is reported from shell midden deposits dated to about 2000 BC in the Bagumbayan site on Masbate (Bay-Petersen 1982), and plain, slipped and incised sherds occur at around the same date in the Edjek site on Negros (Hutterer and Macdonald 1982:223). Plain and red-slipped sherds also occur in the Sangasanga shelter in the Sulu Archipelago (Spoehr 1973), but in this case with an unacceptably early radiocarbon date of 5500 BC.

In general, the Philippine Early Neolithic sites have continuing evidence for pig and deer hunting as well as for the use of flake tools (with an opal phytolith gloss at Dimolit), but to my knowledge the stone reaping knives are

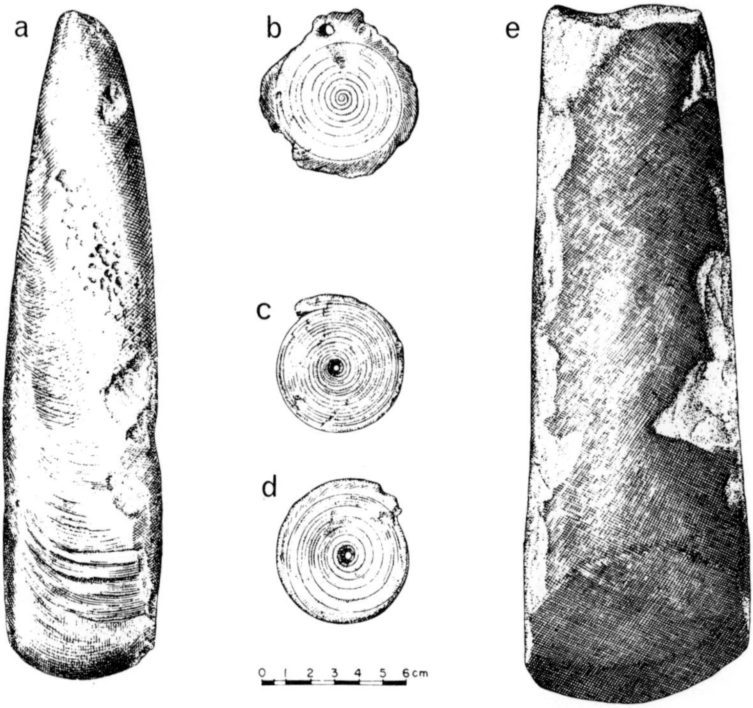

Fig. 7.11. Burial goods from Duyong Cave, Palawan, c. 3000 BC. (a) Shell adze; (b–d) *Conus* shell discs and pendant; (e) stone adze. From Fox 1970. Courtesy: National Museum of the Philippines.

not found here at all, and the pottery spindle whorls do not occur south of Luzon. As I noted for the Yüan-shan culture, grain reaping may have been carried out with organic tools, or it may have faded away towards equatorial latitudes, and the latter is an option which I will elaborate upon in due course. Weaving may have been replaced by barkcloth production in many areas (a conclusion also reached by Ngo T.P. 1985 to explain the shift away from cord-marked pottery to the south of Taiwan), but since weaving was so widespread ethnographically an initial retraction followed much later by an expansion, perhaps with more suitable fibres of mainland origin such as cotton, may have occured. Another item which seems to decline in frequency in the southern Philippines and southwards is the stone adze; these are common in Taiwan and Luzon, but their great rarity southwards (except in Java and Bali) seems to me to tell a story. With respect to cereal cultivation, forest clearance and textile production, it may be detected that rather significant changes were taking place as Austronesians expanded towards the equator, and I will expand on these later.

Within Indonesia, the Leang Tuwo Mane'e shelter in the Talaud Islands has yielded plain and red-slipped sherds from thin walled vessels with globular bodies and everted rims (Fig. 7.12) dating from about 2500 BC (Bellwood 1976b, 1981). Large numbers of shellfish continued to be discarded in the Neolithic layers, and the chert industry continued, but without the earlier tendency towards blade production (see Chapter 6, Section IIIA). Stone adzes were totally absent. Across the Celebes Sea in the cave of Agop Atas (Madai) in northern Borneo (see Chapter 6, Section IIB), the early Holocene pebble and flake industry was succeeded, after a long gap in occupation, by a pottery assemblage similar to that from Talaud (Fig. 7.12). This has been dated a little uncertainly by thermoluminescence and radiocarbon to between 2000 and 500 BC. Again, a stone flake industry continues, but there are no adzes. After 500 BC the cave was again abandoned until the Early Metal phase about 2000 years ago. The ring feet which are rather characteristic of the Luzon and Taiwan assemblages are totally absent both in Talaud and at Madai, but a lid fragment was found in Agop Atas. My impression from these sites is that the pottery is becoming simplified in form, but the thinness of many of the sherds suggests that there was no loss of potting skill.

In south-western Sulawesi, pottery appears in small quantities in the upper layers of Toalian sites, perhaps here used by continuing hunter–gatherer populations. In the shelter of Ulu Leang, Glover (1976) has reported the first pottery at about 2500 BC in a continuing Toalian industry with Maros points, and the sherds here are of plain unslipped globular cooking pots with everted rims. From caves in eastern Timor Glover (1978a) has also reported similar pottery from the third millennium BC which he thinks is more comparable to that from Talaud than from the Toalian sites. The Timorese caves have also produced shell beads, bracelets, and one-piece angling hooks of *Trochus* shell (Fig. 7.13), but again no stone adzes (Glover 1972a, 1977a). Perhaps more significantly, pig bones appear from about 2500 BC, and since these animals are not native to Timor there are very good grounds for assuming that domesticated pigs (derived from *Sus scrofa* or *S. celebensis*, Groves 1981) were introduced into the island at this time. Dog, cattle and goats also appear in the Timorese cave record after 1000 BC, but the goats and cattle could be more recent. Plant remains from the Neolithic layers include the Polynesian chestnut (*Inocarpus*), bamboo, gourd, and (after 1000 BC) a single grain of foxtail millet (Glover 1977b).

These Timorese finds are thus of great potential significance, since they allow the suggestion that an agricultural economy involving at least some form of pig husbandry and possibly millet cultivation was introduced into the

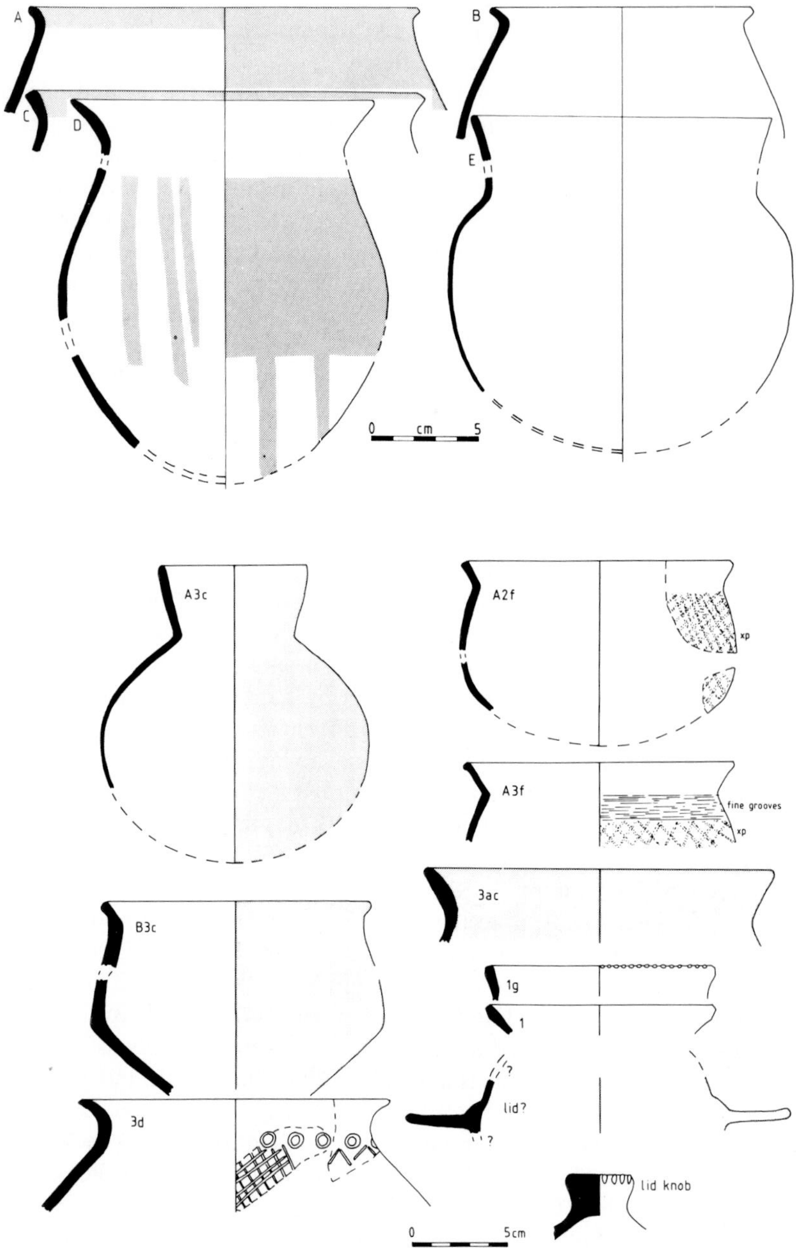

Fig. 7.12. Neolithic pottery from Leang Tuwo Mane'e (top) and Agop Atas (bottom).

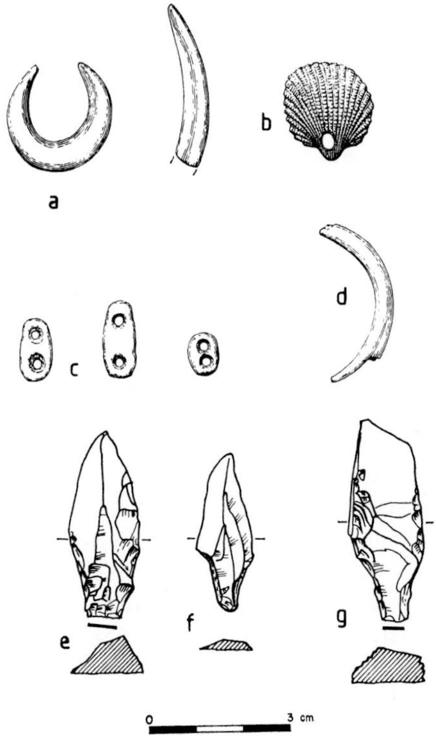

Fig. 7.13. Shell artefacts and tanged stone points from eastern Timor. (a) *Trochus* shell fishhooks from Bui Ceri Uato, c. 1000 BC; (b) pierced *Anadara* shell from Uai Bobo 2, c. 4th millennium BC; (c) *Nautilus* shell spacer beads from Bui Ceri Uato, c. 3rd–2nd millennia BC; (d) fragment of *Trochus* shell armlet from Uai Bobo 2, c. 3rd millennium BC; (e–g) tanged stone points from Uai Bobo 1, c. 500 BC–AD 500. From Glover 1977a. Courtesy: I. C. Glover.

island sometime around 2500 BC. Other discoveries are even more surprising, for Glover was able to show that marsupial cuscuses, civet cats and macaque monkeys were also introduced at about the same time as the pigs. It is not clear whether these animals were tamed or wild at the time of introduction, but this evidence for transport of non-domesticated animals into the faunally-impoverished islands of eastern Indonesia from Neolithic times onwards is particularly interesting. Although possibly historic introductions in many cases, the presence of macaque monkeys, civet cats, deer, and Javan porcupines on various other islands in the Lesser Sundas and Moluccas (Musser 1981; Groves 1984), and of the cassowary in Seram (Wallace 1962:300) should also be noted. Pigs, of course, are perfectly capable of swimming long distances at sea and were often hunted from canoes while doing so (Forrest

1779:142), but there is no good evidence for their establishment on Indonesian islands where they were not native prior to Neolithic times. Domesticated pigs of *scrofa* or *celebensis* origins are now found virtually throughout eastern Indonesia (Groves 1981), and there are also wild populations of *Sus celebensis* on several islands which may descend from an introduced wild or only partially tamed breeding stock (Groves 1984).

The Early Neolithic sites which I have described so far are really the only ones from which there is coherent dated information, with the exception of the West Mouth at Niah with its rather remarkable burial record which I will consider in the next chapter. For Sumatra there is little of a usable archaeological nature, and Java still remains something of a mystery. As I noted for western Indonesia in my previous book (Bellwood 1978a:231), "it will not be possible to write an integrated prehistory of Indonesia until we know much more about this region". Nevertheless, the enormous number of superbly manufactured quadrangular and pick adzes from Java (Duff types 2A and 7A: Fig. 7.14), often made in semi-precious stones such as serpentine, agate or chalcedony, suggests that a very large and wealthy Neolithic population once occupied the island (although some of the finer adzes may actually be of Early Metal phase date). The extensive working floors for adzes and stone bracelets found in several places in central and western Java add support to this view (Heine Geldern 1945). One working floor for quadrangular adzes, excavated some years ago at Kendeng Lembu in eastern Java (Heekeren 1972), produced sherds of thin vessels with round bases and everted rims, some apparantly red-slipped according to Sutayasa (1973). Some rather uncertain stone "sickles" were also found (Heekeren 1972: Plate 95b). There are hints here of affinities with the Early Neolithic sites of the Philippine region, but few details are available. Otherwise, a scatter of cord-marked and incised pottery finds, particularly from western Java, is summarised by Sutayasa (1973, 1979; see also Bellwood 1978a:220–1). As far as Java is concerned only the linguistic evidence suggests settlement by an Austronesian population expanding perhaps from Sulawesi or Borneo, and possibly in the second rather than the third millennium BC.

Pollen diagrams from the highlands of northern and central Sumatra and from western Java provide some interesting but rather equivocal evidence for forest clearance which may be related to settlement of these regions by Austronesian cultivators. A core from the Toba Highlands in northern Sumatra (Maloney 1980) suggests a possibility of clearance by as early as 5000 BC, but the peak values for grass pollen here seem to fall well after 3000 BC. A core from Lake Padang in the Kerinci Valley further south (Flenley 1979:22; 1985; Morley 1982) shows an increase of pollen of regrowth trees about 1000 BC, with a possibility of some clearance about a millennium earlier. Another core from near Bogor in western Java shows an increase in

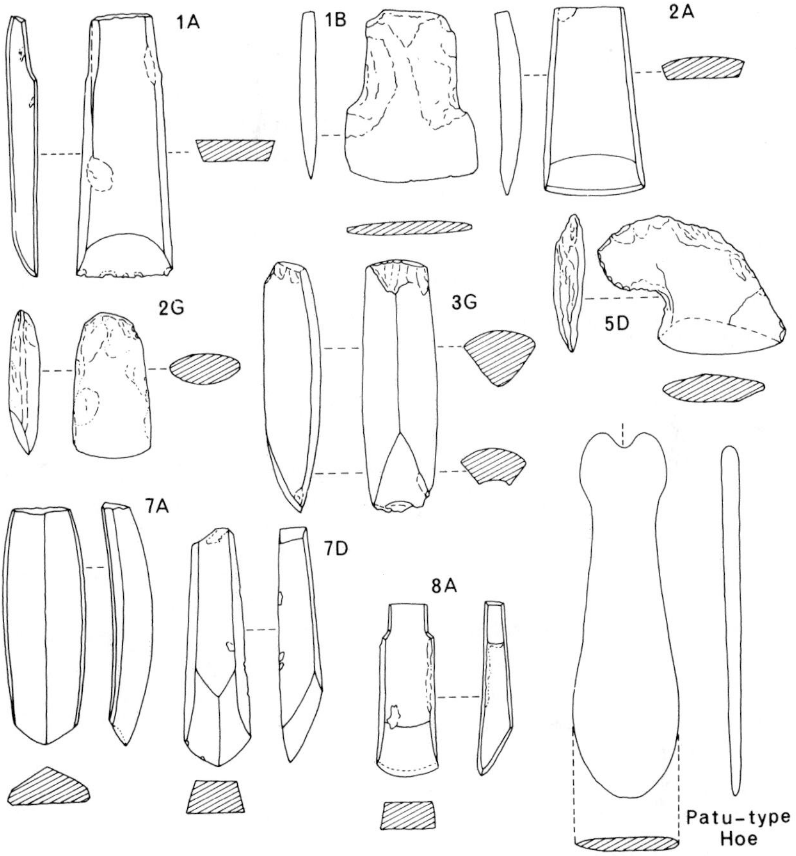

Fig. 7.14. South-East Asian stone adzes, with the terminology used by Roger Duff (1970). Types, popular names and provenances as follows: 1A stepped adze, Luzon; 1B shouldered adze, Kalumpang, Sulawesi; 2A quadrangular adze, Java; 2G oval or "round" adze, Vietnam; 3G Luzon; 5D Tembeling "knife", Pahang; 7A pick adze, Sumatra; 7D beaked adze, Malaya; 8A shouldered adze, Indochina; "patu-type hoe" from Taiwan. Not to scale. From Bellwood 1978a.

pandanus pollen and fern spores at about 3000 BC, although the analysts (Zeist *et al.* 1979) are hesitant about attributing this change to human interference (but see Golson 1985). Nevertheless, the palynological evidence can be used to suggest that favourable highland lake situations in western Indonesia, perhaps actively sought after by early Austronesian settlers, may have been subjected to agricultural clearance from about 2000 BC onwards.

IV. An Integrated View of Early Austronesian Expansion

If the linguistic data from Chapter 4 plus a number of important botanical and ecological observations are added to the above archaeological record, then the course of Austronesian prehistory from the Initial Austronesian settlement of Taiwan (c. 4500–4000 BC) through to about 1500 BC, when Late Neolithic voyagers were beginning the Austronesian settlement of Oceania, can be reconstructed.

During the late fifth millennium BC Neolithic settlers from the mainland of southern China (probably Zhejiang or Fujian) settled Taiwan. Initial Austronesian languages were spoken on this island for at least a millennium before further expansion took place. By about 3000 BC Austronesian settlers moved into Luzon, and Proto-Austronesian (that is the end-point of Initial Austronesian on Taiwan) split into the Formosan and Malayo-Polynesian subgroups. The linguistic reconstruction for Proto-Austronesian reveals an economy with domestic pigs and dogs, and cultivated rice, millet and sugarcane. The archaeological evidence adds pottery, weaving and barkcloth, plus the stone and bone items (reaping knives, projectile points, adzes) already described.

By at least 2500 BC Proto-Malayo-Polynesian (that is the end-point of Initial Malayo-Polynesian) began to break up, probably with settlement expanding into the southern Philippines and Borneo. A best-guess location for Proto-Malayo-Polynesian might therefore be the central or southern Philippines, and the linguistic reconstruction for this stage now adds some very important new items to the economic repertoire: the chicken, breadfruit, the aroids *Alocasia* and *Colocasia* (taro), yams, banana, sago, betel chewing, and the addition of sails to canoes. Of course, none of these items can be proven to have been definitely *absent* from the Proto-Austronesian vocabulary — all that the linguistic evidence can say is that they cannot be demonstrated to have been present. Certainly, it would not be at all surprising if *Colocasia*, the greater yam (*Dioscorea alata*) and the chicken were all present in the Taiwanese economy prior to 3000 BC. But breadfruit, banana, *Alocasia* and sago were most probably first incorporated into the Austronesian crop inventory well to the south.

Archaeologically, it looks as if the activities of cereal cultivation, forest clearance and weaving received temporary setbacks during and after the period of Proto-Malayo-Polynesian, when settlement was expanding into the more forested regions towards the equator. However, these activities were never *totally* abandoned by all Austronesians — they simply declined in importance during the early period of expansion, especially down the Philippine-Sulawesi-Lesser Sunda axis. Some Western Malayo-Polynesians may indeed have maintained a cereal-based economy throughout their prehistory, as I will discuss below.

By about 2500 BC the Central-Eastern Malayo-Polynesians had expanded, presumably through the Moluccas, to at least as far as Timor. Navigational skills and sailing techniques must have been improving by this time as the impending settlement of Oceania makes clear, and rapid coastal expansion was probably preferred to the more laborious process of settling island interiors, which may in some cases have sheltered hostile populations. I am unable to give a reconstruction for the vocabulary of Proto Central-Eastern Malayo-Polynesian, but assume that it would have been similar to that for the earlier Proto-Malayo-Polynesian. Cereal cultivation declined to only minor importance in eastern Indonesia, and the Austronesian settlers of Oceania based their economy purely on tubers, tree fruits, and other vegetatively-reproduced plants.

I will now fill out the botanical background to these Austronesian adaptations by looking at some of the major crop plants, and at the dynamics of shifting cultivation.

A. Rice and Other Cereals

The earliest cultivated rices developed from wild annual forebears between about 18° and 30° north latitude, and it is apparent from studies of modern varieties that both the wild annuals and the early *indica* varieties domesticated from them would have been highly sensitive, during their growth and ripening cycles, to variations in day length (photoperiod) and sunshine incidence. In other words, the first cultivars evolved in a region of sharp wet and dry season distinction, and after wet season germination the ripening process would require dependable and adequate sunshine (about 45 days, Chandler 1979:44) and a precise progression of daylight lengths (Oka and Chang 1960; Vergara 1976; Angladette 1974; Oka 1975; IRRI n.d.; Chang 1985). In effect these cultivars were genetically conditioned for successful growth cycles under specific latitudinal and climatic conditions.

Today, varieties with little or no photoperiod-sensitivity have been developed which will grow successfully in equatorial or high latitudes, but rice yields are still highest in the intermediate tropical latitudes, especially where irrigation is carried out, and they drop off (as do protein and starch contents) as one moves towards the equator (Whyte 1974; Grist 1975; Tanaka 1975; Yamada 1975; Huke 1976) (Fig. 7.15). For the early centuries of Austronesian expansion it may perhaps be assumed that all varieties were sensitive to daylight lengths, and any attempts to grow these in equatorial latitudes would have met with either decreased harvests or no harvests at all (Spencer 1963:84). For instance, excessive cloudiness or rain during the ripening period, high night temperatures, and unvarying day lengths would in combination promote prolific vegetative growth, but grains would tend to be small and in many instances would probably never reach maturity (Oka 1975;

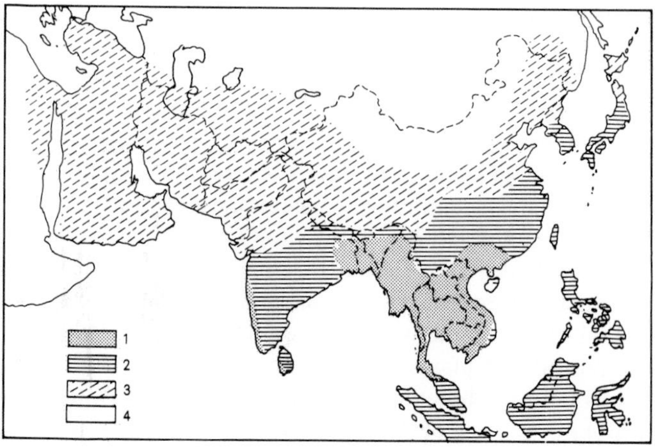

Fig. 7.15. Present-day relationships between rice-cultivation and environment. (1) "Home" area of rice where crop may be raised year after year without climatic modification by man; (2) important rice-producing areas where at least one parameter of climate is frequently less than ideal for succesful crops; (3) areas where climate must be modified to produce a crop; (4) areas with no important rice production. From Huke 1976. Courtesy: International Rice Research Institute.

Grist 1975; Chang 1968). Grains might also ripen in the middle of a very wet period, so that successful harvesting would be difficult or impossible.

All of this means, basically, that equatorial latitudes have never been the most suitable for rice cultivation. It is therefore not surprising that many rice specialists have stressed the difficulties and drops in yields which result from the change from a monsoonal to an equatorial climate (see especially Spencer 1963), and I have also summarised the basic situation in more detail elsewhere (Bellwood 1980b).

The present archaeological record for Indonesia and Malaysia shows that the oldest rice remains are those from Ulu Leang in south-western Sulawesi dated to about AD 500 (Glover 1985), followed by those from Gua Cha in Malaya at about AD 1000 (see Chapter 6, Section IA). Hill (1977) has also suggested that rice was of minor importance in Malaya prior to the period of Funan (early first millennium AD). Even as late as AD 1500 rice seems to have been less important than millet, yams, taro and sago in eastern Indonesia (Spencer 1966), although it clearly was grown in quantity in favourable lowland regions of the Philippines and Sulawesi (e.g. Pelras 1981 for Makassar). However, it is almost universally of great importance today in the islands of western Indonesia, including equatorial Borneo and Sumatra, and may always have been so throughout Austronesian prehistory in the monsoonal islands of Java and Bali.

Given the above observations, I would incline to the following view of the prehistory of Austronesian cereal cultivation. Firstly, the northern popula-

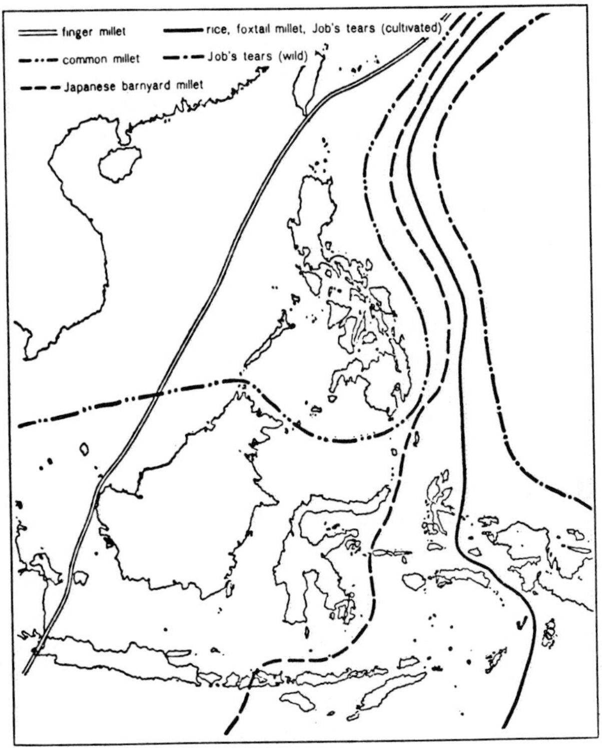

Fig. 7.16. The present eastern limits of cereal crops in the islands of South-East Asia. (Finger millet = *Eleusine coracana*, of Indian origin; common millet = *Panicum miliaceum*; Japanese barnyard millet = *Echinochloa frumentacea*; foxtail millet = *Setaria italica*; Job's tears = *Coix lachryma-jobi*.) From Ishige 1980. Courtesy: National Museum of Ethnology, Osaka.

tions in Taiwan and Luzon have undoubtedly always cultivated rice and foxtail millet in varying proportions. Other cereals of South-East Asian origin, such as the perennial Job's tears and the annual "Japanese barnyard" millet *Echinochloa frumentacea* (Li 1970), were probably also grown on a minor scale as well. A second stage of adaptation followed with expansion into and beyond the southern Philippines after 2500 BC. The groups who moved towards Sulawesi and eastern Indonesia clearly dropped rice to the scale of a very minor crop but probably continued to grow Job's tears and some foxtail millet; I am unsure whether the latter would have suffered the same traumas as rice during an equatorial shift. Foxtail millet, of an apparently ancient and shattering variety, is still of importance in Halmahera (Ishige 1980), in central Sulawesi (Downs 1956) and in other parts of eastern Indonesia (Fig. 7.16). It has also retained considerable importance in Taiwan and Botel Tobago (Arnaud 1974; Fogg 1983).

The other side of this second stage concerns those groups who moved towards western Indonesia, Malaya and southern Vietnam. These appear to have concentrated more on rice and possibly *Echinochloa* (which does not occur in eastern Indonesia; see Fig. 7.16), and although millet has survived ethnographically amongst the Senoi of central Malaya there is a chance that it may be a relatively recent introduction. Rice may have received early setbacks in Borneo — the plant seems to be quite absent in Neolithic sites here such as the Madai and Niah Caves — but it would undoubtedly have come back into its own as soon as settlers reached the ideal soil and climatic conditions of magnificently fertile Java, and non-photoperiod-sensitive varieties better suited to an equatorial climate may already have developed by the time the first Austronesians began to settle Sumatra and Malaya.

B. The Tubers and Tree Fruits

As far as eastern Indonesia and Oceania are concerned the equatorial shift during the second stage described above clearly led to a dominance of fruits and tubers over cereals, and the same may have occurred in parts of Borneo. Of the tubers, the most important are the aroids (Fig. 7.17) and the yams. The greater yam (*Dioscorea alata*) has its homeland in the monsoonal regions of northern Mainland South-East Asia (Burkill 1951), and may have been cultivated by Austronesians throughout their prehistory. Other species of yam were probably first domesticated in Sulawesi and the eastern Indonesia–Melanesia region (Coursey 1972, 1976). Today, yams only survive as staples in parts of Taiwan, Mentawai and Banggai, and wild yams still sustain some of the hunters and gatherers, such as the Negritos and Tasaday.

The taro (*Colocasia*) poses a more difficult origin problem since it grows freely in a wild or feral state along river banks in many parts of South-East Asia and India, and its homeland, if it ever had a restricted one, remains unknown (Barrau 1965; Yen and Wheeler 1968; Plucknett 1976). The same applies to the giant aroid *Alocasia*, which has a similar widespread distribution, although the other giant form, *Cyrtosperma*, does appear to be native to Indonesia. The two latter forms only appear to have been of economic importance in Oceania (*Cyrtosperma* is well suited to atoll cultivation), while *Colocasia* also attained some importance in the islands of South-East Asia; it has been reported as a traditional staple in regions as far apart as Nias, parts of northern Borneo and northern Luzon, and Botel Tobago (near Taiwan). In the latter island it is grown by terraced wet-field techniques similar to those used widely in Oceania (Kano and Segawa 1956). Both the aroids and the yams have probably given way in the face of an expansion of rice cultivation in recent centuries, yet it is clear that they were both of major importance in eastern Indonesia prior to AD 1500 (Spencer 1966).

Fig. 7.17. Left: wild or feral *Colocasia esculenta* (taro), Kelantan, Malaya. The tuber at the base of the plant is the main edible part (see also Fig. 3.2). Right: wild *Alocasia macrorrhiza*, Baturong Forest Reserve, Sabah.

Of the more important fruits, bananas were domesticated locally from Eumusa species in Indonesia, and from Australimusa species in the Moluccas and New Guinea (Simmonds 1966). Wild forms of both still grow on Halmahera today. Coconuts, despite a rather uncertain ancestry, may well have been first domesticated (or at least systematically planted) in the Indonesian–Melanesian region (Child 1964), and coconuts from pre-human contexts have recently been excavated on Aneityum Island in Vanuatu, far out in the western Pacific (Hope and Spriggs 1982). The starch-yielding sago species (*Metroxylon, Corypha, Arenga* and *Caryota*) are also native to equatorial Indonesia and Melanesia (Ruddle *et al.* 1978), while *Eugeissona* is restricted to Borneo and Malaya. All have localised roles in hunter–gatherer and agricultural subsistence in some swampy equatorial lowlands, particularly in eastern Indonesia and Melanesia (e.g. Ohtsuka 1977; Ellen 1978; Ishige 1980). These trees, together with the breadfruit, pandanus, rambutan, durian and other good fruit-bearing species, would all have been available for systematic exploitation by Austronesian societies expanding into equatorial Indo-Malaysian latitudes. Most were probably also exploited by previous hunting and gathering groups, but full domestication and the development of seedless varieties (as in the bananas and breadfruits) would have required at least some conscious selection and planting.

C. Shifting Cultivation

Shifting cultivation of cereals is still practiced widely in Island South-East Asia today, in both equatorial and drier monsoonal climatic regimes. The system obviously varies tremendously from place to place depending on a number of social and ecological factors, but it can support modern populations at densities of up to 60 persons per km^2 (e.g. Freeman 1955; C. Geertz 1963; Spencer 1966; Unesco 1978), or above in certain regions of high fertility such as Java (Chin 1977). Compared to the average densities of 0.005 to 0.12 persons per km^2 given by Unesco (1978) for hunter–gatherers in tropical forests, these figures clearly reveal the demographic significance of this type of agriculture, even if they are small when compared to modern wet rice population densities of up to 2000 persons per km^2 for Java.

Traditional systems of shifting cultivation in Island South-East Asia normally require short cropping cycles of one or two years to be spaced with much longer fallow periods (e.g. Freeman 1955; Rousseau 1977), when secondary forest can re-establish itself and shade out the thick-rooted grasses which would otherwise take over and render future cultivation very difficult (Seavoy 1973b). The whole system depends very much on the nutrients provided by the burning of vegetation prior to planting, and most nutrients in tropical forests are contained in the topsoil and vegetation rather than in the subsoil. If cropping continues for too long the topsoil may be eroded away or depleted in nutrients and grasslands requiring much more labour-intensive methods of cultivation will establish themselves (this has of course happened in many areas). Prolific weed growth can also promote frequent field shifts, since newly-cleared plots require less weeding than old ones (Clarke 1976).

This type of field shifting may eventually require village movement, although it need not necessarily require territorial expansion. For instance, the Mnong Gar of Vietnam need to move their villages every seven years or so (Condominas 1980), but they do so in a cyclical fashion so that an abandoned locality will eventually be re-occupied after many years. The traditional system of the Kayan of Central Borneo appears to have been similar (Hose and McDougall 1912), with village moves occurring every 12 to 15 years. However, the Iban of Sarawak provide a classic example of a unidirectional type of expansion which has allowed single *bilek* families to move as much as 300 km in a single lifetime (Freeman 1955:25, 1970:286), through conscious selection of virgin rainforest for new ricefields which are only used for one or two years until weeds promote their abandonment. This phenomenal expansion is of course relatively recent, and it has involved iron tools and an unlimited expanse of rainforest previously inhabited by only sparse populations, but it does still provide an inkling of how rapidly early Austronesian cultivators could have expanded into virgin agricultural territories 5000 years ago.

Other features of modern shifting cultivation in Island South-East Asia are also of interest for possible reconstructions of how such systems might have been managed in prehistory, since direct archaeological evidence on these points is most unlikely ever to appear. For instance, most groups simply place seeds in holes made by digging sticks in the untilled ash and topsoil, and the system does not require tillage or ploughing if it is maintained at a balanced level with sufficient forest regrowth during fallows. Grasslands and greatly increased population densities do of course require more intensive techniques of tillage and mulching, as in parts of the New Guinea Highlands, but in Island South-East Asia it seems that intensification was directed much more towards the elaboration of wet rice cultivaton, which I will discuss in more detail below. Most modern shifting cultivators also mix their crops in the fields; for instance, the Iban dibble in a few cucumber, pumpkin and gourd seeds with the rice (Freeman 1955). This diversity may help to offset some of the risks associated with dependence on a single crop species, and it may also help to discourage the depredations of crop pests and rats, which often tend to flourish in totally monocultural systems (e.g. Takaya 1980 for modern rice cultivation and rat infestation in lowland Sumatra). Planting in holes rather than direct broadcasting also allows for more conscious selection of seeds, and thus for the development of different varieties.

V. The Stages of Austronesian Agricultural Prehistory

In a previous paper (Bellwood 1980b) I concluded a discussion of Austronesian agricultural prehistory by postulating four main stages of development. I will now expand on these stages with respect to the types of cultivation practiced.

A. Stage 1

Stage 1 is the early phase of cereal dominance at the foundation of Austronesian expansion, centred in southern China, Taiwan and the northern Philippines, and commencing from 4500 BC. Rice may have continued to be grown in localised swamp or alluvial backswamp conditions similar to those in which its annual forebears originated, but favourable areas of this type cannot always be made very extensive without labour-intensive irrigation and water control, and there seems little reason to doubt that cultivation developed more towards the shifting dry land form to feed a slowly but inexorably expanding population. Millet can only be grown by dry land techniques, and the dry (or upland) rices were probably developed at this time by selection for thick and deep roots, loss of photoperiod-sensitivity, and a tendency for early maturity to escape the effects of drought (Chang 1976a; 1985). I therefore visualise this first stage of Austronesian agricultural prehistory as being based on swamp cultivation of rice, and on a more unstable and expansionary system of shifting cultivation of rice, millet and other plants, in a zone of monsoonal climate with a dependable dry season.

B. Stage 2

As I have shown, the expansion towards the equatorial zone after 2500 BC led to a partial replacement of the cereals by the ecologically better-adapted tubers (especially the non-seasonal taro) and fruit or starch-bearing trees. The system of shifting cultivation also underwent changes. In the previous section I have described shifting cultivation in a rather generalised fashion for the whole of Island South-East Asia, but I believe that my Stage 1 systems in the monsoonal regions would have demanded a fairly complete clearance of plots for cereals, with successful burning of vegetation. In the wetter equatorial zone clearance would not have been so easy for a people with only stone tools. Vegetation grows prolifically throughout the year, the rainforest trees are more massive, and, perhaps more importantly, heavy rain can make burning impossible (Freeman 1955; C. Geertz 1963). In Mindanao yields can apparently double when a good dry period allows a burn (Yengoyan, in C. Geertz 1963:22). So there would be obvious pressures towards the development of cultivation systems which would require less forest clearance (cf. the diminishing stone adzes, see Section III), and more emphasis on trees and tubers which do not require such broad expanses of uninterrupted sunlight as cereals.

Systems of this type are of course still widespread in remoter parts of Indonesia and Melanesia today. The Nuaulu of equatorial Seram (Ellen 1978) cultivate taro, yams, bananas and sago (wild sago stands are also exploited) in multi-crop gardens where up to 15 different species may be grown together (including sugar cane, manioc, coconut and others). Since the region has no dependable dry season up to 10 burns may take place before planting can occur, and if we subtract the iron tools which these people now have it is not difficult to see that large-scale garden clearance would not have been a very viable option for Neolithic groups in such an environment. Another example comes from Mentawai, off the western coast of Sumatra, where sago, taro and bananas are grown in swamps with very little clearing and no burning — the cut vegetation is simply used as a mulch (Mitchell and Weitzell 1983). Neither of these groups grows cereals at all, and I rather suspect that systems of this kind, which were eventually taken right through tropical Oceania, began to characterise Austronesian economic patterns increasingly after about 2500 BC in the truly equatorial and ever-wet lowland zone.

It should also be remembered that agricultural systems based on tubers and tree fruits may have developed independently in New Guinea, although the only direct evidence for this at present relates to a tradition of swamp drainage for unknown cultigens which commenced at about 7000 BC in the Wahgi Valley, deep in the highlands of Papua New Guinea (Golson 1977, 1985). I have mentioned the role of New Guinea in this regard several times previously, and I have tried to make it clear that western Melanesia may already have been settled by agricultural groups before the period of Austronesian expansion (the biological and linguistic evidence both provide strong support for this viewpoint). However, while such developments may have been of profound significance for western Melanesia, there is no compelling evidence at the present time which suggests that they had any great effect on the development of agriculture in the Indo-Malaysian Archipelago.

C. Stage 3

As described in my previous paper (Bellwood 1980b), this stage involved the transmission of tuber and fruit cultivation systems by colonising groups of Austronesians into previously uninhabited parts of Oceania after 1500 BC (that is during the Late Neolithic Lapita phase). The details of this are not of direct concern here, but it is significant to point out that the widespread cultivation of taro in bunded wet fields (constructed as valley terraces or in flat swamps) amongst Oceanic Austronesian communities may imply at least a Proto-Oceanic antiquity for this kind of intensive cultivation (cf. Spriggs 1981:170–3). Wet field taro is not common in Island South-East Asia now since rice has acquired dominance as a staple, but it is still the agricultural mainstay on Botel Tobago, off south-eastern Taiwan (Kano and Segawa 1956).

So far I have described three successive stages of Austronesian agricultural prehistory, each representing an adaptation to different environments and crop availabilities. The stages do of course overlap in time, and features of each have survived to the ethnographic present in the regions concerned, despite strong competition from the final stage which I am about to describe. This takes us well beyond the chronological confines of the Early Neolithic, but I have decided to retain it in this chapter so that the agricultural developments can be followed right through.

D. Stage 4

Stage 4 is really the very varied and historically complicated end-piece to Stages 1 and 2 in the Indo-Malaysian Archipelago. By 3000 years ago most

Fig. 7.18. Terraced ricefields in South Amanuban, western Timor. Photo by James Fox.

cultivation systems were probably still based on shifting and localised swamp cultivation, with a predominance of cereals in northern regions (Taiwan, northern Philippines), and perhaps in Java and some of the dry Lesser Sundas. Along the equator, cereal cultivation may have been of importance in the western islands (Borneo, Sumatra), but there is very good evidence that tuber and fruit dominance had long been developed in eastern Indonesia and, of course, in Oceania. Prior to 3000 years ago it is possible that varieties of rice with low photoperiod-sensitivity had developed within the archipelago, and that these rices (like weaving and the backstrap loom) may have been undergoing slight geographical expansions in popularity through a very long period. However, the main features of Stage 4 as recorded historically cannot really be stated to involve changes in crop dominance, and instead it appears that a major but regionally-localised shift towards intensive wet rice cultivation in bunded fields (sawahs) occurred. Such bunded or embanked fields utilise water supplies derived either from wet season rains (rainfed systems) or artificial canals (irrigated systems). Both rainfed and irrigated systems can be laid out as a checkerboard network of bunds on flat land, or they may be terraced into slopes and even very steep hillsides (Figs 7.18, 7.19).

It is most unfortunate that wet rice cultivation, a system which in both irrigated and rainfed forms has obviously transformed islands such as Java,

Fig. 7.19. Rice terraces at Banaue, northern Luzon.

Bali and Luzon, has no clear archaeological or linguistic prehistory in the Indo-Malaysian Archipelago. The apparent antiquity of wet-field taro cultivation in the Pacific Islands (as noted under Stage 3, above) could, if verified, imply at least an equal antiquity for wet-field rice cultivation. Such an eventuality would not be surprising, but on present evidence any great economic importance for this kind of cultivation prior to perhaps 2500 years ago can hardly be assumed. Historical records indicate wet rice cultivation in northern Vietnam from about 200 BC (Wheatley 1965), and here and in northern Thailand there is archaeological evidence that wet rice cultivation in bunded fields may have developed during the Iron Age (after 500 BC), together with the use of water buffalo for ploughing (Higham and Kijngam 1979; Liere 1980; Higham 1983). In Java the oldest inscriptions referring to irrigation (presumably for rice) date from the eighth century AD (Meer 1979). This is about as far as the direct evidence goes, and at this rather vague level it is clearly inappropriate to debate whether rainfed systems preceded irrigated (or vice versa), or whether both forms developed together as a result of local differences in topography.

However, there are other important points to note about wet rice. Most modern systems depend on iron and water buffaloes for successful management, and this has led to ideas that wet rice *must* be an Iron Age phenomenon. This, of course, is not so, since the Polynesians managed quite well to develop and use similar wet taro systems with only stone tools, and no traction animals. Nevertheless, there is no doubt that wet rice cultivation as known today is mainly (but not entirely) related to very large dense populations and the iron–buffalo complex of technology. It is not commonly found in regions of light population, and the system clearly flourishes best on fertile volcanic soils, as in Java and Bali, where it was so closely tied historically with the Hinduised civilisations that an introduction during the first millennium AD must always remain likely (there is no good evidence against this possibility). Wet rice in these islands can support enormous populations since yields can be increased through more careful field preparation, transplanting, and continuous cropping through the year with irrigation (C. Geertz 1963). The sawahs themselves can be cropped indefinitely in many regions without fallows, partly because the irrigation waters carry nutrients, and also because fern-dwelling algae in the sawahs are very efficient fixers of atmospheric nitrogen.

A major point here, of course, is that wet rice cultivation on a given unit of land can feed many more people than dry rice grown by shifting cultivation, but the establishment of the necessary field systems does require a great deal of initial labour. So it is hardly surprising that many shifting cultivators would continue with this system unless obliged to intensify, perhaps owing to population pressure (e.g. Seavoy 1973a for Kalimantan), or in the face of managerial demands for increased production to support a state or bureaucratic apparatus (cf. Earle 1978, 1980 for wet taro intensification in Hawaii). The Hinduised civilisations may well have been able to enforce such managerial demands in Java and Bali, but explanations of this type hardly suffice for wet rice cultivation by the remote Kelabits and Lun Dayeh of inland Borneo (Schneeberger 1979; Padoch 1983), or by the peoples of the northern interior of Luzon whose magnificent terraces are amongst the most spectacular anywhere in eastern Asia (see Fig. 7.19).

The Ifugao terraces of Luzon (Conklin 1980) comprise 20 000 km of embankment, of which 7000 km are stone-faced, and support a relatively small-scale bilateral society with densities of between 100 and 250 persons per km^2. About one-half of Ifugao subsistence needs are also provided by shifting cultivation, and land does not seem to be in short supply. According to Conklin the Ifugao terraces may have developed slowly since about 400 BC (there is actually no evidence to support such a date, and Keesing, 1962, has argued at length that they were all developed after the Spanish conquest of Luzon), and they are clearly not associated in any way with the presence of a centralised authority or a master plan. So in this case we are left with the hypothesis that they have been developed piecemeal by wealthy but tribally organised families of high status, able to command sufficient labour for construction and maintenance. The mountainous Luzon terrain is obviously also suited to terracing in an aesthetic sense, and one cannot entirely discount the importance of such a factor.

Perhaps I can draw one moral from this story — wet rice irrigation can exist on a large scale without bureaucratic intervention of the type associated with the ancient canal irrigation systems of Mesopotamia or China, and this is because it can operate as a piecemeal family or small group system, as with the *subak* irrigation corporations of Bali. There is, therefore, a potentially optative basis to the origins of wet rice cultivation, and this means that the system need not always be associated with a state organisation and a very dense population, although history shows that this has normally been the case. Seemingly aberrant cases such as Luzon and central Borneo are really rather hard to explain without at least a partial model of free choice, and perhaps emulation. In the Borneo case, wet rice cultivation may in fact be a viable alternative to shifting cultivation for small populations who inhabit an equatorial environment with no dependable dry season and have limited supplies of labour and iron tools (Padoch 1983).

Prior to AD 1500, sawah rice may have been the limit of intensification in the Indo-Malaysian Archipelago, although I should perhaps mention the intensive tapping of the juices of the lontar palm (*Borassus sundaicus*) in Roti and Savu in eastern Indonesia (Fox 1977a); a system which was most probably introduced from India. In addition, the modern story of the opening of the lowland swamps of Sumatra, Kalimantan and Irian Jaya to rice cultivation (Collier 1979; Tsubouchi 1980) shows just how productive such apparently useless environments can become with organisation and technology, but this is an unusual option which probably would not have been at all attractive to prehistoric Austronesian cultivators.

8

The Late Neolithic Phase in Island South-East Asia

My previous definition of the Late Neolithic phase (Bellwood 1978a:209–21) in the eastern part of the Indo-Malaysian Archipelago centred on the widespread appearance of decorated (normally stamped and incised) pottery in parts of the Philippines and eastern Indonesia after about 1500 BC, and I also included in this phase the Yüan-shan pottery from northern and eastern Taiwan. Jar burial possibly developed in the Philippines and Sarawak from about 1000 BC(?) onwards, and the phase eventually graded into the Early Metal phase with copper/bronze, iron, glass beads, and widespread jar burial at the end of the first millennium BC. No further discoveries which relate directly to the Late Neolithic phase have been made since 1978, and the large western islands of Indonesia still remain *terra incognita*. However, in the eastern regions it has become clear that the stylistic features of pottery decoration which I used to define the Late Neolithic in 1978 are by no means universal, and in Sabah and Talaud (and possibly also in parts of Luzon) the Early Neolithic plain and red-slipped wares simply continued on to about 2000 years ago (see Chapter 7, Fig. 7.12), when they were replaced quite sharply by an elaborately-decorated array of Early Metal phase wares which I will be describing in due course.

Despite problems such as these I still wish to retain the concept of a Late Neolithic phase for certain stylistically-related assemblages in the eastern part of the archipelago and western Oceania. I will commence in Taiwan with the Yüan-shan culture (see Chapter 7, Section IIA), which was probably developing from its Ta-p'en-k'eng forebear through the Chih-shan-yen phase during the late third millennium BC and which appears to have continued as a fairly stable archaeological entity to as far south as Batan Island until perhaps the first millennium BC. As noted in Chapter 7, it has a ceramic inventory of globular vessels with ring feet, strap handles, red or brown slips, knobbed lids, and an array of incised and stamped decoration (see Chapter 7, Fig. 7.4). The stamped patterns are particularly interesting, and include rows of stamped circles, and also some dentate (comb stamped) or shell-edge stamped motifs (Chang 1969a: Plates 80–6).

I. The Philippines and Eastern Indonesia

It is these stamped patterns which serve to relate the Yüan-shan culture to certain assemblages of the period after 1500 BC found to the south in the Philippines and Indonesia, and also in western Oceania. In the Philippines one such assemblage comes from a disturbed burial cave excavated by Solheim (1968) in Batungan Mountain on the island of Masbate (central Philippines). A carbon date of about 900 BC from an adjacent and perhaps slightly later cave may be pertinent for comparisons with the middle or later phases of the Yüan-shan, and the Batungan assemblage concerned (from cave 1) includes a quantity of red-slipped sherds from carinated vessels, with incised, dentate stamped and stamped circle motifs very like those from the Yüan-shan repertoire (Fig. 8.1). It is unfortunate that such material has never been excavated in a well-dated habitation site in the Philippines[1], and the only dates for what may (with some uncertainty) be similar material from Indonesia come from excavations by Glover in eastern Timor. A few decorated sherds were found here in cave deposits loosely dated to between 1500 BC and AD 500 (Glover 1972a), and the patterns include incised hatched triangles and rows of interlocking semi-circles (Fig. 8.2). The latter form of decoration also occurs more prolifically in two very important sites in western Sulawesi.

These sites, Kalumpang and Minanga Sipakko, lie close together on the middle course of the Karama river in west-central Sulawesi, and they have produced the most remarkable presumed Late Neolithic assemblages of any sites in Indonesia. Unfortunately, neither are dated, and Kalumpang, the most important, was investigated long ago by Stein Callenfels in 1933 and by Heekeren in 1949 (Heekeren 1950a, 1972:184–90; Sutayasa 1973). Both are open sites with no stratigraphic differentiation of the materials found, and the assemblages include quandrangular and lenticular-sectioned stone adzes, some with unusual waisted or knobbed profiles, ground slate projectile points similar to the Taiwanese Neolithic types (but without perforations), a stone barkcloth beater, and some possible stone reaping knives (Fig. 8.3). The pottery is especially remarkable — some of the motifs are shown in Fig. 8.4 — and there are also some knobbed lids and ring feet with cut-out decoration. Of all the Neolithic assemblages excavated in Indonesia, this one, at least in

[1]Recent work by Thiel (1985) at the site of Lal lo in the Cagayan Valley of northern Luzon has produced pottery very similar to Yüan-shan (and also Lapita) types from an apparently similar time-span.

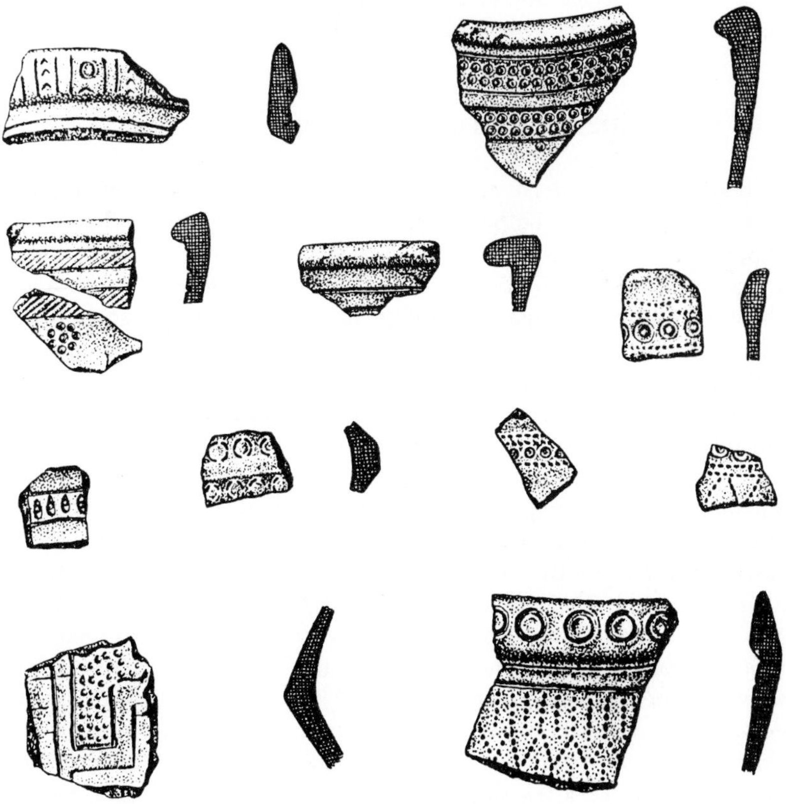

Fig. 8.1. Incised and stamped sherds from the Batungan Caves, Masbate. From Solheim 1968. Courtesy: Social Science Research Institute, University of Hawaii.

its stone repertoire and some aspects of pottery decoration, seems to have the closest resemblance to the Neolithic assemblages of Taiwan.

It is most unfortunate that these two sites have no dates, and it must be admitted that there are certain ceramic parallels from other sites, especially for the knobbed lids and some of the incised decoration, which could make a very recent date for the Kalumpang material seem likely (e.g. Sutayasa 1973; Mulvaney and Soejono 1971). However, Heekeren originally preferred a date of at least 2000 years ago, and given the total absence of metal in these extensive open sites, plus the Taiwanese parallels for the stone points and the Oceanic Lapita parallels for the pottery decoration, I would personally not be too surprised if an age of even 3000 years can one day be demonstrated.

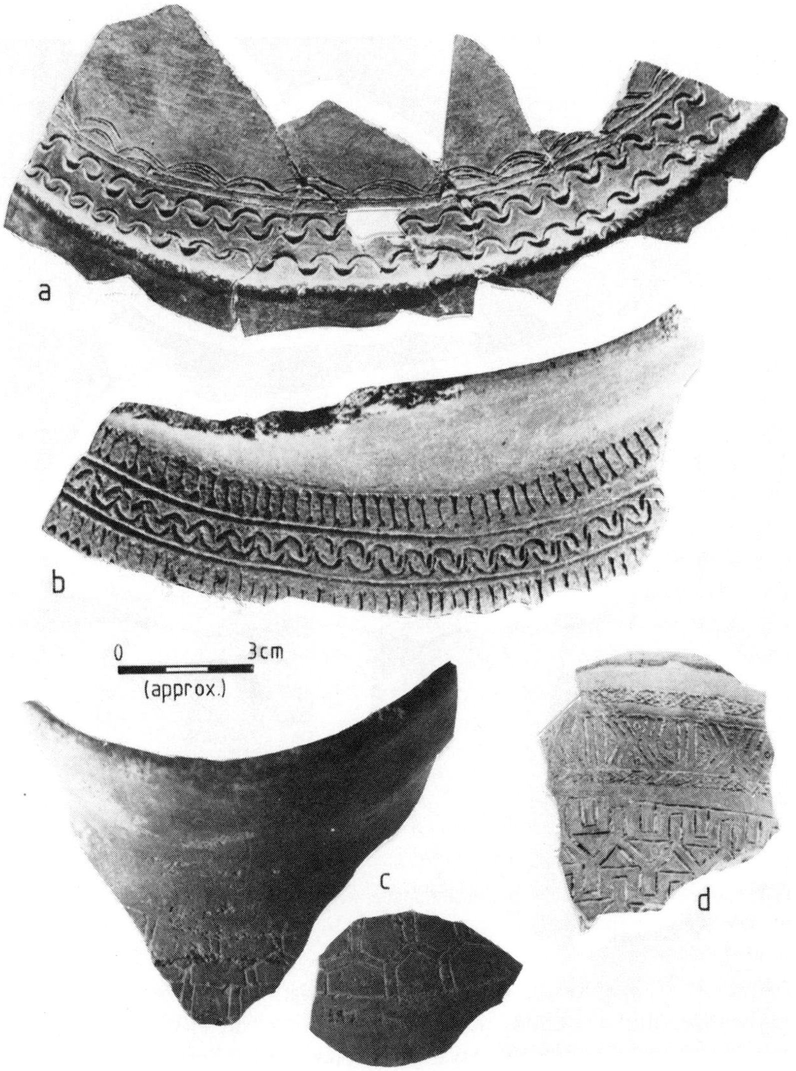

Fig. 8.2. (a, b) Sherds with interlocked semicircle pattern, (a) from eastern Timor, c. 1500 BC–AD 500, and (b) from Ulu Leang 2, southern Sulawesi, undated; (for similar patterns from Kalumpang see Fig. 8.4); (c) red-slipped sherds with incised arcade motifs from Nikiniki I, western Timor, undated. From Glover 1972a. (d) Lapita sherd from Watom Island, New Britain, late 2nd–early 1st millennium BC. Courtesy: I. C. Glover (a–c); Musee de l'Homme, Paris (d).

Fig. 8.3. Stone adzes and points from Kalumpang, west-central Sulawesi. From Heekeren 1972. Courtesy: Martinus Nijhoff.

My main reasons for this view arise in part from a realisation of the significance of the Lapita culture of Oceania — an extremely important window on eastern Indo-Malaysian developments (however obscure they might seem at present) of the mid-second millennium BC.

A. The Lapita Culture of Western Oceania

The existence of the Lapita culture is actually one of my main reasons for holding on to the concept of a Late Neolithic in the Indo-Malaysian Archipelago, despite the lacunae in and problems with the archaeological evidence

Fig. 8.4. Decorated sherds from Kalumpang, west-central Sulawesi. From Heekeren 1972. Courtesy: Martinus Nijhoff.

from this region. In the western Pacific, however, Austronesian colonists between 1500 and 1000 BC left an extremely clear-cut trail of pioneer archaeological sites across about 6500 km of ocean and islands (many previously uninhabited), from the Admiralty Islands (north of New Guinea) to as far east as Samoa, in western Polynesia. This impressive migration probably correlates linguistically with the period of Proto-Oceanic (see Chapter 4, Section VB), and although much of western Melanesia had long been occupied by Papuan-speaking groups it is clear that these tended to be settled mainly in the larger islands of New Guinea, the Bismarcks, and the Solomons. Many small islands, and all territories from perhaps Vanuatu (and certainly Fiji) onwards, were thus available for canoe-borne colonisation by Austronesian groups.

The resulting Lapita culture, which represents colonisation of virgin territory in most locations where it has been found, is generally well-dated and well-studied in terms of artefacts and economy and suffers from few of the chronological problems which beset the often mixed and undated assemblages from Island South-East Asia. Lapita, therefore, can provide an excellent insight into its logical antecedents, which lie somewhere in the eastern regions of Indonesia or the Philippines (the linguistic evidence points to the Moluccas and western New Guinea) in the mid-second millennium BC. No one has yet found these antecedents, and sites like Batungan and Kalumpang are the closest known, but even if many of the elaborations of ceramic decoration were developed within Melanesia itself one can hardly deny the prior existence of cultures with similar economic, technological and navigational skills somewhere on the eastern fringes of the Indo-Malaysian Archipelago.

The Lapita evidence, when viewed from an Indo-Malaysian viewpoint, reveals quite clearly an integrated culture with the following archaeological features (for summaries see Bellwood 1978a:244–55; Green 1979):

a. A range of coiled or slab-built vessels with sand or crushed shell tempers, ranging in form from globular cooking pots through narrow-necked water jars to a variety of open bowls, some with flat bases. Tripods apparently do not occur, although there are some possible cylindrical pot stands from Fiji. Some vessel profiles are sharply carinated, and other accessories include lug and strap handles, and some possible lids and ring feet. Vessel surfaces are often red-slipped, and the decoration, generally in zones around the upper surfaces of some of the vessels, includes a quite astonishing and intricate range of incised and dentate-stamped motifs of rectilinear, curvilinear and even anthropomorphic forms. Paddle-impressed surfaces do occur, but very rarely. The Yüan-shan, Batungan and Kalumpang pottery repertoires clearly have a very wide range of parallels, many quite specific, with the Lapita range, and a red-slipped and incised vessel with decoration precisely paralleled in some Lapita sites (see Fig. 8.2c) was found by Alfred Buhler in his 1935 excavations in the disturbed cave of Nikiniki I in western Timor (Glover 1972b). Tanged blades found in the same site have been dated to between 2300 and 1200 years ago by Glover (1972a:226), according to the results of his own excavations in other sites (see Chapter 7, Fig. 7.13 e–g), but the vessel itself is not precisely datable. Given the diffuseness of present evidence it is not of course possible to regard any of these sites as being especially central to the question of immediate Lapita origins.

b. Economically, the Lapita culture originated within Stage 2 and represents the beginning of Stage 3 of my reconstructed agricultural sequence (see Chapter 7, Section V). Pigs, fowls and dogs (in Fiji) were all present, and a fairly healthy inter-island exchange of obsidian and other items was carried out (Green 1979, 1982). Items of material culture apart from pottery include stone adzes (all untanged) with quadrangular, lenticular and plano-convex cross-sections, shell adzes, and a range of shell ornaments and fishhooks. The shell fishhooks suggest a technological adaptation confined mainly to Oceania, since these artefacts are not found in Indo-Malaysian sites except for a few examples from Timor (see Chapter 7, Fig. 7.13a).

The Mariana Islands of western Micronesia were also settled about 1500 BC (Kurashina and Clayshulte 1983) by users of a thin-walled red-slipped pottery, usually termed Marianas Redware (Bellwood 1978a: Chapter 10). There are indications that this pottery may be closer to the Philippine and Talaud Early Neolithic assemblages than to the decorated Batungan and Lapita repertoires, but whatever the final verdict it does look as if these islands were settled, perhaps from the Philippines, by a separate and possibly slightly earlier movement than that indicated by Lapita in more southerly latitudes.

I have made this excursion into the Lapita culture because sites of this kind, perhaps without the elaborate dentate stamping and the fishhooks, will surely be more fully documented some day in eastern Indonesia. I regard this as an important priority for future research in this region. However, it is necessary to point out that these pottery similarities, which also extend well into Vietnam during the last two millennia BC (Ha Van Tan 1985b), can hardly be used to document significant movements of people, except of course for the Lapita case. The founder movements of Austronesian speakers to the west of Oceania took place earlier, and these Late Neolithic similarities most probably represent continuing contacts between linguistically related populations, perhaps involving some degree of trade, although direct evidence for this is so far absent in the Island South-East Asian archaeological record.

II. The Neolithic of the Niah Caves

As I have noted, the Neolithic period of western Indonesia is virtually a total blank, despite the numerous reports of pottery from scattered sites in Java and Sumatra, often cord-marked or carved-paddle-impressed in contradistinction to that from eastern Indonesia (see Chapter 7, Section III; Bronson and Asmar 1975). Apart from my own work in Sabah, which has produced material more closely related to the Early Neolithic of the Philippines and eastern Indonesia, the only site with a major sequence in this western region is again the West Mouth at Niah in Sarawak. I will now continue the Niah sequence from where I left off in Chapter 6, Section IIA.

According to the original reports of Harrisson (e.g. 1957, 1958, 1959, 1970a), pottery first appeared in the West Mouth sequence at around 2500 or 2000 BC together with quadrangular cross-sectioned adzes, which were preceded by an earlier lenticular-sectioned form (see Chapter 7, Fig. 7.14 2G). The pottery appears to be mainly of simple globular forms with plain or carved-paddle-impressed surfaces, and cord-marking is rather rare (Solheim, Harrisson and Wall 1959; Wall 1962; Majid 1982). Unusual forms include closed water vessels with double spouts (Harrisson 1971), and some elaborate "three-colour ware" which has painted designs enclosed within incised lines (Figs 8.5, 8.6). The three-colour ware is in fact similar to some Early Metal phase pottery from Sabah and the Philippines, but the radiocarbon dates discussed below do suggest that it may be older at Niah.

The only way to look at the Niah sequence for the last three millennia BC is in terms of burial types and their associations. During the Neolithic, an inner portion of the cave behind the area previously occupied was used for burial purposes. About 130 burials were excavated from this "cemetery sector" prior to 1967, and cultural details have been described by Harrisson (1967). All are shallow, and they seem to belong to one continuous phase of activity dated mainly between 3000 BC and about AD 100. A large series of 30 collagen or apatite radiocarbon dates of varying reliability have been reported by Brooks *et al.* (1977).

The main burial types are as follows:

a. Extended burials, totalling 68, laid in shallow graves marked with stakes, with (in most cases) heads pointing into the cave. Many skeletons were coated with hematite or partially burnt, and it is interesting to note that a similar incomplete burning of corpses has been reported ethnographically for Land Dayak groups in Sarawak (Roth 1896:137). At Niah the bodies were placed in log coffins with plank lids or in cigar-shaped caskets of sewn bamboo strips, and in some cases they were also wrapped in pandanus mats before being placed in the containers. Some of the

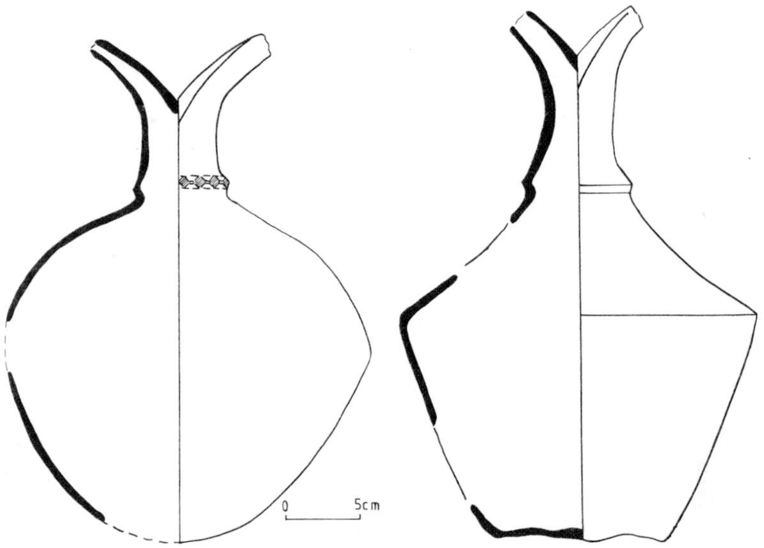

Fig. 8.5. Double-spouted vessels from Lobang Jeragan, near Niah. From Harrisson 1971. Courtesy: Malaysian Branch of the Royal Asiatic Society.

Fig. 8.6. Large three-colour ware vessel (79 cm high) from the West Mouth at Niah; the rectangular meanders are painted in greenish-yellow clay, the incised lines are blackened with charcoal, and the vessel body has been red-slipped. Courtesy: Sarawak Museum.

burials in bamboo caskets were provided with pillows of wood, matting, bamboo or leaves. There are also traces of textiles, perhaps cotton, with two burials which are probably quite late in the sequence. Associated artefacts, possibly grave goods, include a quadrangular adze, sherds of three-colour ware, two bone rings (in burial 133, c. 1200 BC), and a wooden disc-shaped earplug.

Dates from coffin wood and bone collagen or apatite for the extended burials range from about 3800 BC to about AD 100. There are no certain dated associations with pottery, but one burial dated on collagen to about 1000 BC (no. 36) had a copper knife, and another, dated to about 1100 BC (no. 60A) had a blue glass bead. These dates are obviously much too early for these items by perhaps a millennium, and the question arises of whether some of the other collagen dates are also too old. I have no means of demonstrating this since there are no stratigraphic details for any of these burials, and can only point out that three non-bone dates from a mat and two wooden coffins (burials 75 and 60: Harrisson 1975b; Harrisson 1967:154) fall more acceptably between about 1750 and 500 BC. If the collagen dates are taken purely at face value they do suggest that burials were being placed in wooden coffins or bamboo caskets for a millennium or so before the appearance of pottery (at 2500 BC?), and such an early date contradicts the evidence for a predominance of unenclosed flexed burials at this time elsewhere in the archipelago (for example Gua Cha, Gua Lawa, Duyong cave).

b. Cremations and burnt secondary burials. These two categories were separated by Barbara Harrisson, but it seems best to consider them together. Fifty-nine were found (26 fully cremated and 33 less fully burnt), and they were placed in small wooden coffins, pottery jars (Fig. 8.7), or baskets. One was in a Chinese jar, presumably post-dating AD 1000. Associated goods for the whole group included quadrangular adzes, shell rings and perforated discs, some double-spouted jar sherds, and a single copper object. The collagen dates for these burials range between about 2100 and 700 BC, and dated associations include a double-spouted sherd (about 2100 BC, burial 30), two burial jars dated to about 1500 BC (burial 69, and from wood with burial 159, Harrisson 1968), and another burial jar dated to about 750 BC (burial 67). Again, these dates do seem a little early given the patterning elsewhere in the archipelago, but similar dates in the late second millennium BC for double-spouted sherds have been claimed from two other caves near Niah, called Magala and Lobang Jeragan (Harrisson and Harrisson 1968; Harrisson 1971). However, the problem with Magala is that the sherd concerned was found on the surface of the cave, and not in definite association with the bone which was dated.

Fig. 8.7. Lidded burial urn (burial 159: Harrisson 1968) with carved-paddle-impressed decoration from the West Mouth, Niah. Height excluding cover 69.5 cm. This jar was associated with burnt wood, radiocarbon dated to about 1500 BC. Courtesy: Sarawak Museum.

The Niah evidence thus presents some major problems. On the one hand there is a very large series of radiocarbon dates, but mainly on collagen or apatite and of uncertain reliability. On the other hand there are large numbers of artefacts, but it is almost impossible to associate the vast majority of them in any convincing way with the dated bones. Nothing short of massive re-excavation, perhaps now impossible, can resolve this problem. But if the many published opinions are taken at face value then one may be looking at the following sequence, as worked out by my student Aubrey Parke. Firstly, there are apparently preceramic extended burials in coffins or bamboo caskets, and continuing flexed burials, in a period dubiously dated to between about 4000 and 2000 BC. Secondly, there follows a phase from about 2000 BC (or later?) extending to an uncertain point, perhaps late in the first millennium BC, characterised by continuing extended burials, newly-appearing cremations, jar burials, and pottery (including the double-spouted form). Thirdly comes the Early Metal phase, which probably postdates AD 1 at Niah, associated with the same continuing burial forms, copper, and perhaps textiles.

If these dates are correct then the Niah sequence may indeed contain jar burials from the second millennium BC in fully Neolithic contexts, as now appears to be the case in southern Vietnam (Ha Van Tan 1985b). I am also willing in principle to accept second millennium BC dates for the double-spouted and three-colour sherds, but such dates need to be much more firmly established before full acceptance can be given to them.

A few other comments can be added to the Niah story. It is possible that a small domestic dog was present in the Neolithic phase (Clutton Brock 1959; Medway 1977b) together with the domestic pig, although definitive evidence for the latter before the 15th century AD seems to be lacking (Medway 1973; Cranbrook 1979). Neither the dog nor the domesticated species of pig (*Sus scrofa*) are native to Borneo, and the native wild boar (*Sus barbatus*) appears never to have been domesticated. Otherwise, the economic evidence from the West Mouth suggests little real change from pre-pottery times, and it looks as if the site was used predominantly for burial during the Neolithic, and perhaps for occasional visits, rather than as a base for a sedentary agricultural population.

III. The Ban Kao Neolithic Culture of Southern Thailand and Malaya

Malaya represents a totally different Neolithic world — one belonging to *orang asli* populations with cultural affinities directed towards southern Thailand. It is quite possible that Austronesian-speakers did not settle the peninsula before 1000 BC, if as early as this, and the Malayan Neolithic has no obvious connections at all with the ramified island Neolithic which I have just been describing. Instead, it is very closely related to assemblages from western Thailand which have been grouped together as the Ban Kao culture (Sørensen 1972; Bellwood 1978a:166–70). The key site is the burial ground of Ban Kao in Kanchanaburi Province (Sørensen and Hatting 1967), and other assemblages are known from the nearby shelter of Sai Yok, and from locations running down the peninsula towards Malaya.

The intricate details of the Thai aspects of this culture are not of concern here, and I will simply note that extended burials have been excavated at Ban Kao, together with a range of grave goods which include untanged adzes, barbed bone harpoon or spear points (see Fig. 8.15), disc beads and bracelets of shell, and pottery with a fairly complex range of shapes and mainly cord-marked decoration (Fig. 8.8). Some form of slow wheel seems to have been used during manufacture, and Sørensen (1972) has divided the Ban Kao pottery into an early group which has many vessels with tripods, ring feet or high pedestals, and a later group with plainer round or flat-based forms. The

Fig. 8.8. Neolithic pottery from Ban Kao, western Thailand. From Sørensen and Hatting 1967. Courtesy: Munksgaard.

Ban Kao burials themselves are not directly dated, but habitation layers in the site have a convincing spread of radiocarbon dates beteen the late third and mid-second millennia BC (Tauber 1973). Sørensen (supported by Sieveking 1974) accepts these dates as relevant for the burials, although other authors (e.g. Parker 1968; Bayard and Parker 1976; Macdonald 1978) have proposed that all be placed in the Iron Age, after 500 BC. Given the Malayan evidence I certainly support a pre-Iron Age antiquity: only two late burials at Ban Kao have iron, and none have copper or bronze artefacts.

The habitation layers in Ban Kao and Sai Yok fill out the burial inventories with a range of items including shouldered adzes of the common Thai and Vietnamese type (see Chapter 7, Fig. 7.14 8A), stone bracelets, bone fish-hooks and combs, clay barkcloth beaters and spindle whorls, and some possible semi-lunar stone reaping knives (Sørensen 1972:477–82). Sørensen has suggested an economy based on rice cultivation with domesticated pigs and possibly fowls; the case for cattle, certainly domesticated by this time in northern Thailand (Higham and Kijngam 1979), seems to be uncertain. In addition, another site at Nong Chae Sao has yielded the posthole plan of a round-ended raised-floor house (Fig. 8.9), with two burials and a group of four pots placed beneath the floor (Henriksen 1982). The skeletal remains from the Ban Kao burials are similar to those of modern South-East Asian Mongoloid populations, such as the Thai (Sangvichien *et al.* 1969).

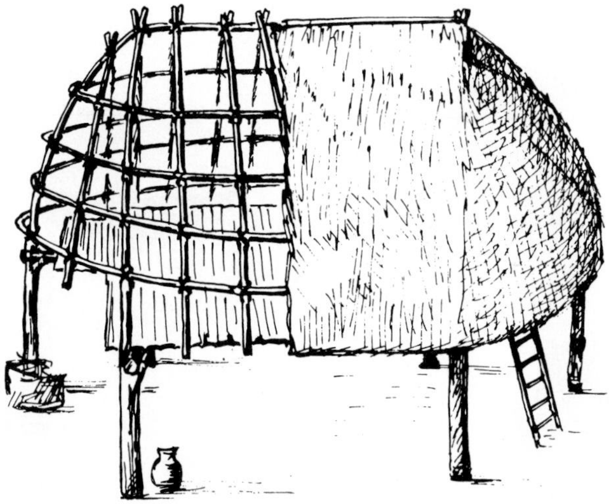

Fig. 8.9. One possible reconstruction for the postholes of a house excavated at Nong Chae Sao, western Thailand. House length c. 9.5 m. From Henriksen 1982. Courtesy: P. Sørensen.

In Malaya there are no known open burial grounds like Ban Kao, and most assemblages come from caves. The Malayan Neolithic pottery as a whole is very similar to that from Ban Kao; some was made on a slow wheel, the same tripod and footed forms occur, and most surface decoration is cord-marked (Peacock 1959). Cord-marking was a very common method of decoration in many regions of Mainland South-East Asia (including Ban Kao) during the Neolithic and Early Metal phases, but it was virtually absent before about 2000 years ago in the island assemblages which I have been discussing — even at Niah the bulk of the paddle-impression is of the carved paddle and not the corded kind.

Vessel tripods almost identical to those from Ban Kao and from another southern Thai site called Buang Bep, with round holes to allow air to escape during firing, have been found unstratified in the caves of Gua Berhala in Kedah (Fig. 8.10) and Gua Bintong in Perlis (Peacock 1964a), and further south at the open site of Dengkil in Selangor (Batchelor 1977). The Dengkil finds come from alluvial deposits disturbed through tin mining, and are radiocarbon dated to older than 2000 years ago. Although not found in stratigraphic relationships the finds from here also include untanged quadrangular and shouldered adzes, a Tembeling knife (see below), and two wooden oars carbon dated to within the first millennium BC.

The major sites of the Ban Kao culture in Malaya are caves in the northern part of the country. At Gua Cha in Kelantan (see Chapter 6, Section IA) the Neolithic deposits began, according to Sieveking (1954), with a discrete working floor for quadrangular adzes found in his Cutting 1. Burials were then placed in the shelter after a period of sterile silt deposition. Sieveking believed that the burials belonged to two periods: an earlier with fairly crude

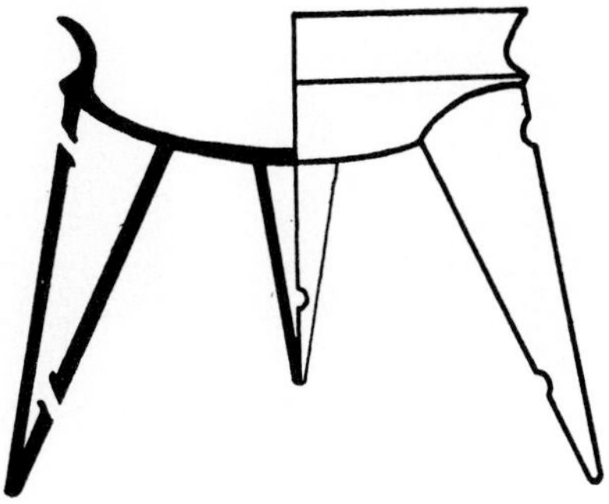

Fig. 8.10. Reconstructed tripod vessel about 28 cm high from Gua Berhala, Kedah. From Peacock 1959. Courtesy: University of Hawaii Press.

Fig. 8.11. Neolithic burial at Gua Cha, Kelantan, with pots at head and on legs (one of the latter contains a rat skull), a T-sectioned nephrite bracelet on the right forearm, a mussel-shell spoon in the left hand, and two quadrangular stone adzes on the pelvis. From Sieveking 1954 (burial 8). Courtesy: National Museum, Kuala Lumpur.

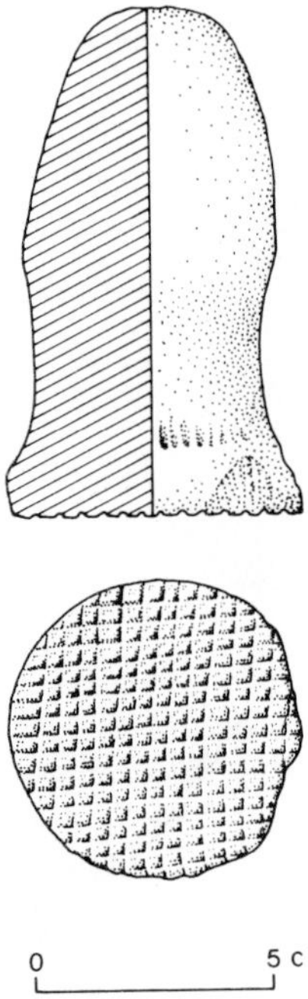

Fig. 8.12. Cylindrical stone barkcloth beater from Gua Cha. After Sieveking 1956c.

cord-marked vessels, and a later with the more elaborate pottery of Ban Kao type. This proposition was not accepted by Peacock (1959), and the 1979 excavations did not throw any further light on this matter. Most of the burials were extended and buried with grave goods (Fig. 8.11) which included D or T-sectioned stone bracelets, quadrangular adzes and one beaked adze (see Chapter 7, Fig. 7.14 7D), a cylindrical stone barkcloth beater (Fig. 8.12), and shell bead necklaces and shell spoons. The pottery presents the most complete Neolithic assemblage known from Malaya and includes footed, round and flat-based forms (no tripods) with a predominance of cord-marked decoration (Fig. 8.13). Many vessels have polished upper surfaces and definite slow wheel striations, and some are red-slipped. Another cave in Kelantan called Gua Musang has similar vessel forms to Gua Cha (Tweedie 1940), and the collections of the National Museum in Kuala Lumpur have sherds with an almost identical red slip from sites as widespread as Gua Cha and Gua Musang in Kelantan, Gua Bintong in Perlis (Collings 1937a), Gua Kajang in Perak (Evans 1918), Gua Kelawar in Kedah (Collings 1936), and Gua Kechil in Pahang (see below).

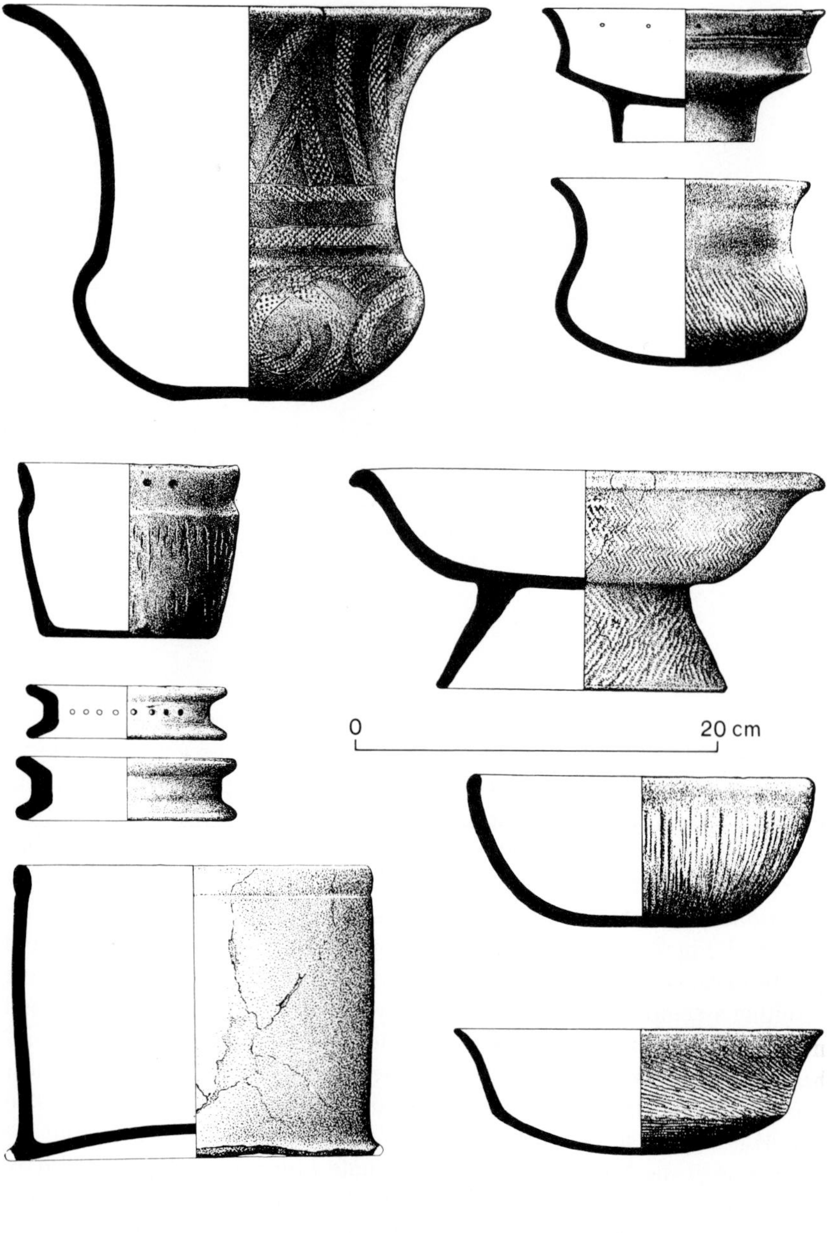

Fig. 8.13. Cord-marked, incised and punctate (top left), and red-slipped (bottom left) pottery from Gua Cha, Kelantan. There are also two potstands at centre left. From Sieveking 1954. Courtesy: National Museum, Kuala Lumpur.

Another very important but unstratified Neolithic collection comes from a cave in the limestone massif of Bukit Tengku Lembu in Perlis (Sieveking 1962) (Fig. 8.14). The pottery here is of the same fabric and manufacture as that from Gua Cha, but forms apparently localised to this region include beakers on high splayed feet and flat-based bell-mouthed jars. Sherds of a vessel of presumed Indian manufacture, possibly Northern Black Polished Ware (or a south Indian form associated with Rouletted Ware according to Bronson 1979b:330; see also Peacock 1964a who questions foreign importation) have been found in the site, but its exact identification and precise association with the rest of the assemblage remain uncertain. Bukit Tengku Lembu has also yielded a bone gouge, a stone bracelet, and some very fine beaked adzes and untanged quadrangular adzes with splayed cutting edges.

On the question of a date for the northern Malayan Neolithic there are a number of rather vague pointers. At Gua Cha the Neolithic burials were laid at an unknown time between 1250 BC and AD 1000 according to radiocarbon dates (Adi 1981), and the T-sectioned stone bracelets from here are closely paralleled in bronze in the northern Thai site of Ban Chiang between 1000 and 300 BC (White 1982). There is also a carbon date of uncertain validity of about 1800 BC for cord-marked pottery from a cave called Gua Harimau in Perak (Dunn 1966), and Bukit Tengku Lembu has the possible Indian sherd of early historic date (600 BC to AD 200?). The site of Gua Kechil in Pahang, which has lower levels with Hoabinhian tools and cord-marked pottery associated together (Dunn 1964), has a non-Hoabinhian upper level with pottery in the same tradition as that from Gua Cha, dated to sometime in the fourth millennium BC by a single radiocarbon date with an 800 year error range (Dunn 1966). However, I suspect that this date is much too old for the upper Gua Kechil assemblage. The site has also produced two bone projectile points (one sharply tanged, Fig. 8.15) and untanged adzes with quadrangular and lenticular cross-sections, but none of this material demands a date on typological grounds older than Ban Kao. Given these pointers one can perhaps place the whole Ban Kao culture within the last two millennia BC, but I hesitate to be more specific.

There are other Neolithic sites in central and northern Malaya which do not fit so well within the general bounds of the Ban Kao culture (the southern half of the country remains fairly blank). I have already referred to the unusual necked axes and pottery from the shell-mounds at Guar Kepah in Pinang (see Chapter 6, Section IA), and I should also refer to an open site of uncertain character partly excavated by Evans (1928a, 1931a) in the alluvium of the Tembeling River at Nyong in Pahang. Artefacts were found here scattered through a 4 m thickness of alluvium, and they included several of the distinctive stone "Tembeling knives" (see Chapter 7, Fig. 7.14 5D)— an unusual tool which may best be regarded as a side-hafted axe or adze, but

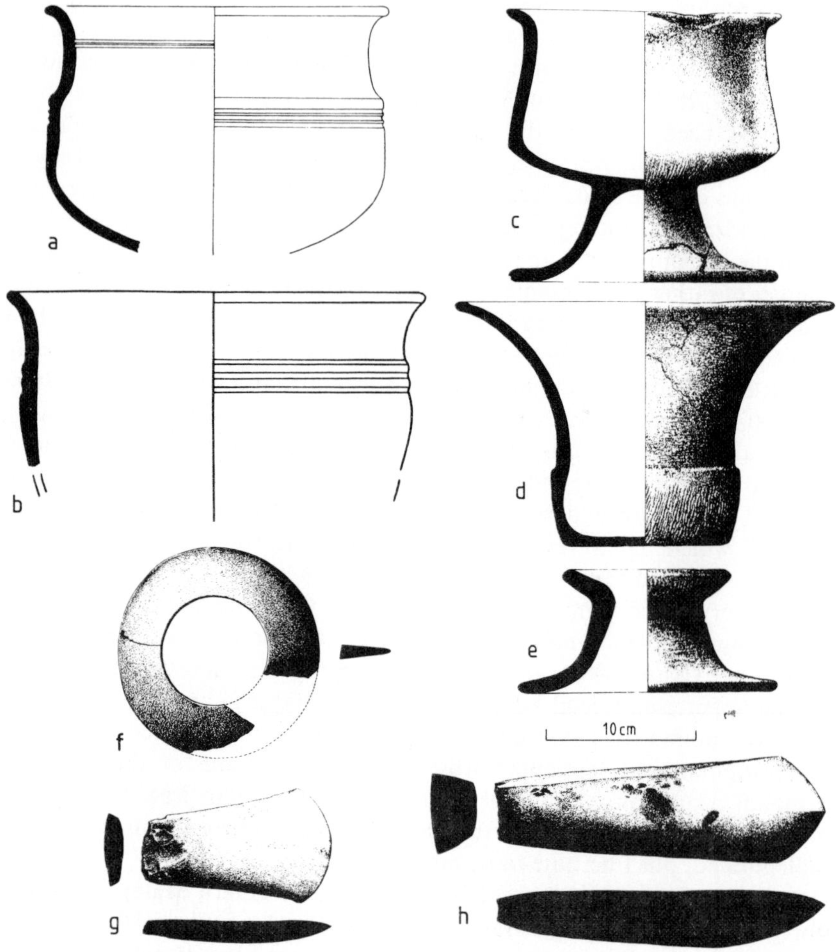

Fig. 8.14. Bukit Tengku Lembu, Perlis. (a) Vessel of possible Northern Black Polished Ware; (b) comparative N.B.P. vessel from Rupar, Punjab, c. 600–200 BC; (c) beaker on splayed foot; (d) bell-mouthed jar; (e) potstand; (f) stone bracelet; (g) axe or adze with splayed cutting-edge; (h) beaked adze. From Sieveking 1962. Courtesy: National Museum, Kuala Lumpur.

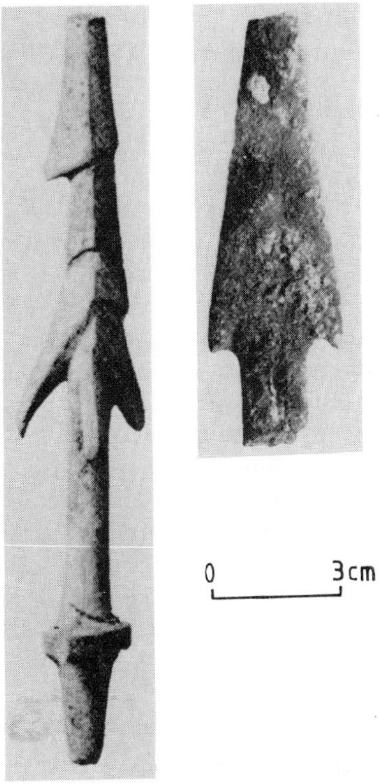

Fig. 8.15. Bone points from Ban Kao (left) and Gua Kechil (right). From Sørensen and Hatting 1967; Dunn 1964. Courtesy: Munksgaard, Malaysian Branch of the Royal Asiatic Society.

which in some cases may have served as a reaping knife. There is also another possible stone reaping knife with two perforations. Other items include adzes of quadrangular and beaked forms, a cylindrical barkcloth beater, and fragments of stone bracelets and a discarded centre ring. The stone assemblage is in fact very well paralleled at Gua Cha, and there are also similar sherds of cord-marked and red-slipped pottery, some made on a slow wheel. However, a few spouts and lugs (both absent in Ban Kao style pottery) suggest that the assemblage may not all belong to one period.

A. The Significance of the Ban Kao Culture

I will now examine the Ban Kao culture, especially its Malayan component, from the overall perspective of the Neolithic cultures of Mainland South-East Asia. In both Malaya and western Thailand there are clear signs that the purely artefactual manifestations of this culture, at least in terms of pottery and polished adzes, were introduced fairly sharply into a Hoabinhian technological landscape. At Gua Kechil there are indications that simple cord-marked pottery preceded the more "classic" wares of the Gua Cha main assemblage and Bukit Tengku Lembu types, but it seems to me that one cannot derive the Ban Kao culture as a whole purely from a local Hoabinhian matrix. This raises the question of the origins of the Ban Kao culture, especially in southern and western Thailand, and I strongly suspect that here an expansion of horticultural and basically Mongoloid populations from northern Thailand has occurred; an expansion perhaps parallel to but separate from that of the Austronesians much further to the east, and which faded rapidly in its genetic impact in some of the remoter portions of the Malay Peninsula. Linguistically, this mainland expansion may be associated with speakers of Austro-Asiatic languages.

The archaeological background to support such an expansion is now quite well-known. I can only touch on this briefly here, but it is clear that from sometime during the third or perhaps even the fourth millennium BC there were developing agricultural societies in northern Thailand and northern Vietnam with cultivated rice, domesticated animals (cattle, pigs and dogs), cord-marked and incised pottery, polished stone adzes, and some form of weaving. By the mid-second millennium BC a number of small-scale societies in this region were producing bronze tools and ornaments, and from about 600 BC onwards the rise of a stratified society in northern Vietnam (the Dong Son culture) with superb metal craftsmanship, an increasingly hierarchical settlement pattern, and an economy based partly on wet rice cultivation in bunded fields, can be seen. Similar developments occurred in northern Thailand from perhaps the end of the first millennium BC.

For present purposes, it is probably sufficient to note that the northern Thai cultures as a whole, particularly as represented in the early levels of such sites as Non Nok Tha and Ban Chiang, present an adequate economic, social and technological milieu for an ultimate derivation of the Ban Kao culture to the south. The latter, of course, has no metal, but Higham's recent papers (e.g. 1983) suggest that bronze working in the north may date from only the late third or second millennium BC, rather than from the fourth as once claimed. It is not my intention here to try to document a northern Thai origin for the Ban Kao culture in any precise way because the intervening regions have not been sufficiently researched. As I hope I have also made clear, the Ban Kao culture cannot be in any way related to the Neolithic cultures of Indonesia and East Malaysia. The Malay Peninsula is perhaps best regarded as a terminus point of overlap for both the earlier mainland Neolithic (that is the Ban Kao culture) and the later north-western limits of Austronesian settlement.

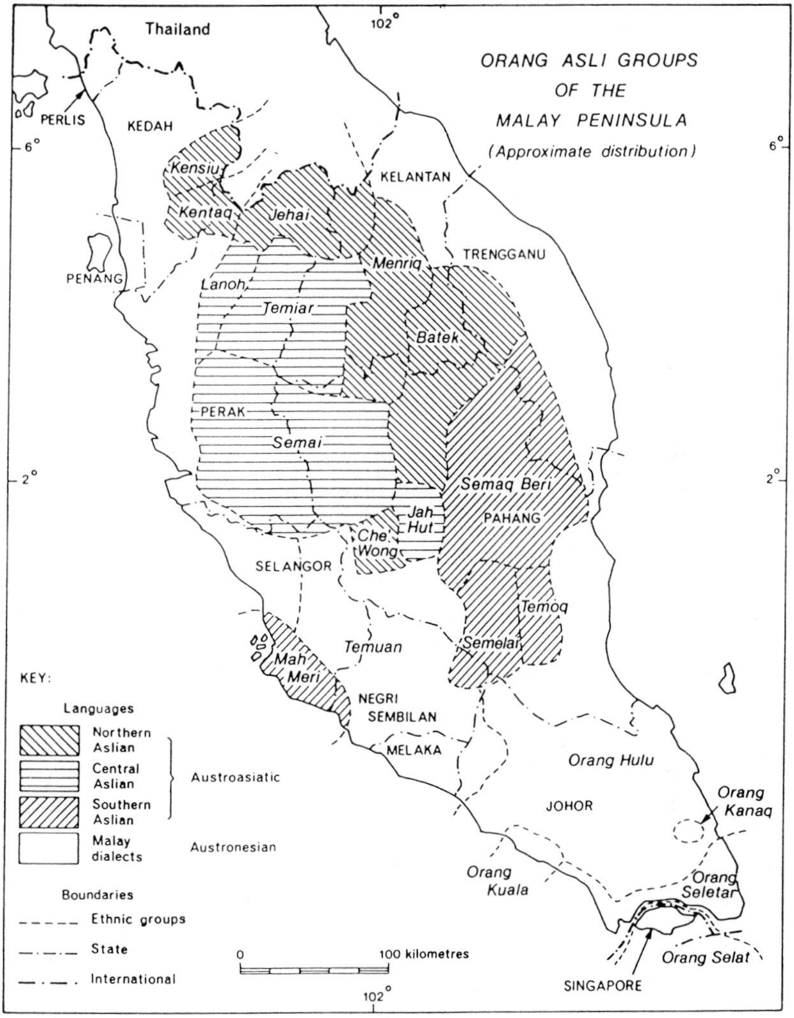

Fig. 8.16. The distribution of Aslian languages and Malay dialects (excluding Malay proper, which is now spoken over most of the peninsula apart from the interior Temiar, Semai and Jehai regions). Courtesy: G. Benjamin; drawn by Joan Goodrum.

There still remains the overall interpretation of the Ban Kao culture in Malaya itself. It is clear that the skeletal remains from Gua Cha do not express the Mongoloid phenotype which is apparent in the Ban Kao or northern Thai skeletons (e.g. Pietrusewski 1982), and at Gua Cha there also seems to be a generalised racial continuity from the Hoabinhian through into the Neolithic. As I noted in Chapter 3, Section IIIB, the Gua Cha population does not appear to have been closely related to the modern short-statured Negritos, and the latter clearly represent an evolutionary development for whom no skeletal record has yet been found. On the other hand, it is not difficult to see the Gua Cha population throughout as ancestral to the modern Senoi; the horticultural *orang asli* population of central Malaya amongst whom there are traces of past gene flow from Mongoloid sources.

A linguistic reconstruction of the course of prehistory in Malaya has been proposed by Benjamin (1976). This article gives dates for linguistic splits which may be too old owing to the use of a very high retention rate for glottochronological reckoning, but the overall sequence is very important. According to Benjamin, the Negritos (Northern Aslian speakers, Fig. 8.16) have always retained their mobile hunting and gathering lifestyle, and have presumably not been associated with Malayan Neolithic developments. The Central and Southern Aslian-speaking Senoi appear to have undergone more rapid linguistic diversification than the Negritos; the Central Aslians owing to the adoption of a sedentary endogamous social pattern based on agriculture and the development of corporate cognatic descent groups, and the Southern Aslians owing to a growing involvement in trade with and influence from the more recent Austronesian settlers of the coastal parts of the Peninsula (see also Benjamin 1983).

Hence it may be inferred that the introduction of agriculture from Thailand, perhaps around 2000 BC, led to increasing sedentarisation and isolation of small Senoi groups, and the later emphasis on trade in the southern part of the peninsula gave rise to a different and more assimilatory trend, as epitomised by such "Malayised" groups as the Temuan. Prior to the 19th century the interior parts of Malaya were probably occupied entirely by Aslian speakers (Benjamin 1976; Dunn 1975), and Austronesian settlement on the peninsula may not be much more than 2000–3000 years old. The documentation for initial Austronesian settlement in Malaya may in fact overlap partly with the Early Metal phase.

9

The Early Metal Phase: A Protohistoric Transition towards Supra-tribal Societies

The Early Metal (or Palaeometallic) phase correlates with the introduction of new technologies and trade items into the Indo-Malaysian Archipelago from Vietnamese, Indian and Chinese sources. In addition, it overlaps chronologically with and merges into the period of the developing Indianised states during the first millennium AD, and in this sense it seems quite reasonable to regard it as basically protohistoric.

However, the difficulties which attend any attempt to gauge the real significance of this phase are considerable. Most of the older reports contain little more than lists of undated artefacts, and the major cultural changes which are presumed to have taken place at this time remain virtually undocumented. My own research in Sabah and the Talaud Islands has provided a partial chronology for certain localised and regional aspects of the phase as a whole, but the vast bulk of the archipelago has not yet received the modern attention it deserves. Perhaps the best contribution to future studies which I can make in this chapter is to present some definitions, and to review the material in related groups which can in certain cases be elevated to the status of localised archaeological cultures.

The Early Metal phase commenced with the introduction of copper-bronze[1] and iron artefacts and their manufacturing technologies, presumably together (there is no separate "Bronze Age"), and almost certainly from

[1]Copper and bronze in archaeological contexts cannot be differentiated by visual inspection alone, and my general use of the term "bronze" may be imprecise in some circumstances, especially in Indonesia. Many so-called "bronze" objects may simply be of copper, but without analysis it is pointless to speculate.

immediate sources on the South-East Asian mainland during the last few centuries BC. I will take 500 BC as an arbitrary starting point, although I personally do not feel that any metal in the archipelago can be conclusively dated as early as this, and future research may push this date closer to AD 1. Artefacts and assemblages attributed to this phase of course exclude those which can unequivocally be associated with the historical Indianised or Islamic states, although I suspect that many assemblages considered to be "Bronze–Iron Age" in the terminology of Heekeren (1958) are in fact fully historical in this sense. However, this is usually hard to prove owing to poor documentation and dating. It should be emphasised that pre-Indianised styles of metal and other artefacts undoubtedly continued in production well after the first appearance of Indian bronzes and inscriptions in the archipelago, and for many of the remoter eastern regions and Borneo it would be quite acceptable to continue the Early Metal phase into ethnographic times, as in the case of the small bronze drums (*moko*) of Javanese or Balinese manufacture used in Alor (Dubois 1944). For practical reasons such a diffuseness of ending might cause this chapter to lengthen into another book, so I will draw an arbitrary termination at AD 1000, and thus leave the archaeology of the China trade, Islam, and the Malay sultanates out of consideration.

For locations of sites described in this chapter see Fig. 9.1.

I. The Dong Son Culture of Northern Vietnam

Bronze working in northern Vietnam commenced around the middle of the second millennium BC, and is associated with the Dong Dau and succeeding Go Mun phases of Vietnamese archaeologists (Ha Van Tan 1980; Hoang and Bui 1980). Together with northern Thailand (Bayard 1981) this region has the earliest evidence for bronze working in South-East Asia, and in recent years there has been considerable discussion about the origins of the tradition, which has no preceding copper phase. Whether indigenous or not these origins are of no real concern here, but the types of bronze artefacts involved in the millennium prior to 500 BC include socketed axes and spearheads, shaft-hole sickles, tanged spearheads and arrowheads, and other small items such as knives, fishhooks and bracelets. At some time between 600 and 400 BC according to recent carbon dates (Barnard 1980:36–7; Ha Van Tan 1980) the classic Dong Son phase of Vietnamese protohistory began, with its bronze drums, high status burials, and the first appearance of iron.

The Dong Son archaeological assemblages are of considerable importance since the earliest metal goods found in the Indo-Malaysian Archipelago are generally of this type, rather than of direct Indian or Chinese inspiration.

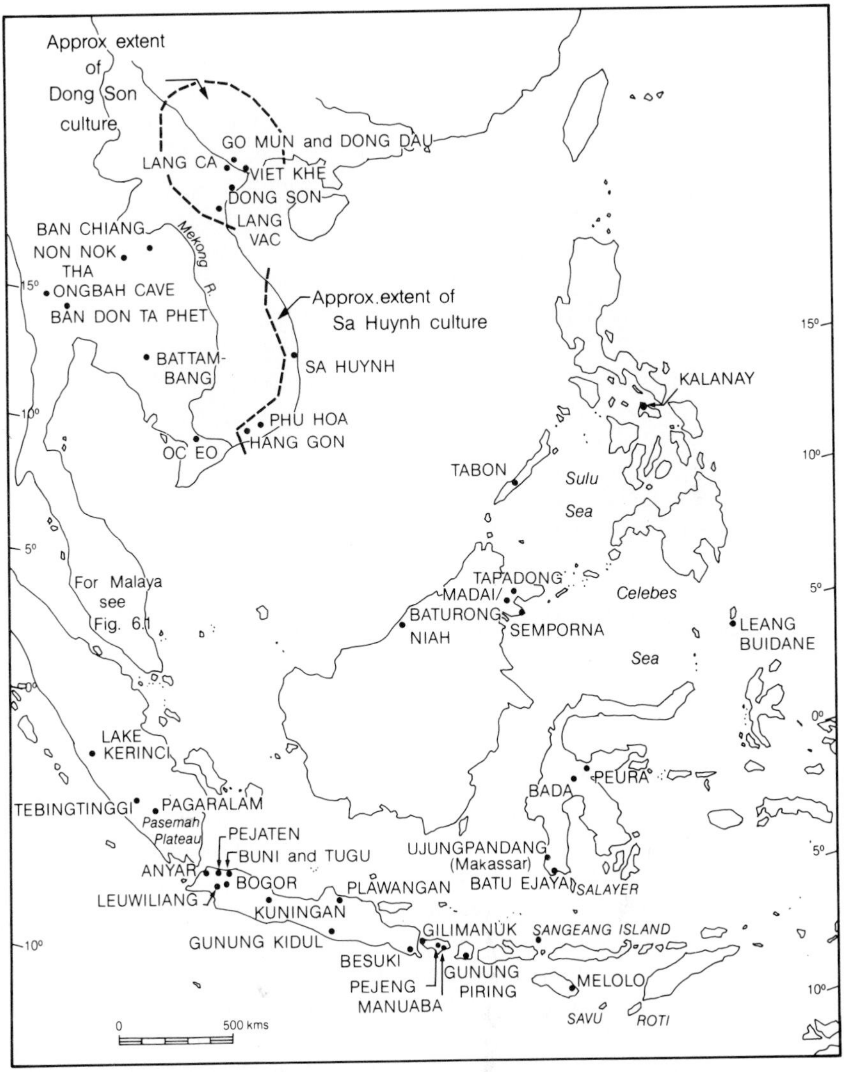

Fig. 9.1. Locations of sites described in Chapter 9.

Bronzes of Dong Son style are found widely in Mainland South-East Asia and southern China, but stylistic and compositional homogeneity, especially of the drums, suggests an outstanding dominance of Dong Son workshops on northern Vietnamese soil at this time. The drums are of Heger type I (Fig. 9.2), and the finest and oldest examples found in Vietnam have remarkable

Fig. 9.2. Bronze drum of Heger type I, 84 cm high, from Sangeang Island, Indonesia (the "Makalamau" drum). Courtesy National Museum, Jakarta.

decorative friezes of human, animal and geometric ornament. Such friezes occur, albeit with considerable simplification and schematisation, in all the later drums of this type, including those exported to Indonesia and Malaysia.

The range of other Dong Son bronze goods, excavated from such sites as the Dong Son settlement itself, and more recently from burials at Viet Khe, Lang Ca and Lang Vac (Janse 1958; Bellwood 1978a:187–9; Ha Van Tan 1980), includes bowls and situlae, miniature drums and bells, socketed axes with splayed or "boot-shaped" blades, socketed hoes, socketed or tanged arrowheads and spearheads, daggers with anthropomorphic handles (see Fig. 9.10), bracelets, belt hooks, and many other items of more idiosyncratic interest. Iron is rather rare, but there are a few spearheads and a cast iron hoe, the latter of possible Chinese manufacture. Imperial Chinese domination of northern Vietnam overlapped with the later stages of the Dong Son culture, and there are some undoubted Chinese imports in a number of the northern Vietnamese sites, but these occurrences cannot be used to support the derivation of Dong Son bronze metallurgy as a whole from China. The local genius expressed in the drum, situla and axe forms, plus the importance of lost wax casting (a technique generally considered to have been absent in

China prior to the third century BC), indicate quite clearly that northern Vietnam was a vital centre of bronze metallurgy which had a dramatic impact on many other regions of South-East Asia. The basic artefact styles overlap only marginally with those of metropolitan China, and not at all with the contemporary bronze and iron industries of India, which lack the emphasis on socketed hafting. However, the rather limited iron industry of Dong Son could have an immediate Chinese origin.

The Dong Son culture has a number of other features which merit attention. I will be returning to certain purely artefactual aspects repeatedly in this chapter, but it is also of great importance to realise that this culture was centrally involved in a transition to a highly stratified and partly urbanised society with an economy based on intensive rice production, presumably in rainfed or irrigated bunded fields with ploughs and buffalo traction (Higham 1983). The intensified production supported an upper ruling echelon whose wealthy burials have been found in many sites, and who in turn were able to support a degree of craft specialisation associated in many other areas with literate civilisations. It is therefore not surprising that such professionally-made items as the magnificent bronze drums, and perhaps Vietnamese techniques for the manufacture of lesser bronze tools and weapons, should have had such an impact on the contemporary societies of Indonesia and Malaysia.

II. The Sa Huynh Culture of Southern Vietnam

I will now move southwards to examine a different mainland culture which may also have been involved in the transmission of metalworking techniques, particularly of iron, into the islands of South-East Asia. The Sa Huynh culture of southern Vietnam belonged to an Austronesian-speaking (Chamic) population of Indo-Malaysian origin, which appears to have settled this region from either Malaya or Borneo (see Chapter 4, Section VA). When this settlement took place is uncertain, but the event may be documented by the Sa Huynh culture itself, which appeared in mature form around 600 BC, although possibly ancestral assemblages from the late second millennium BC are now being reported by Vietnamese archaeologists. Prior to the Sa Huynh culture or its immediate ancestor southern Vietnam was presumably occupied entirely by Austro-Asiatic-speaking populations. The Chams developed the important Indianised civilisation of Champa during the first millennium AD, but later succumbed to the pressures of Vietnamese expansion and now survive as minority hill peoples.

From an Indo-Malaysian point of view it is significant that the Chams of late prehistory were the closest-resident Austronesian groups to the northern

Vietnamese centres of metallurgy, and given their ethnic affiliations they were undoubtedly in a central position to introduce new metalworking techniques acquired on the mainland, particularly of iron, into the Indo-Malaysian Archipelago. However, their direct contacts with the bronze-working centres of the Dong Son region seem to have been rather limited since only two Heger I drums have been found in the south of Vietnam, and these items may have been transmitted into the archipelago by other routes, perhaps through Thailand and Malaya or directly by sea.

Assemblages of the Sa Huynh culture known to date have come mostly from jar burial sites, and this is a custom which may have been brought by the first Chamic settlers themselves from the Indo-Malaysian islands, especially if the Niah and Tabon dates for jar burial from the late second millennium BC onwards can be relied upon (see Chapter 8, Section II). Generally speaking, pottery jar burial was not characteristic of the Dong Son or other contemporary Mainland South-East Asian cultures, and where it does occur, as at the Dong Son site of Lang Vac in northern Vietnam (Ha Van Tan 1980:133), influence from Chamic sources may be suspected. The stone burial jars of northern Laos (Colani 1935; Bellwood 1978a:194–8) do not, in my opinion, represent a likely region of origin for the Sa Huynh or other Indo-Malaysian jar burial traditions, and they appear to be too recent in date.

Major Sa Huynh sites occur in coastal regions from central Vietnam southwards to the Mekong delta; the type site is Sa Huynh itself, but there are others further south at Hang Gon and Phu Hoa, and further north around Da Nang (for summaries see Bellwood 1978a:191–4; Ha Van Tan 1980:136–7; Fontaine 1979, 1980). The finer details of this culture are not of concern here, and I will return to the whole question of jar burial in Indonesia and East Malaysia in more detail below. However, it should be noted that the Sa Huynh burial jars and the associated accessory vessels with their incised and shell-edge stamped zones of decoration (Fig. 9.3) are paralleled very closely in the Early Metal phase jar burial assemblages of the Philippines, northern Borneo, and the Celebes Sea region of northern Indonesia. These links have been strengthened by the discovery of almost identical knobbed pennanular stone earrings (the so-called "lingling-o"), and of a special kind of earring or pendant with two animal heads (presumably deer), in a number of sites in Vietnam, Palawan and Sarawak (Loofs-Wissowa 1980–1; and Majid 1982 for Niah), (Fig. 9.4).

These connections between southern Vietnam and the Borneo–Philippine region in the Early Metal phase (and possibly the preceding Late Neolithic) may be important when considering the evidence in the Sa Huynh sites for iron metallurgy. The iron repertoire as a whole includes many socketed tools such as spades, picks and axes, and there are also unsocketed sickles, tanged

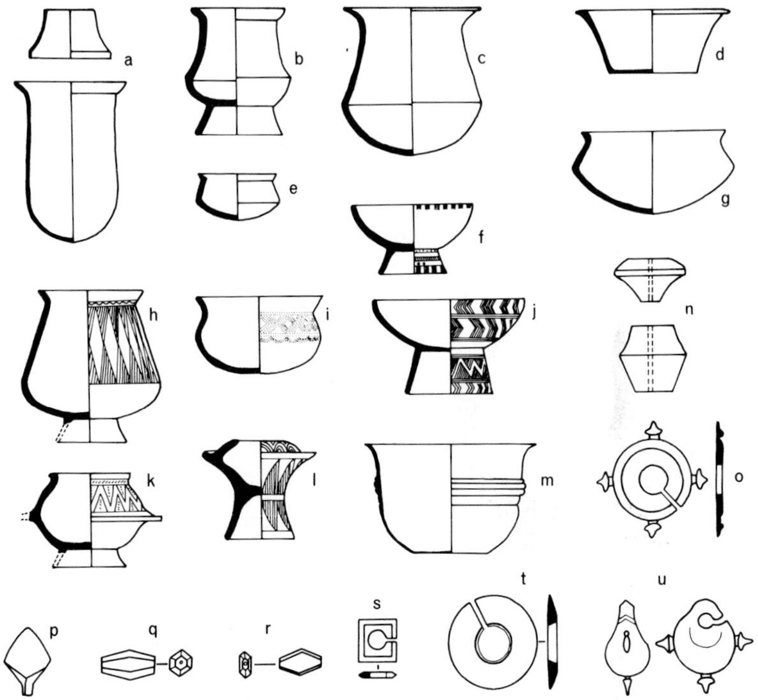

Fig. 9.3. The Sa Huynh assemblage, after Parmentier 1924. (a) Large burial jar 77 cm high with lid; (b–l) pottery vessels between 14 and 21 cm diameter, decorated by incision or punctation; (m) bronze vessel 9 cm diameter; (n) clay spindle whorls 3.5 cm diameter; (o, s–u) stone earrings — (o) and (u) are of lingling-o type — diameters 2–5 cm; (p) iron hoe 17 cm long; (q, r) facetted carnelian beads 19 and 15 mm long. From Bellwood 1978a.

knives, spindle whorls, rings and spiral bracelets. A sword of possible Chinese manufacture was found at Hang Gon (Saurin 1973), and there is a possibility that the technology of iron working was introduced into the area from a Chinese source, although I suspect that a lot of metallurgical analysis will need to be done before this question can be settled. As with Dong Son, neither the bronze nor the iron goods from the Sa Huynh sites resemble Indian models.

In general, the Sa Huynh sites reveal a greater usage of iron than the Dong Son sites, and Sa Huynh bronzes are mainly decorative items rather than tools and weapons (that is bracelets, bells and small vessels). There are also some rare gold beads and silver wire (e.g. Fontaine and Hoang 1975 for Phu Hoa), and most sites have glass, banded agate and a range of carnelian beads (round, cigar-shaped or facetted) which are probably of Indian origin (see

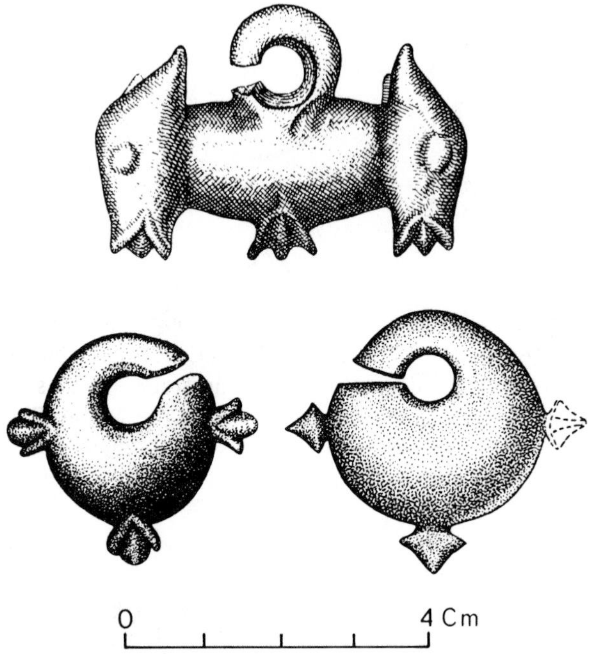

Fig. 9.4. Stone earrings (the bottom two of lingling-o type) from the Tabon Caves, Palawan. Identical ornaments have been found in sites of the Sa Huynh culture in Vietnam (see Fig. 9.30u). From Fox 1970. Courtesy: National Museum of the Philippines.

Fig. 9.3 q, r). Carbon dates from Phu Hoa and Hang Gon suggest an overall date range for the Sa Huynh culture between 600 BC and 0, but Phu Hoa does have some comb-incised pottery similar to that from the Funanese site of Oc Eo (early-mid first millennium AD), and I doubt whether iron or Indian beads were really of common occurrence in southern Vietnam as early as 600 BC — such details cannot be determined from the available reports. Perhaps an overall date range from 600 BC until well into the first millennium AD, thus overlapping with the civilisations of Champa and Funan, will one day be demonstrated for the mature (Iron Age) Sa Huynh culture as a whole, and internal phases still await definition.

III. The Role of India

The bulk of the Palaeometallic sites in the Indo-Malaysian Archipelago overlap in date with the historical evidence for the earliest trading states and the succeeding Indianised kingdoms, and it is necessary here to expand a little on the brief survey of this topic given in Chapter 5, Section II. Of direct Chinese contact with the archipelago prior to AD 1000 there is little to add, except to note that northern Vietnam was made into a province of the Chinese Han Empire in 111 BC, that a quantity of Han dynasty pottery has been found in uncertain contexts in southern Sumatra (Hoop 1940; Heine Geldern 1945; Orsoy de Flines 1969), and that Chinese Buddhist pilgrims were travelling to India by sea via Indonesia from the fifth century onwards. But Chinese trade goods in any quantity are generally absent in the archipelago prior to the Song dynasty.

Indian enterprise, however, presents a very different picture. Sanskrit and Tamil literary references to South-East Asia may go back as far as the third century BC (Wheatley 1961: Chapter XI), and between the first and fifth centuries AD a number of small indigenous trading states developed in southern Indochina and in the northern part of the Malay Peninsula (Fig. 9.5). At this time there appears to have been a land portage for trade goods from the Andaman Sea to the Gulf of Siam across the narrow Kra Isthmus (at the head of the Thai-Malayan Peninsula), but by the fifth century a lot of the traffic was using the more southerly sailing route through the Strait of Malacca (Wheatley 1961; Quaritch Wales 1976; Hall 1982). This change may have caused the decline of the expansive trading state of Funan around the Gulf of Siam and the consequent rise of Champa in southern Vietnam. By the fifth century it is also apparent that extensive areas of the western Indo-Malaysian Archipelago were becoming increasingly important links in the trade routes, and Austronesian-speaking crews may have been in control of much of the shipping (Wolters 1979; Hall 1980) — a circumstance which no doubt played a large role in the settlement of Madagascar at about this time.

Archaeological evidence for Indian–South-East Asian trade contact in the period from about 200 BC to AD 500 is slight but significant, especially for the mainland. I will simply note here, as one of the most noteworthy examples, the presence of Roman and Indian imported items dated from the second century AD onwards at Oc Eo in southern Vietnam; the Indian items include a Gandharan Buddha head, seals, rings, bronzes, and carnelian and agate beads, and there are also some Chinese Later Han dynasty bronze mirror fragments (Malleret 1959–63; Christie 1979a). Indian or local raw materials may also have been worked here into glass and stone beads in Indian styles, as perhaps in the Malayan site of Kuala Selinsing in Perak at a slightly later date (Evans 1932; Lamb 1965). In addition, Oc Eo has a number of ornaments of tin which could have been imported from Laos or Malaya. Indeed, some of the earliest small states on the Malay Peninsula, and particularly in its narrower Thai portion, may have developed partly on the proceeds of an export of tin, as well as of the forest products and spices which bulk larger in the historical records (e.g. Wolters 1967; Dunn 1975).

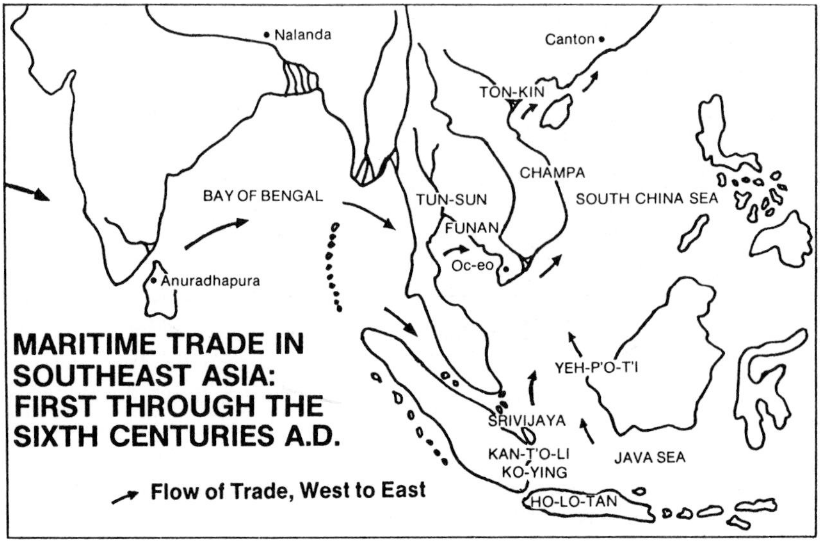

Fig. 9.5. Maritime trade in South-East Asia, 1st through the 6th centuries AD. From Hall 1980. Courtesy: K. R. Hall.

Having made these relevant background observations on the prehistoric metallurgy of the South-East Asian mainland and on the earliest historic trade links into South-East Asia, I will now turn to the archaeological record for Malaysia and Indonesia.

IV. Bronze Artefacts of Dong Son and Local Styles from the Sunda Islands and Malaya

A large number of artefacts of precise Dong Son affinity, especially Heger type I drums, have survived in villages or turned up as chance finds without coherent archaeological contexts in the Malay Peninsula and the Sunda chain of Indonesia. There are now six fragmentary Heger I drums known from Malaya; the Klang (Fig. 9.6) and Tembeling (Batu Pasir Garam) fragments were both dated to the second century BC on stylistic grounds by Loewenstein (1956), and two other damaged drums excavated from beneath a possible burial mound at Kampong Sungei Lang in Selangor have been carbon dated rather uncertainly from an associated wooden plank to between about 500 BC and AD 200 (Peacock 1964b, 1979). There are also two further drum fragments from Kuala Trengganu on the east coast.

No less than 26 drums or parts thereof are known from the Sunda chain of Indonesia, mostly from Java and Sumatra, but with examples occurring

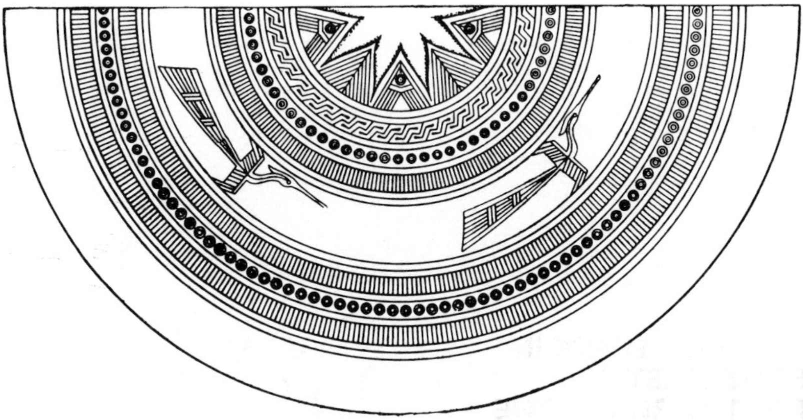

Fig. 9.6. The Heger type I drum from Klang: a semi-diagrammatic rendering of the decoration on one half of the tympanum. From Loewenstein 1956. Courtesy: Malaysian Branch of the Royal Asiatic Society.

to as far east as the Kai Islands south of western New Guinea (see Smith and Watson 1979:514–5 for a list). Some of the more significant Indonesian examples include the "Makalamau" drum from Sangeang Island near Sumbawa (Fig. 9.7) with its figures in possible Han dynasty and Kushan (northern Indian) costumes (Heine Geldern 1947), the drum from Kai with its deer and tiger-hunting frieze, and that from Salayar (Fig. 9.8) with its elephants and peacocks (Schmeltz 1904). All these are scenes which would presumably have been unfamiliar to the inhabitants of the eastern Indonesian islands where the drums eventually came to rest, so on these grounds alone it is clearly most unlikely that they were cast locally. Indeed, in terms of style and a frequent high lead content it looks as if most of these Malayan and Indonesian drums were manufactured in Vietnam prior to the demise of the Dong Son culture in the first century AD, although Heine Geldern (1947) did suggest that the Sangeang drum might have been cast in Funan as late as AD 250.

In terms of distribution within the Indo-Malaysian Archipelago it may be important to stress that Heger I drums have only been found in Malaya and in the islands of the Sunda chain, and have never been reported from Borneo, Sulawesi, the Moluccas or the Philippines (Fig. 9.9). This distribution does of course overlap in the west with that of the earliest recorded Indian contact, and it may be that many of these exotic bronzes were transported secondarily, long after their dates of manufacture, within the trade networks of the earliest historical states in the Thai-Malayan Peninsula and western Indonesia.

A number of other copper or bronze artefacts found in Indonesia might also represent imports from Vietnam. There can be no certainty of this, but

Fig. 9.7. Part of the decorated tympanum of the "Makalamau" drum from Sangeang. Courtesy: National Museum, Jakarta. This scene shows a pile-dwelling with a saddle-shaped roof, partitioned attic (with a kettle-drum at right), main floor, and basement. According to Heine Geldern (1947) the figures on the main floor may be in Chinese Han dynasty costumes. Scenes include paying homage, and kneeling around a drum. The basement has a pig, two chickens and a dog. For a fuller description of this superb drum see Heine Geldern 1947; Heekeren 1958:24–6.

outstanding finds of Dong Son affinity which attract attention in this regard include the male statuette similar to a Dong Son dagger handle (Fig. 9.10) from Satus near Bogor, the miniature Heger I drum from Cibadak in western Java, and perhaps the statuettes and knobbed bracelets from Bangkinang in southern Sumatra (Heekeren 1958: Plates 5 and 9). While details of date and composition for these artefacts are insufficient to prove a Vietnamese origin, it nevertheless seems possible that they were traded, like the Heger I drums, as status items into the chiefly lineages of the Sunda Islands.

The eventual result of this external introduction of bronze goods into the Indo-Malaysian Archipelago was the establishment of local metalworking centres. As I will show in due course, there have been several finds of stone or terracotta valves from the moulds used for casting copper and bronze axes from sites in Java, Sabah and the Talaud Islands, all of which show quite conclusively that some casting of either local or imported raw materials was being carried out during the early-mid first millennium AD. In addition, there are large numbers of the axes themselves, especially from Java and Bali

Fig. 9.8. The Salayer drum (top and side views), with its distinctive friezes of elephants and peacocks; 92 cm high, tympanum diameter 103 cm. From Schmeltz 1904.

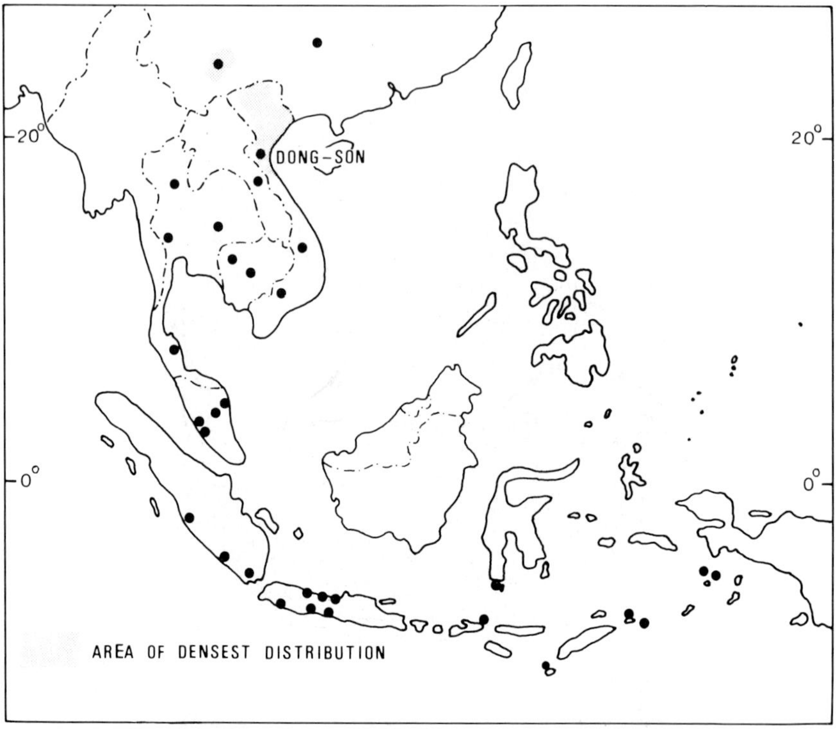

Fig. 9.9. The schematic distribution of Heger type I drums. From Bellwood 1978a. According to R. B. Smith (in Smith and Watson 1979: Appendix II), regional totals as known in 1973 were as follows: North Vietnam 67; Yunnan and Guizhou 21; South Vietnam 2; Thailand and Cambodia 16; Malaya 6; Sunda islands of Indonesia 26.

(Soejono 1972), and these can hardly all be regarded as imports. However, it should be noted that the "swallowtail" form which occurs commonly in these two islands (Fig. 9.11), and also in a hoard from Peura in central Sulawesi (Sukendar 1980:11–12), is present in the Dong Son site of Lang Vac in Vietnam (Ha Van Tan 1980:133). Naturally, there is always a possibility that these axes were traded from Indonesia back into Vietnam, but this suggestion can hardly be sustained without some analytical backing.

Apart from the axes, the evidence for the beginning of one or more local and possibly Indonesian casting traditions comes in the form of a number of quite splendid copper or bronze objects, some perhaps of early first millennium AD date, which are not in a classic Dong Son style. In one group is the almost 2 m high hourglass-shaped drum from Pejeng in Bali (not a Heger type), and a number of similar but smaller drums from this island and Java

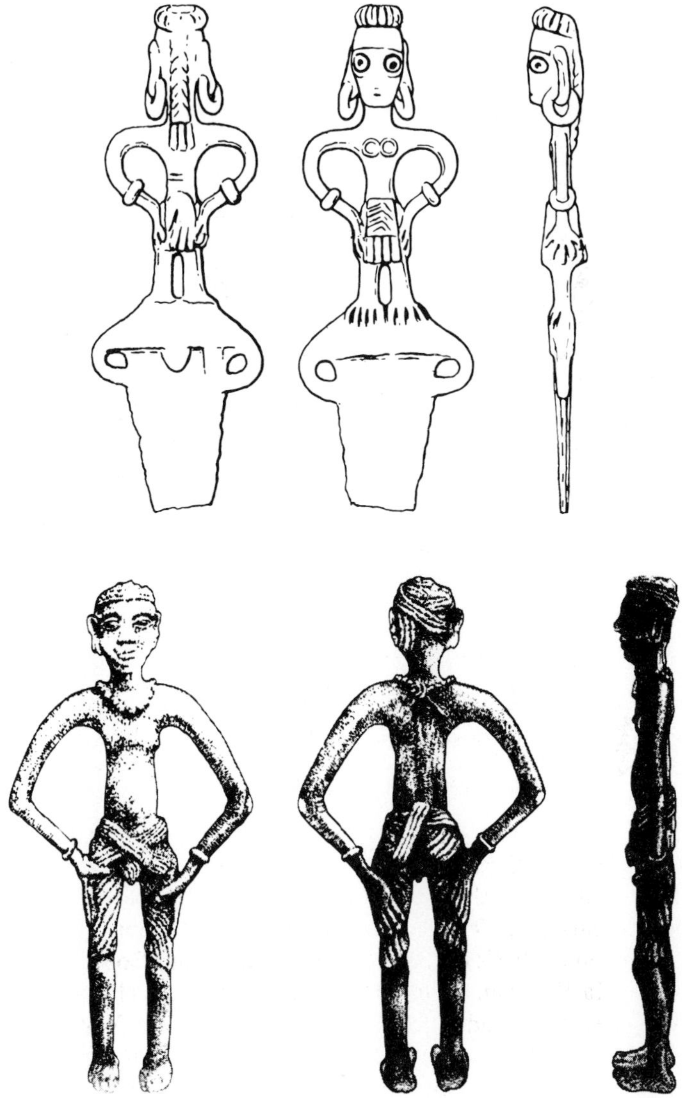

Fig. 9.10. Top: bronze dagger handle from Dong Son, 11 cm high. From Goloubew 1929. Courtesy: École Francaişe d'Extrême-Orient. Bottom: copper or bronze statuette from Satus near Bogor, 25 cm high. From Heekeren 1958. Courtesy: Martinus Nijhoff.

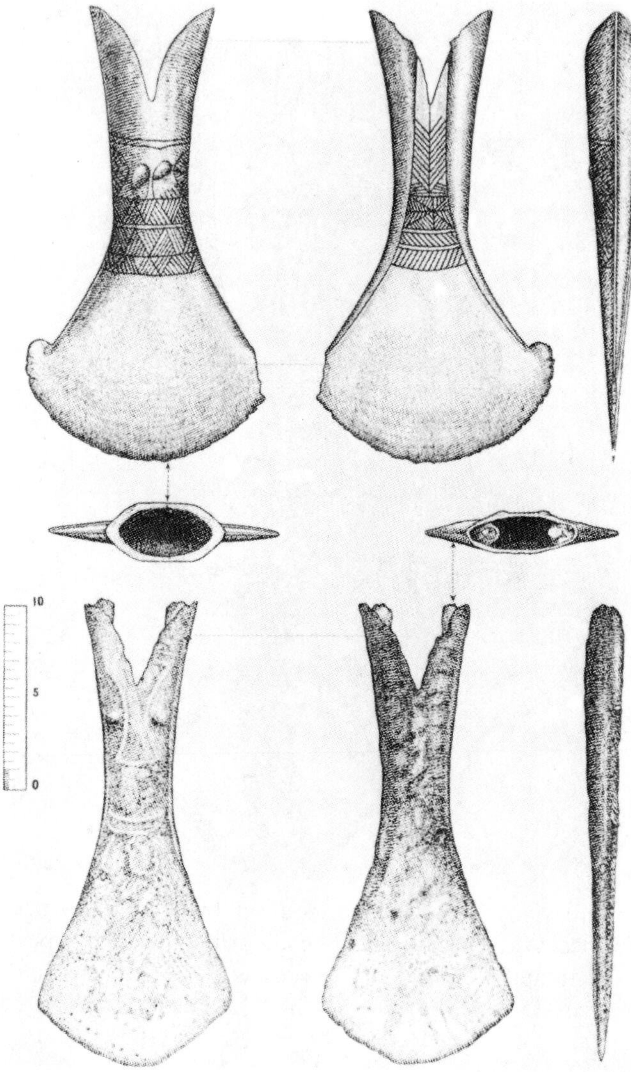

9.11. "Swallowtail" bronze axes from Java (scale in cm). From Heekeren 1958. Courtesy: ıus Nijhoff.

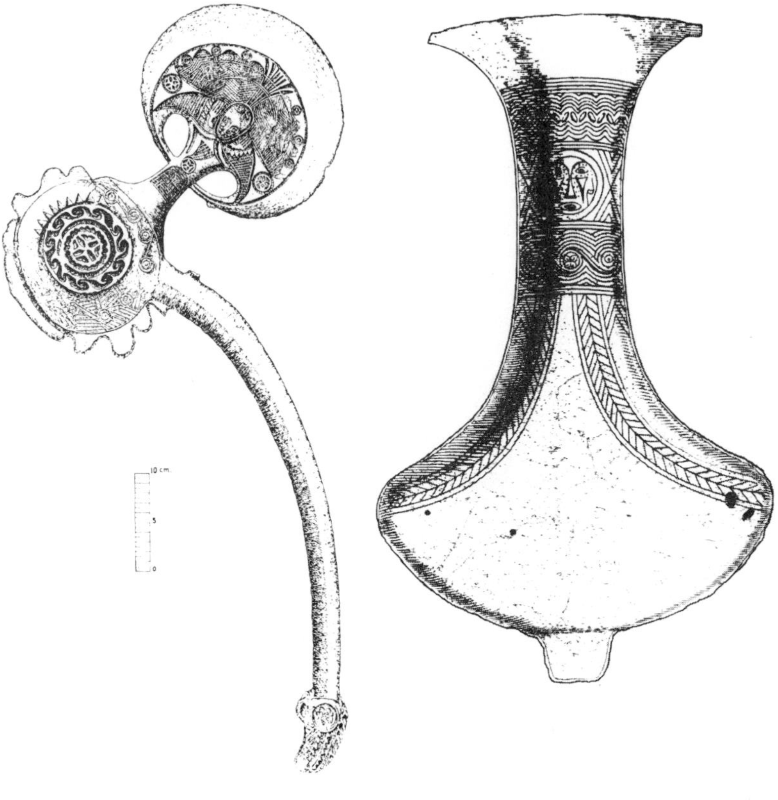

Fig. 9.12. Left: bronze ceremonial axe from Roti. Right: bronze flask, possibly from southern Sulawesi (purchased in Ujungpandang), 69 cm high; (scale is for axe only). From Heekeren 1958. Courtesy: Martinus Nijhoff.

which have been placed in a stylistic sequence by Bernet Kempers (1978). Three mould pieces for the casting of a small drum of Pejeng type have also been found at Manuaba in Bali, but these are unfortunately undated. Other items related in style, and characterised like the Pejeng drum by the use of a face-mask in a dominant position in the decoration (Bernet Kempers 1959), include an unusual flask from Ujungpandang (Makassar), a ceremonial axe from Savu in eastern Indonesia (Bintarti 1981a), and two ceremonial axes from Roti, Fig. 9.12 (although one of the latter does show a typical Dong Son tangent and circle motif).

A second stylistic group, in this case of flasks and large clapperless bells, is distinguished by an unusual and elaborate type of incised spiral decoration

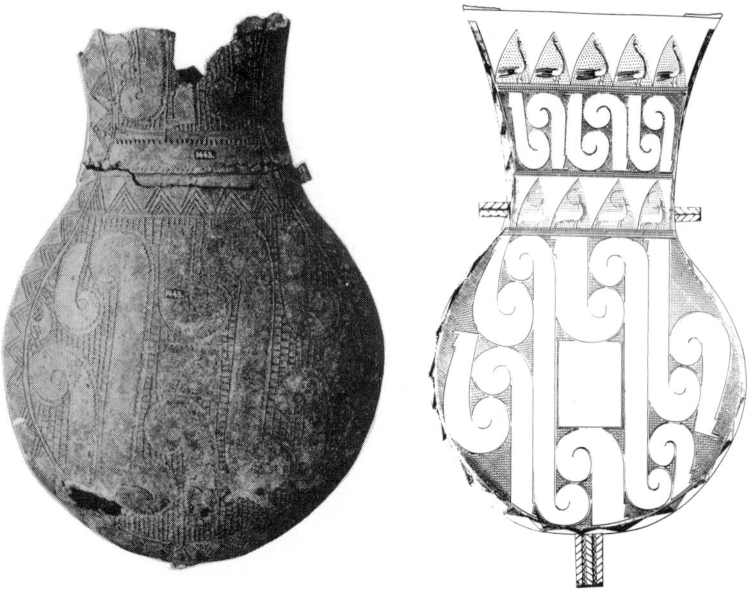

Fig. 9.13. Bronze flasks from Indonesia. Left: from Kerinci, Sumatra, 51 cm high. Right: from Madura, 84 cm high (this specimen has a tin content of 15.2%). From Heekeren 1958. Courtesy: Martinus Nijhoff.

which is again outside the Dong Son repertoire. The flasks come from Kerinci in Sumatra, from Madura, and from Kandal in Cambodia (Fig. 9.13), and the bells include one from Battambang in Cambodia, three (one now lost) from Klang in Selangor, and a newly-discovered example from Kampong Pencu near the Muar River in Johor (Fig. 9.14). The Muar bell has been dated by thermoluminescence on a fragment of the clay casting core preserved in its narrow neck to less than 1800 years old (Adi 1983:61). Although this date is not very precise, it at least does not contradict a view that these bells and flasks belonged to a first millennium AD casting tradition which was not Vietnamese, but which may have been of ultimate Vietnamese technological derivation. Indeed, a bronze bell which might conceivably represent a prototype for these specimens was excavated by Janse at Dong Son (Loewenstein 1956: Fig. 22).

It is unfortunately not possible to pinpoint any actual manufacturing centres outside northern Vietnam in this early period. Malaya does have large resources of alluvial tin, but has no definite sources of copper or any archaeological traces of ancient bronze casting. By AD 500 it is quite possible that drums were being cast in Bali and Java, and the Roti axes could be from

Fig. 9.14. Left and centre: bronze bells from Klang (Kelang), Selangor (centre specimen is 56.5 cm high). From Loewenstein 1956. Right: bronze bell from Kampong Pencu, Johor (58 cm high). From Adi 1983. Courtesy: Malaysian Branch of the Royal Asiatic Society; National Museum, Kuala Lumpur.

this region. But for the bells and flasks there is a huge region of potential manufacture from Cambodia to Madura, and a bell very similar to the ones described has also been found at Dabona in Yunnan.

So far, I have been describing an array of Indo-Malaysian bronze objects which are mostly divorced from satisfactory archaeological contexts, apart from the drums from Kampong Sungei Lang. It is now time to fill out the record of the Early Metal phase in terms of broader cultural variation in the archipelago.

V. The Slab Graves and Iron Industry of Malaya

Apart from the drums and bells already considered, the Early Metal phase in Malaya is also associated with a number of slab-lined graves (Fig. 9.15), presumably for extended inhumations (although bones always seem to have dissolved), found in southern Perak and northern Selangor (Evans 1928b, 1931b; Collings 1937b; Linehan 1951). The general range of associated artefacts from the graves includes glass and carnelian beads, a stone bark-cloth beater, a bronze bowl, and a most unusual industry of iron tools. The pottery is wheel-made, either plain or slipped with a resinous coat, and

Fig. 9.15. A slab grave (2.3 m long) excavated at Sungkai, southern Perak. From Collings 1937b. Courtesy: National Museum of Singapore.

usually with impressed lip patterns, Similar pottery was also found with part of a socketed iron spearhead under the mound which contained the two Sungei Lang bronze drums (Peacock 1979).

The iron industry has been found in several other sites apart from the slab graves, and it appears to be very much a unity in terms of style and the associations of different tool forms in hoards, which occur commonly in Malaya. The forms have been clearly described by Sieveking (1956a), and include axes (some with very long shafts, known colloquially as *tulang mawas*), knives and sickles, all with shaft holes. In addition, there are some socketed spearheads and tanged knives (Fig. 9.16). The tools appear to be of low carbon steel according to Sieveking, and this suggests that the iron was roasted purposefully in a bed of charcoal after the initial smelting process. Tools of this type were also found with the Klang bells as well as with the dated Sungei Lang drums, and the latter association does place in doubt Loewenstein's belief (1956) that the iron industry as a whole could not date before the end of the first millennium AD[2].

Sieveking saw the Malayan iron industry as having an origin in the socketing tradition for bronze tools represented in the Dong Son culture of Vietnam; a tradition which he believed was transmitted in iron towards Malaya via southern Vietnam after the first century AD. At the time he was

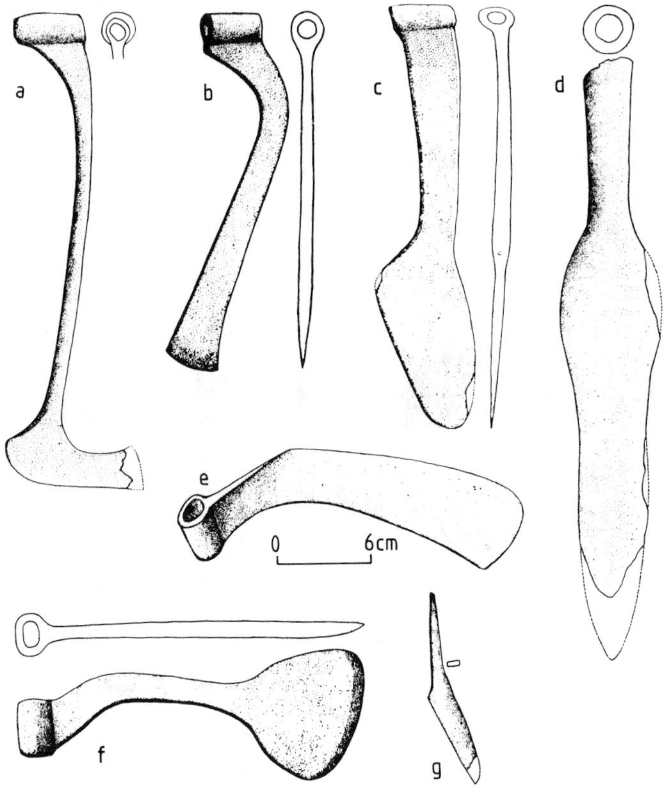

Fig. 9.16. The iron industry of the Malayan Early Metal phase. (a) *Tulang mawas* from Tersang, Raub, Pahang; (b, f) shaft hole axes from Bukit Jong, Pahang; (c) shaft hole knife (?) from Tanjong Rambutan, Perak; (d) socketed spearhead from Bukit Jati, Klang, Selangor; (e) shaft hole sickle from Bukit Jong, Pahang; (g) tanged knife from Batu Kurau, Perak. From Sieveking 1956a. Courtesy: Malaysian Branch of the Royal Asiatic Society.

---

[2]Loewenstein based his estimate on the observation that the glass beads from the slab graves were similar to those from Kuala Selinsing in Perak. This site is undoubtedly one of the most enigmatic in the whole of Malaysia; the original assemblage excavated by Evans (1932) included a wheel-made comb-incised ware like that from Oc Eo (early-mid first millennium AD?), a carnelian seal with an inscription in Pallava script, evidence for local blue glass and agate bead manufacture, glass bracelets, and lead slag. The site was evidently an estuarine pile village, and it has also produced human burials in canoe coffins (Sieveking 1956b). Evans originally favoured a date between AD 600 and 1100 for Kuala Selinsing, but Beck (Appendix in Collings 1937b) dated the beads to between AD 1 and 400. Stargardt (1980) also mentions an unpublished carbon date in the second century AD from the site. The point here is that the Malayan iron industry does evidently overlap in time with Kuala Selinsing, which may in turn have been a satellite settlement of an early Indianised state on the peninsula. But the great range of possible dates for the site clearly prohibits any real assessment of its significance.

writing there was little archaeological evidence to support such a connection, but recent excavations have produced the very respectable socketed iron industry of the Sa Huynh culture of southern Vietnam (Section II), and from just above the top of the Malay Peninsula in south-western Thailand there are prolific iron industries from Ongbah Cave and Ban Don Ta Phet. Ongbah Cave (Sørensen 1973) has yielded a tanged iron industry in association with boat-shaped coffins and Heger I drums, and one carbon date of about 200 BC. The site of Ban Don Ta Phet (Glover 1983; Glover *et al.* 1984) is an open burial ground, presumably for extended burials, although as with the Malayan cists no bone has survived. The iron industry here, which has a larger socketed component than that from Ongbah and also a shaft-hole sickle or bill-hook a little like the Malayan ones, is associated with a rich array of Indian carnelian and etched agate beads, and appears to date again from around 2000 years ago.

One feature of these early Mainland South-East Asian iron industries is that they are all characterised by different and localised tool forms, especially in terms of hafting. This localisation is more marked than in the case of the bronze industries, where there is the integrating phenomenon of the long-distance trade of status items such as drums and other decorated ceremonial objects. Iron objects give an impression of being localised in style to regional industries, and hence manufactured on the spot for use as everyday tools and weapons with only limited trade or status value. This naturally suggests that iron working was a process which could be carried out easily by local small communities, and that knowledge of its manufacture spread very rapidly from about 2000 years ago as the superior economic potential and easier availability of this metal when compared to bronze was realised.

A final point to note about the Malayan slab graves is that they provide the oldest archaeological evidence which might tentatively be associated with the Austronesian coastal settlement of Malaya. Linguistically (see Chapter 4, Section VA), an origin for the Malays, and also for the other smaller *orang Melayu asli* groups such as the Temuan and Jakun (Carey 1976), may perhaps be located in Sumatra (where slab graves also occur) or western Borneo during the first millennium BC. But there is very little archaeological evidence to throw light on this, and the whole period between the *aslian* Neolithic as represented at Gua Cha and the Indianised monuments of Kedah, which may all postdate AD 1000, is in urgent need of further research.

VI. The Early Metal Phase in Sumatra, Java and Bali

In this section I will describe the slab graves and stone monuments of southern Sumatra and Java, the sarcophagi of eastern Java and Bali, and a number of other important Early Metal phase excavated assemblages. I do not intend to go deeply into the question of megaliths, and will not be concerned with such matters as the oft-proposed unity of megalithic cultures (e.g. Christie 1979b), or with Heine Geldern's theories that different types of megaliths can be ordered into "older" and "younger" strata (Heine Geldern 1937, 1945). I discussed some of these questions briefly in a previous book (Bellwood 1978a:225–8), and one of the problems is that most of the celebrated "megalithic" cultures of Indonesia, for instance on Nias (Schnitger 1964; Mulia 1981), amongst the Bataks of northern Sumatra (Schnitger 1964), in parts of Borneo (Sierevelt 1929; Harrisson 1973; Schneeberger 1979), in central and southern Sulawesi (Crystal 1974), and in some of the Lesser Sunda Islands (Sukendar 1985) are all of recent or ethnographic date and have no archaeologically-documented antecedents. It is perhaps time for prehistorians to join the ethnologists and art historians in examining the antecedents of these recent cultures, but so far there has been little progress in this respect.

A. Sumatra

One of the main concentrations of prehistoric stone monuments in Indonesia lies on the Pasemah Plateau around Pageralam in southern Sumatra (Hoop 1932; Heekeren 1958:63–79). Recent surveys have also shown that a fairly simple megalithic tradition ("dolmens", mortars, occasional standing stones) occurs widely in the adjacent Lampung district at the southern tip of the island (Sukendar 1979). The Pasemah monuments, however, are really very striking and have attracted attention since 1850. The structures include groups and avenues of upright stones, stone blocks with carefully hollowed cup-like mortars, troughs with human heads carved on their ends (Fig. 9.17), simple terraced platforms (often referred to as "graves"), "dolmens" of uncertain function with large capstones, slab graves, and some quite remarkable stone carvings of humans and animals.

The slab graves excavated by Hoop (1932) at Tegurwangi (Fig. 9.18) contained large numbers of glass beads and a few metal objects — copper or bronze spirals, a gold pin, and a corroded iron lance — which cannot in themselves be closely dated. As in the Malayan slab graves the acid soils had dissolved all traces of bone, but one of the Tegurwangi graves and two megalithic chamber graves at nearby Tanjungara (Bie 1932) (Fig. 9.19) still preserved traces of polychrome wall-paintings showing human figures and water buffaloes.

The Pasemah human and animal statues are carved in relief or in the round on large stone blocks in a dynamic style. Men are shown riding on elephants or buffaloes (Fig. 9.20), wearing bracelets, anklets, helmets with peaks at the back, loincloths, tunics and earplugs. Necklaces of oblong plaques and what appear to be facetted beads are also shown. Animal and human heads are

Fig. 9.17. Left: stone trough with heads carved on ends, Pageralam, Pasemah. Right: mortar stone, Gunungmegang, Pasemah.

Fig. 9.18. Excavated slab grave at Tegurwangi, Pasemah. From Hoop 1932. Courtesy: W. J. Thieme.

Fig. 9.19. Stone chamber graves with massive capstones at Tanjong Ara, Pasemah.

often carved in considerable detail, while bodies are often disproportionately small or simply left out, depending perhaps on the original shape of the stone. Some reliefs also show combat themes of men fighting tigers or snakes, although the elephants and water buffaloes are more often in situations demonstrating human control, and possibly domestication or taming.

The most important chronological indicators on these carvings are the Heger I drums shown on the Batugajah and Airpurah reliefs (Fig. 9.21). These could indicate a date in the early or mid-first millennium AD, although Bronson (1979a) has suggested that many of the Pasemah monuments may overlap in time with the period of the Srivijaya Kingdom on the plains to the east around Palembang (that is after AD 670).

B. Java and Bali

In Java and Bali many sites have produced Early Metal phase assemblages in association with slab graves, or with the more elaborate carved sarcophagi which occur from eastern Java through Bali to Sumbawa and Sumba (Soejono 1969, 1982b; Glover 1979). Only the slab graves at Kuningan in western Java lack metal associations, and all other sites appear to belong to the first millennium AD or later. In the listing of the Javanese material given by Heekeren (1958:46–54) it is apparent that knowledge of these sites is extremely vague, although Hoop (1935) did present a clear report of some

Fig. 9.20. Man astride a buffalo, with necklace, helmet and anklets, Pematang, Pasemah. From Hoop 1932. Courtesy: W. J. Thieme.

Fig. 9.21. Relief carving of a man flanking an elephant, wearing anklets and carrying a drum of Heger type I. From Batugajah, Pasemah, but now in the museum grounds in Palembang. For a similar carving at Wonotunggal in north-central Java see Satari 1981.

slab graves excavated around Gunung Kidul near Wonosari in central Java. Well-preserved examples of these at Kajar and Bleberan (Fig. 9.22) produced evidence for extended burials with a lot of iron tools (mainly tanged knives, a dagger, axes and chisels), bronze rings, and glass and facetted carnelian beads (Fig. 9.23). The slab graves and carved sarcophagi examined by Heekeren (1931) near Besuki in eastern Java produced no coherent archaeological assemblages, but similar monuments at Pakauman were apparently associated with Chinese imported ceramics of ninth century date or later. Therefore, many of these graves may overlap in date with the Javanese historical civilisations, as Hoop thought possible for the Gunung Kidul sites.

The distinctive sarcophagi of Bali were carved from soft tuff or breccia (Heekeren 1955; 1958:54–8; Soejono 1977; Sukarto 1979). They have separate bodies and high domed lids, and usually have knobbed projections on their ends, sometimes carved into human or turtle-like heads (Fig. 9.24). A range of sizes was produced to accommodate both flexed and extended burials, and the goods include glass and carnelian beads, some rather indeterminate iron objects, unusual ornaments and finger-sheaths made of spiralled bronze wire (e.g. Soejono 1977: Foto 67–70), and socketed bronze axes of a unique crescent-bladed type. The whole assemblage presents a

Fig. 9.22. Excavated slab grave with extended burial from Bleberan, central Java. From Hoop 1935.

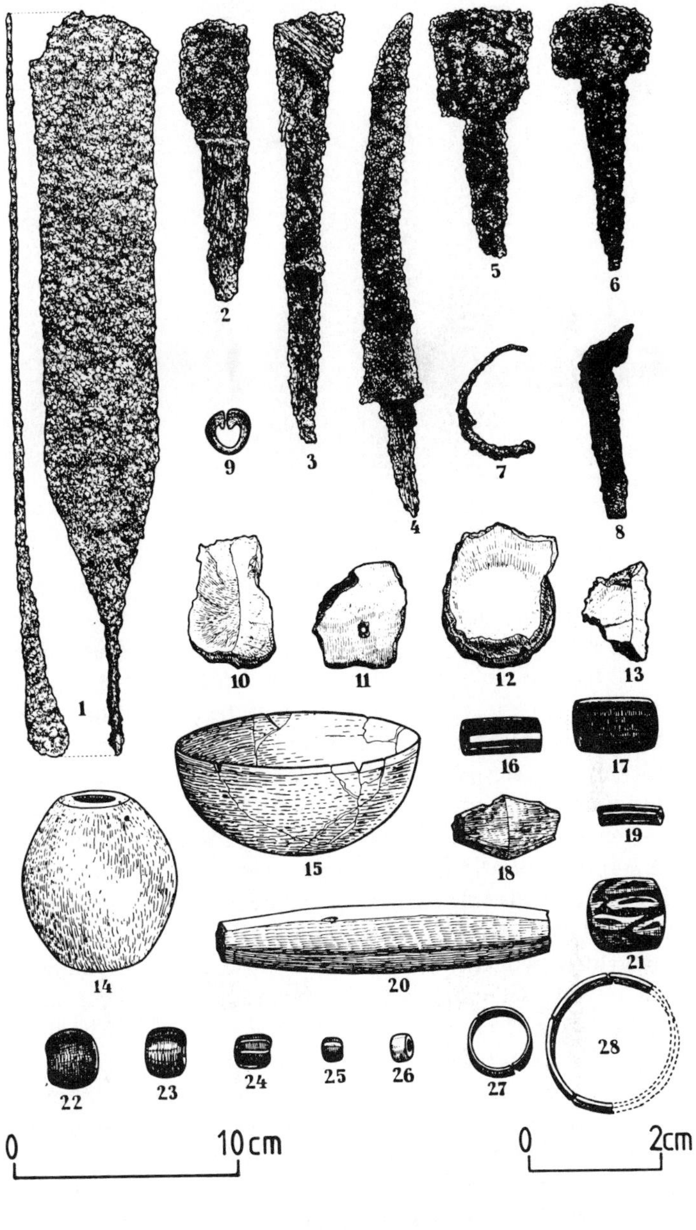

Fig. 9.23. Artefacts from slab graves at Gunung Kidul, central Java. The tanged iron tools include a *keris* (dagger: no. 4), and a range of stone and glass bead shapes are shown; (left-hand scale for 1–13, 15; right-hand scale for 14, 16–28). From Hoop 1935.

Fig. 9.24. Balinese stone sarcophagi. Pejeng Museum.

highly localised appearance, with no obvious parallels with other regions which can be used for dating purposes.

There are also a number of localities in western Java with complexes of stone paved terraces and platforms which appear to belong to a pre-Hindu–Buddhist architectural tradition. Bintarti (1981b) has recently described an excellent example at Gunung Padang, south of Cianjur, and others occur in the north-western corner of the island at Lebak Sibedug (Hoop 1932: plate 204) and Arca Domas (Tricht 1929). These structures probably served as open air temples or gathering places, rather like the *marae* of Polynesia, and stone human statues of fairly simple shape, which many authors have called "Polynesian", are also known from localities widely distributed over Java (Mulia 1980). Unfortunately, it is impossible to date these monuments and statues, although one statue of this type near Bandung carries an inscription, possibly secondary, of AD 1341, (Suleiman 1976:8). The apparent Polynesian similarities are either coincidental or may reflect some form of shared early Austronesian architectural and artistic inheritance.

Apart from the research on the stone graves and other monuments, which have always attracted much archaeological attention in western Indonesia, there have been a number of excavations in other types of site belonging to the Early Metal phase in Java and Bali. As I will show later, the practice of jar burial was predominant mainly in the more easterly parts of Indonesia, but jar burials have been uncovered with an inhumation burial at Anyar in western Java (Heekeren 1956a), and apparently alone at Tebingtinggi in southern Sumatra (Heekeren 1958:83). Recent Indonesian excavations at a site called Plawangan in north-central Java (Sukendar and Awe 1981) have also produced an interesting mixture of extended burials and burials in jars with inverted-vessel lids. The assemblage from this site includes iron knives, a bronze fishhook and ring, glass beads, and incised and stamped pottery. Other Javanese sites which have produced important Early Metal phase assemblages include Leuwiliang near Bogor, and Pejaten to the south of Jakarta (Sutayasa 1979; Panggabean 1981), where baked clay casting moulds for bronze axes and knives are apparently radiocarbon dated to before AD 200. However, none of these sites can as yet be placed within a coherent reconstruction of Javanese prehistory, and the most urgent requirements are for a fuller publication record and many more well-documented radiocarbon dates.

The so-called "Buni cultural complex" of looted graves on the western coast of northern Java (Sutayasa 1972, 1973, 1979) also has obvious future potential for archaeological investigation. Brief records of the grave-goods, apparently found with extended burials, include gold and carnelian beads, stone adzes, undefined metal artefacts, and a range of carved-paddle-impressed and incised pottery with a variety of forms, including ring-footed vessels, high-necked flasks and knobbed lids. The Buni complex is also of great significance because it has produced three platters of the very distinctive south Indian Rouletted Ware (Walker and Santoso 1977), Fig. 9.25, and gold eye covers possibly of south Indian inspiration or origin (O'Connor and Harrisson 1971). Since this rather exciting and possibly imported material has been found in the same part of western Java as the oldest Sanskrit inscriptions (for example the Purnavarman inscription at Tugu, possibly of fifth century date; Noorduyn and Verstappen 1972), it is apparent that the Buni sites, despite their tragic looting, may contain information directly relevant to the initial period of contact between India and Java, presumably in the first few centuries AD.

I will also mention here the related assemblage from Gilimanuk on western Bali (Soejono 1979), where recent excavations have uncovered extended burials and two jar burials, with associated pottery apparently like that from Buni. Other grave-goods include socketed bronze axes of a localised heart-shaped form, a tanged iron spearhead, an iron dagger with a bronze handle (like Mainland South-East Asian bimetallic forms from Ban Chiang and Shizhaishan), beads of gold, glass and carnelian, and a range of other items of which gold eye covers like those of the Buni complex are the most striking. No stone tools were found with the burials, and as a whole the assemblage may belong to the early or mid-first millennium AD.

The Buni Complex in particular brings back the question of the geographical origins of initial Indian contact with western Indonesia. The Rouletted

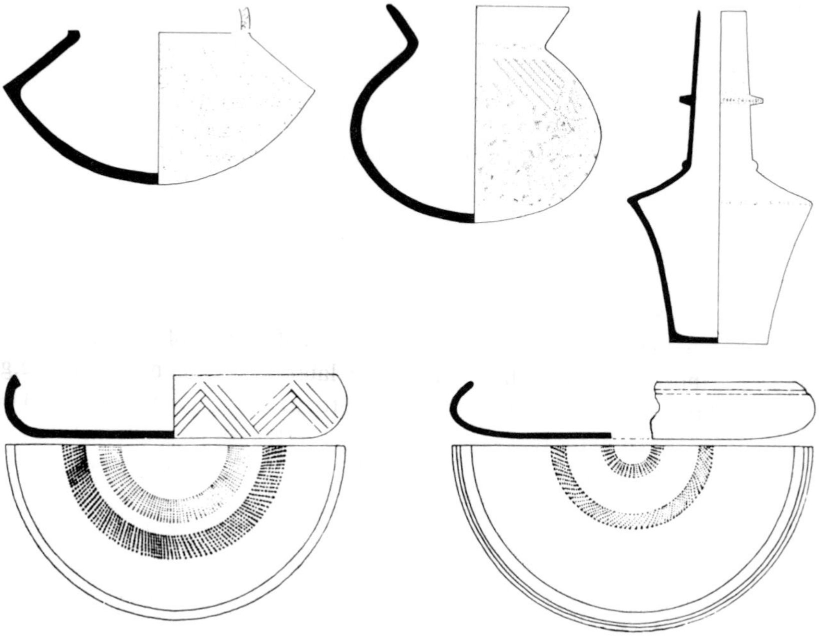

Fig. 9.25. Pottery from the Buni complex, north-western Java. Top: two paddle-impressed vessels and a high-necked flask (not to scale, but the flask is 30 cm high). From Summerhayes and Walker 1982. Bottom: Rouletted Ware from Kobak Kendal (left) and Cibutak (right), both c. 28 cm diameter. From Walker and Santoso 1977. Courtesy: M. Walker.

Ware was originally dated to the first and second centuries AD by Wheeler *et al.* (1946), owing to its association with Roman imports at Arikamedu in Tamil Nadu. Since then it has been recovered from excavations along the whole eastern coast of the subcontinent, from Anuradhapura in Sri Lanka (Deraniyagala 1972) to sites as far north as Sisupalgarh in Orissa (Lal 1949) and Chandraketugarh in West Bengal. It is in these northerly sites that very distinctive north Indian etched agate beads occur which, as I will show, have also been found in sites of the Early Metal phase in Talaud and the Philippines. On the other hand, the sites with Rouletted Ware in south India and Sri Lanka also have utilitarian pottery decorated with carved-paddle-impressed and stamped patterns which find suggestive parallels in the pottery of the Buni complex and Gilimanuk. It would be premature to suggest a definite link from this type of pottery on present evidence, and Solheim (1969, 1981b) has always favoured a southern Chinese origin for the South-East Asian paddle-impressed wares as a whole (which belong in his "Bau-Malay" pottery complex), but I believe that the possibility of an Indian link does deserve careful consideration.

The earliest historically-recorded Indian influences on western Indonesia apparently came from south India (see Chapter 5, Section II), but the archaeological materials which I have just reviewed are of course too diffuse geographically to allow more precision. It is quite possible that trade connections between India and western Indonesia were initiated from both directions and to points all along the eastern Indian coastline — only a great deal of future research, especially in Java, is going to improve this rather unsatisfactory conclusion.

The related question also arises of whether the slab graves of western Indonesia could have an origin in the Iron Age slab graves of southern India, which are now very well dated from the later first millennium BC (e.g. Krishnaswami 1945; Sarkar 1982) through into the first few centuries AD. The problem here, of course, is that the iron goods and Black and Red wheel-made pottery associated with these south Indian burials have no parallels in Indonesia (some of the Indian pottery does resemble the forms of the Malayan Neolithic wares, but this may be purely coincidental), and there are slab graves in Neolithic contexts dated back into the second millennium BC in central and eastern Taiwan (Stamps 1977). My own inclination would be to regard the slab graves as a regional development amongst the linked societies of Malaya and western Indonesia, especially where suitable stone was easily available.

Some fundamental questions still remain totally unanswered as far as the Early Metal phase in western Indonesia is concerned. For instance, when did the intensive wet-rice economy (my agricultural Stage 4; see Chapter 7, Section VD) first develop in the region, and when did domesticated cattle and water buffalo first appear? By the ninth century AD, societies of sufficient power and organisation had developed in central Java to be able to build the stupendous temples of the Borobudur and Candi Larajonggrang at Prambanan — undoubtedly amongst the greatest Buddhist and Hindu monuments ever constructed. At present, one simply cannot make the leap from the rather insignificant grave assemblages to highly developed states of this kind. Perhaps the archaeological record has vast lacunae, or possibly central Java was subjected to a colossal programme of Indianisation and economic development through a brief period in the mid-first millennium AD for which archaeological evidence, apart from that of the temples themselves, may always be difficult to find (especially in the absence of urbanisation, and in a situation of constant reuse and reorganisation of rice fields). I do not claim to know the answer to these very obvious archaeological problems, but I do regard Java as one of the most important foci for future archaeological research in South-East Asia.

VII. The Early Metal Phase in East Malaysia and Eastern Indonesia

The Early Metal phase in the north-eastern part of the Indo-Malaysian Archipelago is now becoming better known as a result of a number of recent cave and open site excavations, many of which have yielded evidence for a fairly homogeneous tradition of secondary burial in large jars or pottery bone boxes. The pottery assemblages of this phase all demonstrate fairly close relationships, and the period as a whole, with its copper/bronze and iron associations, may be dated from about 200 BC to AD 1000. The tradition of jar burial continued after AD 1000 into ethnographic times in some remoter parts of Borneo, Sulawesi and the Philippines, but in association with imported Chinese and South-East Asian glazed ceramics which really lie outside my upper chronological limit.

Important dated assemblages of the Early Metal phase are known from the central and southern Philippines, Sabah, and the Talaud Islands, but most of eastern Indonesia, especially Sulawesi and the Moluccas, remains rather poorly known. In central Sulawesi there is a presumably related tradition of large stone jars and human carvings, and in the Lesser Sundas and Java the jar burial tradition appears to overlap to some extent with the distribution of the Heger type I drums. However, these drums have never been found in direct association with a jar burial site.

The jar burial tradition is seen at its most elaborate in the islands around the Celebes and Sulu Seas (northern Borneo, Talaud, central and southern Philippines), and here it involved the placing of previously-exposed secondary burials in large jars or bone boxes provided with lids (Fig. 9.26). Small accessory vessels were placed in or around the jars, together with beads, bracelets and metal artefacts, to list the most common grave-goods. The jars were placed either on the floors of fairly remote caves (in which situations they have invariably become smashed and their contents mingled) or in pits dug into open sites (where they have normally survived fairly complete).

The jar burial assemblages which occur around the Celebes and Sulu Seas are generally fairly uniform in burial mode, but in many of the southern Indonesian sites the jar burials occur together with extended burials, as noted in Section VIB for the sites of Plawangan in Java and Gilimanuk in Bali. In general, the tradition of jar burial gave way fairly rapidly to extended inhumation burial in those regions which were influenced by the Indianised and the later Islamic states, and also in those parts of the Philippines which were closest to the Chinese trade networks. The whole tradition thus achieved its apogee in the first millennium AD, and in eastern Sabah and the Philippines the second millennium witnessed a widespread change to a tradition of log coffin burial.

Fig. 9.26. Pottery bone box containing human teeth from Bato Puti Cave, Tabon Cave complex, Palawan. From Fox 1970. Courtesy: National Museum of the Philippines.

A. The Talaud Islands

In order to present the jar burial sites most coherently I will begin with sites in the Talaud Islands and Sabah which I have excavated and can describe accurately, and then move to similar but often more problematic sites in the Philippines and southern Indonesia. The first site to be discussed is the small cave of Leang Buidane on Salebabu Island in the Talaud group of north-eastern Indonesia (Bellwood 1976b, 1976c, 1981). The jar burials here were originally placed on the floor of the cave, but were smashed, presumably deliberately (Bellwood 1981:71), in antiquity. The bone containers comprised a range of large globular jars with round bases, and occasional tripod or ring feet, together with flat-based cylindrical vessels and roughly rectangular pottery boxes (Fig. 9.27). All these large containers appear originally to have been lidded. The human bones (Bulbeck 1978) were mainly of young individuals under 40 years of age, and the ratio of 36 individuals (on teeth) to a minimum of 32 large vessels suggests that only one individual was placed in each container. The bones were mainly skulls, mandibles and limb bones, and pelvic bones and vertebrae appear to have been discarded or lost. The

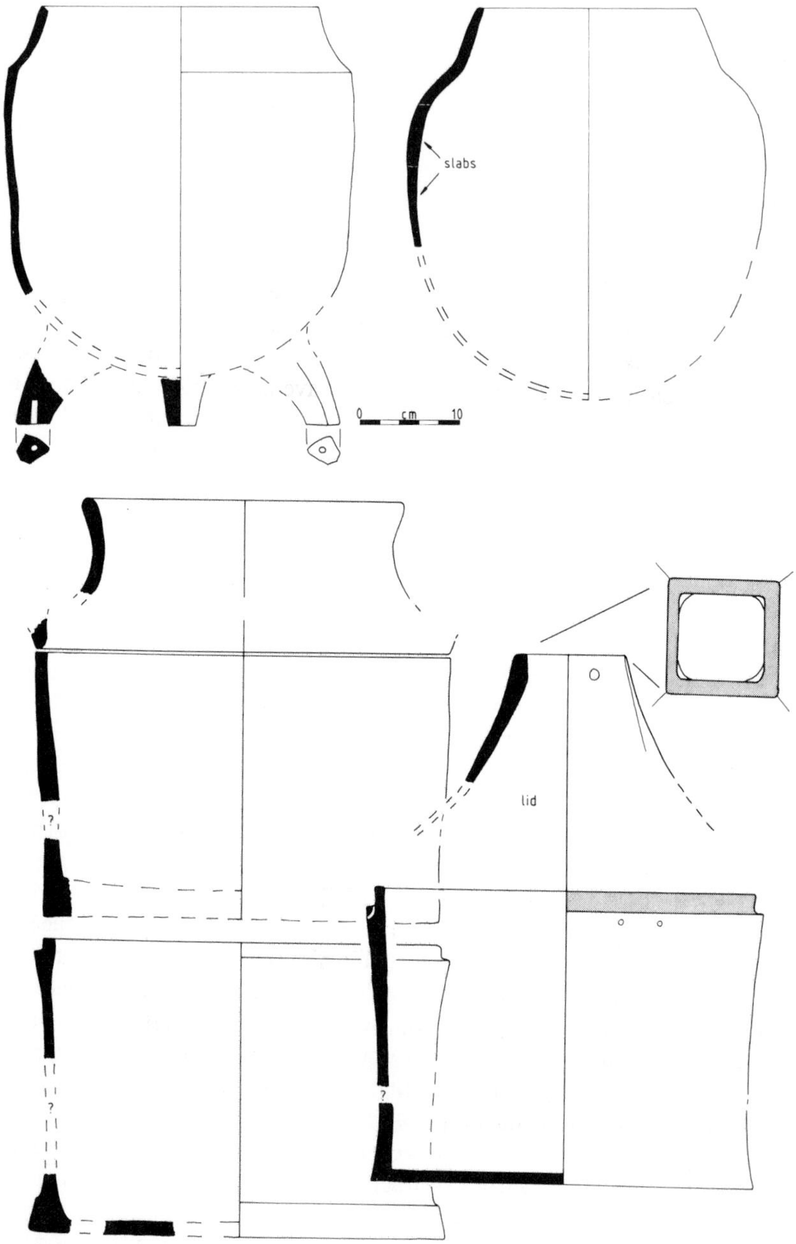

Fig. 9.27. Large burial jars from Leang Buidane, Talaud. The lower three vessels are cylindrical with vertical walls, and two have lids. Stippling = red slip.

teeth revealed some evidence for betel staining, occasional tooth evulsion for females during life, and a Mongoloid morphology presumably directly ancestral to that of the present population. In my original reports I dated this site to between AD 700 and 1200 according to a number of rather oblique chronological indicators, but as a result of my more recent work in Sabah I would now incline to an earlier commencement date.

The accessory vessels and other items found with the remains of the jar burials form a homogeneous stylistic group, and define a Buidane culture which appears to have been current throughout Talaud for much of the first millennium AD. The small pots include round-based carinated vessels with quite elaborate horizontal zones of incised decoration (Fig. 9.28), distinctive high-necked flasks with a polished red slip, and a range of common cooking vessels. The carinated vessels in particular have an angular cross-sectioned rim which is also characteristic of this phase in Sabah, and the Buidane ceramic range is also very closely paralleled in a southern Philippine site visited in the 1920's by the Guthe Expedition, but unfortunately in a now unknown location (Solheim 1964b:94–101, the "unknown site"). However, the concept of a Buidane culture is best confined to the Talaud Islands themselves, since all the sites of this period reveal a gradual fall-off in similarity with distance across the whole region from the central Philippines to Sumba, and at present it would be unwise to class the material at a level greater than that of the individual region or island group.

The other artefacts found in Leang Buidane include shell bracelets and beads, part of a glass bracelet, beads of agate and carnelian, coral flask stoppers, and a penannular pottery earring. The stone beads are particularly interesting; the majority are either spherical or elongated facetted red carnelians with a precision in drilling which indicates a definite Indian origin, although the shapes are chronologically complacent and belong to types common in both India and South-East Asia throughout the past 2000 years. However, there are three black agate beads with designs etched in white (Fig. 9.29), and these are paralleled very precisely from the late first millennium BC in major Gangetic and Indus sites such as Hastinapura (Lal 1954–5: Plate LV), Taxila (Dikshit 1952:35), Kausambi and Chandraketugarh. There is also a banded agate bead of a type common from the Harappan onwards, and the single glass bracelet fragment is also likely to be an Indian import. The etched agates are, to my mind, fairly conclusive evidence for at least some contact between India and eastern Indonesia which may have begun by as early as 200 BC, although the beads may of course have been in use for many years prior to their eventual burial.

Leang Buidane has also produced metal artefacts; there are a number of indeterminate pieces of iron, and the copper or bronze objects include bracelet fragments, a bronze cone, and a copper socketed axe. Three baked clay valves of the bivalve moulds for axes and other cuprous objects were also

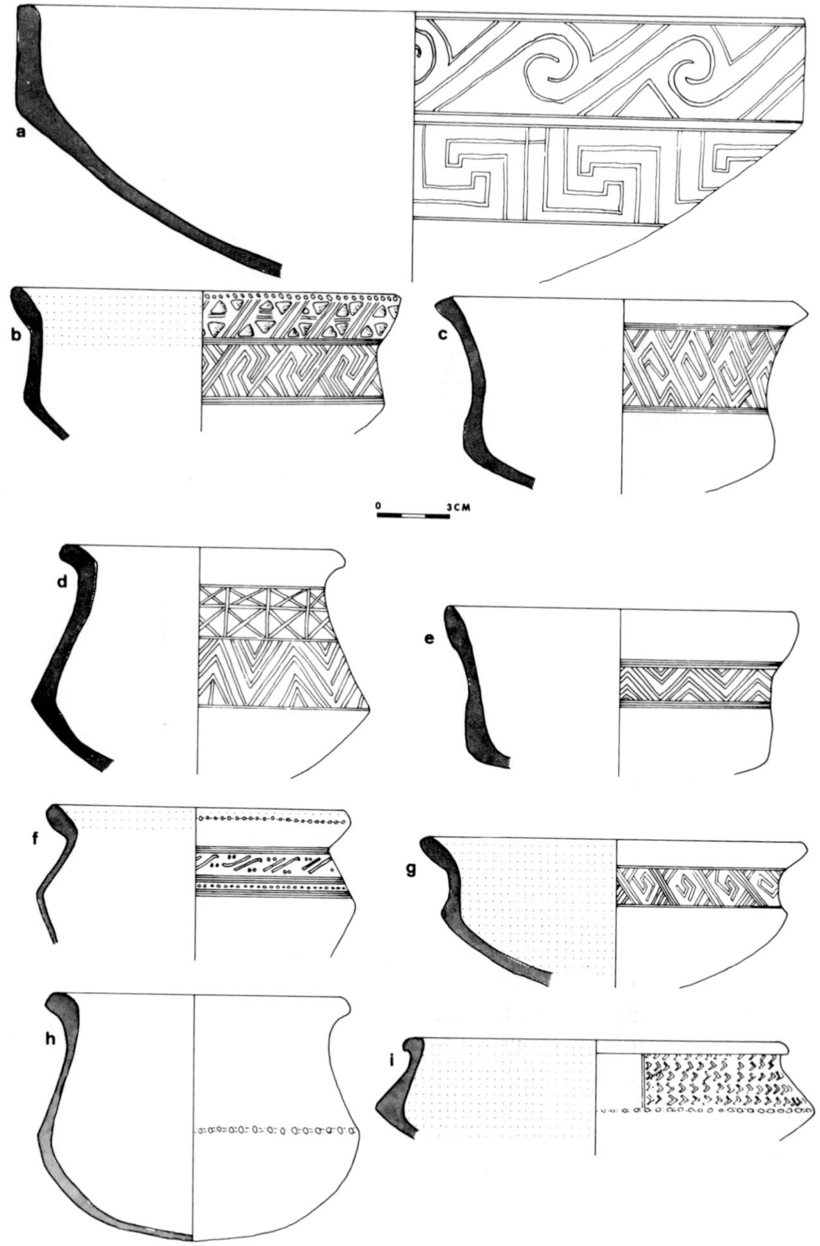

Fig. 9.28. Small carinated vessels from Leang Buidane with friezes of incised geometric decoration. (a) Probably a lid for a burial jar. Stippling = red slip. From Bellwood 1976b.

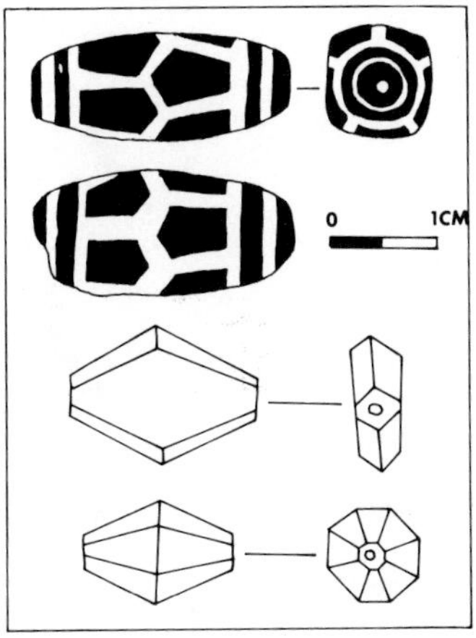

Fig. 9.29. Indian beads from Leang Buidane. Top: white-etched black agate, with identical specimen beneath from Sirkap Mound, Taxila (c. 1st century AD). Bottom: flattened lozenge and octagonal bicone of red carnelian. From Bellwood 1976b (Taxila bead from Beck 1941: Pl. II, 17).

found, and these indicate that metal casting was carried out locally, although this may have been confined to recasting of artefacts which were originally imported. In general, the Buidane metallurgy fits conformably within the range reported from this date in Sabah and the Philippines, and the copper and bronze working seems to be restricted to bivalve mould techniques, without the use of wax.

B. Eastern Sabah

The cave of Agop Atas in the Madai massif in eastern Sabah (Bellwood 1984) has produced a habitation layer of the Early Metal phase which is firmly dated by radiocarbon to the early to mid first millennium AD. This layer is separated by an interval of non-occupation from the underlying Late Neolithic layer described in Chapter 7, Section III. The cave was clearly intensively inhabited, and several of the layers contain postholes, perhaps for sleeping platforms. The pottery (Fig. 9.30) has basically the same rim and vessel forms as Buidane, and the repertoire of incised decoration, carved-paddle and corded impression, and burnished red slip is very similar between the two sites. The distinctive red-slipped and high-necked flasks also occur at Agop Atas, and in another contemporary assemblage from Hagop Bilo shelter in the nearby Baturong massif (see Fig. 9.33b). Other objects found in Agop Atas include copper or bronze fragments, a forged iron tanged

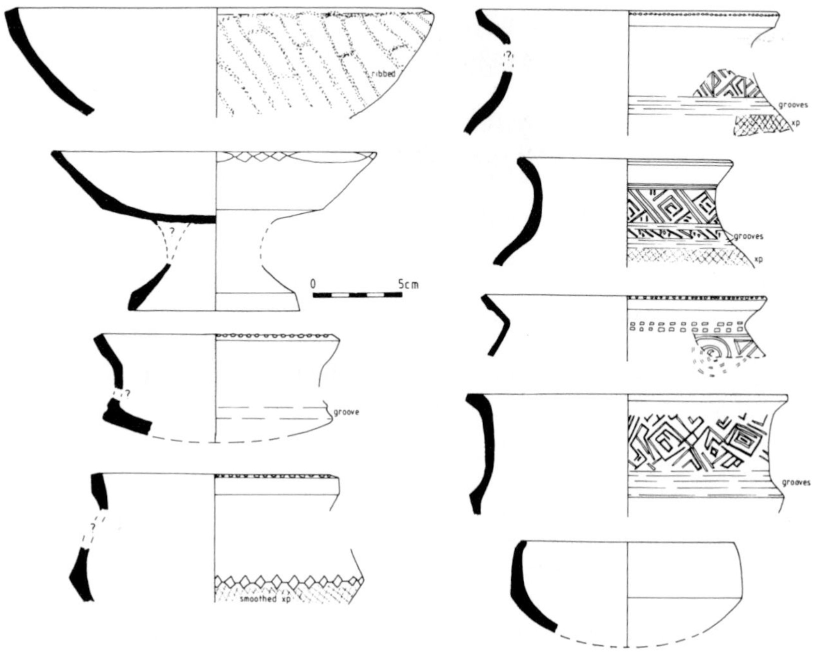

Fig. 9.30. A selection of vessels from Agop Atas — only a part of the total range of variation is represented here (xp = cross-carved-paddle-impressed).

spearhead, a small iron knife, and a few carnelian beads; the latter of somewhat cruder manufacture than those from Buidane.

Jar burial assemblages of this phase in Sabah occur in Pusu Samang Tas Cave in a remote part of the Madai massif (Harrisson, T. and B. 1971), in caves on Bukit Tengkorak near Semporna (which have the same pottery bone box forms as Leang Buidane), and in a cave in the Tapadong massif on the Segama River (Harrisson 1965). The Tapadong assemblage probably dates between AD 500 and 1000, and has produced 11 stone adzes with trapezoidal cross-sections, plus a copper or bronze socketed axe and a casting valve of soft stone. This find demonstrates that local casting was carried out, as in Talaud, although stone adzes clearly continued in use well into the Early Metal phase. Adzes identical to those from Tapadong are also known from surface collections in Mindanao (Lynch and Ewing 1968).

The overall significance of the well-dated Agop Atas and Buidane assemblages is that they demonstrate the existence of iron and copper/bronze working, together with imported Indian beads and a fairly florid style of pottery known to many authors as "Sa Huynh Kalanay" (after Solheim 1964a, 1967), from a date probably quite early in the first millennium AD. The beads and the available carbon dates make it difficult to push the beginnings of the Early Metal phase around the Celebes Sea back to before AD 1, although the traditions of jar burial and the friezes of incised decoration on pottery may go back into the Late Neolithic in Sarawak and Palawan.

C. The Central and Southern Philippines

The best-known ceramic and metal (copper/bronze and iron) complex of the Early Metal phase in the central Philippines is undoubtedly that termed Kalanay by Solheim (1964b), from his excavations in Kalanay cave on Masbate and from earlier collections made by the Guthe Expedition. This material is not of direct concern here, although it should be noted that the whole range shows considerable similarity to the Agop Atas and Buidane assemblages.

The extensive complexes of caves on the west-central coast of Palawan (including the Tabon Caves) have produced prolific jar burial assemblages which still remain only partially published (Fox 1970; Kress 1978). Much of this material is virtually identical to that from Agop Atas and Buidane, although detailed comparison remains impossible. Fox placed the beginnings of the jar burial tradition at Tabon with the Manunggul chamber A assemblage, which he dated to the beginning of the first millennium BC on the basis of two radiocarbon dates. This assemblage contained no metal, and Fox was therefore willing, perhaps rightly, to place in it the Late Neolithic. The pottery is especially fine, and appears to lack the sharply carinated forms of the Tabon Early Metal phase. However, it does have at least one pottery coffin, and some vessels have red-painted curvilinear designs enclosed by incised lines — a technique well represented in the Early Metal sites in Sabah, and also in the Sa Huynh culture in southern Vietnam. So I am a little uncertain about such an early date for this assemblage, and clearly the absence of metal is not a reliable indicator of a Neolithic date. Like all jar burial caves this one was also disturbed and the jars smashed (Fox 1970: Plate X), and the carbon dates need not necessarily date the jar burial event. However, my doubts here may be entirely misplaced, and these problems cannot be resolved at the present time[3].

Although Fox suggested that copper and bronze objects first appeared in the Palawan sequence at about 500 BC, the only dated site for the Early Metal

[3]New discoveries of jar burials in southern Vietnam dating from the late second millennium BC (Ngo S. H. 1985) could provide some support for an equal antiquity of the tradition at Niah and Tabon.

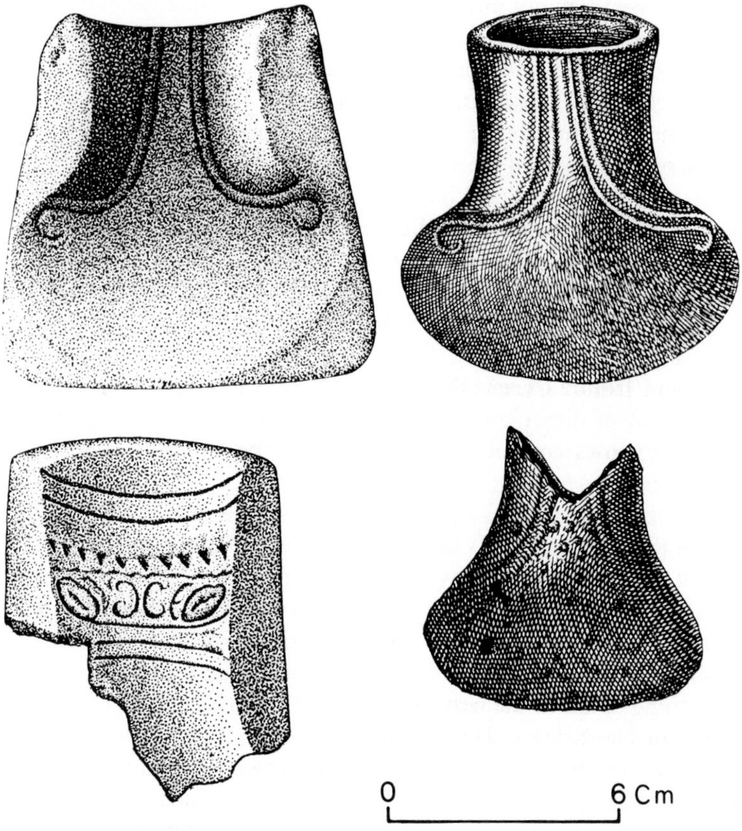

Fig. 9.31. Baked clay casting moulds and copper or bronze axes from the Tabon Caves, Palawan. From Fox 1970. Courtesy: National Museum of the Philippines.

phase at Tabon is Manunggul chamber B, which has a radiocarbon date of about 200 BC. This assemblage produced iron, glass bracelets, glass and carnelian beads, and also five acid-etched agate beads similar to those from Buidane. Copper or bronze items occur in other jar burial caves in the area, and include socketed axes (Fig. 9.31) and spearheads, a tanged and barbed arrowhead, and a possible barbed harpoon. Axe casting moulds, gold beads, and jade lingling-o earrings have also been found. In general I suspect that the Tabon jar burial sequence after analysis will resemble the sequence from the Sabah sites and belong mainly in the first millennium AD.

Another central Philippine site worthy of mention is the open jar burial site of Magsuhot on Negros Island, where Tenazas (1974) excavated three large burial jars placed side by side in a large pit lined with broken potsherds. Pottery of Kalanay type, human and animal figurines of baked clay, and bones of pig and chicken were found with the jar burials, which were sealed in by an earth fill. Only one jar contained human bones — of a young woman and two children. Another pit contained an enormous lidded burial jar with a weight of 52 kg, together with a pottery bone box and no less than 70 accessory vessels. The burial jar was connected to the surface by a tube of stacked pots, and it contained an iron knife, but no identifiable bones. This site is of interest because it reveals the wealth of information which can survive with undisturbed jar burial sites, and while undated it would fit well into a mid or late first millennium AD context.

D. Southern Indonesia and Sulawesi

The most remarkable of the jar burial sites of Indonesia is undoubtedly the large urnfield of Melolo on eastern Sumba. This open site was investigated at various times in the 1920s and 1930s, and produced an array of close-set large burial urns. These contained fragmentary secondary burials, stone adzes, stone and shell beads and shell bracelets, and small accessory pots of which the only kind adequately reported is an elegant high-necked flask with incised geometric and anthropomorphic designs filled in with a white paint (Heekeren 1956b), Fig. 9.32. It appears that some of these flasks were provided with a burnished red slip.

Although Heekeren (1972:191) has classified the Melolo assemblage as Neolithic owing to the absence of metal, it is more likely to be of first millennium AD date; some of the flat-based flasks are paralleled very precisely in the Buni pottery of western Java (see Fig. 9.25), and the flask forms in general are paralleled in a number of other sites of the Early Metal phase. I suspect that this may be a significant observation for future research because the form is not, to my knowledge, found in any Indo-Malaysian assemblage (outside Taiwan) which can conclusively be considered as Neolithic. Indeed, the high-necked flask, often with a globular body and sometimes a burnished red slip, can perhaps be regarded as a clear marker of the Early Metal phase; for instance at Leang Buidane in Talaud, at Agop Atas and Hagop Bilo in Sabah, at Gunung Piring on Lombok, at Leang Bua on Flores, at Batu Ejaya in southern Sulawesi (Harris 1979), at Gilimanuk on Bali, and at Anyar in western Java (Fig. 9.33). The form clearly transcends local cultural areas, and at Gilimanuk, Leang Bua and Gunung Piring it is found in association with inhumation rather than jar burials.

Melolo is really the only jar burial site in eastern Indonesia which merits close attention at present, but there are some further generalisations about the Early Metal phase in the archipelago as a whole which can be made.

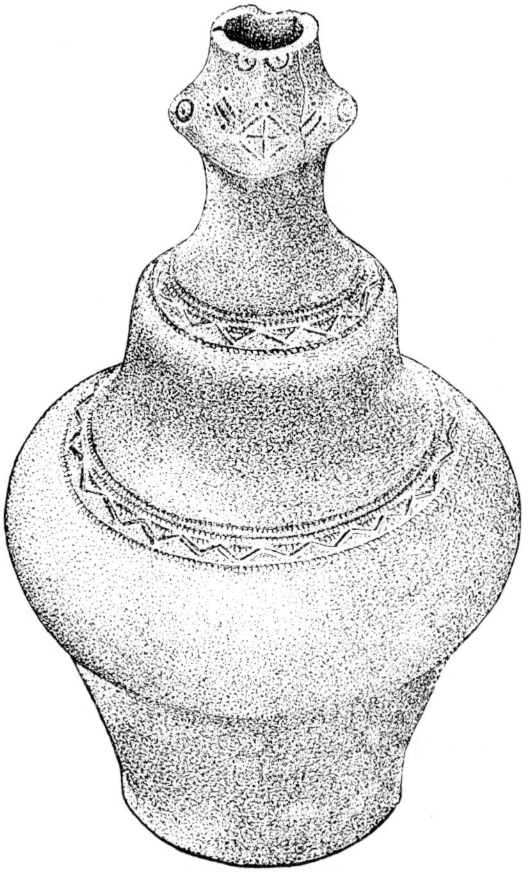

Fig. 9.32. Flask with human face carved on neck from Melolo, Sumba. From Heekeren 1956b. Courtesy: Indonesian National Research Centre for Archaeology.

Firstly, it is clear that the sites around the Celebes and Sulu Seas — the Tabon Caves, the "Kalanay" sites, and the sites of eastern Sabah and Talaud — do share very closely related pottery assemblages with iron and copper/bronze during the first millennium AD. Jar burial is the predominant rite in this region, and another common characteristic is the small pottery bone box.

In southern Indonesia the picture becomes rather more confused, and here comprises the relatively "pure" jar burial site at Melolo, the mixed-rite sites such as Anyar, Plawangan and Gilimanuk, and also Gunung Piring on Lombok which appears to have only inhumations. Between these two regions on the islands of Sumatra, Borneo (except Sabah), Sulawesi and the Moluccas there are unfortunately many blanks, although jar burial assemblages

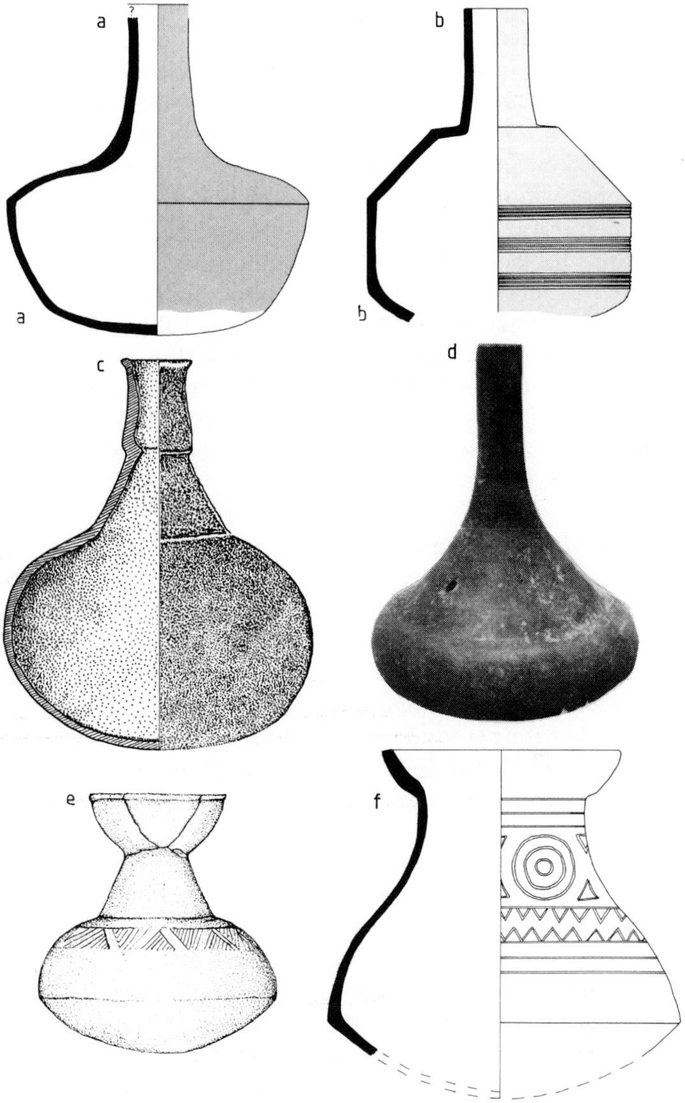

Fig. 9.33. (a–d) High-necked flasks of the Early Metal phase: (a) from Leang Buidane, Talaud (red-slipped), 18 cm high; (b) from Hagop Bilo, Sabah (red-slipped), 20 cm high; (c) from Gunung Piring, Lombok, 25 cm high; (d) from Anyar, Java (on footring), 29 cm high; (e, f) narrow-necked vessels of similar shape from Gunung Piring, Lombok (left, 15 cm high) and Leang Buidane, Talaud (right, 19 cm high). (c, e) From Gunadi *et al.* 1978; (d) from Heekeren 1956a. Courtesy: Indonesian National Research Centre for Archaeology (c, e); Anthropos-Institut (d).

from caves in southern Sulawesi (Mulvaney and Soejono 1970, 1971) have bone boxes and pottery loosely related to the Tabon–Sabah–Talaud sites, which may date well into the first millennium AD. However, it is clear that even the most basic cultural and chronological framework for the Early Metal phase does not yet exist for the great bulk of the archipelago, and until this is established understanding of the period is unlikely to advance very far.

The same observation still applies to the remarkable complex of large stone jars and human statues in central Sulawesi (Kaudern 1938). I have little to add to my previous description of these monuments (Bellwood 1978a:228), and dates are still elusive, but an extensive survey in the Bada district to the west of Lake Poso (Sukendar 1980) has brought to light more stone jars and statues, and demonstrated their association with iron and carved-paddle-impressed pottery. However, the absence of a chronological scheme for Sulawesi subsequent to the Toalian industry makes accurate dating virtually impossible, and the apparent absence of Chinese pottery can only suggest a date older than 500 years.

E. The Origins of the Jar Burial Tradition

I have already discussed the evidence, of varying reliability, which indicates that jar burial was practised in Late Neolithic contexts at Niah in Sarawak, in the Tabon Caves, and in northern Luzon. Possible commencement dates fall in the late second and early first millennia BC, and if these dates are correct then they provide strong grounds for regarding the tradition as an indigenous development in Island South-East Asia. However, it must still be realised that the bulk of the jar burial sites are certainly not older than 200 BC.

Of course, no conclusive evidence exists to support a watertight case for or against a local origin of the jar burial tradition, but some comparative observations may be of interest. Although infant burial in jars occurs in some early Chinese, Japanese, and Thai Neolithic sites (e.g. White 1982 for Ban Chiang; Kidder 1974 for Jomon Japan), it is apparent that the South-East Asian mainland prehistoric sequence (outside southern Vietnam) is almost totally devoid of this tradition, and always stressed extended inhumation in post-Hoabinhian contexts. On the other hand, a coherent tradition of jar burial does occur in the Late Jomon and Yayoi periods of south-western Japan (100 BC to AD 300), and here it appears that bones were often placed in two jars laid horizontally mouth-to-mouth (Mori 1956; Chard 1974). Although this pattern is not to my knowledge found in the Indo-Malaysian Archipelago there are records of vertical mouth-to-mouth jar burials on Batan Island between Luzon and Taiwan (Solheim 1960), at Plawangan on Java (Sukendar and Awe 1979) and at Gilimanuk on Bali (Soejono 1969: Plate 24). In addition, the Yayoi pottery style, which is different in many respects from that of the preceding Jomon periods, does include flasks, cut-outs in ring feet, red-slipped surfaces and incised scroll patterns which overlap to some extent with the repertoire of the Early Metal phase in the Philippines. While I would not suggest Japan as a source for the Indo-Malaysian jar burials, I do feel that some degree of contact between the two archipelagic regions may have taken place from the late first millennium BC onwards.

In India there is a widespread tradition of mouth-to-mouth urn burial in Chalcolithic sites spread across the country from Karnataka to West Bengal, but of more relevance is the tradition of burial in single upright urns found in association with the Black and Red pottery of the Iron Age cultures of southern India and Sri Lanka (e.g. Rea 1915; Sitrampalam 1980). Many specific features of this tradition — the practice of secondary burial with grave goods in the urns, the use of bone boxes and legged coffins, and the occasional occurrence of stone jar lids (as in some Philippine sites) — clearly do have definite Indo-Malaysian parallels. The historical and archaeological data already reviewed indicate that Indian contact with South-East Asia was taking place from perhaps the end of the first millennium BC onwards, so some exchange of ideas may have been occurring. However, it is also apparent that the basic artefact forms, especially in metal and pottery, differ so considerably between the two regions that an actual Indian source for the Indo-Malaysian jar burials would be unthinkable. I am therefore still strongly inclined to keep to my previous conclusion (Bellwood 1978a:213) that the Austronesian jar burial tradition was an indigenous development.

10
A Final Overview

I now wish to reiterate a number of outstanding questions, and to review my conclusions on those aspects of the prehistory of the Indo-Malaysian Archipelago which I regard as having central significance for its overall human story. Few of the major problems will ever be elucidated and explained to the satisfaction of all scholars — hence perhaps, the attraction and vitality of the multifaceted discipline of prehistory. Many pieces of the total jigsaw will doubtless be added in the future by devoted analyses of stone tools, words and skulls, but the whole will probably always remain a sum of more than its individual archaeological, linguistic and biological parts.

If we commence at the remote and misty beginning, then there are obviously many questions concerning *Homo erectus* which have hardly even begun to be answered. Did these hominids enter the archipelago sufficiently early to take advantage of Late Pliocene land bridges and travel with the stegodons to Sulawesi and the Lesser Sundas? Did they make stone tools, as did their African and Chinese cousins? Did they belong to one single chronospecies or even one single lineage as the present record suggests, or were there "side branches" which became extinct? Was Sundaland a continent throughout this period, or were there long periods of island separation? If the latter, what were the biological and cultural effects of the separations? Were these early hominids restricted to monsoon forest and parkland environments, or were they able to colonise the equatorial rainforests as well?

There are also major biological questions which concern more recent populations. For instance, just how "sealed" was the presumed evolutionary trajectory in Sundaland from *Homo erectus* to ancestral Australoids of *sapiens* grade? Total isolation of an evolving human population in this region for the enormous period of time involved seems unlikely, as does the converse of total extinction of *Homo erectus* followed by (or perhaps even caused by) a *Homo sapiens* immigration from an outside source. The latter option seems to me to be quite impossible since there is really no logical source for the Australoids apart from Sundaland and the adjacent South-East Asian mainland, unless we resort to special pleading for India or Africa, both far distant and lacking convincing biological support. We may have to settle for the time being for a middle road — the Australoids clearly have a continuous but probably not an entirely sealed ancestry from *Homo erectus* in the western part of the Indo-Malaysian Archipelago.

For the period after 40 000 years ago there is better evidence for human movement both out from and into the archipelago. Early Australoids were able to expand into New Guinea and Australia, and it is possible that many of the Wallacean Islands were first settled at about this time. It also looks as if newcomers entered the archipelago from time to time long before the period of Austronesian expansion. The evidence is sparse, but it includes the suggestion of links between southern China and Australia at about 30 000 years ago (Chapter 3, Section IIID), and possibly certain archaeological assemblages such as the Tingkayu lanceolates and the later flake and blade industries. All these hints point to the east Asian mainland and Japan, rather than to India.

Environmentally related questions also arise. I have suggested that the equatorial and densely forested regions were always less important for human settlement than the more open intermediate tropical belts where there is a long dry season. This contrast seems to hold for all periods, from early hunting and gathering through the Neolithic to the present day, where it is of course crystal clear. But were the equatorial rainforests really only inhabited to any extent from the early Holocene onwards? I believe that the evidence from Malaya, Sumatra and Borneo lends support to such a view, but we still need to know what happened to these lowland rainforests in the dry glacial periods — were they reduced in extent or broken up by "dry season corridors"? If so, was there periodic Pleistocene occupation of these drier zones? Furthermore, did the presumed expansion of rainforest and the rise in sea-level in the early Holocene cause the observed cases of animal extinction, or (less likely in my view) were human hunters partly to blame?

The early Holocene climatic amelioration leads on to further questions, since this was apparently more marked and rapid on a world-wide scale than any climatic and environmental change which had occurred in the previous 100 000 years. I regard this change as having been crucial for the radiation of annual cereals in certain key regions of the northern hemisphere, and of course for their ultimate domestication. One offshoot of this economic transition in the southern Chinese region was the phenomenon of Austronesian expansion after 4000 BC. As I have tried to make clear, I do not now regard the Indo-Malaysian region itself as a zone of pristine agricultural origins, although it is obvious that many useful trees and tubers were brought under systematic cultivation there. The major question mark still hangs over New Guinea, where agriculture could have evolved independently in unique highland environments, and have sown the seeds of Papuan demographic resistance to Austronesian expansion.

There is also the question of the significance of the post-glacial rise in sea-level which I, together with other scholars, once regarded as a stimulus for demographic crowding in Sundaland and for ultimate and local developments there towards agriculture (Bellwood 1978a:422). I have now changed my mind about this, since I doubt whether the mangrove coasts of late glacial Sundaland ever supported large populations, and furthermore the sea-level rise would have increased rather than reduced the extent of coastline (Bellwood 1983b:75; and see Chapter 1, Section IVD). The drowning of Sundaland may have been a major environmental event, but there is really no good evidence that human populations were particularly affected by it.

It will by now be clear that I regard the main period of Austronesian expansion between 3000 and 1000 BC as the foundation for major biological, linguistic and cultural changes in the prehistory of the archipelago. I have reviewed the agricultural background to this expansion, and also the economic changes which early Austronesian groups underwent as they expanded southwards towards and across the equator. I choose the term "expansion" with some care, since I do not think there is good evidence for long-distance migration of the Polynesian type until the Oceanic islands were being settled after 1500 BC. The expansion was also quite a slow affair in real terms; after all, it required almost 4000 years for Austronesians to reach New Zealand and Madagascar if 3000 BC be taken as a reasonable date for the first movements southwards from Taiwan. I have also mentioned viewpoints which are in opposition to mine, and which postulate foundation developments of the Southern Mongoloid phenotype and the Austronesian languages in the Indo-Malaysian Archipelago itself, or even (in the case of the languages) in western Melanesia. I look forward to future debate on these matters, and have expressed my own views more forcefully in a recent paper (Bellwood 1983a).

My opinion on the overall "shape" of Indo-Malaysian prehistory should by now be apparent (Fig. 10.1). Basically, I see few indications of major cultural change in the region prior to the period of Austronesian expansion, apart from those kinds of regional variation in stone tool-making techniques which are perhaps no more than one would expect given the time span involved and the inherent capacity of humans to communicate. With the exception of periodic trickles of new peoples and occasional items of cultural baggage I doubt whether the archipelago witnessed any major replacements of population or dramatic spurts of local development from the period of *Homo erectus* through into the early Holocene.

However, the long pre-agricultural millennia of relative stability came to a dramatic close in the period of Austronesian expansion. As agriculturalists by virtue of prior cultural developments outside the Indo-Malaysian region, the Austronesians had a culturally inbuilt and demographically founded drive for expansion which eventually took them to Easter Island and New

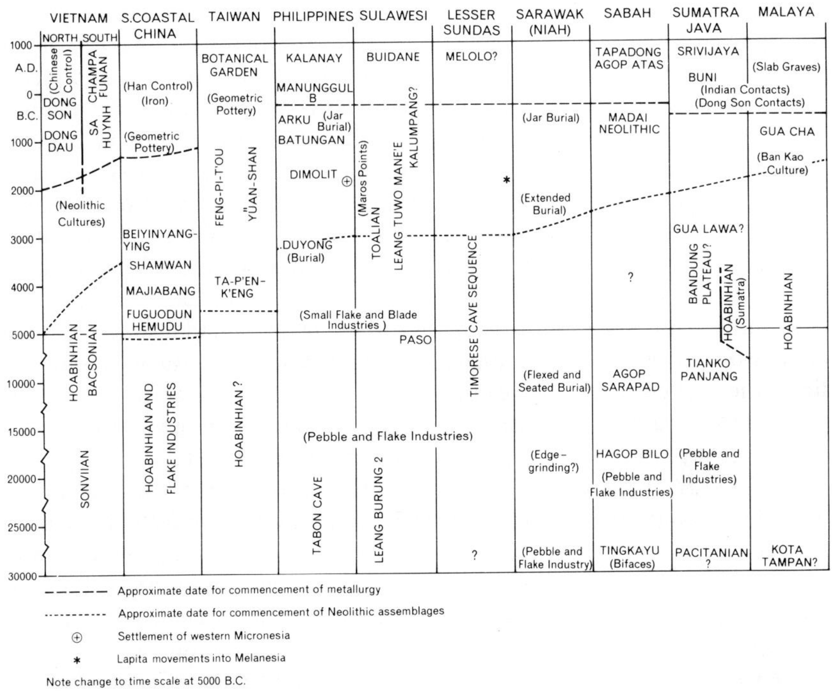

Fig. 10.1. Chart of selected archaeological developments during the past 30 000 years in Vietnam, China and the Indo-Malaysian Archipelago. Note the change of scale at 5000 BC.

Zealand. Agriculture on the whole allows for much higher population densities than hunting and gathering, and it is clearly an economic system which can utilise and even encourage the breeding of an increasing labour force in the form of children and adolescents. Although populations of agriculturalists who inhabit constrained geographical ranges have been forced either to control population growth or to intensify production in the past, it is clear that the early Austronesians, like the 19th century Iban of Sarawak, did not face such constraints. Confronted by fertile environments with good agricultural potentials occupied only by hunters and gatherers, they "chose" expansion. Many of their descendants are still expanding their geographical ranges at the ultimate expense of forest hunters and gatherers in some regions to this day.

There are also two observations of Oceanic significance which arise from my review of earlier Austronesian prehistory in the Indo-Malaysian Archipelago. The first is that the Austronesian societies of eastern Indonesia and Melanesia were heavily affected (more so than those in the west and north of Indonesia) by two-way contact with pre-existing societies. However, it is not yet clear whether agriculture had spread from a putative and independent New Guinea source into eastern Indonesia prior to Austronesian settlement. If it had, it would go far towards explaining the biological and cultural variation observed in this region. A second observation must be that the spread of the ancestral Polynesian Lapita culture through Melanesia after about 1600 BC correlates in linguistic terms with the period of Proto-Oceanic. Hence the problems which arose through acceptance of an erroneous date of 3000 BC for Proto-Oceanic (Bellwood 1978a:423), and thereby having the early Polynesians somehow "lost" in a millennium and a half of archaeological void in Melanesia, can now be forgotten. The original problem lay in an unwillingness to recognise the rapidity of change in the Austronesian languages of this region.

As far as the later phases of Austronesian prehistory are concerned I have little to add to my opinions as presented in Chapters 8 and 9. Clearly, it is important to find out more about the development and spread of metallurgy, and there is still little coherent information about the archaeology and the societies of western Indonesia just prior to the period of intensive Indian influence in the first millennium AD. Questions concerning the evolution of complex societies provide just as much stimulus and excitement for prehistorians as do questions concerning the origins of agriculture, and I believe that the former represent perhaps the largest untapped field of research facing Indonesian, and especially Javanese, prehistorians at the present time.

Finally, what of the future for prehistoric research in the Indo-Malaysian Archipelago? Firstly, it is becoming very obvious that high-quality archaeological excavations with full publication of data are absolutely essential. This may seem obvious to many archaeologists, but the South-East Asian record has generally looked a little foggy from this angle. Secondly, new data must be assessed against well-formulated models of Indo-Malaysian prehistory which are based on the whole South-East Asian and Oceanic scene, and which draw (when applicable) on information from archaeology, historical sources, linguistics, biological anthropology, cultural anthropology and the natural sciences. I hope that I have presented such a model in this book, and that it will encourage, guide, and also be modified by future research.

Appendix

Pinyin and Wade-Giles Equivalents for Chinese Placenames

Pinyin	Wade-Giles (Traditional province spellings in brackets)
Anhui	An-hui (Anhwei)
Beiyinyangying	Pei-yin-yang-ying
Dali	Ta-li
Dingcun	Ting-ts'un
Fujian	Fu-chien (Fukien)
Fuguodun	Fu-kuo-tun
Gehe	K'o-ho
Gongwangling	Kung-wang-ling
Guangdong	Kuang-tung (Kwangtung)
Guangxi	Kuang-hsi (Kwangsi)
Guanyindong	Kuan-yin-tung
Guizhou	Kuei-chou (Kweichow)
Hangzhou	Hang-chou
Hemudu	Ho-mu-tu
Henan	Ho-nan (Honan)
Hubei	Hu-pei (Hupeh)
Hunan	Hu-nan (Hunan)
Jiangsu	Chiang-su (Kiangsu)
Jiangxi	Chiang-hsi (Kiangsi)
Lantian	Lan-t'ien
Liujiang	Liu-chiang
Maba	Ma-pa
Majiabang	Ma-chia-pang
Shaanxi	Shen-hsi (Shensi)
Shanxi	Shan-hsi (Shansi)
Shandong	Shan-tung (Shantung)
Shizhaishan	Shih-chai-shan
Sichuan	Ssu-ch'uan (Szechwan)
Song (dynasty)	Sung
Xianrendong	Hsien-jen-tung
Xihoudu	Hsi-hou-tu
Yuanmou	Yüan-mou
Yunnan	Yün-nan (Yunnan)
Zhejiang	Che-chiang (Chekiang)
Zhoukoudian	Chou-k'ou-tien
Ziyang	Tsu-yang (Tzeyang)

References

Abbreviations

AJPA	*American Journal of Physical Anthropology*
AP	*Asian Perspectives*
APAO	*Archaeology and Physical Anthropology in Oceania*
APAS	*Asian and Pacific Archaeology Series*
BIPPA	*Bulletin of the Indo-Pacific Prehistory Association*
BPA	*Berita Penelitian Arkeologi* (Jakarta: Pusat Penelitian Arkeologi Nasional)
BRM	*Bulletin of the Raffles Museum*, Singapore
BTLV	*Bijdragen tot de Taal-, Land- en Volkenkunde*
CA	*Current Anthropology*
FMJ	*Federation Museums Journal*
JFMSM	*Journal of the Federated Malay States Museums*
JHE	*Journal of Human Evolution*
JHKAS	*Journal of the Hong Kong Archaeological Society*
JMBRAS	*Journal of the Malaysian Branch of the Royal Asiatic Society*
JSEAS	*Journal of Southeast Asian Studies*
MQRSEA	*Modern Quaternary Research in Southeast Asia*
PQCS	*Philippine Quarterly of Culture and Society*
SMJ	*Sarawak Museum Journal*
TITLV	*Tijdschrift voor Indische Taal-, Land- en Volkenkunde*
TKNAG	*Tijdschrift van het Koninklijk Nederlandsch Aardrijkskundig Genootschap*
WA	*World Archaeology*

Adi Haji Taha. 1981. *The re-excavation of the rockshelter of Gua Cha, Ulu Kelantan, West Malaysia.* Unpublished M.A. thesis, Australian National University.

——— 1983. "Recent archaeological discoveries in Peninsular Malaysia 1976–82". *JMBRAS* 56(1):47–63.

Aharon, P. 1983. "Surface ocean temperature variations during the late Wisconsian stages". In CLIMANZ, pp. 3–4.

Aigner, J. 1978a. "Pleistocene faunal and cultural stations in South China". In Ikawa-Smith, F. (ed.) 1978:129–60.

——— 1978b. "Important archaeological remains from North China". In Ikawa-Smith, F. (ed.) 1978:163–232.

——— 1978c. "The Palaeolithic of China". In Bryan, A. L. (ed.). *Early man in America from a Circum-Pacific perspective*, pp. 25–41. Edmonton: Dept. Anthropology, University of Alberta.

——— 1979. "Pleistocene ecology and Palaeolithic assemblages in South China". *JHKAS* 8:52–72.

——— 1981. *Archaeological remains in Pleistocene China.* Munich: Verlag C. H. Beck.

Aikens, C. M. and Higuchi, T. 1981. *The prehistory of Japan.* London: Academic Press.

Alkire, W. 1972. "Concepts of order in Southeast Asia and Micronesia". *Comparative Studies in Society and History* 14(4):484–93.

Allen, J., Golson, J., and Jones, R. (eds). 1977. *Sunda and Sahul.* London: Academic Press.

Ambary, H. M. 1981. "Notes on research on sites from the Srivijaya period". In *Studies on Srivijaya*, pp. 1–12. Jakarta: Pusat Penelitian Arkeologi Nasional.

Andaya, B. and Andaya, L. 1982. *A history of Malaysia.* London: Macmillan.

Andel, T. H. van, Heath, G. R., Moore, T. C., and McGeary, D. F. R. 1967. "Late Quaternary history, climate and oceanography of the Timor Sea". *American Journal of Science* 265:737–58.

Anderson, P. 1983. "The reproductive role of the human breast". *CA* 24:25–46.

Anderson, P. C. 1980. "A testimony of prehistoric tasks: diagnostic residues on stone tool working edges". *WA* 12:181–94.

Anggraeni, N. 1976. "Peninggalan-peninggalan prasejarah di sekitar danau Cangkuang (Leles)". *Kalpataru* 2:55–70.

Angladette, A. 1974. "Rice in humid tropical Asia". In Unesco 1974:415–38.

An Zhi-min. 1981. "The Neolithic archaeology of China". *Early China* 5:35–45.

——— 1983. "C-14 dating and Chinese Neolithic". Paper presented at 31st CISHAAN Congress, September 1983, Tokyo.

Appell, G. N. 1978. "The Rungus Dusun". In King, V. T. (ed.) 1978:143–71.

Arnaud, V. 1974. "La culture du millet chez les Yami". *Journal d'agriculture tropicale et de botanique appliquée* 21:275–311.

Arnold, G. 1958. "Nomadic Penan of the Upper Rejang (Plieran), Sarawak". *JMBRAS* 31(1):40–82.

Ashton, P. S. 1972. "The Quaternary geomorphological history of western Malesia and lowland forest phytogeography". In Ashton, P. and M. (eds) 1972:35–49.

Ashton, P. and Ashton, M. (eds). 1972. *The Quaternary era in Malesia.* University of Hull, Department of Geography, Miscellaneous Series 13.

Atlas. 1938. *Atlas van tropisch Nederland.* The Hague: Nijhoff.

Atlas. 1980. *Atlas of primitive man in China.* New York: Van Nostrand Reinhold.

Audley-Charles, M. G. 1981. "Geological history of the region of Wallace's Line". In Whitmore, T. C. (ed.) 1981:24–35.

Audley-Charles, M. G., Carter, D. J. and Milsom, J. S. 1972. "Tectonic development of eastern Indonesia in relation to Gondwanaland dispersal". *Nature (Physical Science)* 239:35–9.

Audley-Charles, M. G. and Hooijer, D. A. 1973. "Relation of Pleistocene migrations of pygmy stegodonts to island arc tectonics in eastern Indonesia". *Nature* 241:197–8.

Azis, B. S. 1981. "Tradisi kapak perimbas di Indonesia". *Amerta* 4:11–21.

Ball, S. C. 1933. *Jungle fowls from the Pacific Islands.* Bulletin of the Bernice P. Bishop Museum 108.

Bandi, H. G. 1951. "Die Obsidianindustrie der Umgebung von Bandung in Westjava". In *Südseestudien*, pp. 127–61. Basle: Museum für Volkerkunde.

Bard, S. M. 1975. "Chung Hom Wan". *JHKAS* 6:9–25.

Barnard, N. (ed.). 1972. *Early Chinese art and its possible influence in the Pacific Basin.* 3 volumes. New York: Intercultural Arts Press.

——— 1980. *Radiocarbon dates and their significance in the Chinese archaeological scene.* Canberra: privately published.

Barrau, J. 1965. "Histoire et préhistoire horticoles de l'Océanie tropicale". *Journal de la Société des Océanistes* 21:55–78.

—— 1968. "L'humide et le sec". In Vayda, A. P. (ed.), *Peoples and cultures of the Pacific*, pp. 113–32. New York: Natural History Press.
—— 1974. "L'Asie du Sud-Est, berceau cultural". *Études Rurales* 53–6:17–39.
Barth, F. 1952. "The southern Mongoloid migration". *Man* 52:5–8.
Bartlett, H. H. 1934. *The sacred edifices of the Batak of Sumatra.* University of Michigan Museum of Anthropology, Occasional Contribution 4.
Bartstra, G–J. 1974. "Notes about Sangiran". *Quartär* 25:1–12.
—— 1976. *Contributions to the study of the Palaeolithic Patjitan culture of Java, Indonesia.* Leiden: E. J. Brill.
—— 1977. "Walanae formation and Walanae terraces in the study of South Sulawesi". *Quartär* 27–8:21–30.
—— 1978a. "The Patjitan culture: a preliminary report on new research". In Ikawa-Smith, F. (ed.) 1978:29–36.
—— 1978b. "Recent Palaeolithic research in Java". *MQRSEA* 4:63–70.
—— 1978c. "Note on new data concerning the fossil vertebrates and stone tools in the Walanae valley in South Sulawesi". *MQRSEA* 4:71–2.
—— 1982a. "The river-laid strata near Trinil". *MQRSEA* 7:97–130.
—— 1982b. "*Homo erectus erectus*: the search for his artefacts". *CA* 23:318–20.
—— 1983. "Some remarks upon fossil man from Java, his age, and his tools". *BTLV* 139:421–34.
Bartstra, G–J., Basoeki and Santoso, B. 1976. "Solo valley research 1975". *MQRSEA* 2:23–36.
Batchelor, B. C. 1977. Post "Hoabinhian" coastal settlement indicated by finds in stanniferous Langat River alluvium near Dengkil, Selangor, Peninsular Malaysia. *FMJ* 22.
—— 1979. "Discontinuously rising Late Cenozoic sea levels, with special reference to Sundaland, Southeast Asia". *Geologie en Mijnbouw* 58:1–20.
Bayard, D. 1980. "The roots of Indochinese civilization". *Pacific Affairs* 53(1):89–114.
—— 1981. "Temporal distribution and alloy variation in early bronzes from Non Nok Tha". *CA* 22:697–9.
Bayard, D. and Parker, R. H. 1976. "Interpretation of Sai Yok and Ban Kao sites, central Thailand". *AP* 19(2):289–94.
Bay-Petersen, J. 1982. "Excavations at Bagumbayam, Masbate, central Philippines". *Southeast Asian Studies Newsletter* (British Institute in South-East Asia) 8:1–3.
Beaty, C. B. 1978. "The causes of glaciation". *American Scientist* 66:452–9.
Beck, H. C. 1941. *The beads from Taxila.* Archaeological Survey of India, Memoir 65.
Bellwood, P. S. 1976a. "Prehistoric plant and animal domestication in Austronesia". In Sieveking, G., Longworth, I. H. and Wilson, K. E. (eds), *Problems in economic and social archaeology*, pp. 153–68. London: Duckworth.
—— 1976b. "Archaeological research in Minahasa and the Talaud Islands, north-eastern Indonesia". *AP* 19:240–88.
—— 1976c. "The significance of excavated bronze objects and casting moulds from the Talaud islands". In Barnard, N. (ed.), *Ancient Chinese bronzes and Southeast Asian metal and other archaeological artefacts*, pp. 413–20. Melbourne: National Gallery of Victoria.
—— 1978a. *Man's conquest of the Pacific.* Auckland: Collins.
—— 1978b. "The sultanate of Brunei". *Hemisphere* 22(11):18–21.
—— 1980a. "The peopling of the Pacific". *Scientific American* 243(5):74–85.
—— 1980b. "Plants, climate and people: the early horticultural prehistory of Austronesia". In Fox, J. J. (ed.) 1980:57–74.
—— 1981. "The Buidane culture of the Talaud islands". *BIPPA* 2:69–127.
—— 1983a. "The great Pacific migration". *Yearbook of Science and the Future* (1984), pp. 80–93.

——— 1983b. "New perspectives on Indo-Malaysian prehistory". *BIPPA* 4:71–83.
——— 1984. "Archaeological research in the Madai-Baturong region, Sabah". *BIPPA* 5:38–54.
Bellwood, P. S. and Adi Haji Taha. 1981. "A home for ten thousand years". *Hemisphere* 25(5):310–3.
Bellwood, P. S. and Omar, M. 1980. "Trade patterns and political developments in Brunei and adjacent areas, AD 700–1500". *Brunei Museum Journal* 4(4):155–79.
Bemmelen, R. W. van. 1949. *The geology of Indonesia.* 2 volumes. The Hague: Government Printing Office.
Benedict, P. K. 1942. "Thai, Kadai and Indonesian: a new alignment in Southeastern Asia". *American Anthropologist* 44:576–601.
——— 1975. *Austro-Thai language and culture.* New Haven: HRAF Press.
——— 1976. "Austro-Thai and Austro-Asiatic". In Jenner, P. N. *et al.* (eds) 1976:1–36.
Benjamin, G. 1976. "Austroasiatic subgroupings and prehistory in the Malay Peninsula". In Jenner *et al.* (eds) 1976:37–128.
——— 1980. Semang, Senoi and Malay: culture history, kinship and consciousness in the Malay Peninsula. Unpublished typescript.
——— 1983. "In the long term: three themes in Malayan cultural ecology". To appear in Hutterer, K. and Rambo, T. (eds), *Cultural values and tropical ecology in Southeast Asia.* Ann Arbor: Center for South and Southeast Asian Studies, University of Michigan.
Berger, A. (ed.). 1981. *Climatic variations and variability: facts and theories.* Dordrecht: D. Reidel.
Bergman, P. A. M. and Karsten, P. 1952. "Fluorine content of Pithecanthropus and of other species from the Trinil fauna". *Koninklijke Nederlandse Akademie van Wetenschappen,* Proceedings Series B, vol. 55:150–2.
Bergsland, K. and Vogt, H. 1962. "On the validity of glottochronology". *CA* 3:115–53.
Bernet Kempers, A. J. 1959. *Ancient Indonesian art.* Harvard University Press.
——— 1978. *Monumental Bali.* The Hague: van Goor Zonen.
Bie, C. W. P. de. 1932. "Verslag van de ontgraving der steenen kamers in de doesoen Tandjoeng Ara, Pasemah-Hoogvlakte". *TITLV* 72:626–35.
Bijlmer, H. J. T. 1929. *Outlines of the anthropology of the Timor-Archipelago.* Weltevreden: G. Kolff.
Bilsborough, A. 1973. "A multivariate study of evolutionary change in the hominid cranial vault and some evolutionary rates". *JHE* 2:387–404.
Binford, L. R. 1983. *In pursuit of the past.* London: Thames and Hudson.
Bintarti, D. D. 1981a. *The bronze object from Kabila, West Sabu.* Aspek-Aspek Arkeologi Indonesia 8. Jakarta: Pusat Penelitian Arkeologi Nasional.
——— 1981b. "Punden berundak di Gunung Padang, Jawa Barat". *Amerta* 4:28–37.
Birdsell, J. B. 1949. "The racial origin of the extinct Tasmanians". *Records of the Queen Victoria Museum, Launceston* 2:105–22.
——— 1967. "Preliminary data on the trihybrid origins of the Australian Aborigines". *APAO* 2:100–55.
——— 1972. *Human evolution.* Chicago: Rand McNally.
——— 1977. "The recalibration of a paradigm for the first peopling of Greater Australia". In Allen, J. *et al.* (eds) 1977:113–68.
Biswas, B. 1973. "Quaternary changes in sea level in the South China Sea". *Bulletin of the Geological Society of Malaysia* 6:229–55.
Blust, R. A. 1974. "Eastern Austronesian: a note". *Working Papers in Linguistics,* vol. 6, no. 4:101–7. Dept. Linguistics, University of Hawaii.
——— 1976. "Austronesian culture history: some linguistic inferences and their relations to the archaeological record". *WA* 8:19–43.

——— 1977. "The Proto-Austronesian pronouns and Austronesian subgrouping: a preliminary report". *Working Papers in Linguistics*, vol. 9, no. 2. Dept. Linguistics, University of Hawaii.

——— 1978. "Eastern Malayo-Polynesian: a subgrouping argument". In Wurm, S. A. and Carrington, L. (eds) 1978, fascicle 1:181–234.

——— 1980. "Early Austronesian social organization: the evidence of language". *CA* 21:205–47.

——— 1981a. "Variation in retention rate among Austronesian languages". Paper presented at the 3rd International Conference on Austronesian Linguistics, Bali, January 1981.

——— 1981b. "The reconstruction of Proto-Malayo-Javanic: an appreciation". *BTLV* 137:456–69.

——— 1981c. "Linguistic evidence for some early Austronesian taboos". *American Anthropologist* 83:285–319.

——— 1982a. "The linguistic value of the Wallace Line". *BTLV* 138:231–50.

——— 1982b. Review of Sneddon 1978. In *Language* 58(4):921–6.

Boaz, N.T. 1977. "Paleoecology of early hominidae in Africa". *Kroeber Anthropological Society Papers* 50:37–62.

——— 1979. "Hominid evolution in eastern Africa during the Pliocene and early Pleistocene". *Annual Review of Anthropology* 8:71–85.

Booth, P. B. and Taylor, H. W. 1976. "Genetic distance analysis of some New Guinea populations: an evaluation". In Kirk, R. L. and Thorne, A. G. (eds) 1976:415–30.

Bosch, F. D. K. 1961. "The problem of the Hindu colonization of Indonesia". In Bosch, F. D. K., *Selected studies in Indonesian archaeology*, pp. 1–22. The Hague: Nijhoff.

Boserup, E. 1965. *The conditions of agricultural growth.* London: Allen and Unwin.

——— 1980. *Population and technological change.* University of Chicago Press.

Bottema, S. and Zeist, W. van 1981. "Palynological evidence for the climatic history of the Near East, 50 000–6000 BP". In *Préhistoire du Levant*, pp. 111–32. Paris: CNRS Colloque International no. 598.

Bowler, J. M., Jones, R., Allen, H., and Thorne, A. G. 1970. "Pleistocene human remains from Australia: a living site and human cremation from Lake Mungo, western New South Wales". *WA* 2:39–60.

Brace C. L. 1964. "A non-racial approach towards the understanding of human diversity". In Montagu, M. (ed.), *The concept of race*, pp. 103–52. New York: Free Press.

——— 1976. "Tooth reduction in the Orient". *AP* 19:203–19.

——— 1980a. "Tooth-size and Austronesian origins". In Naylor, P. (ed.) 1980:167–80.

——— 1980b. "Australian tooth-size clines and the death of a stereotype". *CA* 21:141–64.

Brace, C. L. and Hinton, R. J. 1981. "Oceanic tooth-size variation as a reflection of biological and cultural mixing". *CA* 22:549–69.

Braches, F. and Shutler, R. 1983–4. "Early vertebrates and the theory of the emergence of Java". *Southeast Asian Studies Newsletter* (British Institute in South-East Asia) 13:1–2; 16:1–3.

Brandt, R. W. 1976. "The Hoabinhian of Sumatra: some remarks". *MQRSEA* 2:49–52.

Brain, C. K. 1978. "Some aspects of the South African Australopithecine sites and their bone accumulations". In Jolly, C. (ed.), *Early hominids of Africa*, pp. 131–61. London: Duckworth.

Bronson, B. 1976. Comment to Hutterer, K. L. 1976. *CA* 17:230.

——— 1977. "The earliest farming: demography as cause and consequence". In Reed, C. A. (ed.) 1977:23–48.

——— 1979a. "The archaeology of Sumatra and the problem of Srivijaya". In Smith, R. B. and Watson, W. (eds) 1979:395–405.

——— 1979b. "The late prehistory and early history of central Thailand with special reference to Chansen". In Smith, R. B. and Watson, W. (eds) 1979:315–36.

——— In press. "Radiocarbon dates for Southeast Asia". In Ehrich, R. (ed.), *Chronologies Old World Archaeology.* University of Chicago Press.

Bronson, B. and Asmar, T. 1975. "Prehistoric investigations at Tianko Panjang cave, Sumatra". *AP* 18:128–45.
Bronson, B. and Wisseman, J. 1976. "Palembang as Srivijaya: the lateness of early cities in southern Southeast Asia". *AP* 19:220–39.
Brooks, S. T., Hegler, R. and Brooks, R. H. 1977. "Radiocarbon dating and palaeoserology of a selected burial series from the Great Cave of Niah, Sarawak, Malaysia". *AP* 20:21–31.
Brothwell, D. R. 1960. "Upper Pleistocene human skull from Niah Caves, Sarawak". *SMJ* 9:323–49.
Brown, D. E. 1970. *Brunei: the structure and history of a Bornean Malay sultanate.* Brunei Museum.
——— 1978. "Brunei in contemporary perspective". *SMJ* 47:135–60.
Brues, A. M. 1977. *People and races.* New York: Holt, Rinehart and Winston.
Budd, W. F. 1983. "Changes in the earth's orbital radiation regime". In CLIMANZ, pp. 125–9.
Buettner-Janusch, J. 1966. Review of Coon, C. S. 1966. *AJPA* 25:182–8.
Bulbeck, D. 1978. *Analysis of a skeletal assemblage from Leang Buidane, Talaud Islands, Indonesia.* Unpublished B. A. Hons thesis, Australian National University.
——— 1981. *Continuities in Southeast Asian evolution since the Late Pleistocene.* Unpublished M. A. thesis, Australian National University.
——— 1982. "A re-evaluation of possible evolutionary processes in Southeast Asia since the Late Pleistocene". *BIPPA* 3:1–21.
Burkill, I. H. 1951. "The rise and decline of the greater yam in the service of man". *Advancement of Science* 7:443–8.
Butzer, K. 1976. "Pleistocene climates". In West, R. C. and Haag, W. G. (eds) 1976:27–44.
Campbell, B. G. 1966. *Human evolution.* London: Heinemann.
Capell, A. 1962. "Oceanic linguistics today". *CA* 3:371–428.
——— 1969. *A survey of New Guinea languages.* Sydney University Press.
Carey, I. 1976. *The orang asli.* Kuala Lumpur: Oxford University Press.
Carter, D. J., Audley-Charles, M. G. and Barber, A. J. 1976. "Stratigraphical analysis of island arc-continental margin collision in eastern Indonesia". *Journal of the Geological Society of London* 132:179–98.
Casparis, J. G. de. 1975. *Indonesian palaeography.* Leiden: Brill.
Chai, C. K. 1967. *Taiwan aborigines: a genetic study of tribal variations.* Cambridge, Mass: Harvard University Press.
Chandler, R. F. 1979. *Rice in the tropics.* Boulder, Colorado: Westview Press.
Chang, J. H. 1968. "The agricultural potential of the humid tropics". *Geographical Review* 58:333–61.
Chang, K. C. 1969a. *Fengpitou, Tapenkeng and the prehistory of Taiwan.* New Haven: Yale University Publications in Anthropology 73.
——— 1969b. Review article on *Changpinian: a newly discovered preceramic culture from the agglomerate caves on the east coast of Taiwan*, by Sung Wen-hsun. *AP* 12:133–6.
——— 1970. "Prehistoric archaeology of Taiwan". *AP* 13:59–78.
——— 1972. "Neolithic cultures in the coastal areas of Southeast China". In Barnard, N. (ed.) 1972, vol. 2:431–58.
——— and collaborators. 1974. "Man in the Choshui and Tatu river valleys in central Taiwan". *AP* 17:36–55.
——— 1977a. *The archaeology of ancient China.* Revised 3rd edition. New Haven: Yale University Press.
——— 1977b. "A new prehistoric ceramic style in the southeastern coastal area of China". *AP* 20:179–82.
——— 1981. "The affluent foragers in the coastal areas of China". *Senri Ethnological Studies* 9:177–86.

Chang, T. T. 1976a. "The rice cultures". *Philosophical Transactions of the Royal Society of London*, Series B, 275:143–55.
——— 1976b. "The origin, evolution, cultivation, dissemination and diversification of Asian and African rices". *Euphytica* 25:425–41.
——— 1983. "The origin and early cultures of the cereal grains and food legumes". In Keightley, D. N. (ed.) 1983:65–94.
——— 1985. "Ethnobotany of rice in Insular Southeast Asia". Paper given at the 12th Congress of the Indo-Pacific Prehistory Association, Peñablanca, Philippines.
Chapman, V. 1981. *The Australian-Indonesian archaeological expedition to Sulawesi, 1969.* Unpublished M. A. thesis, Australian National University.
Chappell, J. 1974. "Late Quaternary glacio- and hydro-isostasy, on a layered earth". *Quaternary Research* 4:429–40.
——— 1978. "Theories of Upper Quaternary Ice Ages". In Pittock, A. B. *et al.* (eds), *Climatic change and variability*, pp. 211–25. Cambridge University Press.
——— 1982. "Sea levels and sediments: some features of the context of coastal archaeological sites in the tropics". *Archaeology in Oceania* 17:69–78.
——— 1983. "A revised sea-level curve for the last 30 000 years from Papua New Guinea". *Search* 14:99–101.
Chappell, J. and Thom, B. G. 1977. "Sea levels and coasts". In Allen, J. *et al.* (eds) 1977:275–92.
Chard, C. S. 1974. *Northeast Asia in prehistory.* University of Wisconsin Press.
Chasen, F. N. and Tweedie, M. W. F. (eds). 1940. *Proceedings of the Third Congress of Prehistorians of the Far East.* Singapore: Government Printer.
Chekiang Province and Chekiang Provincial Museum. 1978. "Excavations (first season) in Yu-Yao County, Chekiang Province". *K'ao Ku Hsüeh Pao* 1978, 1:94, 106–7 (English sections).
Chen, Chi-lu. 1968. *Material culture of the Formosan aborigines.* Taipei: Taiwan Museum.
Cheng, Te-k'un. 1969. *Archaeology in Sarawak.* Cambridge University Press.
Cherry, R. 1978. "An analysis of the lithic industry of Buad Island, Samar". *PQCS* 6:3–80.
Child, R. 1964. *Coconuts.* London: Longmans.
Chin, S. C. 1977. "Shifting cultivation — a need for greater understanding". *SMJ* 46:107–28.
Chivers, D. J. 1977. "The lesser apes". In Prince Rainier III and Bourne, G. H. (eds), *Primate conservation*, pp. 539–98. London: Academic Press.
Chretien, C. D. 1956. "Word distribution in southeastern Papua". *Language* 32:88–108.
Christie, A. H. 1979a. "Lin-i, Fu-nan, Java". In Smith, R. B. and Watson, W. (eds) 1979:281–7.
——— 1979b. "The megalithic problem in South East Asia". In Smith, R. B. and Watson, W. (eds) 1979:242–52.
Clark, J. A., Farrell, W. E. and Peltier, W. R. 1978. "Global changes in postglacial sea-levels: a numerical calculation". *Quaternary Research* 9:265–87.
Clarke, B. 1975. "Causes of biological diversity". *Scientific American* 233(2):50–60.
Clarke, W. C. 1976. "Maintenance of agriculture and human habitats within the tropical forest ecosystem". *Human Ecology* 4:247–59.
Clason, A. T. 1980. "Mesolithic hunter-gatherers in Sulawesi". *BIPPA* 2:65–8.
——— In press. "The faunal remains of Paso in northern Sulawesi". *MQRSEA.*
CLIMANZ. 1983. *Proceedings of the First CLIMANZ Conference.* Canberra: Department of Biogeography and Geomorphology, Australian National University.
CLIMAP. 1976. "The surface of the Ice-Age earth". *Science* 191:1131–7.
Climate and Rice. 1976. *Climate and Rice.* Los Banños, Philippines: International Rice Research Institute.
Clutton Brock, J. 1959. "Niah's Neolithic dog". *SMJ* 9:143–5.
Coedes, G. 1975. *The Indianized states of Southeast Asia.* Canberra: Australian National University Press.

Cohen, M. N. 1977. *The food crisis in prehistory.* New Haven: Yale University Press.

——— 1980. "Speculations on the evolution of density measurement and population regulation in *Homo sapiens*". In Cohen, M. N., Malpass, R. S. and Klein, H. G. (eds), *Biosocial mechanisms of population regulation*, pp. 275–303. New Haven: Yale University Press.

Colani, M. 1935. *Mégalithes du Haut-Laos.* 2 volumes. Publications de l'École Française d'Extrême-Orient nos 25, 26.

Cole, F. C. 1945. *Peoples of Malaysia.* New York: Van Nostrand.

Collier, W. L. 1979. *Social and economic aspects of tidal swamp land development in Indonesia.* Canberra: Development Studies Centre Occasional Paper 15, Australian National University.

Collings, H. D. 1936. "Report of an archaeological excavation in Kedah, Malay Peninsula". *BRM* Series B, vol. 1, no. 1:5–16.

——— 1937a. "An excavation at Bukit Chuping, Perlis". *BRM* Series B, vol. 1, no. 2:94–119.

——— 1937b. "Recent finds of Iron Age sites in southern Perak and Selangor". *BRM* vol. 1, no. 2:75–92.

Condominas, M. 1980. "The Mnong Gar of Vietnam". In Harris, D. R. (ed.) 1980:209–51.

Conklin, H. C. 1980. *Ethnographic atlas of Ifugao.* New Haven: Yale University Press.

Coon, C. S. 1962. *The origin of races.* London: Jonathan Cape.

——— 1966. *The living races of man.* London: Jonathan Cape.

Cooper, J. M. 1941. *Temporal sequence and the marginal cultures.* Washington DC: Catholic University of America, Anthropological Series 10.

Coursey, D. G. 1972. "The civilizations of the yam". *APAO* 7:215–33.

——— 1976. "Yams". In Simmonds, N. W. (ed.), *Crop plant evolution*, pp. 70–4. London: Longmans.

Coutts, P. J. F. and Wesson, J. P. 1980. "Models of Philippine prehistory: a review of the flaked stone industries". *PQCS* 8:203–59.

Covey, C. 1984. "The earth's orbit and the Ice Ages". *Scientific American* 250(2):42–50.

Cowan, H. J. K. 1965. "On Melanesian and the origin of Austronesian". *CA* 6:217.

Cranbrook, Earl of (formerly Lord Medway). 1979. "A review of domesticated pig remains from archaeological sites in Sarawak". *SMJ* 48:79–86.

——— 1981. "The vertebrate faunas". In Whitmore, T. C. (ed.) 1981:57–69.

——— In press a. "A review of fossil and prehistoric remains of rhinoceroses in Borneo". *Sabah Museum Annals.*

——— In press b. "A note on canid remains from the Madai caves, Kunak, provisionally identified as the dhole". *Sabah Museum Annals.*

Cronin, T. M., Szabo, B. J., Ager, T. A., Hazel, J. E. and Owens, J. P. 1981. Quaternary climates and sea levels of the U.S. Atlantic coastal plain". *Science* 211:233–40.

Crystal, E. 1974. "Contemporary megalithic practices of the Sa'dan Toraja of Sulawesi, Indonesia". In Donovan, C. B. and Clelow, C. W. (eds), *Ethnoarchaeology*, pp. 117–28. Monograph 4, Archaeological Survey, Institute of Archaeology, University of California, Los Angeles.

Cunningham, C. E. 1967. "Soba: an Atoni village of West Timor". In Koentjaraningrat (ed.), *Villages in Indonesia*, pp. 63–89. New York: Cornell University Press.

Curtis, G. H. 1981. "Establishing a relevant time scale in anthropological and archaeological research". *Philosophical Transactions of the Royal Society of London*, Series B, 292:7–19.

Dahl, O. C. 1951. *Malagache et Maanyan.* Oslo: Egede Instituttet.

——— 1973. *Proto-Austronesian.* Scandinavian Institute of Asian Studies Monograph 15.

Dalrymple, R. E. 1984. "The *waruga* burial tombs of North Sulawesi". *Hemisphere* 28(5):267–72.

Darlington, P. J. 1957. *Zoogeography: the geographical distribution of animals.* New York: Wiley.
Davis, S. J. H. 1982. "Climate change and the advent of domestication". *Paléorient* 8(2):5–16.
Day, M. H. 1977. *Guide to fossil man.* 3rd edition, University of Chicago Press.
Day, M. H. and Molleson, T. I. 1973. "The Trinil Femora". In Day, M. H. (ed.), *Human evolution*, pp. 127–54. London: Taylor and Francis.
Dentan, R. K. 1968. *The Semai.* New York: Holt, Rinehart and Winston.
Deraniyagala, S. 1972. "The citadel of Anuradhapura 1969: excavations in the Gedige area". *Ancient Ceylon* 2:48–169.
Dewar, R. E. 1977. *Archaeology as ecological anthropology in central Taiwan.* Ann Arbor: University Microfilms International.
Diamond, J. M. 1977. "Distributional strategies". In Allen, J. *et al.* (eds) 1977, pp. 295–315.
Dickerson, R. E. 1928. *Distribution of life in the Philippines.* Manila: Bureau of Printing.
Diffloth, G. 1974. "Austro-Asiatic languages". *Encyclopaedia Britannica* 15th edition, *Macropaedia* 2:480–4.
——— 1979. "Aslian languages and Southeast Asian prehistory". *FMJ* 24:3–18.
Dikshit, M. G. 1952. "Beads from Ahichchhatra, U.P." *Ancient India* 8:33–63.
Dobby, E. H. G. 1976. *Southeast Asia.* 11th Edition. University of London Press.
Donk, J. van. 1976. "O^{18} record of the Atlantic Ocean for the entire Pleistocene epoch". *Geological Society of America Memoir* 145:147–64.
Doran, E. Jr. 1981. *Wangka: Austronesian canoe origins.* College Station: Texas A&M University Press.
Dortch, C. E. 1977. "Early and late stone industrial phases in Western Australia". In Wright, R. V. S. (ed.) 1977:104–32.
Dortch, C. E. and Bordes, F. 1977. "Blade and Levallois technology in Western Australian prehistory". *Quartär* 27–8:1–20.
Downs, R. E. 1955. "Head hunting in Indonesia". *BTLV* 111:40–70.
——— 1956. *The religion of the Bare'e-speaking Toradja of central Celebes.* The Hague: Excelsior.
Dubois, C. 1944. *The people of Alor.* Minneapolis: University of Minnesota Press.
Duff, R. 1970. *Stone adzes of Southeast Asia.* Christchurch: Canterbury Museum Bulletin 3.
Dunn, F. L. 1964. "Excavations at Gua Kechil, Pahang". *JMBRAS* 37(2):87–124.
——— 1966. "Radiocarbon dating of the Malayan Neolithic". *Proceedings of the Prehistoric Society* 32:352–3.
——— 1975. *Rain forest collectors and traders.* Malaysian Branch, Royal Asiatic Society, Monograph 5.
Dunn, F. L. and Dunn, D. F. 1977. "Maritime adaptations and the exploitation of marine resources in Sundaic Southeast Asian prehistory". *MQRSEA* 3:1–28.
Duplessy, J. C. 1981. "Oxygen isotope studies and Quaternary marine climates". In Berger, A. (ed.) 1981:181–92.
——— 1982. "Glacial to interglacial contrasts in the northern Indian Ocean". *Nature* 295:494–8.
Duy, N. and Quyen, N. Q. 1966. "Early Neolithic skulls in Quynh Van, Nghê An, North Vietnam". *Vertebrata Palasiatica* 10:49–57.
Dyen, I. 1962. "The lexicostatistical classification of the Malayopolynesian languages". *Language* 38:38–46.
——— 1965a. *A lexicostatistical classification of the Austronesian languages.* International Journal of American Linguistics Memoir 19.
——— 1965b. "Formosan evidence for some new Proto-Austronesian phonemes". *Lingua* 14:285–305.
——— 1971a. "The Austronesian languages and Proto-Austronesian". In Seboek, T. (ed.) 1971, vol. 1:5–54.

——— 1971b. "The Austronesian languages of Formosa". In Seboek, T. (ed.) 1971, vol. 1:168–99.

——— 1971c. "The Chamic languages". In Seboek, T. (ed.) 1971, vol. 1:200–10.

——— 1971d. "Malagasy". In Seboek, T. (ed.) 1971, vol. 1:211–39.

——— 1975. *Linguistic subgrouping and lexicostatistics.* The Hague: Mouton.

Earle, T. 1978. *Economic and social organization of a complex chiefdom: the Halelea district, Kaua'i, Hawaii.* Ann Arbor: University of Michigan Museum of Anthropology, Anthropological Papers 63.

——— 1980. "Prehistoric irrigation in the Hawaiian Islands". *APAO* 15:1–28.

Ellen, R. F. 1978. *Nuaulu settlement and economy.* The Hague: Nijhoff.

Ellen, R. F. and Glover, I. C. 1974. "Pottery manufacture and trade in the central Moluccas, Indonesia". *Man* (new series) 9:353–79.

Endicott, K. 1979a. *Batek Negrito religion.* Oxford: Clarendon Press.

——— 1979b. "The hunting methods of the Batek Negritos of Malaysia". *Canberra Anthropology* 2(2):7–22.

Evans, I. H. N. 1918. "Preliminary report on cave explorations near Lenggong, Upper Perak". *JFMSM* 7(4):227–34.

——— 1923. *Studies in religion, folk-lore and custom in British North Borneo and the Malay Peninsula.* Cambridge: Cambridge University Press.

——— 1928a. "On a find of stone implements associated with pottery". *JFMSM* 12(5):137–5, 143–4.

——— 1928b. "On slab-built graves in Perak". *JFMSM* 12(5):111–20.

——— 1931a. "Excavations at Nyong, Tembeling river". *JFMSM* 15(2):51–62.

——— 1931b. "A further slab-built grave at Sungkei, Perak". *JFMSM* 15(2):63–4.

——— 1932. "Excavations at Tanjong Rawa, Kuala Selinsing, Perak". *JFMSM* 15(3):79–134.

Fernandez, C. A. and Lynch, F. 1972. "The Tasaday: cave-dwelling food-gatherers of South Cotobato, Mindanao". *Philippine Sociological Review* 20:277–330.

Ferrell, R. 1969. *Taiwan aboriginal groups: problems in cultural and linguistic classification.* Taipei: Institute of Ethnology, Academia Sinica, Monograph 17.

——— 1980. "Phonological subgrouping of Formosan languages". In Naylor, P. (ed.) 1980:241–54.

Fink, J. and Kukla, G. 1977. "Pleistocene climates in central Europe: at least 17 interglacials after the Olduvai event". *Quaternary Research* 7:363–71.

Fitzgerald, C. P. 1972. *The southern expansion of the Chinese people.* Canberra: Australian National University Press.

Fix, A. 1984. "Genetic structure of the Semai". In Crawford, M. H. and Mielke, J. H. (eds), *Current developments in anthropological genetics*, Vol.2, pp. 179–204. New York: Plenum.

Flenley, J. R. 1979. *The equatorial rainforest: a geological history.* London: Butterworths.

——— 1985. "Man's impact on the vegetation of Southeast Asia: the pollen evidence". In Misra, V. N. and Bellwood, P. S. (eds) 1985:297–305.

Flenley, J. R. and Morley, R. J. 1978. "A minimum age for the deglaciation of Mt Kinabalu, East Malaysia". *MQRSEA* 4:57–62.

Flint, R. F. 1971. *Glacial and Quaternary geology.* New York: Wiley.

Flohn, H. 1981. "Tropical climate variations during Late Pleistocene and Early Holocene". In Berger, A. (ed.) 1981:233–42.

Fogg, W. H. 1983. "Swidden cultivation of foxtail millet by Taiwan aborigines". In Keightley, D. N. (ed.) 1983:95–116.

Foley, W. A. 1980. "History of migrations in Indonesia as seen by a linguist". In Fox, J. J. (ed.) 1980:75–80.

Fontaine, H. 1979. "A note on the Iron Age in southern Vietnam". *JHKAS* 8:91–8.

——— 1980. "On the extent of the Sa Huynh culture in continental Southeast Asia". *AP* 23:67–70.

Fontaine, H. and Hoang, Thi Than. 1975. "Nouvelle note sur le champ de jarres funéraires de Phu Hoa". *Bulletin de la Société des Etudes Indochinoises* 51:7–74.

Forman, S. 1977. "East Timor: exchange and political hierarchy at the time of the European discoveries". In Hutterer, K. L. (ed.) 1977:97–112.

Forrest, T. 1779. *A voyage to New Guinea and the Moluccas from Balambangan.* London: G. Scott.

Forth, G. R. 1981. *Rindi.* The Hague: Nijhoff.

Fox, J. J. 1977a. *Harvest of the palm.* Cambridge (Mass.): Harvard University Press.

——— 1977b. "Notes on the southern voyages and settlements of the Sama-Bajau". *BTLV* 133:459–65.

——— (ed.). 1980. *Indonesia: the making of a culture.* Canberra: Research School of Pacific Studies.

——— 1985. "Possible models of early Austronesian social organisation", Paper presented at the 12th Congress of the Indo-Pacific Prehistory Association, Peñablanca, Philippines.

Fox, R. B. 1953. "The Pinatubo Negritos". *Philippine Journal of Science* 81:173–414.

——— 1970. *The Tabon Caves.* Manila: National Museum Monograph 1.

——— 1976. "Notes on the stone tools of the Tasaday". In Yen, D. E. and Nance, J. (eds) 1976:3–12.

——— 1978. "The Philippine Palaeolithic". In Ikawa-Smith, F. (ed.) 1978:59–85.

——— 1979. "The Philippines during the first millennium BC". In Smith, R. B. and Watson, W. (eds) 1979: 227–41.

Frake, C. O. 1956. "Malayo-Polynesian land tenure". *American Anthropologist* 58:170–3.

Francisco, J. R. 1965. "On the date of the coming of the Indian influences in the Philippines". *Philippine Historical Review* 1:136–52.

Franssen, C. J. H. 1941. Praehistorische werktuigen uit de omgeving van Leuwiliang in de Residentie buitenzorg". *TITLV* 81:531–44.

Freeman, D. 1955. *Iban agriculture.* London: Her Majesty's Stationery Office.

——— 1960. "The Iban of western Borneo". In Murdock, G. P. (ed.) 1960b:65–87.

——— 1970. *Report on the Iban.* London: Athlone Press.

——— 1981. *Some reflections on the nature of Iban society.* Canberra: Australian National University, Department of Anthropology.

Freeman, L. 1977. "Palaeolithic archaeology and palaeoanthropology in China". In Howells, W. W. and Tsuchitani, P. J. (eds) 1977:79–114.

Fried, M. 1983. "Tribe to state or state to tribe in ancient China?". In Keightley, D. N. (ed.) 1983:467–93.

Friedlaender, J. L. 1975. *Patterns of human variation.* Cambridge (Mass.): Harvard University Press.

Gajdusek, D. C. 1970. "Psychological characteristics of Stone Age man". *Engineering and Science* 33:26–33, 56–62.

Gates, R. R. 1961. "The Melanesian dwarf tribe of Aiome, New Guinea". *Acta Geneticae Medicae et Gemellologiae* (Rome) 10(3):277–311.

Geertz, C. 1963. *Agricultural Involution.* Berkeley: University of California Press.

——— 1972. "The wet and the dry: traditional irrigation in Bali and Morocco". *Human Ecology* 1:23–39.

Geertz, H. 1963. "Indonesian cultures and communities". In McVey, R. (ed.), *Indonesia*, pp. 24–96. New Haven: Yale University Press.

Geyh, M. A., Kudrass, H–R., and Streif, H. 1979. "Sea level changes during the Late Pleistocene and Holocene in the Strait of Malacca". *Nature* 278:441–3.

Giresse, P. and Davies, O. 1980. "High sea levels during the last glaciation". *Quaternaria* 22:211–36.
Glinka, J. 1978. *Gestalt und Herkunft: Beitrag zur Anthropologischen Gliederung Indonesiens.* St Augustine bei Bonn: Studia Instituti Anthropos 35.
——— 1981. "Racial history of Indonesia". In Suzuki, H. (ed.), *Rassengeschichte der Mensheit 8, Lieferung Asien I: Japan, Indonesien, Ozeanien*, pp. 79–113. München: Oldenbourg.
Glover, I. C. 1971. "Prehistoric research in Timor". In Mulvaney, D. J. and Golson, J. (eds), *Aboriginal man and environment in Australia*, pp. 158–81. Canberra: Australian National University Press.
——— 1972a. *Excavations in Timor.* 2 volumes. Unpublished PhD thesis, Australian National University.
——— 1972b. "Alfred Buhler's excavations in Timor: a re-evaluation". *Art and Archaeology Research Papers* 2:117–42. Institute of Archaeology, University of London.
——— 1976. "Ulu Leang cave, Maros: a preliminary sequence of post-Pleistocene cultural development in South Sulawesi". *Archipel* 11:113–54.
——— 1977a. "The late Stone Age in eastern Indonesia". *WA* 9:42–61.
——— 1977b. "Prehistoric plant remains from Southeast Asia, with special reference to rice". In *South Asian Archaeology 1977*, pp. 7–37. Naples: Istituto Universitario Orientale.
——— 1978a. "Survey and excavation in the Maros district, South Sulawesi, Indonesia". *BIPPA* 1:60–102.
——— 1978b. "Report on a visit to archaeological sites near Medan, Sumatra". *BIPPA* 1:56–60.
——— 1979. "The late prehistoric period in Indonesia". In Smith, R. B. and Watson, W. (eds) 1979:167–84.
——— 1981. "Leang Burung 2: an Upper Palaeolithic rock shelter in South Sulawesi, Indonesia". *MQRSEA* 6:1–38.
——— 1983. "Excavations at Ban Don Ta Phet, Kanchanaburi Province, Thailand 1980:1". *Southeast Asian Studies Newsletter* (British Institute in South-East Asia) 10:1–3.
——— 1985. "Some problems relating to the domestication of rice in Asia". In Misra, V. N. and Bellwood, P. S. (eds) 1985: 265–74.
Glover, I. C. and Glover, E. A. 1970. "Pleistocene flaked stone tools from Timor and Flores". *Mankind* 7:88–90.
Glover, I. C. and Presland, G. 1985. "Microliths in Indonesian flaked stone industries". In Misra, V. N. and Bellwood, P. S. (eds) 1985:185–95.
Glover, I. C., Charoenwongsa, P., Alvey, B. and Kamnounket, N. 1984. "The cemetery of Ban Don Ta Phet, Thailand: results from the 1980–1 excavation season". In Allchin, B. (ed.), *South Asian Archaeology 1981*, pp. 319–30. Cambridge University Press.
Gohara, Y. 1976. "Climatic fluctuations and sea level changes during the latest Pleistocene and early Holocene". *Pacific Geology* 11:87–98.
Goloubew, V. 1929. "L'age du bronze au Tonkin". *Bulletin de l'École Française d'Extrême-Orient* 29:1–46.
Golson, J. 1977. "No room at the top: agricultural intensification in the New Guinea Highlands". In Allen, J. *et al.* (eds) 1977:601–38.
——— 1985. "Agricultural origins in Southeast Asia: a view from the east". In Misra, V. N. and Bellwood, P. S. (eds) 1985:307–14.
Gonda, J. 1973. *Sanskrit in Indonesia.* 2nd edition. New Delhi: International Academy of Indian Culture.
Goodenough, W. 1955. "A problem in Malayo-Polynesian social organization". *American Anthropologist* 57:71–83.
Gorman, C. F. 1970. "Excavations at Spirit Cave, North Thailand: some interim interpretations". *AP* 13:79–108.

—— 1971. "The Hoabinhian and after: subsistence patterns in Southeast Asia during the latest Pleistocene and early Recent periods". *WA* 2:300–20.

—— 1977. "A priori models and Thai prehistory". In Reed, C. A. (ed.) 1977:321–56.

Gorman, C. F. and Pisit Charoenwongsa. 1978. "From domestication to urbanization: a Southeast Asian view of chronology, configuration and change". To appear in *Origins of agriculture and technology; west or east Asia?* Copenhagen: Scandinavian Institute of Asian Studies.

Goudie, A. S. 1983. *Environmental change.* Oxford: Clarendon Press.

Gould, R. A. 1977. "Ethnoarchaeology; or where do models come from?. In Wright, R. V. S. (ed.) 1977:162–8.

—— 1980. *Living archaeology.* Cambridge: Cambridge University Press.

Grace, G. W. 1959. *The position of the Polynesian languages within the Austronesian (Malayo-Polynesian) family.* Memoir no. 16, International Journal of American Linguistics.

—— 1964. "Movements of the Malayo-Polynesians 1500 BC–500 AD; the linguistic evidence". *CA* 5:361–8, 403–4.

—— 1967. "Effect of heterogeneity on the lexicostatistical test list: the case of Rotuman". In Highland, G. A., Force, R. W., Howard, A., Kelly, M. and Sinoto, Y. H. (eds), *Polynesian culture history*, pp. 289–302. Honolulu: Bishop Museum.

—— 1981. "Indirect inheritance in the aberrant Melanesian languages". In Hollyman, J. and Pawley, A. K. (eds) 1981:255–68.

Green, R. C. 1979. "Lapita". In Jennings, J. D. (ed.), *The prehistory of Polynesia*, pp. 27–60. Cambridge (Mass.): Harvard University Press.

—— 1981. "Location of the Proto-Polynesian homeland: a continuing problem". In Hollyman, J. and Pawley, A. K. (eds) 1981:133–58.

—— 1982. "Models for the Lapita cultural complex". *New Zealand Journal of Archaeology* 4:7–19.

Greenberg, J. H. 1971. "The Indo-Pacific hypothesis". In Seboek, T. (ed.) 1971:807–76.

Grist, D. H. 1975. *Rice.* 5th edition. London: Longmans.

Groves, C. P. 1976. "The origin of the mammalian fauna of Sulawesi". *Zeitschrift für Säugetierkunde* 41:201–16.

—— 1981. *Ancestors for the pigs.* Canberra: Australian National University, Department of Prehistory.

—— 1984. "Of mice and men and pigs in the Indo-Australian Archipelago". *Canberra Anthropology* 7:1–19.

Gudschinsky, S. 1964. "The ABC's of lexicostatistics (glottochronology)". In Hymes, D. (ed.), *Language in culture and society*, pp. 612–23. New York: Harper and Row.

Gunadi Nitihaminoto, Harry Truman Simandjuntak, Suwarno, Timbul Hartono and Budijanto. 1978. *Laporan ekskavasi Gunung Piring (Lombok Selatan). BPA* 17.

Haile, N. S. 1968. "The Quaternary geomorphic history of North Sarawak". *SMJ* 16:277–81.

—— 1971. "Quaternary shorelines in West Malaysia and adjacent parts of the Sunda shelf". *Quaternaria* 15:333–43.

—— 1973. "The geomorphology and geology of the northern part of the Sunda shelf". *Pacific Geology* 6:73–90.

—— 1978. "Reconnaisance palaeomagnetic results from Sulawesi, Indonesia". *Tectonophysics* 46:77–85.

Hall, D. G. E. 1968. *A history of Southeast Asia.* 3rd edition. London: Macmillan.

Hall, K. R. 1976. "State and statecraft in early Srivijaya". In Hall, K. R. and Whitmore, J. K. (eds), *Explorations in early Southeast Asian history*, pp. 61–105. Ann Arbor: Michigan Papers on South and Southeast Asia 11.

—— 1977. "The coming of Islam to the archipelago: a reassessment". In Hutterer, K. L. (ed.) 1977:213–32.

——— 1980. "The origin of maritime trade in Southeast Asia". *The Elmira Review* 2:35–43.

——— 1982. "The 'Indianization' of Funan". *JSEAS* 13:81–106.

Hallam, S. J. 1977. "The relevance of Old World archaeology to the first entry of man into the New World: colonization as seen from the Antipodes". *Quaternary Research* 8:128–48.

Hamilton, A. 1976. "The significance of patterns of distribution as shown by forest plants and animals in tropical Africa for the reconstruction of Upper Pleistocene palaeoenvironments". *Palaeoecology of Africa* 9:63–97.

Hamilton, W. 1979. *Tectonics of the Indonesian region.* U.S. Geological Survey, Professional Paper 1078.

Hanbury-Tenison, R. 1980. *Mulu: the rainforest.* London: Weidenfeld and Nicholson.

Haq, B. K., Berggren, W. A. and Couvering, J. A. van. 1977. "Corrected age of the Pliocene–Pleistocene boundary". *Nature* 269:483–8.

Harris, D. R. 1977. "Alternative pathways toward agriculture". In Reed, C. A. (ed.) 1977:179–244.

——— (ed.) 1980. *Human ecology in savanna environments.* London: Academic Press.

Harris, T. 1979. *Prehistoric pottery from Batu Edjaya, South-west Sulawesi: a descriptive analysis.* Unpublished B. A. Hons thesis, Australian National University.

Harrisson, B. 1967. "A classification of Stone Age burials from Niah Great Cave, Sarawak". *SMJ* 15:126–200.

——— 1968. "A Niah Stone-Age jar-burial C14 dated". *SMJ* 16:64–6.

Harrisson, B. and Harrisson, T. 1968. "Magala — a series of Neolithic and Metal Age burial grottos at Sekaloh, Niah, Sarawak". *JMBRAS* 41(2):148–75.

Harrisson, T. 1957. "The Great Cave of Niah". *Man* 57:161–6.

——— 1958. "Niah: a history of prehistory". *SMJ* 8:549–95.

——— 1959. "New archaeological and ethnological results from Niah Caves, Sarawak". *Man* 59:1–8.

——— 1962. "Borneo death". *BTLV* 118:1–41.

——— 1965. "A stone and bronze tool cave in Sabah". *Journal of the Sabah Society* 4:151–59.

——— 1970a. "The prehistory of Borneo". *AP* 13:17–46.

——— 1970b. *The Malays of South West Sarawak before Malaysia.* London: Macmillan.

——— 1971. "Prehistoric double-spouted vessels excavated from Niah caves, Borneo". *JMBRAS* 44(2):35–78.

——— 1973. "Megalithic evidences in East Malaysia: an introductory summary". *JMBRAS* 46(1):123–39.

——— 1975a. "Tampan: Malaysia's Palaeolithic reconsidered". *MQRSEA* 1:53–70.

——— 1975b. "Early dates for 'seated' burial and burial matting at Niah caves, Sarawak". *AP* 18:161–5.

——— 1978. "Recent status and problems for Palaeolithic studies in Borneo and adjacent areas". In Ikawa-Smith, F. (ed.) 1978:37–57.

Harrisson, T. and Harrisson, B. 1971. *The prehistory of Sabah.* Kota Kinabalu: Sabah Society.

Harrisson, T. and Medway, Lord. 1962. "A first classification of prehistoric bone and tooth artefacts". *SMJ* 10:335–62.

Harrisson, T., Hooijer, D. A. and Medway, Lord. 1961. "An extinct giant pangolin and associated mammals from Niah Caves, Sarawak". *Nature* 189:166.

Harvey, M. 1982. "Subgroups in Austronesian". In Halim, A., Carrington, L. and Wurm, S. A. (eds), *Papers from the Third International Conference on Austronesian Linguistics*, Vol. 2, pp. 47–99. Canberra: Pacific Linguistics Series C. No. 75.

Hassan, F. A. 1977. "The dynamics of agricultural origins in Palestine". In Reed, C. A. (ed.) 1977:589–610.

Haudricourt, A. G. 1954. "Les origines asiatiques des langues Malayo-Polynésiennes". *Journal de la Société des Océanistes* 10:180–3.

——— 1965. "Problems of Austronesian comparative philology". *Lingua* 14:315–29.

Ha Van Tan. 1978. "The Hoabinhian in the context of Vietnam". *Vietnamese Studies* 46:127–97.

——— 1980. "Nouvelles recherches préhistoriques et protohistoriques au Viêtnam". *Bulletin de l'École Française d'Extrême-Orient* 68:113–54.

——— 1985a. "Late Pleistocene climate in Southeast Asia: new data from Vietnam". Paper given at the 12th Congress of the Indo-Pacific Prehistory Association, Peñablanca, Philippines.

——— 1985b. "Prehistoric pottery in Vietnam and its relationships with Southeast Asia". Paper given at the 12th Congress of the Indo-Pacific Prehistory Association, Peñablanca, Philippines.

Hayden, B. 1977a. "Stone tool functions in the Western Desert". In Wright, R. V. S. (ed.) 1977:178–88.

——— 1977b. "Sticks and stones and ground edge axes: the Upper Palaeolithic in Southeast Asia?". In Allen, J. *et al.* (eds) 1977:73–109.

——— 1979. *Palaeolithic reflections.* Canberra: Australian Institute of Aboriginal Studies.

——— 1981. "Research and development in the Stone Age: technological transitions among hunter-gatherers". *CA* 22:519–48.

Heaney, L. 1985. "Zoogeographic evidence for Middle and Late Pleistocene landbridges in the Philippines". Paper given at the 12th Congress of the Indo-Pacific Prehistory Association, Peñablanca, Philippines.

Heekeren, H. R. van. 1931. Megalithische overblijfselen in Besoeki, Java". *Djawa* 11:1–18.

——— 1935–6. "Prehistorisch grottenonderzoek in Basoeki (Java)". *Djawa* 15:123–9, 16:187–93.

——— 1937. "Ontdekking van het Hoa-binhien op Java". *TITLV* 77:269–76.

——— 1949. "Rapport over de ontgraving van de Bola Batoe, nabij Badjo (Bone, Zuid-Celebes)". *Oudheidkundig Verslag* for 1941–7, pp. 89–108.

——— 1950a. "Rapport over de ontgraving te Kamasi, Kalumpang (West Central-Celebes)". *Oudheidkundig Verslag* for 1949, pp. 26–48.

——— 1950b. "Rock paintings and other prehistoric discoveries near Maros (South West Celebes)". *Laporan Tahunan* for 1950: 22–35. Jakarta: Dinas Purbakala Republik Indonesia.

——— 1955. "Proto-historic sarcophagi on Bali". *Berita Dinas Purbakala* 2:1–15. Jakarta.

——— 1956a. "Notes on a proto-historic urn-burial site at Anjar, Java". *Anthropos* 51:194–201.

——— 1956b. *The urn cemetery at Melolo, East Sumba.* Berita Dinas Purbakala no. 3, Jakarta.

——— 1958. *The Bronze–Iron Age of Indonesia.* The Hague: Nijhoff.

——— 1972. *The Stone Age of Indonesia.* 2nd edition. The Hague: Nijhoff.

Heekeren, H. R. van and Knuth, E. 1967. *Archaeological excavations in Thailand. Vol. 1: Sai Yok.* Copenhagen: Munksgaard.

Heffernan, K. 1980. *Molluscan resources and Talaud economy: ecological and cultural parameters in the study of refuse.* Unpublished B. A. Hons thesis, Australian National University.

Heine Geldern, R. von. 1937. "L'art prébouddique de la Chine et de l'Asie du Sud-Est et son influence en Océanie". *Revue des Arts Asiatiques.* 11:177–206.

——— 1945. "Prehistoric research in the Netherlands Indies". In Honig, P. and Verdoorn, F. (eds) 1945:129–67.

——— 1947. "The drum named Makalamau". *India Antiqua,* 1947:167–79. Leiden.

Henriksen, M. A. 1982. "The first excavated prehistoric house site in Southeast Asia". In Izikowitz, K. G. and Sørensen, P. (eds), *The house in East and Southeast Asia,* pp. 17–24. Copenhagen: Scandinavian Institute of Asian Studies Monograph 30.

Henry, D. O. 1983. "Adaptive evolution within the epipalaeolithic of the Near East". In Wendorf, F. and Close, A. E. (eds), *Advances in World Archaeology,* Vol. 2, pp. 99–160, New York, Academic Press.

Henry, D. O., Leroi-Gourhan, A. and Davis, S. 1981. "The excavation of Hayonim Terrace". *Journal of Archaeological Science* 8:33–58.

Hickson, S. J. 1889. *A naturalist in North Celebes.* London: J. Murray.

Higham, C. F. W. 1983. "The Ban Chiang culture in wider perspective". *Proceedings of the British Academy* 69:229–61.

Higham, C. F. W. and Kijngam, A. 1979. "Ban Chiang and northeast Thailand: the palaeoenvironment and economy". *Journal of Archaeological Science* 6:211–33.

Hill, R. D. 1977. *Rice in Malaya.* Kuala Lumpur: Oxford University Press.

Hislop, J. A. 1954. "Notes on the migration of bearded pig". *FMJ* 1 and 2:134–7.

Ho, P. T. 1977. "The indigenous origins of Chinese agriculture". In Reed, C. A. (ed.) 1977:413–84.

Hoang, X. C. and Bui, V. T. 1980. "The Dong Son culture and cultural centres in the Metal Age of Vietnam". *AP* 23:55–66.

Hoffman, C. L. 1981. "Some notes on the origin of the 'Punan' of Borneo". *Borneo Research Bulletin* 13(2):71–4.

Holloway, R. L. 1980. "Indonesian 'Solo' (Ngandong) endocranial reconstructions". *AJPA* 53:285–95.

——— 1981. "The Indonesian *Homo erectus* brain casts revisited". *AJPA* 55:503–21.

Hollyman, J. and Pawley, A. K. (eds). 1981. *Studies in Pacific languages and cultures.* Auckland: Linguistic Society of New Zealand.

Holmer, N. M. 1968. "Two viewpoints bearing on linguistic affinity in Southeast Asia". *Philippine Journal of Science* 97:93–113.

Honig, P. and Verdoorn, F. (eds). 1945. *Science and scientists in the Netherlands Indies.* New York: Board for the Netherlands, Surinam and Curaçao.

Hooijer, D. A. 1950a. *Man and other mammals from Toalean sites in southwestern Celebes.* Verhandelingen der Koninklijke Nederlandse Akademie van Wetenschappen, Afdeling Natuurkunde, Tweede Sectie 46, no. 2, pp. 1–158.

——— 1950b. "Fossil evidence of Australomelanesian migrations in Malaysia?". *South Western Journal of Anthropology* 6:416–22.

——— 1952. "Australomelanesian migrations once more". *South Western Journal of Anthropology* 8:472–7.

——— 1956. "The lower boundary of the Pleistocene in Java and the age of *Pithecanthropus*". *Quaternaria* 3:5–10.

——— 1963. "Further 'Hell' mammals from Niah". *SMJ* 11:196–200.

——— 1967–8. "Indo-Australian pygmy elephants". *Genetica* 38:143–62.

——— 1968. "The Middle Pleistocene fauna of Java". In Kurth, G. (ed.), *Evolution und Hominization*, pp. 86–90. 2nd edition. Stuttgart: Gustav Fischer.

——— 1975. "Quaternary mammals east and west of Wallace's Line". *MQRSEA* 1:37–46.

——— 1981. "What, if anything new, is *Stegodon sumbaensis Sartono*?". *MQRSEA* 6:89–90.

——— 1982. "The extinct giant land tortoise and the pygmy stegodont of Indonesia". *MQRSEA* 7:171–6.

Hoop, A. N. van der. 1932. *Megalithic remains in South-Sumatra.* Zutphen: Thieme.

——— 1935. "Steenkistgraven in Goenoeng Kidoel". *TITLV* 75:83–100.

——— 1940. "A prehistoric site near Lake Kerinchi, Sumatra". In Chasen, F. N. and Tweedie, M. W. F. (eds) 1940:200–4.

Hope, G. S. 1980. "Historical influences in the New Guinea flora". In Royen, P. van (ed.), *The Alpine flora of New Guinea*, pp. 223–48. Vaduz: J. Cramer.

Hope, G. S. and Spriggs, M. 1982. "A preliminary pollen sequence from Aneityum Island, southern Vanuatu". *BIPPA* 3:88–94; 4:v.

Hose, C. 1926. *Natural man: a record from Borneo.* London: Macmillan.

Hose, C. and McDougall, W. 1912. *The pagan tribes of Borneo.* 2 volumes. London: Macmillan.

Howells, W. W. 1970. "Anthropometric grouping analysis of Pacific peoples." *APAO* 5:192–217.

——— 1973a. *Evolution of the genus Homo.* Reading (Mass.): Addison-Wesley.

——— 1973b. *Cranial variation in man*. Papers of the Peabody Museum, Harvard University, vol. 67.

——— 1973c. *The Pacific Islanders*. New York: Scribner's.

——— 1976. "Physical variation and history in Melanesia and Australia". *AJPA* 45:641–50.

——— 1977. "Hominid fossils". In Howells, W. W. and Tsuchitani, P. J. (eds) 1977:66–78.

——— 1980. "Homo erectus — who, when and where: a summary". *Yearbook of Physical Anthropology* 23:1–23.

Howells, W. W. and Tsuchitani, P. J. (eds). 1977. *Palaeoanthropology in the Peoples' Republic of China*. Washington DC: National Academy of Science.

Huang Weiwen, Li Chunchu, Wang Honshou and Huang Yukun. 1982. "Re-examination of a microlithic site at Xiqiaoshan, Nanhai County, Guangdong". *CA* 23:487–92.

Hudson, A. B. 1970. "A note on Selako: Malayic Dayak and Land Dayak languages in western Borneo". *SMJ* 18:301–18.

Hudson, A. B. and Hudson, J. M. 1978. "The Ma'anyan of Paju Epat". In King, V. T. (ed.) 1978:215–32.

Hughes, D. R. 1967. "Osteological evidence suggestive of the origin of the Mongoloid peoples". *APAS* 1:1–10.

Huke, R. 1976. "The geography and climate of rice". In Climate and Rice, pp. 31–50.

Hutterer, K. L. 1976. "An evolutionary approach to the Southeast Asian cultural sequence". *CA* 17:221–42.

——— 1977. "Reinterpreting the Southeast Asian Palaeolithic". In Allen, J. *et al.* (eds) 1977:31–71.

——— (ed.) 1977. *Economic exchange and social interaction in Southeast Asia*. Ann Arbor: Michigan Papers on South and Southeast Asia 13.

Hutterer, K. L. and Macdonald, W. K. (eds). 1982. *Houses built on scattered poles*. Cebu City: University of San Carlos.

Ikawa-Smith, F. (ed..) 1978. *Early Palaeolithic in South and East Asia*. The Hague: Mouton.

——— 1979. "Technological traditions in Late Pleistocene and early Holocene Japan". Paper read at 14th Pacific Science Congress, Khabarovsk, August 1979.

——— 1982. "The early prehistory of the Americas as seen from Northeast Asia". In Ericson, J. E. *et al.* (eds), *Peopling of the New World*, pp. 15–33. Los Altos: Ballena Press.

Imbrie, J. and Imbrie, K. P. 1979. *Ice Ages: solving the mystery*. Short Hills N. J.: Enslow Publishers.

IRRI n.d. *Effects of temperature and photoperiodism on rice growth*. International Rice Research Institute, Slide-Tape Instructional Unit GM-5. Los Baños, Philippines.

Isaac, G. 1977a. "Squeezing blood from stones". In Wright, J. V. S. (ed.) 1977:5–12.

——— 1977b. *Olorgesailie*. Chicago University Press.

——— 1980. "Casting the net wide". In Konigsson, L–K. (ed.) 1980:226–51.

Ishige, N. (ed.). 1980. *The Galela of Halmahera*. Osaka: Senri Ethnological Studies 7.

Jacob, T. 1967a. *Some problems pertaining to the racial history of the Indonesian region*. Utrecht: Drukkerij Neerlandia.

——— 1967b. "Racial identification of the Bronze Age human dentitions from Bali, Indonesia". *Journal of Dental Research* 46:903–10.

——— 1972a. "The problem of head hunting and brain eating among Pleistocene men in Indonesia". *APAO* 7:81–91.

——— 1972b. "The absolute date of the Djetis beds at Modjokerto". *Antiquity* 46:148.

——— 1975. "Morphology and palaeoecology of early man in Java". In Tuttle, R. H. (ed.) 1975:311–26.

——— 1976. "Early populations in the Indonesian region". In Kirk, R. L. and Thorne, A. G. (eds) 1976:81–93.

——— 1978a. "New finds of Lower and Middle Pleistocene hominines from Indonesia". In Ikawa-Smith, F. (ed.) 1978:13–22.

——— 1978b. "The puzzle of Solo Man". *MQRSEA* 4:31–40.

——— 1979. "Hominine evolution in South East Asia". *APAO* 14:1–10.

——— 1980. "The Pithecanthropus of Indonesia: phenotype, genetics and ecology". In Konigsson, L–K. (ed.) 1980:170–9.

Jacob, T., Soejono, R. P., Freeman, L. G. and Brown, F. H. 1978. "Stone tools from mid-Pleistocene sediments in Java". *Science* 202:885–7.

Jacobs, M. 1974. "Botanical panorama of the Malesian archipelago". In Unesco 1974:263–94.

Janse, O. R. T. 1958. *The ancient dwelling site of Dong Son (Thanh-Hoa, Annam)*. Bruges: St Catherine Press.

Jenner, P. N., Thompson, L. C. and Starosta, S. (eds). 1976. *Austroasiatic Studies.* Honolulu: University of Hawaii Press.

Jett, S. C. 1970. "The development and distribution of the blowgun". *Annals of the Association of American Geographers* 60:662–88.

Jia Lanpo. 1980. *Early man in China.* Beijing: Foreign Languages Press.

Johanson, D. C. 1980. "Early African hominid phylogenesis: a re-evaluation". In Konigsson, L–H. (ed.) 1980:31–69.

Johanson, D. C. and Edey, M. A. 1981. *Lucy.* London: Granada.

Kahler, H. 1978. "Austronesian comparative linguistics and reconstruction of the earlier forms of the language". In Wurm, S. A. and Carrington, L. (eds) 1978, fascicle 1:3–18.

Kamminga, J. 1979. "The nature of use-polish and abrasive smoothing on stone tools". In Hayden, B. (ed.), *Lithic use wear analysis*, pp. 143–57. New York: Academic Press.

Kano, T. and Segawa, K. 1956. *An illustrated ethnography of Formosan aborigines. Vol. 1: The Yami.* Tokyo: Maruzen.

Katili, J. A. 1974. *Geological environment of the Indonesian mineral deposits.* Bandung: Direktorat Geologi, Publikasi Teknik, Seri Geologi Ekonomi 7.

——— 1975. "Volcanism and plate tectonics in the Indonesian island arcs". *Tectonophysics* 26:165–88.

——— 1978. "Past-present geotectonic positions of Sulawesi". *Tectonophysics* 45:289–322.

Katili, J. A. and Hartono, H. M. S. 1979. "Van Bemmelen's contribution to the growth of geotectonics". *Geologie en Mijnbouw* 58:107–16.

Kaudern, W. 1938. *Megalithic finds in central Celebes.* Ethnographical Studies in Celebes vol. V. Göteborg: privately published by the author.

Kay, R. F. 1981. "The nut-crackers: a new theory of the adaptations of the Ramapithecines". *AJPA* 55:141–52.

Kedit, P.M. 1978. *Gunung Mulu report: Sarawak Museum Field Report 1.* Unpublished paper.

Keeley, L. H. 1980. *Experimental determination of stone tool uses.* University of Chicago Press.

Keers, W. 1948. *An anthropological survey of the Eastern Little Sunda Islands.* Amsterdam: Konihklijke Vereeniging Indisch Instituut.

Keesing, F. M. 1962. *The ethnohistory of northern Luzon.* Stanford University Press.

Keesing, R. 1981. *Cultural anthropology.* New York: Holt, Rinehart and Winston.

Keightley, D. N. (ed.). 1983. *The origins of Chinese civilization.* Berkeley: University of California Press.

Kennedy, K. A. R. 1977. "The deep skull of Niah". *AP* 20:32–50.

Kennedy, R. 1937. "A study of Indonesian civilization". In Murdock, G. P. (ed.), *Studies in the science of society presented to Albert Galloway Keller*, pp. 268–97. New Haven: Yale University Press.

Kern, H. 1889/1917. "Taalkundige gegevens ter bepaling van het stamland der Maleisch-Polynesische volken". In Kern, H., *Verspreide geschriften*, vol. 6, pp. 105–120 (1917). The Hague: Nijhoff.

Kidder, J. E. 1974. "Jar burials of the Middle Jomon period". In Ghosh, A. K. (ed.), *Perspectives in palaeoanthropology*, pp. 259–72. Calcutta: Mukhopadhyay.

Kim, Byung-mo. 1982. *Megalithic cultures in Asia*. Seoul: Hanyang University Press.

King, V. T. (ed.) 1976. "Migration, warfare and culture contact in Borneo: a critique of ecological analysis". *Oceania* 46:306–27.

——— (ed.) 1978. *Essays on Borneo societies*. Oxford: Oxford University Press.

Kirk, R. L. 1979. "Genetic differentiation in Australia and its bearing on the origin of the first Americans". In Laughlin, W. S. and Harper, A. B. (eds), *The first Americans: origins, affinities and adaptations*, pp. 221–37. New York: G. Fischer.

——— 1980a. "Population movements in the Southwest Pacific: the genetic evidence. In Fox, J. J. (ed.) 1980:45–56.

——— 1980b. "Languages, genes and people in the Pacific". In Erikson, A. W. (ed.), *Population structure and genetic disorders*, pp. 113–37. London: Academic Press.

——— 1981. *Aboriginal man adapting*. Oxford: Clarendon Press.

——— 1982. "Microevolution and migration in the Pacific". In *Human genetics part A: the unfolding genome*, pp. 215–25. Proceedings of the VI International Congress of Human Genetics, Jerusalem, 1981. New York: Alan R. Liss.

Kirk, R. L. and Thorne, A. G. (eds). 1976. *The origin of the Australians*. Canberra: Australian Institute of Aboriginal Studies.

Klein, J., Lerman, J. C., Damon, P. E. and Ralph, E. K. 1982. "Calibration of radiocarbon dates". *Radiocarbon* 24(2):103–50.

Koenigswald, G. H. R. von. 1949. "Vertebrate stratigraphy". In Bemmelen, R. W. van 1949, pp. 91–3.

——— 1951. "Introduction". In Weidenreich, F. 1951, pp. 211–21.

——— 1952. "Evidence of a prehistoric Australomelanesoid population in Malaya and Indonesia". *South Western Journal of Anthropology* 8:92–6.

——— 1956. *Meeting prehistoric man*. London: Scientific Book Club.

——— 1958. "Remarks on the prehistoric fauna of the Great Cave". *SMJ* 8:620–6.

Koenigswald, G. H. R. von and Ghosh, A. K. 1973. "Stone implements from the Trinil beds". *Koninklijk Nederlands Akademie van Wetenschappen, Proceedings Series* B 76:1–34.

Koenigswald, G. H. R. von and Weidenreich, F. 1939. "The relationship between *Pithecanthropus* and *Sinanthropus*". *Nature* 144:926–9.

Konigsson, L–K. (ed.). 1980. *Current argument on early man*. Oxford: Pergamon Press.

Koyama, S. 1977. "Archaeological surveys at the sites of Shih-pa-chang and Ta-ch'iu-yüan, Nan-t'ou, Taiwan". *Institute of History and Philology, Academia Sinica, Special Publication* 70:349–87. Taipei.

Krantz, G. S. 1980. *Climatic races and descent groups*. North Quincy, (Mass): Christopher Publishing House.

Kress, J. 1977a. "Contemporary and prehistoric subsistence patterns on Palawan". In Wood, W. (ed.), *Cultural-ecological perspectives on Southeast Asia*, pp. 29–48. Ohio University, Center for International Studies, Southeast Asia series no. 41.

——— 1977b. "Tom Harrisson, North Borneo and Palawan". *AP* 20:75–86.

——— 1978. "The ceramics from Pilanduk cave and Sa'agung rockshelter, Quezon Municipality, Palawan Island". *AP* 21:58–85.

Krishnaswami, V. D. 1949. "Megalithic types in South India". *Ancient India* 5:35–45.

Kukla, G. 1977. "Pleistocene land–sea correlations. 1: Europe". *Earth-Science Reviews* 13:307–74.

——— 1981. "Pleistocene climates on land". In Berger, A. (ed.) 1981:207–32.

Kumamoto. 1983. *Batan Island and northern Luzon*. University of Kumamoto (Japan), Faculty of Letters.

Kumar, A. 1974. "Indonesia and Malaysia". In Basham, A. L. (ed.), *The civilizations of Monsoon Asia*, pp. 135–78. Sydney: Angus and Robertson.
——— 1979. "Developments in four societies over the sixteenth to eighteenth centuries". In Aveling, H. (ed.), *The development of Indonesian society: from the coming of Islam to the present day*, pp. 1–44. Brisbane: Queensland University Press.
Kupper, H. 1930. "Palaeolitische werktuigen uit Atjeh, Nord Sumatra". *TKNAG* 47:985–9.
Kurashina, H. and Clayshulte, R. N. 1983. "Site formation processes and cultural sequence at Tarague, Guam". *BIPPA* 4:114–22.
Kurten, B. 1971. *The age of mammals.* London: Weidenfeld and Nicolson.
Kutzbach, J. E. 1981. "Monsoon climate of the early Holocene". *Science* 214:59–61.
Lal, B. B. 1949. "Sisupalgarh 1948: an early historical fort in eastern India". *Ancient India* 5:62–105.
——— 1954–5. "Excavations at Hastinapura and other explorations in the Upper Ganga and Sutlej basins". *Ancient India* 10–11:5–151.
Lamb, A. 1965. "Some observations on stone and glass beads in early Southeast Asia". *JMBRAS* 38(2):87–124.
Lamb, H. H. 1982. "Reconstruction of the course of post-glacial climate over the world". In Harding, A. (ed.), *Climatic change in later prehistory*, pp. 11–32. Edinburgh University Press.
Leach, E. R. 1954. *Political systems of highland Burma.* London: Bell.
Leakey, M. 1981. "Tracks and tools". *Philosophical Transactions of the Royal Society of London*, Series B, 292:95–102.
Lebar, F. M. (ed.). 1972. *Ethnic groups in Insular Southeast Asia. Vol. 1: Indonesia, Andaman Islands and Madagascar.* New Haven: HRAF Press.
Lebar, F.. M., Hickey, G. C. and Musgrave, J. K. 1964. *Ethnic groups of Mainland Southeast Asia.* New Haven: HRAF Press.
Lee, R. B. 1980. "Lactation, ovulation, infanticide and women's work: a study of hunter–gatherer population regulation". In Cohen, M. N. *et al.* (eds) 1980:321–48.
Le Gros Clark, W. E. 1964. *The fossil evidence for human evolution.* Chicago University Press.
Leslie, D. 1981. "Muslims in early China". *Hemisphere* 25(6):343–8.
Lestrel, P. E. 1975. "Hominid brain size versus time: revised regression estimates". *JHE* 5:207–12.
Leur, J. C. van. 1967. "On early Asian trade". In Leur, J. C. van (ed.), *Indonesian trade and society*, pp. 1–144. The Hague: van Hoeve.
Li, H–L. 1970. "The origins of cultivated plants in Southeast Asia". *Economic Botany* 24:3–19.
——— 1983. "The domestication of plants in China: ecogeographical considerations". In Keightley, D. H. (ed.) 1983:21–64.
Li, K–C. 1983. *K'en-ting: an archaeological laboratory near southern tip of Taiwan.* Ann Arbor: University Microfilms International.
Li, P. J–K. 1983. "Male and female forms of speech in Atayal". Paper presented at 15th Pacific Science Congress, Dunedin, February 1983.
Lie-Injo, L. E. 1976. "Genetic relationships of several aboriginal groups in Southeast Asia". In Kirk, R. L. and Thorne, A. G. (eds) 1976:277–306.
Liere, W. J. van. 1980. "Traditional water management in the lower Mekong valley". *WA* 11:265–80.
Lincoln, G. A. 1975. "Bird counts either side of Wallace's Line". *Journal of the Zoological Society of London* 177:349–61.
Lincoln, P. 1978. "Reefs-Santa Cruz as Austronesian". In Wurm, S. A. and Carrington, L. (eds) 1978, fascicle 2:929–67.

Linehan, W. 1951. "Traces of a Bronze Age culture associated with Iron Age implements in the regions of Klang and the Tembeling, Malaya". *JMBRAS* 24(3):1–59.
Littlefield, A., Lieberman, L. and Reynolds, L. T. 1982. "Redefining race: the potential demise of a concept in physical anthropology". *CA* 23:641–56.
Liu, T. and Ding, M. 1983. "Discussion on the age of 'Yuanmou Man' ". *Acta Anthropologica Sinica* 2(1):48–58.
Loeb, E. M. 1935. *Sumatra.* Wiener Beiträge zur Kulturgeschichte und Linguistik III.
Loeb, E. M. and Broek, J. O. M. 1947. "Social organization and the longhouse in Southeast Asia". *American Anthropologist* 49:414–25.
Loewenstein, J. 1956. "The origin of the Malayan Metal Age". *JMBRAS* 29(2):5–78.
Loofs-Wissowa, H. H. E. 1980–1. "Prehistoric and protohistoric links between the Indochinese Peninsula and the Philippines". *JHKAS* 9:57–76.
Loomis, W. F. 1967. "Skin pigment regulation of vitamin biosynthesis in man". *Science* 157:501–6.
Lopez, C. 1967. "Origins of the Philippine languages". *Philippine Studies* 15:130–66.
Lovejoy, C. O. 1970. "The taxonomic status of the *Meganthropus* mandibular fragments from the Djetis beds of Java". *Man* (new series) 5:228–36.
——— 1981. "The origin of man". *Science* 211:341–50.
Lynch, F. X. and Ewing, J. F. 1968. "Twelve ground stone implements from Mindanao, Philippine Islands". *APAS* 2:7–20.
Lynch, J. 1982. "Melanesian diversity and Polynesian homogeneity: the other side of the coin". *Oceanic Linguistics* 20:95–130.
Mabbett, I.W. 1977. "The 'Indianization' of Southeast Asia". *JSEAS* 8:1–14, 143–61.
Macdonald, W. K. 1978. "The Bang site, Thailand: an alternative analysis". *AP* 21:30–51.
Maceda, M. N. 1974. "Artificial cranial deformation". In *First Regional Seminar on Southeast Asian prehistory and archaeology*, pp. 27–36. Manila: National Museum of the Philippines.
Macintosh, N. W. G. 1972. "Radiocarbon dating as a pointer in time to the arrival and history of man in Australia and islands to the northwest". In *Proceedings of the 8th International Conference on Radiocarbon Dating, New Zealand*, Vol. I, pp. XLIV–LVI. Wellington: Royal Society of New Zealand.
Macintosh, N.W.G. 1978. "The Tabon Cave mandible". *APAO* 13:143–59.
Macintosh, N. W. G. and Larnach, S. L. 1976. "Aboriginal affinities looked at in world context". In Kirk, R. L. and Thorne, A. G. (eds) 1976:113–26.
Macknight, C. C. 1973. "The emergence of civilization in South Celebes and elsewhere". In Reid, A. and Castles, L. (eds), *Pre-colonial state systems in Southeast Asia*, pp. 126–35. Malaysian Branch, Royal Asiatic Society, Monograph 6.
Maglio, V. J. 1973. "Origin and evolution of the Elephantidae". *Transactions of the American Philosophical Society* 63(3):1–149.
Maglioni, R. 1952. "Archaeology in South China". *Journal of East Asiatic Studies* 2:1–20.
Majid, Z. 1982. *The West Mouth, Niah, in the prehistory of Southeast Asia.* SMJ 31.
Malleret, L. 1959–63. *L'archéologie du delta du Mékong.* 4 volumes. Paris: École Française d'Extrême-Orient.
Maloney, B. K. 1980. "Pollen analytical evidence for early forest clearance in north Sumatra". *Nature* 287:324–6.
Manabe, S. and Hahn, D. 1977. "Simulation of the tropical climate of an Ice Age". *Journal of Geophysical Research* 82:3889–3911.
Manning, A., McKinnon, E. E. and Treloar, F. E. 1980. "Analysis of gold artefacts from the Kota Cina site, near Medan, Sumatra". *JMBRAS* 53(2):102–16.
Marcus, L. F. and Newman, W. S. 1983. "Hominid migrations and the eustatic sea level paradigm: a critique". In Masters, P. M. and Flemming, N. C. (eds), *Quaternary coastlines and marine archaeology* pp. 63–86. London: Academic Press.

Maringer, J. and Verhoeven, Th. 1970a. "Die oberflächenfunde aus dem Fossilgebiet von Mengeruda und Olabula auf Flores, Indonesien". *Anthropos* 65:530–46.

——— 1970b. Die Steinartefakte aus der Stegodon-Fossilschicht von Mengeruda auf Flores". *Anthropos* 65:229–47.

Maringer, J. and Verschuuren, J. 1981. "Zum Paläolithikum der Insel Timor, Indonesien". *Anthropos* 76:584–8.

Marrison, G. E. 1975. "The early Cham language and its relationship to Malay". *JMBRAS* 48(2):52–60.

Marschall, W. 1968. "Metallurgie und frühe Besiedlungsgeschichte Indonesiens". *Ethnologica* 4:31–263.

Massing, A. W. 1981. "The journey to paradise". *Borneo Research Bulletin* 13(2):85–104.

Matsuo, T. 1975. "Rice cultures in China". In Rice in Asia 1975:157–69.

Matsu'ura, S. 1982. "A chronological framing for the Sangiran hominids". *Bulletin of the National Science Museum, Tokyo,* Series D (Anthropology), Vol. 8:1–53.

Matthews, J. M. 1965. "Stratigraphic disturbance: the human element". *Antiquity* 39:295–8.

Mayr, E. 1945. "Wallace's Line in the light of recent zoogeographic study". In Honig, P. and Verdoorn, F. (eds) 1945:241–50.

McDonald, P. 1980. "An historical perspective to population growth in Indonesia". In Fox, J. J. (ed.) 1980:81–94.

McFarland, C. D. 1981. *A linguistic atlas of the Philippines.* Manila: Linguistic Society of the Philippines.

McKinley, R. 1978. "Pioneer expansion, assimilation and the foundation of ethnic unity among the Iban". *SMJ* 47:15–28.

Meacham, W. 1975. "Tung Kwu". *JHKAS* 6:55–66.

——— 1976–8. "C14 dates from Vietnam". *JHKAS* 7:93–7.

——— 1977. "Continuity and local evolution in the Neolithic of South China". *CA* 18:419–40.

——— (ed.). 1978. *Sham Wan, Lamma Island.* Hong Kong Archaeological Society, Journal Monograph 3.

——— 1980. *Archaeology in Hong Kong.* Hong Kong: Heinemann Asia.

——— 1983. "Origins and development of the Yüeh coastal Neolithic". In Keightley, D. N. (ed.) 1983:147–76.

Medway, Lord. 1965. "Niah cave animal bone VIII: rhinoceros in late Quaternary Borneo". *SMJ* 12:77–82.

——— 1972. "The Quaternary mammals of Malesia: a review". In Ashton, P. and M. (eds) 1972:63–83.

——— 1973. "The antiquity of domesticated pigs in Sarawak". *JMBRAS* 46(2):167–78.

——— 1977a. "The Niah excavations: and an assessment of the impact of early man on mammals in Borneo". *AP* 20:51–69.

——— 1977b. "The ancient domestic dogs of Malaysia". *JMBRAS* 50(1):14–27.

——— 1978. "The wild pig remains from the West Mouth, Niah cave". *SMJ* 25:21–39.

Meer, N. C. van Setten van der. 1979. *Sawah cultivation in ancient Java.* Canberra: Australian National University Press.

Merimee, T. J., Zapf, J. and Froesch, E. R. 1981. "Dwarfism in the Pygmy". *New England Journal of Medicine* 305, No. 17:905–8.

Metzner, J. K. 1982. *Agriculture and population pressure in Sikka, Isle of Flores.* Canberra: Australian National University Press.

Mijsberg, W. A. 1932. "Recherches sur les restes humaines trouvés dans les fouilles des abris-sous-roche de Goea Lawa à Sampoeng et des sites préhistoriques à Bodjonegoro". In *Hommage du Service Archéologique des Indes Néerlandaises au Ier Congrès des Préhistoriens d'Extrême-Orient à Hanoi,* pp. 39–54. Batavia: Albrecht.

——— 1940. "On a Neolithic Palae-Melanesian lower jaw fragment found at Guak Kepah, Province Wellesley, Straits Settlements". In Chasen, F. N. and Tweedie, M. W. F. (eds) 1940:100–18.

Miksic, J. N. 1979. *Archaeology, trade and society in northeast Sumatra.* Ann Arbor: University Microfilms International.

Miles, D. 1972. "Land, labour and kin groups among Southeast Asian shifting cultivators". *Mankind* 8:185–97.

Minchen Chow, Rich P. and Zhang Y–P. 1983. "Wandering continents and their backboned animals — 1". *Hemisphere* 27(4):227–32.

Misra, V. N. and Bellwood, P. S. (eds). 1985. *Recent advances in Indo-Pacific prehistory.* New Delhi: Oxford and IBH.

Mitchell, A. and Weitzell, V. 1983. "Monkeys and men in the land of mud". *Hemisphere* 27(5):308–14.

Mizukoshi, M. 1971. "Regional divisions of monsoon Asia by Köppen's classification of climate". In Yoshino, M. M. (ed.), *Water balance of monsoon Asia: a climatological approach*, pp. 259–73. Honolulu: University of Hawaii Press.

Mohr, E. C. J. 1945. "Climate and soil in the Netherlands Indies". In Honig, P. and Verdoorn, F. (eds) 1945:250–4.

Molengraaff, G. A. F. 1921. "Modern deep-sea research in the East Indian Archipelago." *Geographical Journal* 57:95–118.

Molony, C. H. and Tuan, D. 1976. "Further studies on the Tasaday language". In Yen, D. E. and Nance, J. (eds) 1976:13–96.

Mori, T. 1956. "Archaeological study of jar-burials in Eneolithic Japan". In *Proceedings 4th Far-Eastern Prehistory and the Anthropology Division of the 8th Pacific Science Congresses combined*, part 1, fascicle 2, section 1, pp. 225–45. Quezon City.

Morlan, V. J. 1971. "The preceramic period of Japan: Honshu, Shikoku and Kyushu". *Arctic Anthropology* 8:136–70.

Morley, R. J. 1982. "A palaeoecological interpretation of a 10 000 year pollen record from Danau Padang, Central Sumatra, Indonesia". *Journal of Biogeography* 9:151–90.

Mountain, M-J. 1983. "Preliminary report of excavations at Nombe rockshelter, Simbu Province, Papua New Guinea". *BIPPA* 4:84–99.

Movius, H. L. 1944. *Early man and Pleistocene stratigraphy in South and East Asia.* Cambridge, Mass: Papers of the Peabody Museum 19(3).

——— 1948. "The Lower Palaeolithic cultures of southern and eastern Asia". *Transactions of the American Philosophical Society* (new series) 38(4):329–420.

——— 1955. "Palaeolithic archaeology in southern and eastern Asia, exclusive of India". *Cahiers d'Histoire Mondiale* 2:157–82, 520–53.

Mulia, R. 1980. "Beberapa catatan tentang arca-arca yang disebut arca tipe Polinesia". In *Pertemuan Ilmiah Arkeologi*, pp. 599–646. Jakarta: Pusat Penelitian Arkeologi Nasional.

——— 1981. *Nias: the only older megalithic tradition in Indonesia.* Bulletin of the Research Centre of Archaeology in Indonesia 16.

Muller, J. 1975. "Pollen-analytical studies of peat and coal from northwest Borneo". *MQRSEA* 1:83–6.

Mulvaney, D. J. 1970. "The Patjitanian industry: some observations". *Mankind* 7:184–7.

——— 1985. "Australian backed-blade industries in perspective". In Misra, V. N. and Bellwood, P. S. (eds) 1985:211–7.

Mulvaney, D. J. and Soejono, R. P. 1970. "The Australian–Indonesian archaeological expedition to Sulawesi". *AP* 13:163–78.

——— 1971. "Archaeology in Sulawesi, Indonesia". *Antiquity* 45:26–33.

Murdock, G. P. 1960a. *Social structure.* New York: Macmillan.

——— (ed.). 1960b. *Social structure in Southeast Asia.* New York: Viking Fund Publication in Anthropology 29.
——— 1964. "Genetic classification of the Austronesian languages: a key to Oceanic culture history". *Ethnology* 3:117–26.
Musser, G. G. 1981. "The giant rat of Flores and its relatives east of Borneo and Bali". *Bulletin of the American Museum of Natural History* 169: article 2.
——— 1982. "The Trinil rats". *MQRSEA* 7:65–86.
Naerssen, F. H. van. 1977. "Economic history in early Indonesia". In Naerssen, F. H. van and Iongh, R. C. de, *The economic and administrative history of early Indonesia*, pp. 1–84. Leiden: Brill.
Nance, J. 1975. *The gentle Tasaday.* New York: Harcourt Brace Jovanovitch.
Naylor, P. (ed.). 1980. *Austronesian studies: papers from the 2nd Eastern conference on Austronesian languages.* Michigan Papers on South and Southeast Asia 15.
Needham, R. 1954. "Penan and Punan". *JMBRAS* 27(1):73–83.
Neel, J. V. 1967. "Genetic structure of primitive human populations". *Japanese Journal of Human Genetics* 12:1–16.
Ngo Sy Hong 1985. "Sa Huynh Culture: recent discoveries". Paper given at the 12th Congress of the Indo-Pacific Prehistory Association, Peñablanca, Philippines.
Ngo The Phong 1985. "Some archaeological questions of the northern Vietnamese coastal areas in relation to Austronesian origins". Paper given at the 12th Congress of the Indo-Pacific Prehistory Association, Peñablanca, Philippines.
Nicholl, R. (ed.). 1975. *European sources for the history of the sultanate of Brunei in the sixteenth century.* Brunei Museum.
Nicolaisen, I. 1976. "The Penan of Sarawak". *Folk* 18:205–36.
——— 1977–8. "The dynamics of ethnic classification: a case study of the Punan Bah of Sarawak". *Folk* 19–20:183–200.
Nimmo, H. 1967. Review of Sopher, D. 1965. *Philippine Studies* 25:209–12.
——— 1968. "Reflections on Bajau history". *Philippine Studies* 16:32–59.
——— 1972. *The sea people of Sulu.* London: Intertext.
Ninkovitch, D. and Burckle, L.H. 1978. "Absolute age of the base of the hominid-bearing beds in eastern Java". *Nature* 275:306–8.
Nix, H. A. and Kalma, J. D. 1972. "Climate as a dominant control in the biogeography of northern Australia and New Guinea". In Walker, D. (ed.), *Bridge and barrier*, pp. 61–91. Canberra: Australian National University Press.
Noorduyn, J. and Verstappen, H. T. 1972. "Purnavarman's river-works near Tugu". *BTLV* 128:298–307.
Nothofer, B. 1975. *The reconstruction of Proto-Malayo-Javanic.* The Hague: Nijhoff.
O'Connor, S. J. and Harrisson, T. 1971. "Gold-foil burial amulets in Bali, Philippines and Borneo". *JMBRAS* 44(1):71–7.
Ohtsuka, R. 1977. "The sago-eaters: an ecological discussion with special reference to the Oriomo Papuans". In Allen, J. *et al.* (eds) 1977:465–92.
Oka, H-I. 1975. "The origin of cultivated rice and its adaptive evolution". In Rice in Asia 1975, pp. 21–34.
Oka, H-I. and Chang, W. T. 1960. "Survey of variations in photoperiodic response in wild *Oryza* species". *Botanical Bulletin, Academia Sinica* 1:1–14. Taipei.
Olivier, G. 1956. *Les populations du Cambodge.* Paris: Masson.
Ollier, C. 1980. "The geological setting". In Fox, J. J. (ed.) 1980:5–19.
Omar, M. 1981. *Archaeological excavations in protohistoric Brunei.* Brunei Museum.
Omoto, K. 1981. "The genetic origins of the Philippine Negritos". *CA* 22:421–2.

Oppenoorth, W. F. F. 1932. "*Homo javanthropus* een Pleistocene mensch van Java". *Dienst van den Mijnbouw, Wetenschappelijke mededelingen* 20:49–63.

——— 1936. "Een prehistorisch cultuur-centrum langs de Solo-Rivier". *TKNAG* 53:399–411.

Orban-Segebarth, R. and Procureur, F. 1983. "Tooth size of *Meganthropus palaeojaanicus*" *JHE* 12:711–20.

Orchiston, D. W. 1978. "The supposed Javan affinities of the tula 'adze-flake' from Australia". *MQRSEA* 4:1–18.

Orchiston, D. W. and Siesser, W. G. 1982. "Chronostratigraphy of the Plio-Pleistocene fossil hominids of Java". *MQRSEA* 7:131–50.

Orsoy de Flines, E. W. van. 1969. *Guide to the ceramic collection.* 2nd edition. Jakarta: Museum Pusat.

Padoch, C. 1983. "Agricultural practices of the Kerayan Lun Dayeh". *Borneo Research Bulletin* 15(1):30–3.

Panggabean, R. I. 1981. "Manik-manik situs Pasir Angin, Jawa Barat". *Amerta* 4:22–7.

Parker, R. H. 1968. Review of Sørensen, P. and Hatting, T. 1967. *Journal of the Polynesian Society* 77:307–13.

Parmentier, H. 1924. "Dêpots de jarres à Sa Huynh (Quang-ngai, Annam)". *Bulletin de l'École Française d'Extrême-Orient* 24:325–43.

Pawley, A. K. 1974. "Austronesian languages". *Encyclopaedia Britannica*, 15th edition, *Macropaedia* 2:484–94.

——— 1981. "Melanesian diversity and Polynesian homogeneity: a unified explanation for language". In Hollyman, K. and Pawley, A. K. (eds) 1981:269–309.

Pawley, A. K. and Green, R. C. 1975. "Dating the dispersal of the Oceanic languages". *Oceanic Linguistics* 12:1–67.

——— 1984. "The Proto-Oceanic language community". *Journal of Pacific History* 19(3):123–46.

Peacock, B. A. V. 1959. "A short description of Malayan prehistoric pottery". *AP* 3:121–56.

——— 1964a. "The Kodiang pottery cones". *FMJ* 9:4–18.

——— 1964b. "A preliminary note on the Dong-s'on bronze drums from Kampong Sungei Lang". *FMJ* 9:1–3.

——— 1971. "Early cultural development in South-East Asia with special reference to the Malay Peninsula". *APAO* 6:107–23.

——— 1979. "The later prehistory of the Malay Peninsula". In Smith, R. B. and Watson, W. (eds) 1979:199–214.

Pearson, R. 1968. "Archaeological investigations in eastern Taiwan". *AP* 12:137–56.

——— 1969. *Archaeology of the Ryukyu Islands.* Honolulu: University of Hawaii Press.

——— 1969. "Archaeological survey in south-eastern Taiwan". *Bulletin of the Institute of Archaeology, Academia Sinica* 30:317–30. Taipei.

——— 1981. "Social complexity in Chinese coastal Neolithic sites". *Science* 213:1078–86.

Pearson, R. and Lo, S-C. 1983. "The Ch'ing-lien-kang culture and the Chinese Neolithic". In Keightley, D. N. (ed.) 1983:119–46.

Pelras, C. L. 1981. "Célèbes-sud avant l'Islam selon les premiers témoignages étrangers". *Archipel* 21:153–84.

Perry, W. J. 1918. *The megalithic culture of Indonesia.* Manchester University Press.

Peterson, J. T. 1978. *The ecology of social boundaries.* University of Illinois Press.

Peterson, R. M. 1969. "Wurm II climate at Niah cave". *SMJ* 17:67–79.

Peterson, W. 1974. "Summary report of two archaeological sites from north-eastern Luzon". *APAO* 9:26–35.

——— and the University of Philippines Field School. 1979. "Archaeological research in the Novaliches Watershed, Philippines". *AP* 22:120–39.

Pfeffer, P. 1974. "Fauna of humid tropical Asia". In Unesco 1974:295–306.
Piazza, A., Menozzi, P. and Cavalli-Sforza, L. L. 1981. "Synthetic gene frequencies of man and selective effects of climate". *Proceedings of the National Academy of Sciences* 78:2638–41. Washington.
Pietrusewsky, M. 1977. "Etude des relations entre les populations du Pacifique". *L'Anthropologie* 81:67–97.
——— 1982. "The ancient inhabitants of Ban Chiang". *Expedition* 24(4):42–50.
——— 1983. "Multivariate analysis of New Guinea and Melanesian skulls: a review". *JHE* 12:61–76.
Pilbeam, D. 1980. "Major trends in human evolution". In Konigsson, L–K (ed.) 1980:261–85.
——— 1984. "The descent of hominoids and hominids". *Scientific American* 250(3):60–9.
Pinkley, G. 1935–6. "The significance of Wadjak man". *Peking Natural History Bulletin* 10(3):183–200.
Plucknett, D. L. 1976. "Edible aroids". In Simmonds, N. W. (ed.), *Crop plant evolution*, pp. 10–12. London: Longmans.
Polak, B. 1975. "Character and occurrence of peat deposits in the Malaysian tropics". *MQRSEA* 1:71–82.
Polunin, I. 1953. "The medical natural history of Malayan aborigines". *Medical Journal of Malaya* 8:55–175.
Polunin, I. and Sneath, H. A. 1953. "Studies of blood groups in Southeast Asia". *Journal of the Royal Anthropological Institute* 83:215–51.
Pope, G. G. 1977. "Hominids from the Lower Pleistocene of South China". *Kroeber Anthropological Society Papers* 50:63–72.
——— 1983. "Evidence on the age of the Asian hominidae". *Proceedings of the National Academy of Sciences* 80:4988–92.
——— 1984. "The antiquity and palaeoenvironment of the Asian hominidae". In Whyte, R. O. (ed.), *The evolution of the Asian environment*, Vol. II, pp. 822–47. Centre of Asian Studies, University of Hong Kong.
Prentice, D. J. 1970. "The linguistic situation in North Borneo". In Wurm, S. A. and Laycock, D. S. (eds), *Pacific linguistic studies in honour of Arthur Capell*, pp. 369–408. Canberra: Pacific Linguistics Series C, No. 13.
Presland, G. 1980. "Continuity in Indonesian lithic traditions". *The Artefact* 5:19–45.
Puech, P. F. 1983. "Tooth wear, diet, and the artefacts of Java Man." *CA* 24:381–2.
Quaritch Wales, H. G. 1976. *The Malay Peninsula in Hindu times*. London: Bernard Quaritch.
Rambo, T. 1979. "Human ecology of the *orang asli*". *FMJ* 24:41–74.
Rausa-Gomez, L. 1967. "Sri Vijaya and Madjapahit". *Philippine Studies* 15:63–107.
Rea, A. 1915. *Catalogue of the prehistoric antiquities from Adichanallur and Perumbair*. Madras: Government Press.
Reed, C. A. (ed.). 1977. *Origins of agriculture*. The Hague: Mouton.
Reed, R. R. 1976. "Indigenous urbanization in Southeast Asia". In Yeung, C. M. and Lo, C. P. (eds), *Changing Southeast Asian cities*, pp. 14–27. Singapore: Oxford University Press.
Reid, A. 1980. The structure of cities in Southeast Asia". *JSEAS* 11(2):235–50.
Reid, L. A. 1982. "The demise of Proto-Philippines". In Halim, A. *et al.* (eds), *Papers from the Third International Conference on Austronesian Linguistics*, Vol. 2, pp. 201–16. Canberra: Pacific Linguistics Series C, No. 75.
——— 1985. "Benedict's Austro-Thai hypothesis: an evaluation". Paper given at the 12th Congress of the Indo-Pacific Prehistory Association, Peñablanca, Philippines.
Rhoads, J. G. and Friedlaender, J. S. 1975. "Language boundaries and biological differentiation on Bougainville". *Proceedings of the National Academy of Sciences* 72:2247–50. Washington.

Rice in Asia. 1975. Edited by the Association of Japanese Agricultural Scientific Societies. Tokyo: University of Tokyo Press.
Rightmire, G. P. 1980. "*Homo erectus* and human evolution in the African Middle Pleistocene". In Konigsson, L–K. (ed.) 1980:70–85.
Rindos, D. 1980. "Symbiosis, instability, and the origins and spread of agriculture". *CA* 21:751–72.
Riscutia, C. 1975. "A study of the Modjokerto infant cranium". In Tuttle, R. H. (ed.) 1975:377–8.
Robinson, J. T. 1968. "The origin and adaptive radiation of the Australopithecines". In Kurth, G. (ed.), *Evolution und Hominization*, pp. 150–75. Stuttgart: Gustav Fischer.
Robequain, C. 1954. *Malaya, Indonesia, Borneo and the Philippines*. London: Longmans, Green.
Rodwell, S. 1984. "China's earliest farmers: the evidence from Cishan". *BIPPA* 5:55–63.
Roth, H. L. 1896. *The natives of Sarawak and North Borneo*. 2 volumes. London: Truslove and Hanson.
Rousseau, J. 1977. "Kayan agriculture". *SMJ* 46:129–58.
——— 1978. "The Kayan". In King, V. T. (ed.) 1978:78–91.
Ruddle, K., Johnson, D., Townsend, P. K. and Rees, J. D. 1978. *Palm sago*. Canberra: Australian National University Press.
Rutter, O. 1929. *The pagans of North Borneo*. London: Hutchinson.
Sangvichien, S., Sirigaroon, P., Jorgensen, J. B. and Jacob, T. 1969. *Archaeological excavations in Thailand. Vol. 3 part 2: The prehistoric Thai skeletons*. Copenhagen: Munksgaard.
Santa Luca, A. P. 1980. *The Ngandong fossil hominids*. New Haven: Yale University Publications in Anthropology 78.
Sarkar, H. 1982. "Megalithic culture of India". In Kim, B–M. (ed.) 1982:127–63.
Sartono, S. 1969. "*Stegodon timorensis:* a pygmy species from Timor". *Koninklijk Nederlands Akademie van Wetenschappen, Proceedings Series B* 72:192–202.
——— 1973. "On an additional *Stegodon timorensis* Sartono". *Geological Survey of Indonesia, Publikasi Teknik, Seri Palaeontologi* 5:1–10.
——— 1975. "Implications arising from *Pithecanthropus* VIII". In Tuttle, R. H. (ed.) 1975:327–60.
——— 1976. "Genesis of the Solo terraces". *MQRSEA* 2:1–21.
——— 1979a. "The age of the vertebrate fossils and artefacts from Cabenge in South Sulawesi". *MQRSEA* 5:65–82.
——— 1979b. "The discovery of a pygmy stegodont from Sumba". *MQRSEA* 5:57–64.
——— 1979c. "The stratigraphy of the Sumbung Mekan site in central Java". *MQRSEA* 5:83–8.
Sartono, S., Sémah, F., Astadiredja, K. A. S., Sukendarmono, M. and Djubiantono, T. 1981. "The age of *Homo modjokertensis*". *MQRSEA* 6:91–102.
Satari, S. 1981. "New finds from north-central Java". *SPAFA Digest* 2(2):23–8.
Sather, C. 1978. "The Bajau Laut". In King, V. T. (ed.) 1978:172–92.
Sauer, C. O. 1952. *Agricultural origins and dispersals*. New York: American Geographical Society.
Saurin, E. 1973. "La champ de jarres de Hang Gon près Xuan Loc (Sud Viêt-Nam). *Bulletin de l'École Française d'Extrême-Orient* 60:329–58.
Schanfield, M. S. and Gerschowitz, H. 1973. "Non random distribution of Gm haplotypes in East Asia". *American Journal of Human Genetics* 25:567–74.
Schmeltz, J. D. E. 1904. "Einige vergleichende Bemerkungen über die Kesseltrommel von Saleyer". *Internationales Archiv für Ethnographie* 16:158–61.
Schneeberger, W. F. 1979. *Contributions to the ethnography of Central Northeastern Borneo*. Bern University: Institute of Ethnology.
Schneider, W. M. 1978. "The Selako Dayak". In King, V. T. (ed.) 1978:59–77.

Schnitger, F. M. 1964. *Forgotten kingdoms in Sumatra.* (Reprint of 1939 edition). Leiden: Brill.

Schrire, C. 1982. *The Alligator Rivers: prehistory and ecology in western Arnhem Land.* Canberra: Department of Prehistory, Australian National University, Terra Australis 7.

Schulte Nordholt, H. G. 1971. *The political system of the Atoni of Timor.* The Hague: Nijhoff.

Scott, W. H. 1968. *Prehispanic source materials for the study of Philippine prehistory.* Manila: University of Santo Tomas Press.

Scrivenor, J. B., Burkill, I. H., Smith, M. A., Shaw, H. K. A., Richards, P. W. and Zeuner, F. E. 1942–3. "A discussion of the biogeographic division of the Indo-Australian archipelago". *Proceedings of the Linnaean Society of London* 154:120–65.

Seavoy, R. E. 1973a. "The transition to continuous rice cultivation in Kalimantan". *Annals of the Association of American Geographers* 63:218–25.

——— 1973b. "The shading cycle in shifting cultivation". *Annals of the Association of American Geographers* 63:522–8.

Seboek, T. (ed.). 1971. *Linguistics in Oceania.* 2 volumes. Current Trends in Linguistics vol. 8. The Hague: Mouton.

Sémah, A–M. 1982a. "Variations de la vegetation au Plio-Pleistocene sur les sites de Sangiran et Sambungmacan par l'analyse pollinique". *1er Congrès International de Paléontologie Humaine,* pp. 559–77. Nice.

——— 1982b. "A preliminary report on a Sangiran pollen diagram". *MQRSEA* 7:165–70.

Sémah, F. 1982. "Pliocene and Pleistocene geomagnetic reversals recorded in the Gemolong and Sangiran domes (central Java)". *MQRSEA* 7:131–50.

Sémah, F., Sartono, S., Zaim, Y. and Djubiantono, T. 1981. "A palaeomagnetic study of Plio-Pleistocene sediments from Sangiran and Simo (central Java)". *MQRSEA* 6:103–10.

Serizawa, C. 1982. *Catalogue of archaeological collections.* Faculty of Arts and Letters, Tohoku University, Sendai.

Serjeantson, S. W. 1984. "Migration and admixture in the Pacific: insights provided by human leucocyte antigens". *Journal of Pacific History* 19(3):160–71.

Serjeantson, S. W., Kirk, R. L. and Booth, P. B. 1983. "Linguistic and genetic differentiation in New Guinea". *JHE* 12:77–92.

Serjeantson, S. W., Ryan, D. R. and Thompson, A. R. 1983. "The colonization of the Pacific: the story according to human leucocyte antigens". *American Journal of Human Genetics* 34:904–18.

Service, E. R. 1970. "The law of evolutionary potential". In Sahlins, M. D. and Service, E. R., *Evolution and culture,* pp. 93–122. Ann Arbor: University of Michigan Press.

Shackleton, N. J. 1977. "Carbon-13 in *Uvigerina*: tropical rainforest history and the equatorial Pacific carbonate dissolution cycles". In Anderson, N. R. and Malahoff, A. (eds), *The fate of fossil fuel* CO_2 *in the oceans,* pp. 401–27. New York: Plenum Publishing Corporation.

——— 1982. "The deep-sea sediment record of climatic variability". *Progress in Oceanography* 11:199–218.

Shackleton, N. J. and Opdyke, N. D. 1973. "Pacific core V28-238". *Quaternary Research* 3:39–55.

——— 1977. "Oxygen isotope and paleomagnetic evidence for early northern hemisphere glaciation". *Nature* 270:216–9.

Shutler, R. and Marck, J. C. 1975. "On the dispersal of the Austronesian horticulturalists". *APAO* 10:81–113.

Sierevelt, A.M. 1929. "Rapport over oudheden van Apo Kajan, Borneo". *Oudheidkundig Verslag* for 1929, pp. 162–4.

Siesser, W. G. and Orchiston, D. W. 1978. "Micropalaeontological re-assessment of the age of *Pithecanthropus* mandible C from Sangiran, Indonesia". *MQRSEA* 4:25–30.

Sieveking, G. de G. 1954. "Excavations at Gua Cha, Kelantan 1954. Part 1". *FMJ* 1 and 2:75–143.

——— 1956a. "The Iron Age collections of Malaya". *JMBRAS* 29(2):79–138.

——— 1956b. "Recent archaeological discoveries in Malaya (1955)". *JMBRAS* 29(1):200–11.

——— 1956c. "The distribution of stone bark-cloth beaters in prehistoric times". *JMBRAS* 29(3):79–85.

——— 1962. "The prehistoric cemetery at Bukit Tengku Lembu, Perlis". *FMJ* 7:25–54.

——— 1974. Review of Sørensen, P. and Hatting, T. 1967. *Antiquity* 48:149–51.

Simmonds, N. W. 1966. *Bananas.* 2nd edition. London: Longmans.

Simmons, R. T. 1962. "Blood group genes in Polynesians and comparisons with other Pacific peoples". *Oceania* 32:198–210.

——— 1967. "The biological origin of the Australian Aboriginals". In Kirk, R. L. and Thorne, A. G. (eds) 1976:307–28.

Simons, E. L. 1981. "Man's immediate forerunners". *Philosophical Transactions of the Royal Society of London*, Series B, 292:21–42.

Simpson, B. B. and Haffer, J. 1978. "Speciation patterns in the Amazonian forest biota". *Annual Review of Ecology and Systematics* 9:497–518.

Simpson, G. G. 1947. *This view of life.* New York: Harcourt, Brace and World (1964 reprint).

——— 1977. "Too many lines: the limits of the Oriental and Australian zoogeographical regions". *Proceedings of the American Philosophical Society* 121:107–20.

Sirk, U. 1978. "Problems of high-level subgrouping in Austronesian". In Wurm, S. A. and Carrington, L. (eds) 1978, fascicle 1:255–73.

Sitrampalam, S. K. 1980. *The megalithic culture of Sri Lanka.* Unpublished PhD thesis, Deccan College, Pune.

Smith, R. B. and Watson, W. (eds). 1979. *Early South East Asia.* New York: Oxford University Press.

Sneddon, J. H. 1978. *Proto-Minahasan.* Canberra: Pacific Linguistics Series B, No. 54.

Snell, C. A. R. D. 1938. *Menschelijke skeletresten uit de duinformatie van Java's zuidkust nabij Poeger.* Surabaya: G. Kolff.

——— 1948. "Human skulls from the urn-field of Melolo, East Sumba". *Acta Neerlandica Morphologiae Normalis et Pathologicae* 6(3):1–20.

Soejono, R. P. 1969. *On prehistoric burial methods in Indonesia.* Bulletin of the Archaeological Institute of the Republic of Indonesia 7.

——— 1972. *The distribution of types of bronze axes in Indonesia.* Bulletin of the Archaeological Institute of the Republic of Indonesia 9.

——— 1977. *Sarkofagus Bali dan Nekropolis Gilimanuk.* Jakarta: Pusat Penelitian Purbakala dan Peninggalan Nasional.

——— 1979. "The significance of excavations at Gilimanuk (Bali)". In Smith, R. B. and Watson, W. (eds) 1979:185–98.

——— 1982a. "New data on the Palaeolithic industry in Indonesia". In *1er Congres International de Paleońtologie Humaine*, pp. 78–92. Nice.

——— 1982b. "On the megaliths in Indonesia". In Kim, B–M. (ed.). 1982:73–98.

Sofro, A. S. M. 1982. *Population genetic studies in Indonesia.* Australian National University: PhD dissertation.

Solheim, W. G. II. 1960. "Jar burial in the Babuyan and Batanes Islands and in central Philippines, and its relation to jar burial elsewhere in the Far East". *Philippine Journal of Science* 89(1):115–48.

——— 1964a. "Pottery and the Malayo-Polynesians". *CA* 5:360, 376–84, 400–3.

——— 1964b. *The archaeology of central Philippines.* Manila: Bureau of Printing.

——— 1967. "Two pottery traditions of late prehistoric times in Southeast Asia". In Drake, F. S. (ed.), *Symposium on historical, archaeological and linguistic studies on southern China, Southeast Asia, and the Hong Kong region*, pp. 15–22. Hong Kong University Press.
——— 1968. "The Batungan cave sites, Masbate, Philippines". *APAS* 2:21–62.
——— 1975a. "Reflections on the new data of Southeast Asian prehistory: Austronesian origins and consequence". *AP* 18:146–60.
——— 1975b. "The Nusantao and South china". *JHKAS* 6:108–15.
——— 1979a. "New data on late Southeast Asian prehistory and their interpretation". *JHKAS* 8:73–87.
——— 1979b. "A look at 'L'art prébouddhique de la Chine et de l'Asie du Sud-Est et son influence en Océanie' forty years after". *AP* 22:165–205.
——— 1980. "Searching for the origins of the *orang asli*". *FMJ* 25:61–76.
——— 1981a. "Philippine prehistory". In Casal, G. *et al.*, *The people and art of the Philippines*, pp. 17–84. Los Angeles: Museum of Cultural History.
——— 1981b. "Notes on 'Malay pottery' in East Malaysia and neighbouring areas". *SMJ* 29:3–16.
Solheim, W. C. II, Harrisson, B. and Wall, L. 1959. "Niah 'Three Colour Ware' and related prehistoric pottery from Borneo". *AP* 3:167–76.
Solheim, W. C. II, Legaspi, A. M. and Neri, J. S. 1979. *Archaeological survey in southeastern Mindanao.* Manila: National Museum Monograph 8.
Sondaar, P. Y. 1981. "The *Geochelone* faunas of the Indonesian archipelago". *MQRSEA* 6:111–9.
Sopher, D. E. 1965. *The sea nomads.* Singapore: National Museum.
Sørensen, P. 1972. "The Neolithic cultures of Thailand (and north Malaysia) and their Lungshanoid relationships". In Barnard, N. (ed.) 1972, vol. 2:459–506.
——— 1973. "Prehistoric iron implements from Thailand." *AP* 16:134–73.
Sørensen, P. and Hatting, T. 1967. *Archaeological excavations in Thailand, Vol. 2, Ban Kao.* Copenhagen: Munksgaard.
Spencer, J. E. 1963. "The migration of rice from mainland Southeast Asia into Indonesia". In Barrau, J. (ed.), *Plants and the migrations of Pacific peoples*, pp. 83–90. Honolulu: Bishop Museum Press.
——— 1966. *Shifting cultivation in Southeast Asia.* University of California Press.
Spencer, J. E. and Thomas, W. L. 1971. *Asia East by South: a cultural geography.* 2nd edition. New York: John Wiley and Sons.
Spoehr, A. 1973. *Zamboanga and Sulu.* Ethnology Monograph 1, Department of Anthropology, University of Pittsburgh.
Spriggs, M. J. T. 1981. *Vegetable kingdoms.* Unpublished PhD thesis, Australian National University.
Stamps, R. B. 1977. "An archaeological survey of the P'uli basin, west central Taiwan". *Institute of History and Philology, Academia Sinica, Special Publication* 70:237–301. Taipei.
Stargardt, J. 1980. "Sud-Est asiatique, art et archéologie. 2: La formation des états indianisés". *Encyclopaedia Universalis, Supplement* 1980:1350–3. Paris.
Steenis, C. G. G. J. van. 1961. "Preliminary revisions of some genera of Malaysian Papilionaceae I". *Reinwardtia* 5:419–56.
——— 1965. "Concise plant-geography of Java". In Backer, C. A. and Bakhuizen van den Brink, R. E. (eds), *Flora of Java*, vol. 2, pp. 1–72. Groningen: Noordhoff.
Stein Callenfels, P. V. van. 1932. "Note préliminaire sur les fouilles dans l'abri-sous-roche du Guwa Lawa à Sampung". In *Hommage du Service Archéologique des Indes Néerlandaises au 1er Congrès des Préhistoriens d'Extrême-Orient à Hanoi*, pp. 25–9. Batavia: Albrecht.

——— 1936a. "An excavation of three kitchen middens at Guak Kepah, Province Wellesley". *BRM* Series B, vol. 1, no. 1:27–37.

——— 1936b. "A remarkable stone implement from the Malay Peninsula". *BRM* Series B, vol. 1, no. 1:38–40.

——— 1936c. "L'industrie osseuse de Ngandong". *L'Anthropologie* 46:359–62.

——— 1938. "Mededeelingen het Proto-Toaliaan". *TITLV* 68:597–84.

Stein Callenfels, P. V. van and Evans, I. H. N. 1928. "Report on cave excavations in Perak". *JFMSM* 12(6):145–60.

Stein Callenfels, P. V. van and Noone, H. D. 1940. "A rock-shelter excavation at Sungei Siput, Perak". In Chasen, F. N. and Tweedie, M. W. F. (eds) 1940:119–25.

St John, S. 1974. *Life in the forests of the Far East.* Reprint of 1862 original, 2 volumes. Kuala Lumpur: Oxford University Press.

Stutterheim, W. F. 1956. "Some remarks on pre-Hinduistic burial customs in Java". In Stutterheim, W. F., *Studies in Indonesian archaeology*, pp. 63–90. The Hague: Nijhoff.

Sudjoko. 1981. *Ancient Indonesian technology.* Aspek-Aspek Arkeologi Indonesia 9. Jakarta: Pusat Penelitian Arkeologi Indonesia.

Sukarto, K. Atmodjo, M. M. 1979. "Notes on a protohistoric sarcophagus at Selasih in Bali". *Majalah Arkeologi* 2(4):61–74.

Sukendar, H. 1979. *Laporan penelitian kepurbakalaan daerah Lampung. BPA* 20.

——— 1980. *Laporan penelitian kepurbakalaan di Sulawesi Tengah. BPA* 25.

——— 1985. "Living megalithic tradition in eastern Indonesia". Paper given at the 12th Congress of the Indo-Pacific Prehistory Association, Peñablanca, Philippines.

Sukendar, H. and Awe, R. D. 1981. *Laporan penelitian Terjan dan Plawangan, Jawa Tengah. BPA* 27.

Suleiman, S. 1976. *Monuments of ancient Indonesia.* Jakarta: National Research Centre of Archaeology.

Summerhayes, G. and Walker, M. 1982. "Elemental analysis and taxonomy of prehistoric pottery from western Java". In Ambrose, W. and Duerden, P. (eds), *Archaeometry: an Australasian perspective*, pp.60–7. Canberra: Department of Prehistory, Research School of Pacific Studies.

Sung, W–H. 1979. "Prehistoric Taiwan". *JHKAS* 8:88–91.

Sutaba, I. M. 1976. *Megalithic traditions in Sembiran, north Bali.* Aspek-Aspek Arkeologi Indonesia 4. Jakarta: Pusat Penelitian Arkeologi Nasional.

Sutayasa, I. M. 1972. "Notes on the Buni pottery complex, northwest Java". *Mankind* 8:182–4.

——— 1973. "The study of prehistoric pottery in Indonesia". *Nusantara* 4:67–82.

——— 1979. "Prehistory in west Java, Indonesia". *The Artefact* 4:61–75.

Suzuki, P. 1959. *The religious system and culture of Nias, Indonesia.* The Hague: Exelsior.

Swadesh, M. 1964. "Linguistics as an instrument of prehistory". In Hymes, D. (ed.), *Language in culture and society*, pp. 575–84. New York: Harper and Row.

Takaya, Y. 1980. "The agricultural landscape of the Komering river of south Sumatra". In Tsubouchi, Y. *et al.* (eds) 1980: article 4.

Tanaka, A. 1975. "Nutrio-physiology of Southeast Asian rice". In Rice in Asia 1975, pp. 202–9.

Tauber, H. 1973. "Copenhagen radiocarbon dates X". *Radiocarbon* 15(1):86–112.

Teeter, K. V. 1963. "Lexicostatistics and genetic relationships". *Language* 39:638–48.

Tenazas, R. 1974. "A progress report on the Magsuhot excavations in Bacong, Negros Oriental". *PQCS* 2:133–55.

——— 1985. "A note on stone and shell implements from Late Palaeolithic and Neolithic sites in Carcar, Cebu, Philippines". In Misra, V. N. and Bellwood, P. (eds) 1985:207–9.

Terra, H. de. 1943. "Pleistocene geology and early man in Java". *Transactions of the American Philosophical Society* 32:437–64.

Terrell, J. 1981. "Linguistics and the peopling of the Pacific Islands". *Journal of the Polynesian Society* 90:225–58.

Terrell, J. and Fagan, J. 1975. "The savage and the innocent". *Yearbook of Physical Anthropology* 19:2–18.

Thiel, B. 1981a. "Excavations in the Piñacanauan valley, northern Luzon". *BIPPA* 2:40–8.

——— 1981b. *Subsistence change and continuity in Southeast Asian prehistory.* Ann Arbor: University Microfilms International.

——— 1985. "Austronesian origins and expansion: the Philippine archaeological data". Paper given at the 12th Congress of the Indo-Pacific Prehistory Association, Peñablanca, Philippines.

Thomas, D. 1964. Comment appended to Grace, G. W. 1964.

Thomas, D. and Healey, A. 1962. "Some Philippine language subgroupings: a lexicostatistical study". *Anthropological Linguistics* 4(9):22–33.

Thommeret, J. and Thommeret, Y. 1978. "^{14}C datings of some Holocene sea levels on the north coast of the island of Java". *MQRSEA* 4:51–6.

Thorne, A. G. 1977. "Separation or reconciliation? Biological clues to the development of Australian society". In Allen, J. *et al.* (eds) 1977:187–204.

——— 1980a. "The arrival of man in Australia". In Sherratt, A. (ed.), *The Cambridge Encyclopaedia of Archaeology*, pp. 96–100. Cambridge University Press.

——— 1980b. "The longest link in human evolution in Southeast Asia and the settlement of Australia". In Fox, J. J. (ed.) 1980:35–44.

Thorne, A. G. and Wolpoff, M. 1981. "Regional continuity in Pleistocene hominid evolution". *AJPA* 55:337–50.

Tjia, H. D. 1970. "Quaternary shorelines of the Sundaland, Southeast Asia". *Geologie en Mijnbouw* 49:135–44.

——— 1980. "The Sunda shelf, Southeast Asia". *Zeitschrift für Geomorphologie* 24:405–27.

Tobias, P. V. 1981. "The emergence of man in Africa and beyond". *Philosophical Transactions of the Royal Society of London*, Series B, 292:43–55.

Tobias, P. V. and Koenigswald, G. H. R. von. 1964. "A comparison between the Olduvai hominines and those of Java, and some implications for hominid phylogeny". *Nature* 204:515–8.

Trevor, J. C. and Brothwell, D. R. 1962. "The human remains of Mesolithic and Neolithic date from Gua Cha, Kelantan". *FMJ* 7:6–22.

Tricht, B. van. 1929. "Levende antiquiteiten in West Java". *Djawa* 9:43–120.

Tsubouchi, Y., Iljas, N., Takaya, Y. and Rasjid Hanafiah, A. (eds). 1980. *South Sumatra: man and agriculture.* Kyoto University, Center for Southeast Asian Studies.

Tsukada, M. 1966. "Late Pleistocene vegetation and climate in Taiwan (Formosa)". *Proceedings of the National Academy of Sciences* 55:543–8. Washington.

Turner, C. G. II 1983. "Sinodonty and Sundadonty". In Vasilievsky, R. S. (ed.), *Late Pleistocene and early Holocene cultural connections of Asia and America*, pp. 72–6. Novosibirsk: USSR Academy of Science, Siberian Branch.

Turner, C. G. II and Swindler, D. R. 1978. "The dentition of New Britain West Nakanai Melanesians". *AJPA* 49:361–72.

Tuttle, R. H.. (ed.). 1975. *Palaeoanthropology: morphology and palaeoecology.* The Hague: Mouton.

Tweedie, M. W. F. 1940. "Report on excavations in Kelantan". *JMBRAS* 18(2):1–22.

——— 1953. "The stone age in Malaya". *JMBRAS* 26(2):1–90.

Uhlenbeck, E. M. 1971. "Indonesia and Malaysia". In Seboek, T. (ed.) 1971, vol. 1:55–111.

Umbgrove, J. H. F. 1949. *Structural history of the East Indies.* Cambridge University Press.

Unesco. 1974. *Natural resources of humid tropical Asia.* Paris.

Unesco. 1978. *Tropical forest ecosystems.* Paris.
Vergara, B. S. 1976. "Physiological and morphological adaptability of rice varieties to climate". In *Climate and Rice* 1976, pp. 67–86.
Verstappen, H. T. 1975. "On palaeo climates and landform development in Malesia". *MQRSEA* 1:3–36.
Vlekke, B. H. M. 1945. *Nusantara.* Cambridge (Mass.): Harvard University Press.
Vos, J. de., Sartono, S., Hardja-Sasmita, S. and Sondaar, P. Y. 1982. "The fauna from Trinil, type locality of *Homo erectus:* a reinterpretation". *Geologie en Mijnbouw* 61:207–11.
Vos, J. de and Sondaar, P. Y. 1982. "The importance of the Dubois collection reconsidered". *MQRSEA* 7:35–64.
Walker, D. 1978. "Quaternary Australia and New Guinea". In Pittock, A. B., Frakes, L. A., Jenssen, D., Peterson, J. A. and Zillman, J. W. (eds), *Climatic change and variability*, pp. 82–97. Cambridge University Press.
——— 1980. "The biogeographical setting". In Fox, J. J. (ed.) 1980:21–34.
——— 1982. "Speculations on the origin and evolution of Sunda-Sahul rainforests". In Prance, G. (ed.), *Biological diversification in the tropics*, pp. 554–75. New York: Columbia University Press.
Walker, D. and Sieveking, A. de G. 1962. "The Palaeolithic industry of Kota Tampan, Perak, Malaya". *Proceedings of the Prehistoric Society* 28:103–39.
Walker, M. J. and Santoso, S. 1977. "Romano-Indian rouletted pottery in Indonesia". *AP* 20:228–35.
Wall, L. 1962. "Earthenwares: prehistoric pottery common to Malaya and Borneo". *SMJ* 10:417–27.
Wallace, A. R. 1962. *The Malay Archipelago.* (Originally published 1869). New York: Dover.
Wang, S. C. 1984. *The Neolithic site of Chih-shan-yen.* Taipei Municipal Cultural Heritage Commission, Taiwan.
Wasson, R. J. and Cochrane, R. M. 1979. "Geological and geomorphological perspectives on archaeological sites in the Cagayan valley, northern Luzon, the Philippines". *MQRSEA* 5:1–26.
Weidenreich, F. 1945. *Giant early man from Java and South China.* Anthropological Papers of the American Museum of Natural History, vol. 40, part 1.
——— 1946. *Apes, giants and man.* University of Chicago Press.
——— 1951. *Morphology of Solo Man.* Anthropological Papers of the American Museum of Natural History, vol. 43, part 3.
West, R. C. and Haag, W. C. (eds). 1976. *Ecology of the Pleistocene.* Baton Rouge: School of Geoscience, Louisiana State University.
Wetmore, A. 1940. "Avian remains from the Pleistocene of central Java". *Journal of Palaeontology* 14:447–50.
Wheatley, P. 1961. *The Golden Khersonese.* Kuala Lumpur: University of Malaya Press.
——— 1965. "Discursive scholici on recent papers on agricultural terracing and on related matters pertaining to northern Indochina". *Pacific Viewpoint* 6:123–44.
Wheeler, R. E. M., Ghosh, A., and Krishna Deva. 1946. "Arikamedu: an Indo-Roman trading-station on the east coast of India". *Ancient India* 2:17–124.
White, J. C. 1982. *Ban Chiang.* Philadelphia: University of Pennsylvania Press.
White, J. P. and O'Connell, J. F. 1982. *A prehistory of Australia, New Guinea and Sahul.* Sydney: Academic Press.
Whitmore, J. K. 1977. "The opening of Southeast Asia, trading patterns through the centuries". In Hutterer, K. L. (ed.) 1977:139–54.
Whitmore, T. C. 1975. *Tropical rainforests of the Far East.* Oxford: Clarendon Press.
——— 1981. "Palaeoclimate and vegetation history". In Whitmore, T. C. (ed.) 1981:36–42.
——— (ed.). 1981. *Wallace's Line and plate tectonics.* Oxford: Clarendon Press.

Whyte, R. O. 1972. "The Gramineae, wild and cultivated, of monsoonal and equatorial Southeast Asia". *AP* 15:127–51.

——— 1974. "Grasses and grasslands". In Unesco 1974, pp. 239–62.

——— 1975. "An environmental interpretation of the origin of Asian food legumes". *Indian Journal of Genetics and Plant Breeding* 35(1):61–8.

——— 1983. "The evolution of the Chinese environment". In Keightley, D. N. (ed.) 1983:3–20.

Willems, W. 1939. "Merkwaardige praehistorische schelpartefacten van Celebes en Java". *Cultureel Indiä* 1:181–5.

Williams, B. V. 1979. "Hai Dei Wan". *JHKAS* 8:27–51.

Williams, M. A. J. 1975. "Late Pleistocene tropical aridity synchronous in both hemispheres?". *Nature* 253:617–8.

Wilson, P. 1980. *Man the promising primate.* New Haven: Yale University Press.

Winstedt, R. 1953. *The Malays: a cultural history.* 3rd edition. London: Routledge and Kegan Paul.

Winters, N. J. 1974. "An application of dental anthropological analysis to the human dentition of two Early Metal Age sites, Palawan, Philippines". *AP* 17:28–35.

Wisseman, J. 1977. "Markets and trade in pre-Madjapahit Java". In Hutterer, K. L. (ed.) 1977:197–212.

Witkamp, H. 1920. " 'Kjokkenmoddinger' ter Oostkust van Sumatra". *TKNAG* 37:572–4.

Wolpoff, M. H. 1980. *Palaeoanthropology.* New York: Knopf.

——— 1982. "*Ramapithecus* and hominid origins". *CA* 23:501–22.

Wolpoff, M. H., Wu, X. J. and Thorne, A. G. 1984. "Modern *Homo sapiens* origins: a general theory of hominid evolution involving the fossil evidence from East Asia". In Smith, F. H. and Spencer, F. (eds), *The origins of modern humans*, pp. 411–83. New York: Liss.

Wolters, O. W. 1967. *Early Indonesian commerce: a study of the origins of Srivijaya.* Ithaca: Cornell University Press.

——— 1979. "Studying Srivijaya". *JMBRAS* 52(2):1–32.

Woo, J-K. (see also Wu Rukang). 1980. "Palaeoanthropology in the New China". In Konigsson, L-K. (ed.) 1980:182–206.

Wood, B. A. 1978. *Human evolution.* London: Chapman and Hall.

Wood, J. 1978. "Population structure and genetic heterogeneity in the upper Markham valley of Papua New Guinea". *AJPA* 48:463–70.

Wouden, F. A. E. van. 1968. *Types of social structure in eastern Indonesia.* (Translation of 1935 original edition). The Hague: Nijhoff.

Wright, H. E. Jr. 1976. "Pleistocene ecology — some current problems". In West, R. C. and Haag, W. C. (eds) 1976:1–12.

——— 1977. "Environmental change and the origin of agriculture in the Old and New Worlds". In Reed, C. A. 1977:281–318.

——— 1983. "Climatic change in the Zagros Mountains — revisited". In Braidwood, L. R., Braidwood, R. J., Howe, B., Reed, C. A. and Watson, P. J. (eds.), *Prehistoric archaeology along the Zagros flanks*, pp. 505–10. University of Chicago Oriental Institute Publications 105.

Wright, R. V. S. 1975. "Stone artefacts from Kow Swamp". *APAO* 10:161–80.

——— (ed.). 1977. *Stone tools as cultural markers.* Canberra: Australian Institute of Aboriginal Studies.

Wu Rukang. 1982. *Recent advances of Chinese palaeoanthropology.* Hong Kong University Press, Occasional Papers Series no. 2.

Wurm, S. A. 1978. "The emerging linguistic picture and linguistic prehistory of the southwestern Pacific". In McCormack, W. C. and Wurm, S. A. (eds), *Approaches to language anthropological issues*, pp. 191–221. The Hague: Mouton.

——— 1982. *Papuan languages of Oceania.* Tübingen: Gunter Narr Verlag.

—— 1983. "Linguistic prehistory in the New Guinea area". *JHE* 12:25–35.

Wurm, S. A. and Carrington, L. (eds). 1978. *Second International Conference on Austronesian Linguistics.* 2 fascicles. Canberra, Australian National University: Pacific Linguistics Series C, No. 61.

Wurm, S. A. and Hattori, S. (eds). 1983. *Language atlas of the Pacific area, Part II.* Canberra: Australian Academy of the Humanities.

Wurm, S. A. and Laycock, D. C. 1961. "The question of language and dialect in New Guinea". *Oceania* 32:128–43.

Yamada, N. 1975. "Rice production in Southeast Asia and some nearby countries". In Rice in Asia, pp. 35–156.

Yen, D. E. 1977. "Hoabinhian horticulture: the evidence and the questions from northwest Thailand". In Allen, J. *et al.* (eds) 1977:567–600.

Yen, D. E. and Nance, J. (eds). 1976. *Further studies on the Tasaday.* Makati, Philippines: Panamin Foundation.

Yen, D. E. and Wheeler, J. M. 1968. "Introduction of taro into the Pacific: the indications of chromosome numbers". *Ethnology* 7:259–67.

Yi, S. and Clark, G. A. 1983. "Observations on the Lower Palaeolithic of Northeast Asia". *CA* 24:181–202.

Zaklinskaya, E. D. 1978. "Palynological information from Late Pliocene–Pleistocene deposits recovered by deep-sea drilling in the region of the island of Timor". *Review of Paleobotany and Palynology* 26:227–41.

Zeist, W. van, Polhaupessy, N. A. and Stuijts, I. M. 1979. "Two pollen diagrams from western Java: a preliminary report". *MQRSEA* 5:43–56.

Zingeser, M. R. 1979. "The '*Pithecanthropus* IV' diastemata: malocclusion in a fossil man". *JHE* 8:523–5.

Index

References in italics are to illustrations (pertinent illustrations on pages or in page sequences already indexed are not listed separately).

B

E

F

G

K

L

M

N

O

P

R

S

T

U

V

W

X

Y

Z

7 8 9 0 1 2 3 4
B C D E F G H I J